Mallorca

Northern
Mallorca
p117

Western
Mallorca
p89

The Interior
p137

Palma & the
Badia de Palma
p48

Eastern
Mallorca
p150

Southern
Mallorca
p165

Hugh McNaughtan, Damian Harper

Contents

PORT DE SÓLLER P109

SOBRASSADA (LOCAL SAUSAGE) P30

Contents

VULCANO/SHUTTERSTOCK ©

SÓLLER P105

Welcome to Mallorca

The ever-popular star of the Mediterranean, Mallorca has a sunny personality thanks to its ravishing beaches, azure views, remote mountains and soulful hill towns.

Lyrical Landscapes

For Miró it was the pure Mediterranean light. For hikers and cyclists it is the Serra de Tramuntana's formidable limestone spires and bluffs. For others it is as fleeting as the almond blossom snowing on meadows in spring, or the interior's vineyards in their autumn mantle of gold. Wherever your journey takes you, Mallorca never fails to seduce. Cars conga along the coast in single file for views so enticing, the resort postcards resemble cheap imitations. Even among the tourist swarms of mid-August, you can find pockets of silence – trek to hilltop monasteries, pedal through honey-stone villages, sit under a night sky and engrave Mallorca's lyrical landscapes onto memory.

Return to Tradition

Mallorca's culture took a back seat to its beaches for decades, but the tides are changing. Up and down the island, locals are embracing their roots and revamping the island's old manor houses, country estates and long-abandoned *fincas* (farmhouses, estates) into refined rural retreats. Spend silent moments among the olive, carob and almond groves and you'll soon fall for the charm of Mallorca's hinterland. Summer is one long party and village *festes* (festivals) offer an appetising slice of island life.

Coastal Living

Mallorca tops Europe's summer holiday charts for many reasons, but one ranks above all others: the island's stunning coast. Beyond the built-up resorts, coves braid the island like a string of beads – each one a reminder of why the island's beaches have never lost their appeal. Go west for cliff-sculpted drama and sapphire seas, or head north for hikes to pine-flecked bays. Scope out deserted coves in the east, or dive off bone-white beaches in the south. With a room overlooking the bright-blue sea, sundown beach strolls to the backbeat of cicadas and restaurants open to the stars, you'll soon click into the laid-back groove of coastal living.

Mediterranean Flavours

Eating out in Palma has never been more exciting, with chefs – inspired as much by their Mallorcan grandmothers as Mediterranean nouvelle cuisine – adding a pinch of creativity and spice to the city's food scene. Inland, restaurants play up hale-and-hearty dishes, such as suckling pig spit-roast, to perfection, pairing them with locally grown wines. On the coast, bistros keep flavours clean, bright and simple, serving the catch of the day with big sea views.

Why I Love Mallorca

By Damian Harper, Writer

My parents did the right thing and bought a house in Fornalutx when I was four. Every summer spent in Mallorca was blissful: building camps with friends in the torrent, leaping from high rocks into the waters of the Port de Sóller, listening to the donkeys clop up the steps of Calle del Monte. Nowadays it's what I took for granted then that transfixes me most: the mesmerising night sky, the Tramuntana glowing like coals at sunset, the timeless terracotta hues of the stone houses and the deep azures of the Mediterranean. And each time I return, there's something else that enthrals me.

For more about our writers, see p224

Above: Cala Llombards, Southern Mallorca (p173)

Mallorca

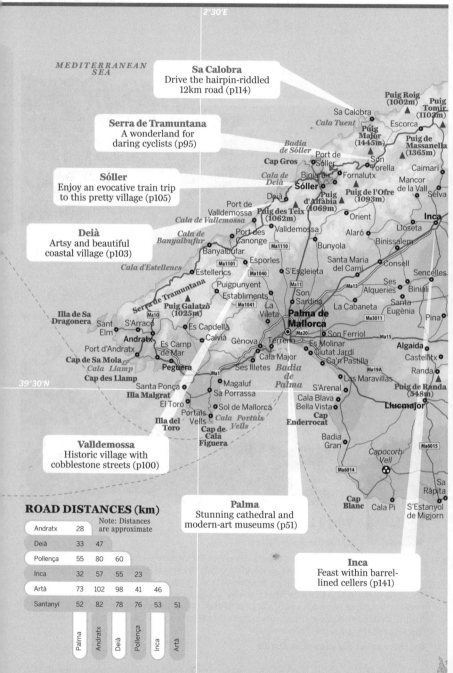

Sa Calobra
Drive the hairpin-riddled 12km road (p114)

Serra de Tramuntana
A wonderland for daring cyclists (p95)

Sóller
Enjoy an evocative train trip to this pretty village (p105)

Deià
Artsy and beautiful coastal village (p103)

Valldemossa
Historic village with cobblestone streets (p100)

Palma
Stunning cathedral and modern-art museums (p51)

Inca
Feast within barrel-lined cellers (p141)

ROAD DISTANCES (km)

Note: Distances are approximate

	Palma	Andratx	Deià	Pollença	Inca	Artà
Andratx	28					
Deià	33	47				
Pollença	55	80	60			
Inca	32	57	55	23		
Artà	73	102	98	41	46	
Santanyí	52	82	78	76	53	51

Cap de Formentor
Breathtaking peninsula high above the Med (p127)

Platja des Coll Baix
Isolated and near-perfect wilderness beach (p134)

Pollença
Pilgrimage town with medieval streets (p120)

Cala Ratjada
Unspoiled east coast beaches (p156)

Artà
Castle lookout and great food (p152)

Parc Natural de S'Albufera
Best birdwatching in the Mediterranean (p135)

Illa de Cabrera
Pristine archipelago with stunning coves (p172)

0   20 km
0   10 miles

MEDITERRANEAN SEA

ELEVATION

1000m
700m
500m
300m
200m
100m
0

Mallorca's
Top 17

Palma Catedral

1 Resembling a vast ship moored at the city's edge, Palma Catedral (p51) dominates the skyline and is the island's architectural tour de force. On the seaward side, the flying buttresses are extraordinary. A kaleidoscope of stained-glass windows and an intriguing flight of fancy by Gaudí inhabit the interior, alongside an inventive rendering of a biblical parable by contemporary artist Miquel Barceló. You'll find yourself returning here, either to get your bearings, or simply to admire it from every angle.

Medieval Artà

2 Set back from eastern Mallorca's busy summer coast, Artà (p152) has enduring year-round charms. Its stone buildings line narrow medieval streets that gently climb up a hillside before ascending steeply to one of the island's most unusual church-castle complexes. The far-reaching views here are compelling, while back in town fine restaurants, hotels and an agreeably sleepy air make it an ideal base for your exploration of the island, including nearby Parc Natural de la Península de Llevant.

The Road to Sa Calobra

3 Even local drivers mutter three Hail Marys before braving the scenic helter-skelter of a road to Sa Calobra (p114). It translates as 'The Snake' and slither it does, for all 12 brake-screeching, hair-raising, white-knuckle kilometres. Drivers teeter perilously close to the edge to glimpse a ravine that scythes through the wild, bare peaks of the Tramuntana to arrive at a sea of deepest blue. But if you think the looping hairpin bends are tough behind the wheel, spare a thought for the mountain bikers that grind it up here!

Staying on a Farm

4 Light years away from the busy coastal resorts, Mallorca's hinterland is sprinkled with *fincas* (estates) where it can be peaceful enough to hear an olive hit the ground. Whether endearingly rustic or revamped in boutique-chic style, properties such as Ca N'Aí (p19) take you that bit closer to the spirit of rural Mallorca. Days unfold unhurriedly here, with lazy mornings by the pool, strolls through olive groves and citrus orchards, and dinners under the stars to the tinkling of goat bells.

SIMON DANNHAUER/SHUTTERSTOCK ©

JCOLU/GETTY IMAGES ©

Deià

5 The mountains of Serra de Tramuntana rise like a natural amphitheatre above Deià (p103), a bird's nest of a village perched high above the iridescent Mediterranean. Mallorca has countless pretty towns, but none surpass this peach: its gold-stone buildings climb a pyramid-shaped hill and glow like warm honey as day fades to dusk. It has long been the muse of artists and writers, not least the poet Robert Graves. Head to nearby Son Marroig, once the romantic abode of an Austrian archduke, to see the Mediterranean aflame at sunset.
Above: Son Marroig (p100)

Valldemossa

6 In any poll of the prettiest villages in the Balearics, Valldemossa (p100) is always a contender, if not outright winner. Draped like a skirt around the eastern foothills of the Serra de Tramuntana, the village has the usual Mallorcan cobblestone lanes, flowerpots, pretty church and stone architecture. But Valldemossa gains extra cachet with its former royal monastery, which once housed Frédéric Chopin and George Sand; aside from giving Valldemossa's residents something to gossip about in perpetuity, their stay bequeathed to the town one of Mallorca's most uplifting music festivals, Festival Chopin.

Palma's Art Trail

7 The crisp Mediterranean light drew some of Europe's most respected painters throughout the 20th century, but two in particular – Joan Miró and Mallorcan Miquel Barceló – will be forever associated with the island. Miró's former home, the Fundació Pilar i Joan Miró (p86), contains a fine range of his works, while Barceló adorned Palma's cathedral with flair and distinction. Elsewhere, works by Picasso and Dalí can be found in Palma's galleries, Es Baluard, Palau March or the Museu Fundació Juan March.
Above: Es Baluard (p66)

Touring the Coast of Cap de Formentor

8 The narrow, precipitous peninsula of Cap de Formentor (p127) is one of the most dramatic mountain ranges in southern Europe. Here, peaks thrust upwards like the jagged ramparts of some epic Mediterranean fortress, while forests of Aleppo pines add light and shadow to austere rocky outcrops that drop abruptly to some of the most beautiful and isolated beaches and coves on the island. However you travel the road running its length, prepare for drama and photo opportunities on every sweeping bend.

The Pollença Sanctuaries

9 Of all the towns of the Mallorcan interior, it is Pollença that rises above the rest. Its two hilltop sanctuaries and pilgrimage points look down on a medieval roofscape of stone and terracotta. Climb the 365 steps of the Calvari (p120) or walk through woods of holm oak and pine to Santuari de la Mare de Déu des Puig for spirit-lifting views. At ground level, wander the town's tangle of lanes, mooch around its Sunday market and watch the world go leisurely by from a front-row cafe on the Plaça Major.

Above right: Calvari (p120)

Cruising to the Illa de Cabrera

10 The only national park in the Balearics, Parc Nacional Marítim-Terrestre de l'Arxipèlag de Cabrera (p172) is a special place and Illa de Cabrera is the jewel in its crown. The largest of 19 uninhabited islands that make up the marine park, Cabrera is blissfully peaceful – its wild headlands and secluded beaches are protected by laws that limit the number of daily visitors to sustainable levels. Boat excursions to the island from Colònia de Sant Jordi stop off at Sa Cova Blava, an exquisitely blue marine cave of rare beauty.

Cycling in the Serra de Tramuntana

11 The winding, climbing, plunging and largely smooth roads of the Serra de Tramuntana (p95), where road and track racing professionals like to limber up for the Tour de France, are a cyclist's wonderland. This wild mountainscape of serpentine bends and cliffs that sheer down to the Mediterranean offers the most challenging terrain on this bikeable island. Among the top rides are the 55km loop from Pollença to Monestir de Lluc and, for the fast and fit, the awesome 12km ascent from Sa Calobra.

Cala Ratjada's Beaches

12 Amid the overdevelopment that blights so much of eastern Mallorca, beautiful bays and half-moon coves peek out to remind us why people eternally come here in search of the perfect stretch of sand. The beaches within striking distance of Cala Ratjada (p156) – particularly Cala Mesquida, Cala Mitjana and Cala Matzoc – are some of the best on the island, with pearly white sand and turquoise waters set against a backdrop of pine trees and sand dunes.

Bottom: Cala Mesquida (p158)

Taking the Slow Train to Sóller

13 Palma and Sóller rank highly as attractions in their own right, but the antique wooden train (p81) that rattles between them is like rewinding 100 years. Scenes of rural Mallorca flash past like film stills, as the train zips through fertile valleys and climbs languidly into the foothills of the Serra de Tramuntana. Traversing tunnels and narrow valleys before emerging high above pretty Sóller, this memorable ride is a poignant reminder that it is the journey itself that matters.

Water Sports

14 One look at Mallorca's unfathomably blue sea has water-sports enthusiasts itching to slip into a wetsuit or leap on a board. Scuba divers are in their underwater element in Formentor's caverns and around the southern islands – Illa de Sa Dragonera (p93) and Illa de Cabrera (for divers with requisite permission) – where wrecks, cave drops and waters swirl with rays, octopuses and barracuda. Coasteering, kayaking and – deep breath now – cliff jumping lure adventure seekers north. Kite surfers go with the winds off the Badia de Pollença.

Bottom: Cala Llombards (p173)

HOLGER LEUE/GETTY IMAGES ©

EL LOBO/SHUTTERSTOCK ©

Birdwatching in Parc Natural de S'Albufera

15 Twitchers flock to Parc Natural de S'Albufera (p135), a tranquil nature park and one of the Mediterranean's premier sites for birdwatching, as the home of 300 bird species, including 64 who breed here. The trails that wind amid the wetlands of this protected area are best explored on foot or by bike. Look out for herons, osprey and egrets from the observation decks discreetly tucked between the reeds, and bring binoculars for the best chances of spotting waterbirds in the marshes.

Above left: European bee-eater

Platja des Coll Baix

16 Isolated coves are the most alluring of Mallorca's many charms, but few can rival the Platja des Coll Baix (p134). Accessible only by sea or on foot through fragrant woods, this hidden beach on the pine-draped headland of Cap des Pinar is a stunning white crescent, backed by cliffs and pummelled by sea that shimmers unfathomable shades of cobalt blue and turquoise. Here the soundtrack is an increasingly rare one – water lapping against the shore, the trill of birdsong and (if you time it right) complete silence.

Eating at a Celler in Inca

17 A suckling pig turns slowly on a spit, the burble of animated conversation rises above the clamour of pans and the chink of glasses, waiters bustle between tables, bringing generous helpings of *conill amb ceba* (rabbit with onions), *frit mallorquí* (a lamb offal fry-up) and *llom amb col* (tender pork loin in cabbage parcels). You eat heartily and drink deep of local wine below the beams and next to giant barrels in the *celler* restaurants of Inca (p141) – this is Mallorcan dining at its most authentic.

Above: Celler Ca'n Ripoll (p142)

Need to Know

For more information, see Survival Guide (p202)

Currency
Euro (€)

Language
Spanish, Mallorquin (a dialect of Catalan)

Visas
Generally not required for stays of up to 90 days; not required for members of EU or Schengen countries. Some nationalities will need a Schengen visa.

Money
ATMs are widely available in towns and resorts. Credit cards are accepted in most hotels, restaurants and shops.

Mobile Phones
Local SIM cards are widely available and can be used in European and Australian mobile phones. Other phones may need to be set to roaming.

Time
Central European Time Zone (GMT/UTC plus one hour)

When to Go

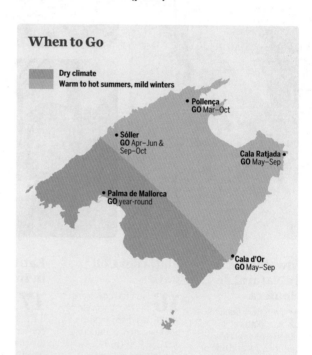

Dry climate
Warm to hot summers, mild winters

• Pollença
GO Mar–Oct

• Sóller
GO Apr–Jun & Sep–Oct

Cala Ratjada •
GO May–Sep

• Palma de Mallorca
GO year-round

• Cala d'Or
GO May–Sep

High Season
(Jul–Aug)

➡ Clear skies, sunny days and warm seas.

➡ Temperatures soar as do room rates. Book well ahead or try for a last-minute deal online.

➡ Fiesta time! The island's towns host high-spirited parties, parades and music festivals.

Shoulder
(Easter–Jun, Sep & Oct)

➡ Most hotels and restaurants open at Easter and stay open until October.

➡ Days are often still mild and crowds are few.

➡ Ideal season for hiking, climbing, mountain biking and canyoning.

Low Season
(Nov–Easter)

➡ Many hotels and restaurants close. Palma is the exception.

➡ Pack layers for cooler-than-expected evening temperatures.

➡ You'll have the island's trails, beaches and sights to yourself.

Useful Websites

LonelyPlanet (www.lonely-planet.com/mallorca) Destination information, hotel bookings, traveller forum and more.

ABC Mallorca (www.abc-mallorca.com) Lifestyle portal for both residents and tourists.

Balearsnatura.com (www.balearsnatura.com) Excellent resource for the natural parks of the Balearic Islands.

Consell de Mallorca (www.infomallorca.net) Excellent website from the island's regional tourist authorities.

TIB (www.tib.org) Public transport fares, times and routes across the island.

Top Fincas (www.topfincas.com) Directory and booking service for Mallorca's rural properties.

Important Numbers

International access code	☑00
Spain country code	☑34
International directory inquiries	☑11825
Emergency	☑112
Policía Nacional	☑91

Exchange Rates

Australia	A$1	€0.72
Canada	C$1	€0.71
Japan	¥100	€0.83
New Zealand	NZ$1	€0.66
UK	UK£1	€1.16
USA	US$1	€0.95

For current exchange rates, see www.xe.com.

Daily Costs

Budget: Less than €100

➡ Basic digs in a hostel, guesthouse or last-minute deal on resort hotel: €45–60

➡ Breakfast in hotel, three-course *menú del día* lunch: €15–20

➡ Bus ticket to nearby towns and beaches: €2–5

Midrange: €100–250

➡ Double room in midrange hotel: €75–150

➡ Cafe lunch, dinner at local restaurant: €30–40

➡ Car rental: from €30 per day

Top End: More than €250

➡ Double room in top-end hotel: €150 and up

➡ Sit-down lunch and dinner at first-rate restaurant: €80–100

➡ Boat tour or guided activity: around €50

Opening Hours

We've provided high-season hours; hours will generally decrease in the shoulder and low seasons. Many resort restaurants and hotels close from November to March.

Banks 8.30am–2pm Monday to Friday; some also open 4–7pm Thursday and 9am–1pm Saturday

Bars 7pm–3am

Cafes 11am–1am

Clubs midnight–6am

Post offices 8.30am–9.30pm Monday to Friday, 8.30am–2pm Saturday

Restaurants lunch 1–3.30pm, dinner 7.30–11pm

Shops 10am–2pm & 4.30–7.30pm or 5–8pm Monday to Saturday; big supermarkets and department stores generally 10am–9pm Monday to Saturday

Arriving in Mallorca

Palma de Mallorca Airport (PMI) Bus 1 runs every 15 minutes from the airport (ground floor of Arrivals) to Plaça d'Espanya in central Palma (€5, 15 minutes); buy tickets from the driver. A taxi for the same 15-minute journey from the centre will set you back between €18 and €22. Some hotels can arrange transfers.

Ferry Port, Palma Bus 1 (the airport bus) runs every 15 minutes from the ferry terminal (Estació Marítima) to Plaça d'Espanya. Tickets cost €3 and the journey takes 10 to 15 minutes. Expect to pay €10 to €12 for a taxi to the city centre.

Tap Water

Tap water is safe to drink across Mallorca, but is often unpalatable because of high sodium or chlorine levels; bottled water is cheap to buy.

For much more on **getting around**, see p210

PLAN YOUR TRIP NEED TO KNOW

Accommodation

Where to Stay

Hotels & Hostales

A *hostal* (sometimes called a *pensión*) is a small-scale budget hotel, usually family-run. The better ones can be bright, spotless and characterful. Hotels cover the entire spectrum, from no-frills digs through to design-focused boutique hotels and luxury hotels.

At the budget end, prices vary according to whether the room has a *lavabo* (washbasin), *ducha* (shower) or *baño completo* (full bathroom). At the top end you may pay more for a room with a *balcón* (balcony) or sea view, and you can fork out more for additional comfort in a suite.

Refugis

Simple hikers' huts, or *refugis*, are mostly scattered about the Serra de Tramuntana, and are a cheap alternative to hotels when hiking. Some are strategically placed on popular hiking routes. Many are run by the **Consell de Mallorca's environment department** (www.conselldemallorca.net/refugis), while others are run by the **Institut Balear de la Natura** (http://ibanat.caib.es). Dorm beds generally cost around €12; some also have a couple of doubles and meal service. Call ahead, as more often than not you'll find them closed if you just turn up.

Monasteries

Seeking a meditative retreat? Mallorca has a handful of monasteries (technically hermitages, as their inmates were hermits and not monks) offering basic digs in converted cells, blissful silence, often spectacular views and superb hiking options. Kids are more than welcome, but they might have to keep the noise down. Four favourites:

Santuari de la Mare de Déu des Puig (☑971 18 41 32; s/d/tr €14/22/30) Take in the full sweep of the north coast from this captivating hilltop hermitage in Pollença, where goat bells are your alarm call. Staying here is an ascetic, tranquil experience. First-floor rooms have the edge. Guests can use the refectory and barbecue areas, or you can order food (the paella is terrific).

Petit Hotel Hostatgería Sant Salvador (www.santsalvadorhotel.com; d/ste €75/115) The monks of Sant Salvador, a fortress-like hermitage high above the plains around Felanitx that dates to 1348, packed up for good in 1992, leaving their home to be converted into a distinctive hotel. Their former cells are now simple, spruce rooms, each with an outstanding panoramic view and private bathroom.

Hospedería del Santuari de Lluc (www.lluc.net; s from €34, d from €41, apt from €84) Popular with school groups, walkers and pilgrims, the Santuari de Lluc has 81 rooms and 39 two- and three-bed apartments (with kitchen), varying in size and facilities. Some look over the courtyard, but those with mountain views are best, while the downstairs rooms are dark and best avoided. It's a magical spot in the Tramuntana and breakfast can be booked.

La Victoria Petit Hotel Hostatgeria (www.lavictoriahotel.com; s/d €50/60) A side road just east of the bay of S'Illot winds up high to a magnificent viewpoint and this hermitage – the Ermita de La Victòria – that dates from 1400. The 13 renovated rooms have a crisp feel, all white walls and cream linen with timber window shutters and beams. The massive stone walls and terracotta floors lend it Mediterranean grace and the position is just wow. Some excellent walks head off into the hills and along the coast, so the hotel is nicely positioned for hikers.

Fincas (Rural Estates)

Whether it's a serene *finca* (rural estate, farm-stay), a B&B in a manor high in the Tramuntana or a sea-facing villa, Mallorca's rural properties are hands down the most atmospheric places to stay. Many are historic, stylish country estates with outstanding facilities, including swimming pools, romantic restaurants and organised activities and excursions.

The local tourism authorities subdivide them into three categories: *agroturisme* (working farms), *turisme de interior* (country mansions converted into boutique hotels) and *hotel rural* (country estates converted into luxury hotels).

Booking Your Accommodation

Advance booking is always a good idea, especially in high season (May to September) when beds are snapped up. Increasingly, Palma is becoming a weekend short-break destination, which means that even in low season it can be an idea to at least call ahead. Prices can skyrocket in high season (doubling, sometimes even tripling), while there are usually cracking deals to be had out of season.

Price Ranges

The following price categories relate to a double room with private bathroom:

$ less than €75

$$ €75–200

$$$ more than €200

Top Choices

Best Places to Stay

➡ **Can Cera** (http://cancerahotel.com; d/ste €352/418)

➡ **Es Petit Hotel de Valldemossa** (www.espetithotel-valldemossa.com; s €117-162, d €150-180)

➡ **Can Busquets** (http://hostalcanbusquets.com; s €75, d €86-104, ste €98-116)

➡ **Hotel Barceló** Formentor (www.barcelo.com; d €225-525, ste €575-900)

➡ **Hotel Cap Rocat** (www.caprocat.com; ste from €843)

Best Rural Hotels

➡ **Cases de Son Barbassa** (www.sonbarbassa.com; s/d/ste €181/242/312)

➡ **Ca N'Aí** (www.canai.com; ste from €165)

➡ **Alqueria Blanca** (www.alqueria-blanca.com; s €135-145, d €155-165, ste €185-205)

➡ **Es Castell** (www.fincaescastell.com; s/d/ste €120/165/210)

➡ **Sa Torre** (www.sa-torre.com; apt €140)

Best on a Budget

➡ **Hostal Dragonera** (http://hostaldragonera.es; s €55-65, d €70-80)

➡ **Hostal Nadal** (971 63 11 80; s/d €30/44, without bathroom €24/35)

➡ **Hostal Villaverde** (www.hostalvillaverde.com; s/d €60/79)

➡ **Hostal Pons** (www.hostalpons.com; d €75)

Best for Families

➡ **HPC Hostal Porto Colom** (www.hostalportocolom.com; s/d €70/115)

➡ **Hotel Casal d'Artà** (www.casaldarta.de; s/d/q €60/96/160)

➡ **Hotel Cala Gat** (www.hotelcalagat.com; s/d €93/146)

➡ **Hotel Barceló Formentor** (www.barcelo.com; d €225-525, ste €575-900)

➡ **Pension Bellavista** (www.pensionbellavista.com; s €35-45, d €55-65, tr €65-75, q €70-80)

First Time Mallorca

For more information, see Survival Guide (p202)

Checklist

➡ Ensure your passport is valid for at least six months

➡ Check airline baggage restrictions

➡ Make advance bookings for accommodation, restaurants, travel and tours

➡ Inform your credit-/debit-card company that you'll be travelling abroad

➡ Arrange comprehensive travel insurance

➡ Verify what you need to hire a car (including excess insurance)

What to Pack

➡ Travel adapter plug

➡ High factor sun cream

➡ Mosquito/insect repellent

➡ Flip flops

➡ Hiking boots for Tramuntana trails

➡ Mobile (cell) phone charger

➡ Sunhat and sunglasses

➡ Beach towel

➡ Bathing suit

➡ Dry bag

➡ Camera

➡ Phrasebook

Top Tips for Your Trip

➡ Detour off the well-trodden trail for a spell and you will find peaceful countryside, restful *fincas* (farms) and uncrowded beaches.

➡ Get high: the best views and photo ops are from the monasteries, forts and castles that crown Mallorca's hillsides. Time it right and you'll catch a fiery sunset.

➡ Allow ample time to get from A to Z. Looking at a map of Mallorca is deceptive. Yes, it is an island and fairly compact, but those twisting mountain roads bump up journey times.

➡ Walk. Whether it's pilgrim-style to a monastery, through the back alleys of a cobbled old town or to a hidden bay, many of Mallorca's most alluring sights can only be seen on foot.

➡ Mallorca is made for cycling: many professional teams do their winter training here, and it's the ideal way to meander among wineries and *finca* hotels.

What to Wear

Mallorca is a laid-back island and most people find they over-pack, especially for beach and poolside holidays that require little more than bathing suits and a couple of changes of shorts and T-shirts. Going out is a casual affair and ties and jackets are not required.

Summers are hot, but layers are advisable for the rest of the year when the weather is patchier and evenings are cool. Forget wearing high heels on the cobbled streets of Mallorca's hill towns – flats it is.

Sleeping

Reserving a room is always a good idea – book well in advance (at least two months) if you are travelling in the peak months of July and August, when beds are like gold dust.

From November to Easter, the vast majority of hotels close in coastal resorts. Palma is a year-round option, though, and you'll also find a sprinkling of places open in towns like Pollença and Sóller. See the Accommodation chapter (p18) for more information.

Taxes & Refunds

Spain's IVA (VAT) goods-and-services tax of up to 21% is included in stated prices. Refunds are available on goods costing more than €90, if taken out of the EU within three months. Collect a refund form when purchasing and present it (together with the purchases) to the customs IVA refunds booth when leaving the EU. For more information, see www.globalblue.com.

Bargaining

The only place haggling skills may be called for, or appropriate, is at markets. Otherwise it's not done. If you want something, be prepared to pay the asking rate.

Tipping

➡ **Hotels** Discretionary: porters around €1 per bag and cleaners €2 per day.

➡ **Cafes and bars** Not expected, but you can reward good service by rounding the bill to the nearest euro or two.

➡ **Restaurants** Service charge is included, unless '*servicio no incluido*' is specified, but many still leave an extra 5% or so.

➡ **Taxis** Not necessary, but feel free to round up or leave a modest tip, especially for longer journeys.

LANGUAGE

Travelling in Mallorca without speaking a single word of Spanish or Mallorquin is entirely possible, but picking up a smattering of these languages will go a long way to winning the affection of the locals. English is widely spoken in the beach resorts and in major towns, but in the rural hinterland and small villages you'll find it handy to have a grasp of a few basic phrases, plus it's part of the fun!

Etiquette

Mallorcans are generally easygoing, and used to the different mores of foreigners, but will respond well to those who make an effort.

➡ **Greetings** Shake hands on first meeting and say '*bon dia*' (good day) or '*bona tarda*' (good evening). In more casual situations, greet with two kisses – offer your right cheek first.

➡ **Socialising** Mallorcans, like all Spanish, are a chatty, sociable lot. Don't be shy – try to join in their rapid-fire conversations, and be prepared for people to stand quite close to you when speaking.

➡ **Eating & Drinking** If you are invited to a Mallorcan home, take a small gift of wine, flowers or chocolate. Wait for your host to say *bon profit!* (enjoy your meal) before getting stuck in. Dunking bread in soup is a no-no, but otherwise meals here are fairly relaxed affairs. Join in a toast by raising your glass and saying *salut!*

If You Like...

Art & Culture

Pack up your towel, break from the beach and discover Mallorca's cultured side, with cathedrals, galleries and artsy hill towns.

Catedral Sing a stained-glass rainbow in this Gothic wonder moored on Palma's seafront. (p51)

Museu Fundación Juan March Picasso, Miró, Dalí, Juan Gris and Mallorcan native Miquel Barceló. (p62)

Deià Poet Robert Graves found his muse in this dreamy hill town. (p103)

Real Cartuja de Valldemossa A Carthusian monastery and the former residence of royals and Chopin. (p100)

Ca'n Prunera Modernista mansion with artworks of the Toulouse-Lautrec, Gauguin and Klimt calibre. (p106)

Fundació Pilar i Joan Miró Miró's former home is filled with his works and spirit. (p86)

Scenic Drives & Rides

Mallorca's precipitous coastlines and hairpin-riddled mountains call for slow touring. Slip behind the wheel for gear-crunching drives, heart-pumping bike rides and unforgettable journeys.

Andratx to Monestir de Lluc Mallorca's drive among drives cuts across the spectacularly rugged Serra de Tramuntana high above the Mediterranean. (p98)

Sa Calobra 'The Snake' sounds like a theme-park ride and this roller-coaster road to a once-isolated cove is almost that. (p114)

Cap de Formentor Eighteen kilometres of precipice-hugging, sea-gazing gorgeousness. (p127)

Artà to Ermita de Betlem A 9km route with pine forests, fine views and a soulful hermitage. (p136)

Orient to Alaró Meander through mountainous foothills, olive groves and sleepy rural hamlets. (p114)

Family Adventures

Mallorca's energy-burning activities, beautiful beaches, and romps around castles, aquariums and water parks are sure-fire kid-pleasers.

Palma Aquarium Dip your toes into Mallorca's underwater world. Shark sleepovers notch up the fear factor. (p85)

Coves del Drac Spelunk the stalactite-encrusted depths of Mallorca's most magical caves. (p162)

Castell d'Alaró Play king of the castle at this impossibly perched medieval fortress. (p114)

Aqualand Race the spaghetti-like slides and white-knuckle flumes at one of Europe's biggest water parks. (p86)

Parc Natural de S'Albufera Gentle strolls in bird-rich wetlands. (p135)

North Coast Caving, cliff-jumping, coasteering and scuba diving will keep older kids as busy as bees. (p117)

History

Get versed in Mallorca's rich past. Bronze Age megaliths, Roman ruins, medieval hill towns, stately palaces and patios bring history vividly to life.

Slow train from Palma to Sóller Board the vintage train for a nostalgic ride through the evocative valleys and mountains of the Tramuntana. (p81)

Pollèntia Sprawling Roman ruins with a fantastic theatre amid the trees and an abundance of remains. (p128)

Top: Palma Catedral (p51)
Bottom: Port d'Andratx, Western Mallorca (p92)

Ses Països Piece together the puzzle of Mallorca's Bronze Age *talayots* (watchtowers). (p152)

Palma's patios Get a tantalising snapshot of how the elite once lived. (p49)

Alcúdia Medieval town walls enclose quiet streets, ancient mansions and old stone houses. (p127)

Festes de la Patrona Rewind to 1550 at Pollença's swashbuckling battle between Moors and Christians. (p121)

Coastal Walks

The Mediterranean is a gorgeous turquoise backdrop as you edge along cliffs, hop between coves and trace Mallorca's coastal contours from a mountaintop.

Ermita de la Victòria to Penya Rotja Survey the entire north coast from this pine-cloaked peninsula. (p130)

Cap de Formentor The jaw-dropping northern finale of the Serra de Tramuntana. (p131)

Parc Natural de la Península de Llevant Quiet trails link beaches and pine valleys. (p161)

Cap de Ses Salines to Colònia de Sant Jordi A rocky trail with bountiful swimming spots and bewitching sea views. (p170)

Finca Can Roig to Cala Magraner Traipse to these four pretty, little-visited coves. (p160)

Month by Month

celebrated with particular gusto in Sa Pobla and Artà.

Sant Sebastià

Palma pulls out the party stops on the eve of the feast day of its patron saint (20 January), with live music, fireworks and revelry in city squares.

January

Winter wraps the island in a blanket of calm; some days are mild, some chilly. Beach resorts are in hibernation, with many hotels and restaurants closed; Palma is a notable exception.

Three Kings

The three kings (tres reis) rock up on 5 January, the eve of Epiphany, bearing gifts of gold, frankincense and myrrh. They are the stars of a flamboyant parade in Palma.

Festes de Sant Antoni Abat

The Festes de Sant Antoni Abat (16 and 17 January) are celebrated with concerts, prancing demons, huge pyres and fireworks, and parading farm animals get a blessing. It's

February

Almond trees in bloom cast flurries of white blossom across the countryside. High-spirited carnivals shake the island out of its winter slumber for pre-Lenten feasting and parading. Many places are still closed.

Carnival

The pre-Lenten season kicks off with parades across the island. In Palma a children's procession, Sa Rueta, is followed by the grown-ups' version, Sa Rua, with pumping music, fancy dress and colourful floats.

March

A glorious month, with solemn Easter celebrations, wildflowers flourishing and fantastic birdwatching in the Parc Natural de S'Albufera.

Semana Santa

Follow the Semana Santa (Holy Week) processions around the island. Begin in Palma on Holy Thursday evening, then head to Pollença for its moving Good Friday Davallament (bringing down). On Easter Sunday, head to Montuïri's S'Encuentro.

April

Mallorcan hotels and restaurants dust off the cobwebs, and resorts start to fill up. Milder days make this a perfect month for hiking and mountain biking.

Fira del Vi

Pollença pops a cork on regional wines at its Fira del Vi (Wine Fair) in the Convent de Sant Domingo in late April.

May

Coastal Mallorca has a real spring in its step as resorts come to life.

Sa Fira

Since 1318, Sineu has been the setting for Sa Fira, the island's largest and most authentic livestock and produce market, held on May's first Sunday.

🎆 Es Firó

On the second weekend of May, Sóller stages Es Firó, where the town's heroic defenders, led by the so-called Valiant Women, fight off Muslim pirates, as they did in 1561, to much merriment and festivities.

🎆 Corpus Christi

Corpus Christi (on the Thursday of the ninth week after Easter) is a major celebration in Palma. The weeks leading up to it are marked by concerts in the city's baroque courtyards.

June

Mallorca moves into top gear. Patron saints' festivals, where religious tradition mixes with good old-fashioned pagan partying, are the excuse for knees-up a plenty.

🎆 Nit de Sant Joan

The feast day of St John (24 June) is preceded the night before by fiery festivities on the Nit de Sant Joan. In Palma, it's *correfoc* (fire running), concerts and beach partying till dawn.

July

There's little to interrupt lazy days on the beach and long liquid nights.

🎆 Festa de la Verge del Carme

On 16 July, many coastal towns stage processions for

the Festa de la Verge del Carme, the patron saint of fisherfolk and sailors.

🎆 Festa de Sant Jaume

On 25 July, the inland town of Algaida sees *cossiers* perform traditional dances in the streets of Algaida for the Festa de Sant Jaume. Six men and one woman dance alongside a demon, who ultimately comes unstuck.

August

The heat cranks up, festivals are in full swing and the hotels (and beaches) are full to bursting point.

🎆 Festes de la Patrona

One of Pollença's most colourful festivals culminates in a staged battle between townsfolk and a motley band of invading Moorish pirates during the weeklong Festes de la Patrona.

☆ Festival Chopin

Valldemossa pays tribute to one-time resident, composer Frédéric Chopin, at the stately Real Cartuja de Valldemossa, with top-notch classical concerts, devoted mostly to Chopin, throughout August.

☆ Mallorca Jazz Festival

Sa Pobla is an unlikely setting for one of the Mediterranean's most celebrated jazz festivals, but no matter – it swings with some of the genre's big names every August.

September

September is like the joyous last drink before the hangover. Autumn is good for migrating birds in the Parc Natural de S'Albufera, coastal hikes, bike rides and water-based activities.

🍷 Festes de la Verema

Mallorca's vine-cloaked interior celebrates the grape harvest with the Festes de la Verema in late September. Binissalem gets stuck into a big juicy mess of a grape fight.

October

Last drinks! People bid tearful farewells to new-found friends at resorts across the island.

🎆 Alcúdia Fair

Concerts, produce markets, music and parades come to Alcúdia on the first weekend in October.

November

As the weather turns chilly, most places close for the winter. Autumnal markets sell wine, just-harvested olives and mushrooms.

December

Many resorts around the island are closed for the winter and most of the ports are hushed. Snow is likely to fall on the Puig de Massanella and Puig Major and other high points of the Serra de Tramuntana and may dust some of the mountain villages.

Itineraries

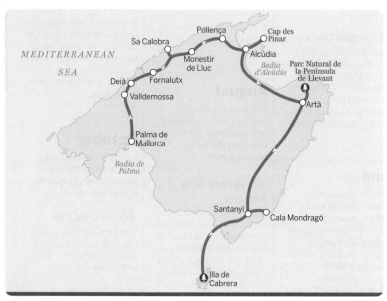

 The Grand Tour

This all-inclusive tour breaks the back of the island, whisking you from Palma's historic attractions along the mountainous coastline of the Serra de Tramuntana via charming mountain villages, seaside inlets, ancient towns and seaboard hikes, before concluding at the gorgeous coves of the Illa de Cabrera.

Spend a few days exploring **Palma**, prowling its colossal cathedral, soulful alleyways and impressive portfolio of galleries and palaces, then head north to the mountains and the stunning town of **Valldemossa**. Continue east along the coast road to restful, artsy **Deià** and the tranquil village of **Fornalutx**, with its unruffled sense of seclusion. Take the epic downhill corkscrew to **Sa Calobra**, then follow the pilgrims seeking spiritual restoration at the **Monestir de Lluc**. From here, aim for ravishing **Pollença** and the ancient sights of walled **Alcúdia**, cultured precursors to a breezy and bracing hike along the sublime **Cap des Pinar**. The ancient settlement of **Artà** lies to the south, a good base from which to explore the outstanding landscapes of the **Parc Natural de la Península de Llevant**. Continue to the charming town of **Santanyí** and nearby **Cala Mondragó**. Conclude your journey with a trip to the beautiful archipelago of **Illa de Cabrera**.

1 WEEK Palma to Pollença

Kicking off in the island's capital, this journey charts a dramatic course through many of Mallorca's signature sights

Warm up with a day or two in sea-splashed **Palma** before drifting southwest to beach belle **Ses Illetes**, harbourside **Port d'Andratx** and low-key **Sant Elm**, before hopping to **Illa de Sa Dragonera**. Dramatic cliff-edge and mountain views unfurl northeast from **Andratx** through alley-woven **Estellencs** and **Banyalbufar** and hill-town stunner **Valldemossa**. Just north, photogenic **Deià** twirls delightfully up a hillside, with the minute village of Lluc Alcari just to the east. Swing north to valley-cupped **Sóller** for backstreet strolls, Modernista treasures, Picasso and Miró. Time permitting, detour to charming hill-toppers **Orient**, **Biniaraix** or **Fornalutx**, or board a rickety vintage tram down to **Port de Sóller**. As the Ma10 weaves inland, take the hair-raising road down to **Sa Calobra** en route to pilgrims' respite **Monestir de Lluc**. See the wild peaks of the Tramuntana unfurl in all their brooding splendour as you descend to the quintessentially Mallorcan town of **Pollença**.

10 DAYS Artà to Illa de Cabrera

Mix gorgeous beaches and sheltered coves with morsels of historic charm, inland wineries and rural vistas.

Linger in fortress-topped **Artà** for a day, then tour the remote coastal loveliness of **Parc Natural de la Península de Llevant**. From Artà, squeeze in a visit to **Capdepera**, a town defined by its castle. Hopscotch along the east coast to beguiling half-moon bays, such as Cala Mesquida near **Cala Ratjada**, and inch south for the Coves d'Artà and medieval Torre de Canyamel around **Platja de Canyamel**. Head further south, pondering the glittering depths of Coves del Drac in **Porto Cristo**, then point your compass inland to vine-streaked **Petra** and **Sineu**, stopping off at wineries along the way. As you wend your way back to the coast, visit handsome Mallorcan estate **Els Calderers** and then head for the boho charms of **Santanyí** and the good-looking port of **Cala Figuera** before aiming for artsy **Ses Salines**, detouring via pretty beaches for a quick swim. Wrap up your trip in **Colònia de Sant Jordi**, springboard to the island-speckled **Parc Nacional Marítim-Terrestre de l'Arxipèlag de Cabrera**.

Off the Beaten Track: Mallorca

BANYALBUFAR

So you've swooned over Deià and visited Valldemossa, but what about Banyalbufar? Centuries-old farming terraces form steps down to the wave-lashed coast – this speck of a village is postcard stuff. (p96)

SA FORADADA

This finger of rock juts out into the Med at the base of Son Marroig. Wander through sheep-dotted olive groves down to the sea and linger for a watercolour sunset. (p100)

CALA BLANCA

Tucked away on the coastline a short drive from Port d'Andratx, Cala Blanca is a quiet, little-visited cove strewn with pebbles, affording moments of serenity and views over the sea to the two headlands and anchored boats offshore. (p92)

Sa Calobra

Cap Gros

Sóller **PUIG D'ALARÓ** ▲

Deià

SA FORADADA ◉ ○ Valldemossa

BANYALBUFAR ○

ILLA DE SA DRAGONERA

Palma de Mallorca

○ Andratx

CALA BLANCA ○ Peguera

Cap des Llamp

Badia de Palma

Llucmajor ○

Cap Enderrocat

Cap de Cala Figuera

ILLA DE SA DRAGONERA

This rippled island reposes like a slumbering dragon off the island's westernmost tip. Trails thread through this nature reserve to quiet capes, far from the beach resort swarms. (p93)

Cap Blanc

PUIG D'ALARÓ

Even in summer those who make it to the top of the rock are few and far between. It's a stiff two-hour climb to the enigmatic remains of a Moorish castle. Or cheat by driving part way. (p114)

MEDITERRANEAN SEA

0 ——————— 20 km
0 ——————— 10 miles

MEDITERRANEAN SEA

Cap de Formentor

Cap des Pinar

Pollença

Badia de Pollença

SANTUARI DE LA MARE DE DÉU DES PUIG

▲ TALAIA D'ALCÚDIA

Parc Natural de S'Albufera

Badia d'Alcúdia

Finca Pública de Son Real

Parc Natural de la Península de Llevant

Santa Margalida

Artà

Cala Ratjada

Manacor

Felanitx

CALES DE MALLORCA

Portocolom

Cala d'Or

Parc Natural de Mondragó

PLATJA DES TRENC

Cap de Ses Salines

Illa des Conills

Illa de Cabrera

TALAIA D'ALCÚDIA

Hike up from the Ermita de la Victoria on a half-hour trek to this astonishing lookout point with 360-degree views over the peninsula and the sea. You may only have wild mountain goats for company. (p134)

SANTUARI DE LA MARE DE DÉU DES PUIG

Silence blankets the courtyards and chapel of this former nunnery, high above Pollença. It's hard to drag yourself away from the views that embrace the full sweep of the north coast. (p120)

CALES DE MALLORCA

Walking is the only way to reach the tiny coves that dot the coastline north of Cales de Mallorca, but chances are you'll have their iridescent waters all to yourself. (p160)

PLATJA DES TRENC

This 3km ribbon of frost-white, dune-backed sand hems Mallorca's southern coast and is lapped by aquamarine water. Even in August, there's space to breathe and go nude if you dare. (p168)

Plan Your Trip
Eat & Drink Like a Local

Stopping to sit down and slowly savour a meal is one of the best things about Mallorca, where eating is not just a functional pastime but one of life's great pleasures. Mallorcans eat late, no matter what the meal, although the large foreign population on the island means that restaurants tend to open an hour or more earlier than they do on the mainland.

The Year in Food
Best in Spring
Sprigs of wild rosemary and thyme add flavour to *anyell de llet* (suckling lamb). *Espàrrecs* (asparagus) and *caragols* (snails) pop up on many menus.

Best in Summer
You can pick *fonoll marí* (samphire), a coastal plant that's marinated and used in salads. Markets and menus fill with a bounty of fresh fruit, veg and fish.

Best in Autumn
Join locals to comb the hills for *esclata-sang*, a mushroom of the milk-fungus family. The island's grape harvest and festivals in late September are great fun, especially the grape-throwing festival in Binissalem.

Best in Winter
Menus go meaty with *sobrassada* (paprika-flavoured cured pork sausage), *llom amb col* (pork wrapped in cabbage with pine nuts and raisins) and *lechona asada* (roast suckling pig).

Food Experiences
Meals of a Lifetime

➡ **Marc Fosh** (p71) Michelin-starred Marc Fosh's flagship restaurant in a stylish converted convent refectory.

➡ **Es Verger** (p114) Superbly tender slow-cooked lamb on the long, winding road up to Castell d'Alaró.

➡ **Es Racó d'es Teix** (p105) Michelin-starred fusion menu and a gorgeous mountain backdrop from the terrace.

➡ **Béns d'Avall** (p108) First-rate seafood paired with an ultra-romantic setting.

➡ **Celler Ca'n Amer** (p142) Rustic charm, cracking Mallorcan menu.

➡ **Cases de Son Barbassa** (p155) Tranquil and romantic *finca* (farm) setting for turbot in champagne with clam and oysters and delightful views.

Cheap Treats

➡ **Forn or confiteria (pastry shop)** You can eat on the hoof, often with change from a €5 note, by popping into one of these pastry shops.

➡ **Ensaïmades** Crispy, croissant-like pastry dusted with icing sugar, and sometimes filled with cream.

➡ **Empanades** Pasties with savoury fillings.

➡ **Cocarrois** Larger version of the *empanades*.

➡ **Tapas and pintxos (mini tapas)** Great way to stave off hunger and absorb local life; hit Palma's Ruta Martiana on a Tuesday or Wednesday evening when a drink and a tapa cost as little as €2.

Dare to Try

➡ **Caragols** Dig into snails cooked in a garlicky, herby broth or served in a rich stew.

➡ **Arròs brut** The name 'dirty rice' is off-putting, but trust us, this soupy wonder – with pork, rabbit and vegetables – is delicious.

➡ **Botifarró** Cured blood sausage (not unlike British black pudding) – surprisingly tasty.

➡ **Percebes** Goose barnacles – claw-like, filter-feeding crustaceans that cling to rocks – look ghastly but taste divine. Perfect finger food.

➡ **Frit Mallorquí** A flavoursome lamb offal and veg fry-up, born out of a desperate need for protein during periods of poverty.

Cooking Courses

Mallorca's fledgling cooking-course scene is just starting to spread its wings, with restaurants and *fincas* occasionally offering the odd class where you can roll up your sleeves and learn the basics. Cooking Holidays Mallorca (p176) holds courses at the Yacht Club Cala d'Or, covering everything from one-day tapas classes to seven-night gourmet breaks. You can learn to make tapas or prepare paella at three-hour courses run by Mallorca Cuisine (p97), northwest of Palma. They also organise winery and market visits.

Local Specialities

You might think of Mallorca's coastline and expect to find nothing but fish on menus, yet traditional dishes are surprisingly gutsy and meat-focused, especially in the rural interior. Pork is a very popular ingredient, working its way into countless wholesome sausages, stews, soups and even some vegetable dishes and desserts. The centuries of hunger Mallorcans endured taught them to appreciate every part of the pig; even today, they use everything but the oink.

It's true that much of the fish eaten on Mallorca is flown in from elsewhere, but many species still fill the waters near the island. *Besugo* (sea bream) and *rape* (monkfish) are some of the most common fish caught here. Especially appreciated is *cap roig,* an ugly red fish found around the Illa de Cabrera.

Although you'll find fish and seafood cooked in a variety of sauces, this is largely a nod to foreign tastes. Mallorcans long ago learned that fresh seafood is best served grilled with just a bit of salt and lemon. Another delicious way to eat it is 'a la sal', or baked in a salt crust.

Paella may have its origins just across the water in Valencia, but this and other rice dishes have been taken to heart by Mallorcans to the extent that some of Spain's best paellas are found on the island.

Mallorcan Wine

Mallorca has been making wine since Roman times and the industry was flourishing by the mid-19th century, but in the late 1880s the Mallorcan vines were ravaged by the imported vine pest phylloxera, which wiped out all the vineyards virtually overnight. It's only in the past few decades that Mallorcan wine has made it back to the world wine map, to be toasted for its quality. Just over 30 cellars, with 2500 hectares between them, make up the island's

---

TAKE IT HOME

For a lingering taste of Mallorca, save room to take home hand-harvested salt from des Trenc, fig bread, *sobrassada,* olives and almonds, wine, Hierbas liqueur and tangy orange preserves from Sóller – a burst of island sunshine when summer is long gone. Here's where you'll find them:

➡ **Enseñat** (p124)

➡ **Típika** (p79)

➡ **Flor de Sal d'es Trenc** (p132) & (p132)

➡ **Fet a Sóller** (p109)

➡ **Colmado Santo Domingo** (p78)

➡ **Malvasia de Banyalbufar** (p97)

moderate production, most of which is enjoyed in Mallorca's restaurants and hotels. The wineries are huddled in the island's two DOs (Denominaciones de Orígen), Binissalem and an area in the interior of the island that includes towns such as Manacor, Felanitx and Llucmajor, where growing conditions are ideal. International varieties such as cabernet sauvignon are planted alongside native varieties, like manto negro, fogoneu and callet. Local white varieties include prensal blanc and girò blanc, which are blended with Catalan grapes like parellada, macabeo and moscatel or with international varieties like chardonnay.

Wine production also takes place on the seaward slopes of the Serra de Tramuntana, particularly around Banyalbufar, where the malvasia grape is enjoying a revival.

Tourist offices across the wine country generally have a list of local wineries and their opening hours.

How to Eat & Drink

English menus are a given in coastal resorts, but not necessarily elsewhere. That said, there is nearly always a waiter who can translate. It's handy to learn a few words of Mallorquin, though, so you can decipher some menu items for yourself. Bottled mineral water (*aigua mineral*) is the norm; order it either with (*amb*) or without (*sense*) gas.

If you're extended the honour of being invited to dine in someone's home, bring a small gift of wine or chocolates and prepare yourself for a feast. A Mallorcan host will go all-out to entertain guests. Family lunches are often big, boisterous affairs – you'll barely get a word in edgeways but have fun trying! Say '*bon profit*' (enjoy your meal) before eating and '*salut!*' (cheers) when drinking a toast.

The one who invites usually foots the bill. Service charge is included, but you might want to reward good service with an additional tip of around 5%.

When to Eat

Most Mallorcans kick-start the day with a shot of *cafè* (black coffee), but they might head out to *esmorzar* (breakfast) around midmorning. This is the ideal time to try a light, sugary *and* fluffy *ensaïmada* (Mallorcan pastry) and wash it down with a *cafè amb llet* (espresso with milk) or a delicious *suc de taronja natural* (freshly squeezed orange juice).

Lunch is the biggest meal of the day. On Sundays, the midday family meal may last until late afternoon. Social dinners are equally drawn out, with each step from appetisers to post-dinner drinks being relished to the fullest. Even when not ordering a *menú*, Mallorcans generally order two courses and a dessert when they go out for lunch.

Mallorcans' stomachs start growling by 7pm or so. This is a great time to stop for tapas. An import from the mainland, tapas aren't as widespread here as in other Spanish cities, but many bars and cafes will have a small selection of snacky things to choose from. Olives or a dish of *ametlla* (almonds) are the ideal accompaniment to a *caña* (beer).

For most Mallorcans, the appropriate dinner time is around 9pm. A meal usually begins with *pa moreno* (brown bread) and perhaps a *pica pica*, when many small appetisers are put out for everyone to share. Next comes the *primer plato*, which may be a salad, pasta, grilled-vegetable plate or something more creative. Desserts are most often a simple *gelat* (ice cream), flan or fruit.

Where to Eat

➡ **Celler** A country wine-cellar-turned-restaurant, with a solid menu of traditional home cooking, a local crowd and relaxed feel.

➡ **Cafe** Takes you through from morning coffee to evening tapas and alcoholic drinks. Great for light bites such as salads and *pa amb oli* (bread with oil).

➡ **Chiringuito** Beach shack serving drinks, snacks and sometimes tapas and seafood.

➡ **Confiteria** A pastry shop, alternatively called a *forn* or a *pastelería*. Find the best *ensaïmades* (round buns) here.

➡ **Gelateria** Ice-cream parlour, often with Italian-style *gelato* (made with milk and fresh fruit).

➡ **Marisquería** Specialises in seafood. Sometimes called a *restaurant de marisc*.

➡ **Restaurant** From simple to gourmet. Anything with ca'n or ca's in its name serves traditional fare in a family-style atmosphere.

Top: *Ensaïmada* (Mallorcan pastry)

Bottom: Mallorcan tapas

MARGARET STEPHEN/LONELY PLANET ©

WESTEND61/GETTY IMAGES ©

➡ **Tabernas** Rustic taverns serving tapas or meals. *Tascas* work to a similar concept.

Vegetarians & Vegans

There has been a rise in restaurants and cafes dishing up vegetarian and vegan fare in recent years. They make the most of the island's fava broad beans, peppers, aubergines, artichokes, cauliflowers and asparagus. Figs, apricots and oranges (especially around Sóller) are abundant.

If you want something light, try *trempó*, a refreshing Mallorcan salad made of chopped tomatoes, peppers and onions, drizzled in olive oil. *Pa amb oli* is another good option, as is *tumbet* (Mallorcan ratatouille). Spanish gazpacho (cold, garlicky tomato soup) and *tortillas* (thick omelettes made with potatoes or veggies) are popular too.

It's worth bearing in mind that many traditional veggie dishes are prepared with salted pork, meat broth or lard. For meat-free meals be sure to stress that you are a vegetarian. *Soy vegetariano/a* (I'm a vegetarian) or *no como carne* (I don't eat meat) should do the trick.

Menu Decoder

arròs bogavante – moist, juicy lobster rice

arròs brut – literally 'dirty rice', a soupy dish made with pork, rabbit and vegetables

arròs negre – rice dish, cooked in and coloured by squid ink, and sometimes served with shellfish. A regional take on paella.

botifarra – flavourful pork sausage; some of the best island sausages

botiffarón – a larger version of *botifarra*

cocas de patata – bread-like pastry dusted with sugar and particularly famous in Valldemossa

conill amb ceba – rabbit with onions

ensaïmada – Mallorcan pastry par excellence; a round bun made with a spiral of sweet dough, topped with powdered sugar and sometimes filled with cream, chocolate or *cabell d'àngel* (pumpkin paste)

gató Mallorquí – dense almond cake

lechona – suckling pig, often roasted on an open spit

llom amb col – pork loin wrapped in cabbage, flavoured with garlic, tomatoes, *sobrassada*, parsley, sultanas and pine nuts

marisquada – heaped tray of steamed shellfish; plan to share

pa amb oli – literally bread with oil; traditional *pa moreno* (rye bread) usually topped with chopped tomatoes, as well as a variety of other toppings. Some are a meal in themselves.

sobrassada – tangy cured pork sausage flavoured with paprika and sea salt

suquet – stew cooked in rich fish stock and filled with fish and/or seafood

trempó – refreshing salad of chopped tomatoes, peppers and onions

tumbet – a kind of vegetable ratatouille made with aubergines, courgettes, potatoes, garlic and tomatoes. Mop up with crusty bread.

Plan Your Trip
Activities

Whether you're hiking along the north coast's ragged clifftops, negotiating the Tramuntana's limestone wilderness by mountain bike or kayaking to secluded coves too tiny to appear on maps, Mallorca's outdoors exhilarates and enthrals. Mountains, canyons and 550km of gorgeous coast are all squeezed into this island. Go forth and explore!

Planning Your Trip

When to Go

Mallorca's outdoor activities are, in theory, possible year-round thanks to the island's relatively mild winters and oft-touted 300 days of sunshine. That said, many organised activities will only be doable from roughly Easter to October, particularly water-based sports.

The ideal conditions for most activities, particularly hiking and cycling, is in spring and autumn. Daytime temperatures in summer can be uncomfortably hot and the traffic on the roads can make cycling a stop-start affair. These drawbacks are partly compensated for by the long daylight hours.

What to Take

Most activities operators in Mallorca can provide you with all of the necessary equipment, while high-quality bicycles can be rented all over the island. Although professional-standard equipment is available for purchase on Mallorca, anyone planning on hiking should bring their own boots – the trails of the Serra de Tramuntana are not the place to be breaking in new footwear.

Best Outdoor Activities

Best Hiking

The twin peninsulas of Cap de Formentor and Cap des Pinar offer coastal hiking at its finest, with pine-cloaked cliffs dropping suddenly to a sea of bluest blue.

Best Cycling

Mountain bikers and road cyclists are in their element in the high peaks of the Serra de Tramuntana, with thigh-crunching climbs, sweeping descents and hairpin bend after looping hairpin bend.

Best Scuba Diving

South Mallorca is a diver's dream. Go to Illa de Sa Dragonera and Illa de Cabrera (for divers with requisite permission) for wrecks, cave drops and pristine water swirling with rays, octopuses and barracuda.

Best Canyoning

The Serra de Tramuntana is rippled through with gorges and canyons. For drama, delve into Gorg Blau Sa Fosca or Torrent d'es Pareis.

Best Windsurfing & Kitesurfing

The thermal winds that whip off the sea rolling into Sa Marina in the Badia de Pollença create the idea conditions for windsurfing and kitesurfing.

On the Land
Hiking

From the bald and dramatic limestone mountains in the west to the rocky coastal trails of the north and east where the lure of the sea is never-ending, Mallorca offers some of the finest hiking anywhere in Europe. The Consell de Mallorca (www.conselldemallorca.net) has become serious about signposting and maintaining the island's trekking routes (many of which have been used for centuries by pack animals and wayfaring pilgrims), so following the route is often (but not always) not too hard.

The Tramuntana cannot rival the Alps in height, but its serrated peaks, crags and ravines are every bit as wild and not to be underestimated, and the hiking season here is longer. A network of *refugis* (mountain refuges) gives weary hikers a place to bed down for the night, as do the hilltop monasteries and hermitages that have been converted into simple accommodation.

While short distances between trails mean you can cover more ground, it's worth bearing in mind that you may need your own wheels to reach many of the trailheads. But once you get there, you'll have them more or less to yourself.

There are hikes for almost every age and fitness level, so don't assume hiking is just for the hardcore.

Best Day Hikes

Just about every tourist office in Mallorca can advise on local day hikes in the area and help you find a route to match your fitness. Five favourites:

➡ **Cap de Ses Salines to Colònia de Sant Jordi** This half-day hike along the south coast takes in captivating seascapes. Plenty of opportunities for swimming.

➡ **Finca Can Roig to Cala Magraner** Slip away from east coast crowds with this glorious, easygoing cove-to-cove walk.

➡ **Sóller to Mirador de Ses Barques** Stride through olive groves to a magical viewpoint, then return via pretty hill town Fornalutx.

➡ **Ermita de la Victòria to Penya Rotja** Walk through forests of pine and gaze out across the north coast from this cliff-hugger of a hike.

➡ **Cala en Gossalba to Fumat** Formentor's most dramatic coastal hike – begins gently and ends spectacularly with 360-degree views from the 334m crag of Fumat.

Multiday Hikes

There are two main long-distance hiking trails in Mallorca. As in the rest of Spain, the two GR (long-distance) trails are signposted in red and white.

➡ Keen hikers can tackle the **Ruta de Pedra en Sec** (Route of Dry Stone, GR221; www.gr221.info), a four- to seven-day walk going from Port d'Andratx to Pollença, crossing the Serra de Tramuntana. At a few points along the GR 221 there are *refugis de muntanya* (rustic mountain huts) where trekkers can stay the night.

➡ Signposting is currently under way on the **Ruta Artà-Lluc** (GR 222), which will eventually link the two towns, although development of this route is slow.

Hiking Maps & Guides

The best hiking maps are the 1:25,000 *Tramuntana Central, Tramuntana Norte* and *Tramuntana Sur* maps by Editorial Alpina (www.editorialalpina.com). These can be picked up at many bookshops around the island. Cicerone's *Walking in Mallorca* details and maps 80 routes.

If you need more than a map, there are some reputable guides on the island:

➡ **Tramuntana Tours** (p209) Respected activities operator based in Sóller and Port de Sóller; its focus is on the Serra de Tramuntana.

PEAK BAGGING

Fancy something really tough? Mallorca's highest peak, Puig Major (1445m), may be an off-limits military zone, but you can trek up to the second-highest, **Puig de Massanella** (1365m). Make sure you take plenty of provisions and a decent map for this 11km, five-hour hike. From the summit, you'll be rewarded with 360-degree views over the buckled Tramuntana to the Badia d'Alcúdia. On clear days you can even spy the island of Menorca on the horizon.

➡ **Món d'Aventura** (p121) This Pollença adventure specialist offers myriad hikes, graded from easy to advanced, including the Ruta de Pedra en Sec.

➡ **Rich Strutt** (p125) An English-speaking guide with over 20 years of experience based in Port de Pollença offering a huge number of day hikes (or longer treks) to choose from for groups of four or more.

Hiking Resources

The Consell de Mallorca publishes two excellent brochures, both of which should be available from the Consell de Mallorca tourist office (p206) in Palma. The brochures' maps are orientative in scope and you'll need to supplement them with detailed hiking maps:

➡ **Rutes per Mallorca (Mallorca Itineraries)** Six treks ranging from 33.2km to 113.5km.

➡ **Caminar per Mallorca (Walking in Mallorca)** Twelve day hikes from 4.5km to 14km.

Cycling

Mallorca's popularity as a destination for road cycling and mountain biking continues to soar, not least thanks to the likes of British cyclist Bradley Wiggins, who trained for the Tour de France in the Tramuntana.

Nearly half of Mallorca's 1250km of roads have been harnessed for cycling, with everything from signposts to separate bike lanes. The lycra peak season in mountainous regions is from March to May and late September to November, when the weather is refreshingly cool.

Mountain bikers will find abundant trails, too, ranging from flat dirt tracks to rough-and-tumble single tracks. Be sure to get a good highway or trekking map before you set out on any cycling expedition.

Bike-rental agencies are ubiquitous across the island, and local tourist offices can usually point you in the right direction. Prices can vary between €10 per day for a basic touring bike and €30 for a high-end mountain or racing bike. Kids bikes and kiddie seats are also widely available.

Best Cycling Routes

There are many great areas for biking; trails cover the island like a web and, depending on your skills and interests, anywhere can be the start of a fabulous ride. That said, here are some of our favourites:

➡ **Palma to Capocorb Vell** (Palma & Southern Mallorca)

➡ **Andratx to Monestir de Lluc** (Western Mallorca)

➡ **Parc Natural de la Península de Llevant** (Eastern Mallorca)

➡ **Cap de Formentor** (Northern Mallorca)

➡ **Port d'Alcúdia & Cap des Pinar** (Northern Mallorca)

➡ **Santa Maria to Binibona, via Santa Eugenia, Binissalem, Lloseta and Caimari** (The Interior)

Cycling Guides

If you don't fancy going it alone, you can hook onto some terrific excursions with guides that know Mallorca like the back of their hands:

➡ **Bike & Kite** (p125) Based in Port de Pollença, Bike & Kite offers guided mountain-bike tours in the north, bike hire and a MTB downhill shuttle service.

➡ **Tramuntana Tours** (p209) As the name suggests, these guys take you into the heart of the Tramuntana.

➡ **Rock and Ride** (☑0664 73 45 12; www.rockandride-mallorca.com) Runs skill courses and publishes an excellent mountain-biking booklet (£10) with maps and GPX files.

Cycling Resources

The **Federació de Ciclisme de les Illes Balears** (www.webfcib.es) can provide contact information for local cycling clubs. A growing number of hotels cater specifically to cyclists, with garages and energy-packed menus.

Mallorca Bike (www.mallorcabike.info) publishes a very useful waterproof bike map, with trails, traffic ratings, gradients, bike shops and more, and costs around €7 from tourist offices and bike-hire companies.

Canyoning

The ultimate Mallorcan adrenaline rush, canyoning is an exhausting but exhilarating mix of jumping into ravines and trudging down gorges and gullies. An average excursion might include boulder hopping, abseiling down waterfalls, shimmying up cliffs and swimming in ice-cold rock pools of crystal blue.

Going with a professional guide is essential. Among the best are Món d'Aventura (p121), Rock and Ride, (p37) Tramuntana Tours (p209) and Experience Mallorca (p135), all of which cater to all levels with tours graded from easy to difficult.

Rock Climbing

The mere thought of Mallorca's sublime limestone walls has climbers' hearts pounding. The island is among Europe's foremost destinations for sport climbers, with abundant overhangs, slabs and crags. Climbing here concentrates on three main areas: the southwest for multi-pitch climbing, the northwest for magnificent crags and the east for superb deep water soloing (DWS).

A holy grail for climbers, Sa Gubia is a huge fist of rock combed through with multi-pitch routes. Other climbing hot spots include the ragged limestone crags of the Formentor peninsula and the coves of Porto Cristo and Cala Barques in the island's east.

Experienced climbers can go it alone. Rock and Ride (p37) offers guided multipitch climbs and intro courses. Rockfax (www.rockfax.com) publishes guides and PDF mini guides on climbing in Mallorca.

Caving

Mallorca's pocked limestone terrain means caving conditions are fantastic. Kitted out with headlamps, spelunkers can penetrate the cool twilight of the numerous cave complexes that burrow into the cliffs of the southern, northern and eastern coasts. A guide is highly recommended.

Experience Mallorca (p135) leads half-day caving excursions year-round. You'll pass through subterranean chambers dripping with stalactites. One minute you're crawling through narrow passageways, the next you are in a cathedral-like vault big enough for 30 people to stand at ease. It's not one for claustrophobes.

Golf

Palma is a popular golfing destination, which is not surprising given the mix of warm Mediterranean climate and fine natural setting. At last count there were around 22 golf courses scattered around the island; some of the best cluster around Capdepera and Artà in the east. Green fees for 18 holes start from €30 and can go as high as €130, although the average is €40 to €75. Cart rental costs €30 to €45. Prices dip in summer when it's often simply too hot to have fun, and can soar in spring and autumn.

ALTERNATIVE ACTIVITIES

When you've cycled, hiked and swum every inch of the island, you can always explore Mallorca vertically.

Mallorca from Above

Mallorca looks tiny as you rise gently above it or glide on thermals. **Illes Balears Ballooning** (p156) offers hot-air balloons for charter, with a bird's-eye view of the entire island. As you approach Port d'Alcúdia you'll often see paragliders drifting high on the thermals. If you're keen to join them, try **Tandem Mallorca** (p132). In addition to tandem flights for beginners, there are also beginners' and intermediate courses year-round.

Cliff Jumping

Yes, cliff jumping sounds more death wish than delightful beach holiday, but with guides who know the rocks inside and out, this suicidal-sounding pursuit is perfectly safe. On the same level as bungee jumping on the Richter scale of nerve-shredding pursuits, you jump off cliffs between 3m and 12m high – not colossal by any means, but it feels that way in the freeze-frame moment when you leap and plunge. Listen for the euphoric whoops in north coast Cala Sant Vicenç, where locals doing dives and even the odd somersault show how it's done properly. Guides from **Experience Mallorca** (p135) can take you to the best spots.

Horse Riding

With its extensive network of rugged trails over hilly countryside and alongside the Mediterranean, Mallorca is a fine place to saddle up. Many towns and resorts have stables where you can join a class (€10 to €20) or a group excursion (about €15 for the first hour, with two five-hour rides generally costing around €25/60 per person). Longer trips are also possible. Some stables also offer pony rides for small children.

Horse-Riding Routes

Cala Ratjada, Colònia de Sant Jordi and Pollença are all popular riding areas; ask at local tourist offices for the nearest stables. Cala Ratjada, in particular, allows you to ride along a largely undeveloped coast towards Cala Mesquida. Rancho Bonanza (p156), Cala Ratjada's main stables, are German-run. Besides countryside and coastal excursions, they arrange pony rides for kids.

Coasteering

A summer alternative to canyoning (being that bit closer to the sea), coasteering is a heart-pumping mix of swimming, climbing, scrambling, abseiling, cliff jumping and traversing the rock horizontally using the sea to catch your falls. Locations reach from Bonaire near Alcúdia in the north to Peguera in the southwest. Adventure specialists offering coasteering provide all the gear you need, such as helmets and life jackets. Món d'Aventura (p121) arranges two different levels – the easier one is suitable for kids. Experience Mallorca's (p135) half-day trips are suitable for over-12s. Skualo (p156) also offers coasteering trips around Cap Pinar from €39 per person.

Water Sports

Diving & Snorkelling

Mallorca is one of southern Europe's premier diving and snorkelling destinations. The combination of super-clear waters and professional dive centres make this an excellent place for a leisure dive or to undertake the open-water PADI diving-accreditation course. Diving is best from May to October.

Mallorca Diving (www.mallorcadiving. com) lists seven reputable dive centres. A one-tank dive will set you back around €45 and a two-hour intro course around €80, while the per-dive rate falls markedly the more dives you take. Diving equipment and insurance are sometimes, but not usually, included in the quoted prices, so always ask. Snorkelling starts from €15 per hour.

Dive Sites

The options around the Mallorcan coast are close to endless, from Port d'Andratx in the southwest to Formentor at the island's northernmost tip. Four favourites:

➡ **Badia de Pollença** (p125) Experienced divers rank this the island's best diving, with caves and decent marine life along the southern wall of the Cap de Formentor peninsula or the southern end of the Cap des Pinar.

➡ **Parc Nacional Marítim-Terrestre de l'Arxipèlag de Cabrera** (p172) A national park, so special permission is required for scuba diving, but also great snorkelling.

➡ **Illa de Sa Dragonera** (p93) The best underwater views off the island's southwest.

➡ **Palma Bay** (p84) Has wrecks and caves for experienced divers to explore.

Sailboarding & Kitesurfing

While the relatively calm wind and waves of Mallorca don't make the island a natural hot spot for fans of windsurfing or kitesurfing (aka kiteboarding), exceptions to the rule are the Badia de Pollença and Port d'Alcúdia, where stiff breezes ensure plenty of action. Three-day beginners' windsurfing courses cost from around €145, with hourly rental starting from €16. Kitesurfing is a more expensive affair – rental will set you back around €120 per day, and a three-day course around €390.

➡ **Bike & Kite** (p125) Kitesurfing lessons and rental in Port de Pollença.

➡ **Sail & Surf Pollença** (p125) Sailing and windsurfing courses and rental in Port de Pollença.

Sailing

Among the 35 marinas that ring Mallorca's coast, many offer yacht charters, sailboat rentals and sailing courses. There are large sailing schools in Palma, Port de Pollença and other resorts; expect a two-day course to cost €400 to €500; the Palma Sea School (p68) is the most professional outfit.

One place that rents yachts is Llaüts (p92) in Port d'Andratx; prices start at €160 per day. Mezzo Magic (p110) in Port de Sóller is also recommended for all-included yacht hire.

Sailing Routes

If you charter or bring your own yacht, your options for sailing are unlimited. Popular routes:

➡ **Palma to Illa de Cabrera** To enter the national park, you'll need prior permission.

➡ **Port d'Andratx to Port de Sóller** The best of the Serra de Tramuntana coast.

➡ **Cala Sant Vicenç to Port d'Alcúdia** Round the inspiring Cap de Formentor.

Sailing Resources

Sailing is a serious business in Mallorca, with plenty of organisations promoting the sport, providing information and ensuring sailors leave the environment as they found it.

➡ **Harbours & Marinas Guide** Free guide to moorings and marinas published annually by Tallers de Molí; available from tourist offices or marinas.

➡ **Conselleria de Medi Ambient** (p81) Contact this organisation for guidelines for anchoring your yacht in open water to protect the sea floor.

➡ **Federación Balear de Vela** (www. federacionbalearvela.org) Another good source of information.

Sea Kayaking

Mallorca's craggy coastline is indented with lovely bays and coves – many of which can only be reached by boat. A sea kayak allows you to tune into the soothing rhythm of the sea and explore rock formations, caves and quiet beaches at your own pace. Marine falcons, cormorants and wild goats are frequently sighted, and you might even spot the odd dolphin or flying fish. The coves of the Parc Natural de la Península de Llevant, inaccessible from the land, are a paradise of pristine waters, pitted rocks and thriving wildlife. The coast around Sóller in the west, Porto Cristo in the east and Port de Pollença in the north is perfect for paddling.

Boat Trips

From Easter to October, glass-bottomed boats drift up and down the eastern coast and can be a fun way to enjoy the water without having the responsibility of sailing your own boat. Most are half-day trips only and rarely last around four hours. All sell return tickets, but on some east-coast routes you can travel one way. If we had to choose just four routes, they would be these:

➡ **Transportes Marítimos Brisa** (p133) Port d'Alcúdia to Cala Sant Vicenç and back, via Cap de Formentor.

➡ **Barcos Azules** (p110) Port de Sóller to Sa Calobra.

➡ **Excursions a Cabrera** (p173) Round-trip tours by speedboat or slower boats from Colònia de Sant Jordi to the Parc Nacional Marítim-Terrestre de l'Arxipèlag de Cabrera.

➡ **Starfish** (p164) From Portocolom to Cala Figuera.

Plan Your Trip
Travel with Children

Mallorca could be the poster child for stimulating and stress-free family travel. Undoubtedly an adults' playground, it's just as packed with diversions and distractions for the littl'uns: castles to scale, warm seas and wild water parks to splash in, caves to explore, beaches to burn energy and warm welcomes all round.

Mallorca for Kids

Resorts up and down the island cater for families with their well-tended seafront promenades, playgrounds, pools, round-the-clock activities and child-friendly hotels and restaurants. And the Mallorcans simply adore tots, so wherever you go, you can be sure they'll not only be welcome, but actively fussed over.

It's the little things that are likely to spark imaginations: eating snail-shaped *ensaïmada* pastries for breakfast, building castles in the sand, taking a (whoa!) helter-skelter ride along the coast to Sa Calobra, or a rickety train ride to Sóller.

There's plenty to appease older children, too: mountain biking, scuba diving, spelunking in sea caves or even cliff jumping – sure to gain them kudos in the classroom back home.

Nappies (diapers), baby food and formula milk are widely available in town and resort supermarkets and chemists.

Children's Highlights
Energy Burners

➡ **Wet and wild** Kids will gleefully exhaust themselves on the slides, rides and tides at theme parks Aqualand (p86) and Western

Best Regions for Kids
Northern Mallorca

Alcúdia and Port de Pollença are natural family-pleasers, with giant gentle bays ideal for long, sandy days. Hit Hidropark (p132) for whizzy slides and Parc Natural de S'Albufera (p135) for gentle bike rides and birdwatching expeditions. Plus, there are loads of activities for teens – from kayaking to spooky caving.

Eastern Mallorca

Tell tales of troglodytes as you duck through the glittering chambers of vast caves – none more impressive than the Coves del Drac (p162). There are castles for fantasy play, pony rides, boat trips, safari encounters and a cluster of lovely, gently shelving bays in the island's east, too.

Palma & Badia de Palma

The island's capital is like a history lesson come to life, whether playing spot-the-gargoyle at the cathedral (p51) or clambering up to Castell de Bellver (p67). Nearby, find giant water parks and an aquarium with brilliantly scary shark sleepovers.

Water Park (p88), while kid-friendly Hidropark (p132) is handy for the northern resorts.

➡ **Back to nature** Treat natural parks such as Península de Llevant (p154) and Cala Mondragó (p175) like vast open-air playgrounds, full of secret coves, ancient stone towers and flocks of beady-eyed goats.

➡ **Pedal pushing** Gentle pedals along the coast and in the bird-rich wetlands of Parc Natural de S'Albufera (p135); mountain biking in the Tramuntana for active teens.

➡ **Float their boat** Pair up with a nipper in a tandem sea kayak to explore the caves and coves around Port de Sóller (p109).

Animal Encounters

➡ **Artestruz** (p169) Ostriches to stroke, feed and admire in full sprint at this one-of-a-kind park near Ses Salines.

➡ **Palma Aquarium** (p85) Some 8000 marine creatures splash around in the tanks here. There are monthly shark sleepovers for little nippers.

➡ **Safari-Zoo** (p162) In the island's east, this is a rare chance to spot giraffe, emus and lions on a safari train.

Natural Wonders

➡ **Coves del Drac** (p162) Wend through watery caverns encrusted with stalactites, millennia in the making.

➡ **Serra de Tramuntana** (p95) Marvel at faces and weird formations in the bizarrely weathered peaks of this mountain range.

➡ **Sa Calobra** (p115) Feel your stomach drop on the roller-coaster road down to Sa Calobra, with snapshot views of sheer cliffs and canyons.

➡ **Coves d'Artà** (p159) A magical cave with a forest of formations, including the 'Queen of Columns' and 'Chamber of Hell'.

➡ **Blue Cave** (p173) Look in wonder at the surreal blue waters on a boat trip to the Illa de Cabrera, part of Mallorca's only national park.

➡ **Parc Natural de S'Albufera** (p135) Bring binoculars to spot wading birds, turtles and even water buffalo in this reed-fringed nature park.

Family Beaches

➡ **Platja de Muro** (p135) Fabulous sweep of silky sand and shallow turquoise sea in the north's Badia d'Alcúdia. It backs onto the Parc Natural de S'Albufera.

➡ **Cala Mondragó** (p175) This southern Blue Flag bay in the Parc Natural de Mondragó is gorgeous, with brilliantly clear water and powder-soft sand. Great for snorkelling.

➡ **Cala Agulla** (Map p157; Cala Agulla) Fringed by pines and dunes, this beautiful arc of a Blue Flag bay sits just north of Capdepera. The water is shallow enough for paddling.

➡ **Platja de Formentor** (p127) Getting to this north-coast beach by boat or the hair-raising coastal road is part of the fun. Tiptoe away from the crowds on the pine-flanked slither of sand.

➡ **Cala Mesquida** (p158) An east-coast favourite, this gently shelving bay has dazzling clear water. It's better for older kids due to stiff winds and waves.

EATING OUT

Eating out with children is a breeze in Mallorca, where large family lunches are a way of life and the mood is laid-back in all but the most formal of places. You'll get lots of smiles if you have kids with you and letting a tot wander around a restaurant – as long as they're not breaking wine bottles or bothering anyone – is usually OK.

Many resort restaurants offer inexpensive children's menus – simple grilled meats, French fries, spaghetti, tortillas and the like, followed by ice cream. If not, most places are generally happy to improvise to suit children's appetites and whip up smaller portions. Kids with more adventurous tastes might like to try *pa amb oli* (bread rubbed with oil and tomatoes with a variety of toppings) and paella, while Sóller orange ice cream always goes down a treat.

You cannot rely on restaurants having high chairs, although many have a couple – getting there early increases your chances of snaffling one. It's worth bringing your own harness, though, as these are often lacking. Few places have nappy-changing facilities.

TOP TIPS

➡ Ask for extra tapas in bars to suit younger taste buds, such as olives or raw carrot sticks.

➡ Adjust your children to Spanish time (ie late nights) as quickly as you can – otherwise they'll miss half the fun.

➡ Unlike in the USA, crayons and paper are rarely given out in restaurants – bring your own.

➡ Kids who share your bed won't incur a supplement – extra beds usually cost €20 to €30.

➡ Ask the local tourist office for the nearest children's playgrounds.

Back in Time

➡ **Castell de Bellver** (p67) The Badia de Palma shrinks to postcard format from this mighty circular castle.

➡ **Ferrocarril de Sóller** (p84) This rattling vintage train from Palma to Sóller is a real blast from the past – a hit with kids and parents.

➡ **Santuari de Sant Salvador** (p152) Ramble along the ramparts of this hilltop castle above Artà.

➡ **Medieval Walls** (p127) Travel back in time with a walk atop the old city walls in Alcúdia.

➡ **Torre des Verger** (p96) Play pirates at this watchtower precariously perched above the sea near Estellencs.

Planning

When to Go

Bear in mind that many kid-geared sights and activities are open only from April to October. The best season to go depends on what you want to see and do. Spring and autumn are dry, warm and fantastic for hiking, cycling and other active pursuits. Families (including locals) descend en masse on the coast during the summer holidays, so if you are going then, you might want to choose a quieter resort, or base yourself slightly inland at a *finca* (farm).

Accommodation

Whether you're looking for a self-catering apartment, a coastal resort for families or a rural farm-stay complete with resident goats and donkeys to pet, we recommend dozens of family-friendly accommodation options.

Many hotels in coastal resorts offer apartments big enough for families or one-bedroom suites with a small sitting area and sofa bed. The vast majority of places will squeeze in a baby's cot for free or a child's bed for a small extra charge – mention it when booking.

The all-inclusive resorts that dominate the southern, eastern and (to a lesser extent) northern coastline, do one thing very well: most places employ kids' entertainers to organise children's activities, from games and discos to craft workshops and outdoor excursions.

Baby Equipment

Most airlines – including Ryanair and easyJet – will take your pushchair from you as you embark for no extra charge (this needs to be tagged at the check-in or bag-drop desk). For additional items such as booster seats and travel cots, they levy a fee (€10/£10 if booked online, €20/£20 if done at the airport). You can take baby food, milk and sterilised water in your hand baggage.

If you would rather not schlep it all with you, companies such as Multi-Hire (www.multi-hire.com) and Baby Equipment Hire

RESOURCES

For general advice on travelling with children, consider the following:
➡ Lonely Planet's *Travel with Children*
➡ www.travelwithyourkids.com
➡ www.familytravelnetwork.com

Mallorca (www.babyequipmenthirema jorca.co.uk) rent out the essentials, and it's often a more cost-effective way of doing it than paying through the nose with airlines.

Baby Food

You can buy baby formula in powder or liquid form, as well as sterilising solutions such as Milton, at *farmacias* (pharmacies). Disposable nappies (diapers) are widely available at supermarkets and *farmacias*. Fresh cow's milk is sold in cartons and plastic bottles in supermarkets in big cities, but can be hard to find in small towns, where UHT is often the only option.

If you've brought baby food with you, just ask for it to be warmed up in the kitchen; most restaurants will have no problem with this.

Childcare

Some of the better hotels can generally arrange babysitters for an hourly fee. You could also check out the website Canguroencasa (www.canguroencasa.com), where you can search for English-speaking babysitters *(canguros)*; click on 'Canguros Baleares'. The going rate is between €5 and €10 per hour.

If you want to explore safe in the knowledge that your kids are in good hands, check out Jelly and Ice Cream (www.jelly-andice-cream.com), who arrange English-speaking childcare with qualified nannies

CHILDREN'S DISCOUNTS

Discounts are available for children (usually aged under 12) on public transport, while under-fives ride for free. You can also expect substantial reductions on sights, though ages vary widely, with free entry ranging from 0 to 16 years. As a rule, under-fours are free and under-12s pay half price, as well as concessions for youths. Most tours (for instance boat tours) offer a 50% reduction for children.

and babysitting. Little Ducklings (www.littleducklings.es), Little Puffs (www.little puffschildcaremallorca.com) and Angels (www.angelsnursingagency.com) also come recommended. Expect to pay around €90 per day, for up to three children.

Car Hire

You can hire car seats for infants and children (usually for a per-day fee) from most car-rental firms, but book them well in advance.

It's worth bearing in mind that most compact cars are short on space, so you may struggle to squeeze in your luggage and pushchair in the boot (trunk). Check the car's dimensions before booking or consider upgrading to a bigger model.

Regions at a Glance

Western Mallorca

Villages
Landscapes
Hiking

Northern Mallorca

Landscapes
Towns
Beaches

Palma & the Badia de Palma

Architecture
Galleries
Food

Medieval Architecture

Palma is like a 3D textbook on Mediterranean architectural history. The Gothic cathedral is the show-stealer, but the old town's tightly packed lanes hide Modernista masterpieces, medieval mansions and baroque *patis* (patios).

Miró, Barceló, Picasso & Dalí

Many of Spain's premier 20th-century artists had a soft spot for Palma. Miró left his playful mark all over the city, Miquel Barceló came from nearby Felanitx, and Picasso and Dalí originals cram the city's stellar galleries.

The Mallorcan Kitchen

Mallorca's culinary star shines brightest in Palma, from the island's best seafood restaurants to the coterie of restaurants overseen by celebrity chef Marc Fosh, to intimate tapas bars around Plaça Major and irresistible pastry shops.

p48

Hilltop Villages

The honey-coloured stone architecture of Western Mallorca's hilltop villages form idyllic stops through a stunning mountain panorama. Explore the time-etched charms of Valldemossa, Deià, Fornalutx, Binaraix and Orient.

Spectacular Uplands

In Mallorca's repertoire of lovely landscapes, the Serra de Tramuntana deserves a standing ovation, with its wild limestone peaks, plunging cliffs and backdrop of azure waters.

Mountain Hikes

The multiday Ruta de Pedra en Sec traversing the Tramuntana is the real biggie, but you can also scramble up Puig de Massanella, trek through Sóller's citrus groves or make the pilgrimage to Monestir de Lluc.

p89

Cap de Formentor

The Serra de Tramuntana reaches a crescendo along this peninsula of dizzying mountain peaks and razor-edge cliffs that plunge to sheltered coves.

Pollença & Alcúdia

The northern coastal hinterland harbours glorious Pollença, with its cobblestone streets and 365 steps to Calvari, and ancient Alcúdia, with Roman ruins and defensive walls.

Superlative Sands

The masses gravitate to the broad beaches and crystal-clear waters of the north's twin bays: Badia de Pollença and Badia d'Alcúdia. Quieter coves punctuate Cala Sant Vicenç, Cap de Formentor and Cap des Pinar.

p117

The Interior

Wine
Food
Architecture

Wineries & Bodegas

Mallorca's wine-producing areas range across the island's vine-cloaked interior; some of the wineries offer tours, others just cellar-door sales.

Mallorcan Country Cooking

From the *celler* restaurants of Inca and Sineu to the rural *fincas* transformed into hotels and restaurants, eating dishes such as *lechona* (roast suckling pig) or *tumbet* (a kind of vegetable ratatouille) in the interior is all about authenticity.

Monasteries & Medieval Towns

Almost every hilltop in inland Mallorca was long ago colonised by a monastery from where the views ripple for miles, while towns like Sineu and Petra are places of quiet, underrated charm.

p137

Eastern Mallorca

Beaches
Caves
Landscapes

Secluded Beaches & Coves

Go off-piste to the wild beaches northeast of Cala Ratjada, home to some of Mallorca's most desirable stretches of coastal real estate. The serene *cales* (coves) south of Porto Cristo are similarly lovely.

Subterranean Cathedrals

The epic formations and stalactite forests of eastern Mallorca's caves rank among the island's most eye-catching phenomena.

The Península de Llevant

North of Artà, the Parc Natural de la Península de Llevant allures birdwatchers and hikers. Cap Ferrutx bookends the peninsula, while Ermita de Betlem affords quiet contemplation.

p150

Southern Mallorca

Beaches
Scenery
Archaeology

Unspoiled Sands

The south has a prize collection of beaches and limpid waters for diving. Loll on the seemingly never-ending sands of Platja des Trenc, or cove-hop to coastal lovelies like Cala Pi, Cala Llombards and the Parc Natural de Mondragó.

Coastal Ramparts

The high cliffs of the coast have spared much of the south from developers' bulldozers, especially from Cap Blanc to Cap de Ses Salines. Illa de Cabrera is a treasure.

Talayotic Sites

The island's prehistory is shrouded in uncertainty; Talayotic sites such as Capocorb Vell and those close to Ses Salines offer insights into pre-Roman Mallorca.

p165

On the
Road

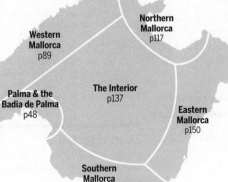

Palma & the Badia de Palma

Best Places to Eat

➜ Marc Fosh (p71)

➜ Can Cera Gastro-Bar (p70)

➜ Es Mollet (p74)

➜ Toque (p73)

➜ Bon Lloc (p72)

Best Bars

➜ Bar Flexas (p75)

➜ Ca La Seu (p75)

➜ La Vinya de Santa Clara (p75)

➜ Idem Café (p76)

➜ Atlantico Café (p76)

Why Go?

Visually magnificent, culturally spoiled, historically fascinating and geographically blessed, Palma should be better known as one of Europe's great destinations. Yes, it's a
playground of the elite, but visitors of all means can enjoy
its wonders: crooked medieval streets lined with aristocratic mansions; galleries packed with the work of renowned
artists; a broad bay bristling with the masts of maritime
wealth; restaurants mixing it with the great innovators of
modern Spanish food; and endless acres of shopping.

Beyond Palma, Mallorca's capital and greatest asset, the
Badia de Palma (Bay of Palma) spreads out in both directions: the flatlands to the east and the wrinkled hills that
presage Mallorca's highest mountains to the west. These
parts are also culturally uneven: one *cala* (cove) may be the
mooring place of the super-wealthy; the next brilliant with
neon, lighting the way for the young British and German
funseekers that come here in droves.

When to Go

Unlike the rest of the island, Palma's energy levels remain
fairly constant throughout the year – most sights, hotels and
restaurants remain open year-round. That said, the city does
have an irresistible feel-good atmosphere when the weather's warm, the yacht harbour is filled with masts and one of
the numerous sailing regattas brings the beautiful people to
town – this applies from April to October.

Scarcely a month passes in Palma without a festival of
some kind: pre-Lenten carnival parades in February, the
crazy pyrotechnics of Nit de Foc in June and December's
Christmas market are top diary dates. The beach resorts of
the Badia de Palma effectively shut down in winter.

What's New

➡ Mercado Gastronómico San Juan (p69) Opened in 2015, this former slaughterhouse in Palma's northern suburbs has quickly established itself as a beacon of the city's ever-evolving food scene, bringing the best Mallorcan produce together in one place.

➡ Skybar at Hotel Hostal Cuba (p76) Yet another stunning vista of photogenic Palma has opened up, with the establishment of this cruisy rooftop hotel-bar.

Palma's Patios

Few experiences in Palma beat simply milling around the backstreets of the city's Old Town, which spreads east of the cathedral. Iron gates conceal the city's *patis* (patios), the grand courtyards where nobles once received guests and horse-drawn coaches clattered to a halt. *Patis* were the intersection of public and private life, and as such they were showpieces – polished until they gleamed and filled with flowers and plants.

There are still around 150 patrician houses with *patis* in Palma today, though most can only be observed through locked wrought-iron gates. They vary in style from Gothic to renaissance, baroque to Modernista, but most have the same defining features: graceful arches and Ionic columns, sweeping staircases with wrought-iron balustrades and a well or cistern. For a closer look, join one of the guided tours run by Mallorca Rutes (p68).

Top Five Galleries

➡ Museu Fundació Juan March (p62) Contemporary art stars, including Mallorca's own Miquel Barceló.

➡ Es Baluard (p66) Picasso, Miró and fine city views at this gallery atop the Renaissance sea wall.

➡ Fundació Pilar i Joan Miró (p86) Total Miró immersion, with 2500 works on show.

➡ Centre Cultural Contemporani Pelaires (p62) In this fetching 17th-century building is Palma's first dedicated contemporary art gallery, still going strong.

➡ Palau March (p53) Paintings by Dalí and sculpture by Moore, Rodin and Chillida in an exquisite palace.

Need to Know

➡ Many of Palma's big attractions close on Monday, including the Fundació Pilar i Joan Miró (p86) and Es Baluard (p66).

➡ Sunday closures include the Catedral (p51) and Palau March (p53).

Getting There & Away

➡ Mallorca's international airport, Son Sant Joan, is in Ca'n Pastilla, just 8km from central Palma. From here, a taxi to the centre of town should cost less than €20, less again if you're headed to the eastern Badia de Palma, and €40 or more if you're bound for Magaluf.

➡ Bus 1 loops around Palma from the airport to Porto Pi on the western side of the city, while bus 21 heads east to S'Arenal. Both cost a flat €5.

Resources

➡ **Ajuntament de Palma** (www.palmademallorca. es) The website of Palma's civil administration has information on most aspects of city life.

➡ **Consell de Mallorca tourist office** (www. infomallorca.net) Easily navigated, up-to-date and terrifically informative.

➡ **Visit Calvia** (www. visitcalvia.com) The lowdown on the resorts to the west of Palma, from Magaluf to Portals Nous.

➡ **EMT Palma public transport** (www.emtpalma. es) Allows you to see and search all routes and fares on the EMT network.

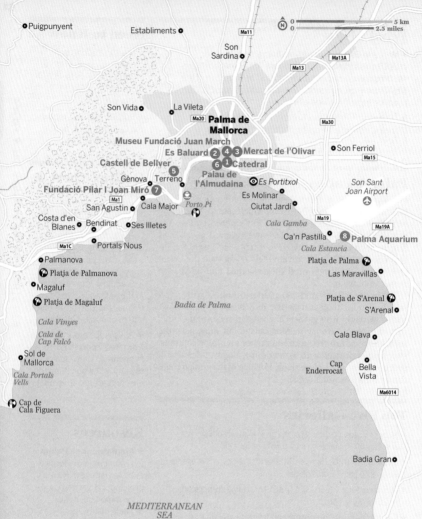

Palma & the Badia de Palma Highlights

1 **Catedral** (p51)
Admiring the work of this stunning confection.

2 **Es Baluard** (p66)
Wandering the ramparts of this historic fortress-museum.

3 **Mercat de l'Olivar** (p69) Tasting the plenty laid out in the stalls of Palma's largest produce market.

4 **Museu Fundación Juan March** (p62) Getting up close to Picasso, Miró and Dalí, minus the crowds.

5 **Castell de Bellver** (p67) Commanding the heights from this 14th-century fortress.

6 **Palau de l'Almudaina** (p53) Walking in the

footsteps of Moorish governors and Spanish royalty.

7 **Fundació Pilar i Joan Miró** (p86) Feeling the inspiration from Miró's hilltop studio.

8 **Palma Aquarium** (p85) Coming face-to-face with the denizens of the Mediterranean deep.

PALMA DE MALLORCA

POP 400,578

Palma is a stunner. Rising in honey-coloured stone from the broad waters of the Badia de Palma, this enduring city dates back to the 13th-century Christian reconquest of the island, and to the Moors, Romans and Talayotic people before that. A richly studded diadem of historical sites, Palma also shelters a seemingly endless array of galleries, restaurants, craft studios and bars – it's without doubt Mallorca's greatest treasure. Wander in any direction from the awe-inspiring Gothic Catedral at its geographic and historical heart and you'll find bent medieval streets lined with aristocratic townhouses, looming baroque churches, teeming public squares, vibrant bohemian neighbourhoods and markets overflowing with all the bounty of the island. You could spend weeks in this city, and still uncover fresh joys every day.

History

Founded by the Romans in 123 BC, Palma (or Palmeria) was built on a prominence naturally commanding the broad Badia de Palma (Bay of Palma), on the site of an earlier, Talayotic settlement. Later falling into dereliction, it was given fresh impetus by the arrival of the island's new Muslim masters in the 10th century. By the 12th century Medina Mayurka (City of Mallorca) was one of the most prosperous Muslim capitals in Europe. The upheaval of Christian reconquest in 1229 didn't interrupt this growth for long – by the 14th century Ciutat de Mallorca or Ciudad Capital (City Capital) had become one of the western Mediterranean's richest trading ports.

By the 16th century, along with the rest of the island, the city was sinking into a protracted period of torpor, suffering from the predations of pirates. The great seaward walls whose remains stand at the Dalt Murada today were largely built in the 16th and 17th centuries, when the city's seasonal torrent, the Riera, was diverted from its natural course along Passeig d'es Born to its present location west of the city walls. The Old Town centre then went into decline, and the bulk of the sea walls were demolished at the beginning of the 20th century to allow rapid expansion of the city. But the heart of the city has been spruced up beyond recognition, since tourist cash began to flow into the island in the 1960s. By the 2000s, a new period of prosperity had manifestly arrived, and property around the Dalt Murada had become among the most expensive in all Spain.

◉ Sights

◎ Old Palma

★**Catedral**   CATHEDRAL
(La Seu; Map p58; www.catedraldemallorca.org; Carrer del Palau Reial 9; adult/child €7/free; ⊙10am-6.15pm Mon-Fri Jun-Sep, to 5.15pm Apr, May & Oct, to 3.15pm Nov-Mar, 10am-2.15pm Sat

---

PALMA IN TWO DAYS

Palma makes a fabulous city break and with a will you can cram a lot into a weekend. Start with the obvious: the colossal Gothic **Catedral** and **Palau de l'Almudaina** (p53). You'll spend hours meandering the Old Town's mazy lanes, and may wish to find some contemplative space at the **Jardí del Bisbe** (p57) and **Banys Àrabs** (p57). Lunch at **Can Cera Gastro-Bar** (p70), within the sedate, 17th-century walls of the former aristocratic mansion now housing the boutique hotel **Can Cera** (Map p58; ☑971 71 50 12; http://cancerahotel.com; Carrer del Convent de Sant Francesc 8; d/ste €352/418; ✳️🔊). Continue touring with the **Basílica de Sant Francesc** (p54) and **Es Baluard** (p66), where you can stop to snack alongside the battlements. For a night out, make for nearby Santa Catalina, with dinner at **Koh** (p73), drinks at **Idem Café** (p76) and clubbing along Passeig Marítim. The following day, head east out of town up to **Castell de Bellver** (p67) and the **Fundació Pilar i Joan Miró** (p86), book lunch at **Ca'n Eduardo** (p74) and spend the afternoon exploring the **Museu Fundació Juan March** (p62), then end with a drink at **Guinness House** (p75). Later, have an *ensaïmada* (a delicate, croissant-like pastry dusted with icing sugar, and sometimes filled with cream) at **Ca'n Joan de S'Aigo** (p71), dinner at **Marc Fosh** (p71) or **La Bodeguilla** (p72), then hit the bars of Sa Gerreria, beginning at **L'Ambigú** (p70).

TOP TREASURES OF PALMA CATHEDRAL

Enter the **Catedral** (p51) from the north flank. You get tickets in the first room and then pass into the **sacristy**, which hosts the main part of the small **Museu Capitular** (Chapter Museum). At the centre of this is a huge gold-plated monstrance, dating to 1585, which comes out for the annual Corpus Christi procession. Interesting items include a portable altar, thought to have belonged to Jaume I. Its little compartments contain saints' relics; other reliquaries include one purporting to hold three thorns from Christ's crown of thorns.

Next come two chapter houses. In the **Gothic chapter house** by Guillem Sagrera, note the tomb of Bishop Gil Sánchez Muñoz (Antipope Clement VIII), the *Tabla de l'Almoina* (Alms Panel) and two paintings by the master Monti-Sion – *El Calvario* (the Calvary) and *Nuestra Señora de la Misericordia* (Our Lady of Mercy) – which allude to a terrible flood in Palma in 1403 that left 5000 dead. The **baroque chapter house** is exquisite, with its delicately carved stonework and 16th-century *relicario de la Vera Cruz* (reliquary of the True Cross) encrusted with gemstones. Your attention will also be drawn to a matching pair of silver candelabras, each weighing 243kg.

On passing through one of the side **chapels** into the cathedral itself, your gaze soars high to the cross vaults, supported by slender, octagonal pillars. The broad **nave** and aisles are flanked by chapels. The walls are illuminated by kaleidoscopic curtains of stained glass, including 87 windows and eight magnificent rose windows. The grandest (the **oculus maior** or 'great eye', featuring a Star of David) comprises 1115 panes of glass shimmering ruby, gold and sapphire, and is the largest Gothic rose window in the world. Visit in the morning to see the stunning effect of its coloured light and shapes, reflected on the west wall. This spectacle is at its best at 8.30am on 2 February and 11 November, when the image of the main rose window appears superimposed below the other.

The cathedral's three strikingly different **apses** show the Eucharist in three stages from left to right: institution, celebration and adoration. The left apse displays the golden wonder of the Corpus Christi altarpiece, an elaborate baroque confection by Jaume Blanquer (1626–41) devoted to the institution of the Eucharist at the Last Supper.

Antoni Gaudí carried out renovations from 1904 to 1914. His most important contribution was the strange **baldachin** that hovers over the main altar. Topped by a fanciful sculpture of Christ crucified and flanked by the Virgin Mary and St John, it looks like the gaping jaw of some oversized prehistoric shark dangling from the ceiling of an old science museum. Some 35 lamps hang from it, and what looks like a flying carpet is spread above. The genius of Barcelona Modernisme seems to have left behind an indecipherable pastiche, but then this was supposed to be a temporary version. The definitive one was never made (typical Gaudí).

Not content with this strangeness, the parish commissioned contemporary Mallorcan artist Miquel Barceló (an agnostic) to remake the **Capella del Santíssim i Sant Pere**, in the right apse. Done in 15 tonnes of ceramics, this dreamscape representing the miracle of the loaves and fishes was unveiled in 2007. On the left, fish and other marine creatures burst from the wall; the opposite side has a jungle look, with representations of bread and fruit. In between the fish and palm fronds, and stacks of skulls, appears a luminous body that is supposed to be Christ, but is modelled on the stocky artist himself.

Other notable elements of the interior include the **giant organ**, built in 1798 (free recitals are held at noon on the first Tuesday of each month), and the two **pulpits**, the smaller of which was partly redone by Gaudí.

year-round) Palma's vast cathedral ('La Seu' in Catalan) is the city's major architectural landmark. Aside from its sheer scale and undoubted beauty, its stunning interior features, designed by Antoni Gaudí and renowned contemporary artist Miquel Barceló, make this unlike any cathedral elsewhere in the world. The awesome structure is predominantly Gothic, apart from the main facade, which is startling, quite beautiful and completely mongrel.

The Catedral occupies the site of what was the central mosque of Medina Mayurka, capital of Muslim Mallorca for three centuries. Although Jaume I and his marauding men forced their way into the city in 1229, work on the Catedral – one of Europe's largest – did not begin until 1300. Rather, the mosque was used in the interim as a church and dedicated to the Virgin Mary. Work wasn't completed until 1601.

The original was a Renaissance cherry on the Gothic cake, but an earthquake in 1851 (which caused considerable panic but no loss of life) severely damaged it. Rather than mend the original, it was decided to add some neo-Gothic flavour. With its interlaced flying buttresses on each flank and soaring pinnacles, it's a masterful example of the style. The result is a hybrid of the Renaissance original (in particular the main doorway) and an inevitably artificial-feeling, 19th-century pseudo-Gothic monumentalism. Mass times vary, but one always takes place at 9am.

★**Palau de l'Almudaina**   PALACE
(Map p58; www.patrimonionacional.es; Carrer del Palau Reial; adult/child €7/4, audio guide/guided tour €3/4; ⊙10am-8pm Apr-Sep, to 6pm Oct-Mar) Originally an Islamic fort, this mighty construction opposite the cathedral was converted into a residence for the Mallorcan monarchs at the end of the 13th century. The King of Spain resides here still, at least symbolically. The royal family are rarely in residence, except for the occasional ceremony, as they prefer to spend summer in the Palau Marivent (in Cala Major). At other times you can wander through a series of cavernous stone-walled rooms that have been lavishly decorated.

The Romans are said to have built a *castrum* (fort) here, possibly on the site of a prehistoric settlement. The Wālis (Governors) of Muslim Mallorca altered and expanded the Roman original to build their own *alcázar* (fort), before Jaume I and his successors modified it to such an extent that little of the Muslim version remains.

The first narrow room you enter has a black-and-white ceiling, symbolising the extremes of night and day, darkness and light. You then enter a series of three grand rooms. Notice the bricked-in Gothic arches cut off in the middle. Originally these three rooms were double their present height and formed one single great hall added to the original Arab fort and known as the **Saló del Tinell** (from an Italian word, *tinello*, meaning 'place where one eats'): this was once a giant banqueting and ceremonial

hall. The rooms are graced by period furniture, tapestries and other curios. The following six bare rooms and terrace belonged to the original Arab citadel.

In the main courtyard, **Patio de Armas**, troops would line up for an inspection and parade before heading out into the city. The lion fountain in its centre is one of the palace's rare Arab remnants. Up the grand Royal Staircase are the **royal apartments**, a succession of lavishly appointed rooms (look up to the beautiful coffered timber *artesonado* ceilings), whose centrepiece is the Saló Gòtic, the upper half of the former Saló del Tinell; here you can see where those Gothic arches wind up. Next door to the apartments is the royal **Capella de Sant'Anna**, a Gothic chapel whose entrance is a very rare Mallorcan example of late Romanesque in rose and white marble.

After the death of Jaume III in 1349, no king lived here permanently again.

In the shadow of the Almudaina's walls, along Avinguda d'Antoni Maura, is S'Hort del Rei (the King's Garden).

★**Palau March**   MUSEUM
(Map p58; ☑971 71 11 22; www.fundacionbmarch.es; Carrer del Palau Reial 18; adult/child €4.50/free; ⊙10am-6.30pm Mon-Fri Apr-Oct, to 2pm Nov-Mar, to 2pm Sat year-round) This house, palatial by any definition, was one of several residences of the phenomenally wealthy March family. Sculptures by 20th-century greats including Henry Moore, Auguste Rodin, Barbara Hepworth and Eduardo Chillida grace the outdoor terrace. Within lie many more artistic treasures from such luminaries of Spanish art as Salvador Dalí and Barcelona's Josep Maria Sert and Xavier Corberó. Not to be missed are the meticulously crafted figures of an 18th-century Neapolitan *belén* (nativity scene).

Entry is through an outdoor terrace display of modern sculptural works, of which centre stage is taken by Corberó's enormous *Orgue del Mar* (1973), or perhaps Rodin's *Torse de l'Homme qui Tombe* (1882).

Inside, more than 20 paintings by Dalí around the themes 'Alchemy and Eternity' catch the eye, as does the *belén's* 1000-plus detailed figures, from angels to kings, shepherds, farm animals and market scenes, making up a unique representation of Christ's birth.

Upstairs, the artist Josep Maria Sert (1874–1945) painted the main vault and music room ceiling. The vault is divided

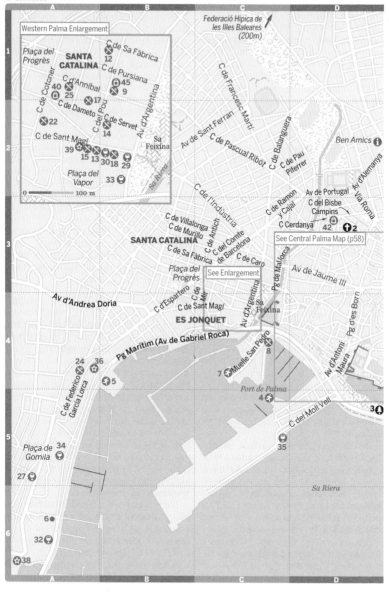

into four parts, the first three representing three virtues (audacity, reason and inspiration) and the last the embodiment of those qualities in the form of Sert's patron, Juan March (1917–98). One of the rooms hosts an intriguing display of maps of the Mediterranean, produced by Mallorcan cartographers in medieval and early modern times.

Basílica de Sant Francesc CHURCH
(Map p58; Plaça de Sant Francesc 7; 6-venue Spiritual Mallorca ticket €5; ⊙10am-2pm & 3-6pm

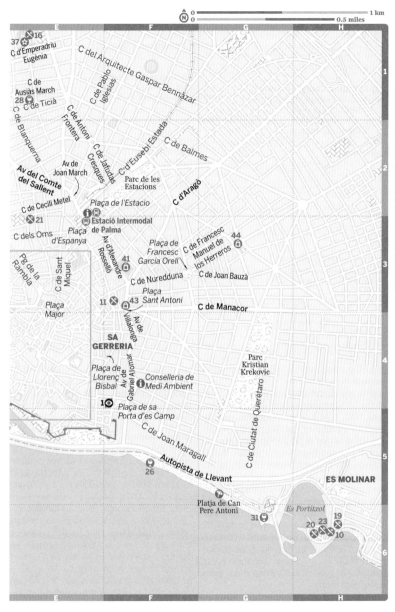

Mon-Sat) One of Palma's oldest churches, the Franciscan Basílica de Sant Francesc was begun in 1281 in Gothic style, while the baroque facade, with its carved postal and rose window, was completed in 1700. In the splendid Gothic cloister – a two-tiered, trap-ezoid affair – the elegant columns indicate it was some time in the making. Inside, the high vaulted roof is classic Gothic, while the glittering high altar is a baroque lollipop, al-beit in need of a polish.

Palma

In the first chapel (dedicated to Nostra Senyora de la Consolació) on the left in the apse is the church's pride and joy, the tomb of the 13th-century scholar and mystic Ramon Llull. Also a fervid evangelist and the inventor of literary Catalan, Llull lays fair claim to the title of Mallorca's favourite son (apart perhaps from tennis genius Rafael Nadal). His alabaster tomb is high up on the right – drop a few coins in the slot for the campaign to have him canonised (he has only made it to beatification). Check out the Capilla de los Santos Mártires Gorkomienses, on the right side of the apse. In 1572, 19 Catholics, 11 of them Franciscans, were martyred in Holland. In this much-faded portrayal of the event, you can see them being hanged, disembowelled, having their noses cut off and more.

Església de Santa Eulàlia CHURCH
(Map p58; Plaça de Santa Eulàlia 2; ☺8am-12.30pm Mon-Sat, 5.20-8.30pm Mon-Fri, 8.15-8.30pm Sat, 4 Masses Sun) One of the first major churches raised after the 1229 conquest, the Església de Santa Eulàlia is a soaring Gothic structure with a neo-Gothic facade (a complete remake was done between 1894

and 1924, following the earthquake of 1851). It is the only such church in Mallorca, aside from the cathedral, with three naves. The baroque *retablo* (altarpiece) is rather worn and you can't get to the chapels in the apse.

Museu Diocesà MUSEUM
(Map p58; www.catedraldemallorca.info; Carrer del Mirador 5; adult/child €3/free; ☺10am-6.15pm Mon-Fri Jun-Sep, to 5.15pm Apr, May & Oct, to 3.15pm Nov-Mar, 10am-2.15pm Sat year-round) Opened in 2007 in its magnificent new home of the Palau Episcopal (Bishop's Residence; a mainly Gothic ensemble dating to the 13th century), the Museu Diocesà, behind the cathedral to the east, is a fascinating excursion for those interested in Mallorca's Christian artistic history. It contains works by Antoni Gaudí, Francesc Comes and Pere Niçard, and a mind-boggling *retaule* (altarpiece) depicting the Passion of Christ (c 1290–1305) and taken from the Convent de Santa Clara.

The episodes of the Passion are shown in precise detail: Palm Sunday, the Last Supper, St Peter's kiss of betrayal. Christ flailed looks utterly unperturbed, while the image of him being nailed to the cross is unsettling. Off to the right, a key work is Comes' *St Jaume de*

Compostela (St James; known to the Spaniards as the Moor-slayer). Niçard's *Sant Jordi* (St George), from around 1468–70, is remarkable for its busy detail. The City of Mallorca (Palma) is shown in the background as St George dispatches the dragon. Below this painting is a scene by Niçard and his boss Rafel Mòger depicting the 1229 taking of Palma. The final room in this wing is the Gothic Oratori de Sant Pau, a small chapel. The stained-glass window was a trial run done by Gaudí in preparation for the windows he did in the cathedral.

Otherwise, a succession of rooms showcases Mallorcan artists such as Pere Terrencs and Mateu López (father and son), while upstairs is a thin collection of baroque art, ceramics and some lovely views over the bay.

Jardí del Bisbe   GARDENS
(Map p58; Carrer de Sant Pere Nolasc 6; ⊗7.30am-1.30pm Mon-Fri) **FREE** Adjoining the Palau Episcopal is the Jardí del Bisbe, a tranquil botanic garden that offers cool respite from a day's hot sightseeing. Stroll among the palms, pomegranates, water lilies, thyme, artichokes and kumquat, orange and lemon trees, or just sit on a bench and contemplate.

Banys Àrabs   HISTORIC BUILDING
(Map p58; Carrer de Serra 7; adult/child €2.50/ free; ⊗9.30am-7pm Apr-Nov, to 5.30pm Dec-Mar) These modest Arab baths, dating from the 10th to 12th centuries, are the single most important remaining monument to the Muslim domination of the island, although all that survives are two small underground

GET YOUR BEARINGS

Use the **Catedral** (p51) as your compass. The heart of the Old Town (the districts of **Sa Portella** and **Sa Calatrava**) has always been centred on its main place of worship, and the one-time seat of secular power opposite it (the **Palau de l'Almudaina** (p53)). Many of Palma's sights are jammed into this warren of tight, twisting lanes and sunny squares, where massive churches jostle noble houses. The bright Mediterranean light and glittering sea are never far away.

To the north lies **Plaça Major** (p65), a typically Spanish public square lined with arcades, shops and cafes. Lively by day, it falls eerily silent at night. To the east, Carrer del Sindicat spokes out towards the avenues that mark the limits of historic Palma, following the zigzag pattern of its now-demolished walls. It crosses a district known as **Sa Gerreria** – for decades run-down and despised, it's now enjoying a revival and boasts some of Palma's more edgy nightlife. Off Plaça Major, the shopping boulevard, **Carrer de Sant Miquel**, leads north towards the vast **Plaça d'Espanya**, the city's major transport hub. Plaça Major and Carrer de Sant Miquel are on high ground that falls away to the west, down to tree-lined **Passeig de la Rambla** boulevard.

West of the cathedral is **Passeig d'es Born**, a classic boulevard for strollers and window shoppers, and one of Palma's major arteries. It borders the historic quarter of **Es Puig de Sant Pere**, buttressed by the fortress-turned gallery **Es Baluard** (p66) to the west, and the shop-lined **Avinguda de Jaume II** to the north. Crossing the **Sa Riera** river brings you to the former sailors' district **Santa Catalina**, with its long, grid-pattern streets and traditional low-slung one- and two-storey houses. As early as the 17th century, windmills were raised in the area still known as **Es Jonquet**, just south of **Carrer de Sant Magí**, the oldest street in the *barri* (district). In recent years gentrification has transformed Santa Catalina into an artsy, bohemian quarter, filled with one-of-a-kind boutiques, galleries, bars and restaurants. Follow the seafront **Passeig Marítim** further west still and you reach the ferry port and Western Palma's major sight: **Castell de Bellver** (p67).

To the east, a 1km walk from the city-centre end of the **Platja de Can Pere Antoni** brings you to **Es Portixol**. The 'little port', once a fishing town beyond Palma and now a delightful dining destination, has a quiet abundance of pleasure craft and is closed off inland by the motorway (at a discreet distance). From central Palma it's an easy walk, cycle or rollerblade here along the **Passeig Marítim**. From Portixol, walking around the next point brings you to **Es Molinar**, a simple, waterfront 'suburban' district of simple fishing folks' houses. Over the bridge is **Ciutat Jardí**, another low-key residential area with a broad, sandy beach.

Central Palma

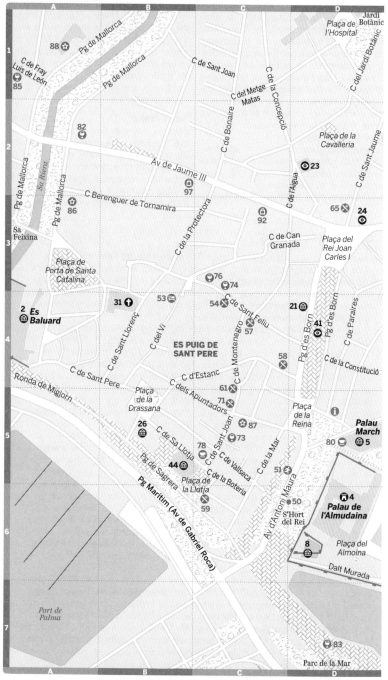

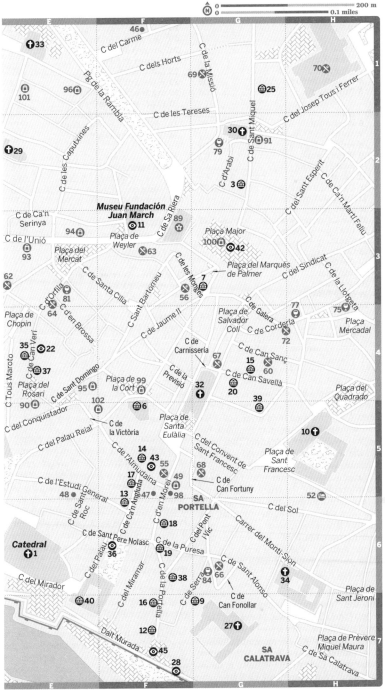

Central Palma

chambers, one with a domed ceiling supported by a dozen columns, some of whose capitals were recycled from demolished Roman buildings. The site may be small, but the two rooms – the caldarium (hot bath) and the tepidarium (warm bath) – evoke a poignant sense of abandonment.

Normally there would also have been a third, cold bath, the frigidarium. As the Roman terms suggest, the Arabs basically took over a Roman idea, here in Mallorca and throughout the Arab world. These ones probably were not public but attached to a private mansion. The baths are set in one of Old Palma's prettiest gardens, where you can sit and relax.

Museu de Mallorca   MUSEUM
(Map p58; http://museudemallorca.caib.es; Carrer de la Portella 5; adult/child €2.40/free; ⊙10am-6pm Tue-Fri, 11am-2pm Sat & Sun) Recently renovated, this excellent city museum is housed in a rambling ensemble of 17th-century mansions on Carrer de la Portella. It showcases a collection of archaeological artefacts,

religious art, antiques and Arabic ceramics – from Talayotic bronzes to intricate Almohad gold jewellery.

Dalt Murada   HISTORIC SITE
(Map p58) Most of Palma's defensive walls were destroyed in the late 19th century to allow the overcrowded city to expand. Only a section of the Renaissance sea wall, the Dalt Murada (begun in 1562, finished in 1801), remains impressively intact. The adjoining Parc de la Mar is an appealing place for a breezy drink at a terrace cafe in summer, despite the nearby coastal road, and is one of the best vantage points for photographing the cathedral in all its glory.

Sa Portella   GATE
(Map p58; Dalt Murada) An original seaward gate in the medieval walls can still be seen.

Arab City Wall   HISTORIC SITE
(Map p54; Carrer de Mateu Enric Lladó) On the eastern rim of the Old Town is a portion of the 12th-century Arab city wall (with some heavy blocks from the Roman wall at the

base), beyond which is a park named after the city gate that once stood here: Porta d'es Camp (Gate of the Countryside). The Muslims knew it as Bab al-Jadid (the New Gate).

Església del Monti-Sion   CHURCH
(Map p58; Carrer del Monti-Sion; ◷ 5.15-7pm) The gaudy baroque facade of the Església del Monti-Sion was converted from a Gothic synagogue. It got a serious baroque makeover, inside and out, in the 16th to 17th centuries, and is now considered one of the high points of the style on the island. Gothic giveaways include the ogive arches in front of the chapels, the key vaulting in the ceiling and the long, low Catalan Gothic arch just inside the entrance.

As you wander in, a priest sitting in a booth by the entry may flip a switch and light up the curves-and-swirls baroque *retablo* (altarpiece) at the back of the church.

Ajuntament   HISTORIC BUILDING
(Town Hall; Map p58; www.palma.ca; Plaça de la Cort 1) Dominating the square that has long been the heart of municipal power in Pal-

ma is the *ajuntament*. The baroque facade (restored in 2016) hides a longer history: the town hall building grew out of a Gothic hospital raised here shortly after the island's conquest. On the top floor of the main facade sits the town clock, En Figuera. The present mechanism dates to 1863 and was purchased in France, but a clock has tolled the hours here for centuries.

You can generally enter the foyer only, in which you will see a Gothic entrance, a fine sweeping staircase and, probably, half a dozen *gegants* (huge figures of kings, queens and other characters that are paraded around town on people's shoulders during fiesta) in storage. More extensive tours are available each Sunday between 11am and noon, but guided tours in English must be prearranged.

Parc de la Mar   PARK
(Map p54) In 1984 the Parc de la Mar (with its artificial lake, fountain and green spaces) was opened. Head slightly east and you'll reach a children's playground.

Museu de sa Juigueta
MUSEUM

(Map p58; ☑654 650780; www.museudesa-juigueta.es; Carrer de la Campana 7; adult/child €3.50/2.50; ⊗9.30am-5pm Tue & Wed, to 12.30pm Thu-Sat; 🖢) The 3000 cars, planes, dolls, robots and other toys on display here represent the tip of a collection of more than 7000 pieces, acquired steadily by a passionate collector from Barcelona. Adjoining is a smart little bar-restaurant (three courses for €13) that not only caters to kids, but turns into a creative play space between 5pm and 8pm in the evening.

Can Bordils
HISTORIC BUILDING

(Map p58; Carrer de l'Almudaina 9) **FREE** This 16th-century mansion with a 17th-century courtyard is home to the Arxiu Municipal, which sometimes holds temporary exhibitions. Unlike many of Palma's (privately owned) historic houses, you can wander in from the street and admire the architecture.

Centre Maimó ben Faraig
MUSEUM

(Map p58; ☑971 22 55 99; Carrer de l'Almudaina 9A; ⊗9.30am-1.30pm Mon-Fri) **FREE** Palma's long Jewish history is given some recognition in this small interpretation centre, attached to the Can Bordils. As well as illustrated panels bringing to life the story of the city's Jews (and, inevitably, their various persecutions), you can see sections of masonry from Roman buildings that once occupied the site.

Can Oms
HISTORIC BUILDING

(Map p58; Carrer de l'Amudaina 7) The 18th-century baroque *pati* of this grand house is one of Palma's most beautiful.

Porta de l'Almudaina
GATE

(Map p58; Carrer de l'Almudaina) The arch over Carrer de l'Almudaina east of Can Bordils is intriguing for history buffs, part of a rare stretch of defensive wall and tower. It is said to have been in use from antiquity until about the 13th century. Although largely medieval in appearance, it is almost certain that this was part of the Roman wall.

Centre Cultural Contemporani Pelaires
CULTURAL CENTRE

(Map p58; www.pelaires.com; Carrer de Can Verí 3; ⊗10am-1.30pm & 4.45-8pm Tue-Fri, 10am-1.30pm Sat) This private cultural centre – Palma's first dedicated contemporary art space – is as interesting for its architecture as for its ever-changing exhibitions. The building, Can Verí, is a beautiful 17th-century town-house that was also used for a while as a convent. Established as a gallery in 1969, the following year it played host to Joan Miró's first solo exhibition.

Convent de Santa Clara
CONVENT

(Map p58; Carrer de Can Fonollar 2; ⊗9am-12.30pm & 4.15-5.30pm Mon-Sat, 9-11am & 4.15-6.45pm Sun) The 'Poor Clares' were one of the first orders to establish a presence in Palma, following the Reconquesta of 1229. The land on which the convent stands was granted them in 1260, although much of the baroque and Gothic structure dates to the 16th and 17th centuries. The current church (the third on the site) was extensively restored from 2007, and the handful of nuns still cloistered here maintains a centuries-old tradition of baking sweets for sale.

You will see a *torno,* a kind of timber turnstile set in a window. Ring for a nun, order what you want and put money into the turnstile. This swivels around and out come your *bocaditos de almendra* (almond nibbles) or *rollitos de anís* (aniseed rolls), at €4 for 200g.

Arc de sa Drassana
HISTORIC BUILDING

(Map p58; off S'Hort del Rei) A grand arch dominated by the Palau de l'Almudaina, the Arc de sa Drassana is one of the city's few extant reminders of its Arab past. When the Riera, the city's river, coursed along what is now Passeig d'es Born and the sea lapped the city walls, this was the seaward entrance into the Arab palace and early shipyards.

◉ Plaça Major & Around

★ Museu Fundación Juan March
GALLERY

(Map p58; ☑91 435 42 40; www.march.es/arte/palma; Carrer de Sant Miquel 11; ⊗10am-6.30pm Mon-Fri, 10.30am-2pm Sat) **FREE** The 17th-century Can Gallard del Canya, a 17th-century mansion overlaid with minor Modernist touches, now houses a small but significant collection of painting and sculpture. The permanent exhibits – some 80 pieces held by the Fundación Juan March – constitute a veritable who's who of contemporary Spanish art, including Miró, Picasso, fellow cubist Juan Gris, Dalí, and the sculptors Eduardo Chillida and Julio González.

After starting with the big names, the collection skips through various movements in Spanish art, such as that inspired in Barcelona by the Dau al Set review (1948–53) and led by Antoni Tàpies. Meanwhile, in

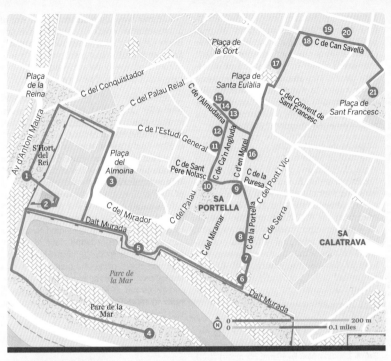

🏃 Town Walk
Historic Palma & Hidden Patios

START S'HORT DEL REI
END BASÍLICA DE SANT FRANCESC
LENGTH 2.5KM; TWO TO THREE HOURS

Begin in ① **S'Hort del Rei** (King's Garden), where ② **Arc de sa Drassana** arches above a pond. Amble north to Miró's bronze sculpture ('the egg'). Climb the steps past Palau March to the immense Gothic ③ **Catedral** (p51). Head down to ④ **Parc de la Mar** (p60), with its lake.

Soak up views along the Renaissance seawall ⑤ **Dalt Murada** (p60). Turn left at medieval gateway ⑥ **Sa Portella** (p60), noting its keystone and coat of arms. Carrer de la Portella hides many historic courtyards: 17th-century ⑦ **Cal Marquès de la Torre** and 19th-century ⑧ **Can Espanya-Serra**, with a neo-Gothic staircase. Swing left onto Carrer de la Puresa, pausing at ⑨ **Can Salas**, one of Palma's oldest *patis* (patios), with carved pillars, a beautiful loggia and 13th-century coat of arms.

Pause in tiny ⑩ **Jardí del Bisbe** (p57) or continue north up Carrer de Ca'n Angluda to ⑪ **Cal Poeta Colom**, named for its one-time resident poet. Further along is grand medieval manor ⑫ **Can Marquès**.

On Carrer de l'Almudaina, the medieval gateway ⑬ **Porta de l'Almudaina** was originally part of the Roman walls. Close by is ⑭ **Can Bordils**, a 17th-century courtyard, and neighbouring ⑮ **Can Oms**, with its Gothic portal. Nearby, on Carrer d'en Morei, ⑯ **Can Oleza** is a baroque patio with loggia, Ionic columns, low arches and wrought-iron balustrade. Pass spired ⑰ **Església de Santa Eulàlia** (p56) to Carrer de Can Savellà, home to Corinthian column-lined ⑱ **Can Vivot** and ⑲ **Can Catlar del Llorer**, one of Palma's oldest Gothic *patis*. Detour one street for hot chocolate at old-school ⑳ **Ca'n Joan de S'Aigo** (p71) before heading back to venerable ㉑ **Basílica de Sant Francesc** (p54).

Valencia, Eusebio Sempere and Andreu Alfaro were leading the way down abstract paths. Sempere's *Las Cuatro Estaciones* (1980) reflects the four seasons in subtle changes of colour in a series of four panels with interlocking shapes made of fine lines. Other names to watch for are Manuel Millares, Fernando Zóbel and Miquel Barceló, who is represented by works including his large-format *La Flaque* (The Pond; 1989).

Església de Sant Miquel   CHURCH
(Church of St Michael; Map p58; Carrer de Sant Miquel 21; ⊙ 9.30am-1.30pm & 5-7.30pm) A striking mix of styles, St Michael's is one of Palma's first four churches, built on the site of a mosque where the island's first Mass was celebrated on 31 December 1229. The facade and entrance, with its long, low arch, is a perfect example of 14th-century Catalan Gothic, as is the squat, seven-storey bell tower. Otherwise the church, with its barrel-vaulted ceiling, is largely the result of a baroque makeover.

Note the statue of Pope John Paul II on the right as you enter.

Claustre de Sant Antoniet   GALLERY
(Map p58; Carrer de Sant Miquel 30; ⊙ 10am-2pm & 3.30-8pm Mon-Fri, 10am-1.30pm Sat) **FREE** The Claustre de Sant Antoniet is a baroque gem that belongs to the BBVA bank. The two-tiered, oval-shaped enclosure was built in 1768 and is now used for temporary art exhibitions. It was originally attached to the **Església de Sant Antoni de Viana**, next door, but was transferred to the stewardship of the church of St Miquel when the Order of Sant Antoni was abolished by Charles III in 1788.

Almacenes El Águila   HISTORIC BUILDING
(Map p58; Plaça del Marqués del Palmer 1) Gaspar Bennàssar (1869–1933) – one of the most influential architects in modern Palma, his native city – played with various styles during his long career, including Modernisme. An outstanding example of this is the Almacenes El Águila, a department store built in 1908. Each of the three floors is different and the generous use of wrought iron in the main facade is a signature of the style.

Círculo de Bellas Artes   CULTURAL CENTRE
(Map p58; www.circulopalma.es; Carrer de l'Unió 3; ⊙ opening hours vary) The 'Circle of Fine Arts', an organisation with roots in the Civil War era, is devoted to nurturing literature and the fine arts in Palma. Casal Balaguer

– a largely baroque mansion on the site of a 13th-century original – is the handsome home of this now-venerable institution. Long neglected, it has been extensively renovated, and now houses exhibition spaces, a museum, library and performance spaces.

CaixaForum   CULTURAL CENTRE
(Map p58; ☑ 971 17 85 00; https://obrasocial-lacaixa.org/en/cultura/caixaforum-palma; Plaça de Weyler 3; adult/child & La Caixa members €4/free; ⊙ 10am-8pm Mon-Sat, 11am-2pm Sun) Housed in the wonderful Modernisme building (the island's first) that was once the Grand Hotel, this cultural centre and gallery is run by one of Spain's biggest building societies, the Barcelona-based La Caixa. The permanent collection of paintings by Hermenegildo Anglada Camarasa is complemented by temporary exhibitions (on themes such as Roman female statuary from the Louvre): pick up a program at reception and flick through it at the cafe, or browse the excellent bookshop.

The Grand Hotel was a city landmark built in 1900–03 by the Catalan master architect Lluís Domènech i Montaner, and the first building in Palma with electricity and a lift. The hotel was shut down during the Civil War and never recovered. As well as the art exhibitions, other frequent activities here include lectures, workshops, film cycles and concerts.

Centre de Cultura
Sa Nostra   CULTURAL CENTRE
(Map p58; www.obrasocialsanostra.com; Carrer de la Concepció 12; ⊙ 10.30am-1.30pm & 5-8pm Mon-Fri) **FREE** The big Balearic building society, Sa Nostra, runs this cultural foundation in Can Castelló, where it stages exhibitions, performances and talks. Keep an eye out for temporary shows, which are often worth a look. The original house dates to the 17th century, with Modernista touches from renovation work in 1909, and it's worth popping in just to check out the fine 18th-century courtyard, which now hosts a stylish cafe.

Just in front of the centre is **Font del Sepulcre**, a Gothic baptismal font left over from a long-disappeared church. Inside it is a 12th-century Muslim-era well. Carrer de la Concepció used to be known as Carrer de la Monederia, as the Kingdom of Mallorca's mint was on this street.

Església de Sant Jaume   CHURCH
(Map p58; Carrer de Sant Jaume 10; ⊙ 11.30am-1.30pm & 5.30-8.30pm) Despite its baroque facade, this is one of Palma's older surviv-

ing Gothic churches. This grey soaring eminence is one of the first four parish churches to be built 'under the protection of the Royal House of Mallorca' from 1327. It is said that the Bonapart family (later Bonaparte) lived here until they moved to Corsica in 1406. Napoleon could have been a Mallorcan!

Plaça Major   SQUARE
(Map p58) Plaça Major is a typically Spanish central square, lined with arcades, shops and cafes. Lively by day, it falls eerily silent at night.

To the east, Carrer del Sindicat spokes out towards the avenues that mark the limits of historic Palma. It crosses a district known as Sa Gerreria. For decades run-down and slightly dodgy, Sa Gerreria is enjoying a revival and it's becoming a trendy hub of the city's nightlife. Off Plaça Major, the shopping boulevard, Carrer de Sant Miquel, leads north towards the vast Plaça d'Espanya. Plaça Major and Carrer de Sant Miquel are on high ground that falls away to the west down to shady Passeig de la Rambla.

Església de Santa Magdalena   CHURCH
(Map p58; Plaça de Santa Magdalena; ⏰7.30am-1.15pm & 5.30-7.30pm) The main claim to fame of the baroque Església de Santa Magdalena is as the resting place of Santa Catalina Thomàs of Valldemossa. Her clothed remains are visible through a glass coffin held in a chapel to the left of the altar and are an object of pilgrimage. It is said that the future saint sat weeping by a great clump of stone one day as none of the convents would accept her because she was too poor.

When someone told her that the convent once attached to the Església de Santa Magdalena would take her in, she was overjoyed. The stone in question is now embedded in the rear wall of the 14th-century **Església de Sant Nicolau** on Plaça del Mercat. The nuns here make pastas de Santa Magdalena and other sweet treats for sale to the public.

Església de Sant Crist de la Sang   CHURCH
(Map p54; Plaça de l'Hospital; ⏰7.30am-1pm & 4-8pm) Within the Hospital General (founded in the 16th century), you can behold the

PATIOS & PALACES

Generations of Palma's aristocratic families have left their mark on the Old Town, most visibly in the form of imposing palaus (palaces or mansions) and their demonstratively handsome patis (patios). Wandering the old medieval streets brings you repeatedly nose-to-wrought iron gate with this tantalising inaccessible legacy: almost all the palaus are in private hands, their cool, colonnaded courtyards barred from the street immediately outside by ornate metal barriers. To the unschooled, these bastions of antique privilege can be hard to tell apart; but to those who know, there are subtleties and stories to be untangled.

Position is one way to distinguish among the rank and provenance of the palaus. Naturally, the longer established families dominated the older areas of the city. The top rung favoured the historic quarter of Palma Alta, around Sa Portella, which became entrenched as the neighbourhood of landed and pedigreed gentry. Those who made their fortune with the taint of Palma's maritime trade, the wealthy merchants and sailors, tended to cluster in Palma Baixa around Es Puig de Sant Pere, where the patis bear visible testament to their line of work: motifs such as boats, and representations of Mercury, god of commerce.

More romantic details also reveal themselves to the canny reader. On the corner of Carrer de la Portella can be seen the serpentine figure of **El Dra de Na Coca**, a dragon reputed to have infested the sewers of the Old Town in the 17th century. As so often is the case in these matters, the beast met its match in the form of a bold knight, who stumbled upon it when paying court to his love, and duly dispatched it. And above the medieval gate known as the **Porta de l'Almudaina** (p62) can be seen a small window that played a signal part in the courtly love rituals of the nobles. Courting gallants would wait below for signs of favour from their beloved.

Of all the patis, that of **Palau March** (p53) – once owned by the wealthy businessman and artistic patron Juan March – is perhaps the most distinctive. Whereas most are closed off, despite their role in publicly demonstrating wealth and taste, the Palau March has an open loggia, affording views of Palma's great **Catedral** (p51) and **Palau de l'Almudaina** (p53).

GALLERY ALLEY

Contemporary-art enthusiasts will get a buzz out of the plethora of galleries that populate the narrow streets just east of the Passeig d'es Born.

➡ **La Caja Blanca** (Map p58; www.lacajablanca.com; Carrer de Can Verí 9; ⊙11am-2pm & 5-8pm Mon-Fri, 11.30am-2pm Sat) **FREE** Edgy Mallorcan and international artists are showcased in this stark, minimalist space. It stages three to four exhibitions annually.

➡ **Galeria K** (Map p58; www.galeria-k.com; Carrer de Can Verí 10; ⊙10.30am-8pm Mon-Fri, 11am-3pm Sat) **FREE** This innovative little gallery presents Spanish and international painters and sculptors.

➡ **Centre Cultural Contemporani Pelaires** (p62) This contemporary art space, Palma's first such dedicated gallery, occupies a lovely 17th-century building.

Gothic facade of this church. It is an object of pilgrimage and devotion, since the *paso* (a sculpted image used in processions) of 'Holy Christ of the Blood' is considered to be miraculous. Just on your left as you enter the church is a 15th-century nativity scene, probably imported from Naples.

If you happen on a Mass, it's moving to see the devotion of the faithful who climb up behind the altar to venerate the image of Christ crucified, with long, flowing *real* hair and embroidered loincloth.

◎ Es Puig de Sant Pere

★**Es Baluard**   GALLERY
(Museu d'Art Modern i Contemporani; Map p58; ☑971 90 82 00; www.esbaluard.org; Plaça de Porta de Santa Catalina 10; adult/temporary exhibitions/child €6/4/free; ⊙10am-8pm Tue-Sat, to 3pm Sun) Built with flair and innovation into the shell of the Renaissance-era seaward walls, this contemporary art gallery is one of the finest on the island. Its temporary exhibitions are worth viewing, but the permanent collection – works by Miró, Barceló and Picasso – give the gallery its cachet. Entry on Fridays is by donation, and anyone turning up on a bike, on any day, is charged just €2.

The 21st-century concrete complex is cleverly built among the fortifications, including the partly restored remains of an 11th-century Muslim-era tower (on your right as you arrive from Carrer de Sant Pere). Inside, the ground floor houses the core of the permanent exhibition, starting with a section on Mallorcan landscapes by local artists and others from abroad; the big names here include Valencia's Joaquín Sorolla, Mallorca's own Miquel Barceló and the Catalan Modernista artist Santiago Rusiñol.

Also on the ground floor and part of the permanent collection is a room devoted to the works of Joan Miró, while on the top floor is an intriguing collection of ceramics by Pablo Picasso; after viewing the latter, step out onto the ramparts for fine views. In sum, it's an impressive rather than extraordinary collection that's well worth a couple of hours of your time.

Sa Llotja   HISTORIC BUILDING
(Map p58; Plaça de la Llotja 5; ⊙11am-2pm & 5-9pm Tue-Sat, 11am-2pm Sun) **FREE** The gorgeous 15th-century sandstone Sa Llotja, opposite the waterfront, was built as a merchants' stock exchange. Designed by the Mallorcan sculptor Guillem Sagrera (who also worked on the cathedral) and completed in 1448, it is the apogee of civilian Gothic building on the island. Its mercantile past well behind it, Sa Llotja is now used for temporary exhibitions.

Inside, six slender, twisting columns lead to the ribs of a lofty groined vault. In each corner of the building rises a fanciful octagonal tower. The flanks are marked with huge arches, fine tracery and monstrous-looking gargoyles leaning out overhead.

Consolat de Mar   HISTORIC BUILDING
(Map p58; Passeig de Sagrera 7) The 'Consulate of the Sea' was founded in 1326 as a maritime tribunal, adjudicating disputes among merchants, sailors and captains. The present building – one of Mallorca's few examples of Renaissance design, albeit an impure one – was completed in 1669. It was tacked onto, and faces, a late-Gothic chapel completed around 1600 for the members of Sa Llotja. The Consolat de Mar houses the presidency of the Balearic Islands regional government.

Passeig d'es Born   AREA
(Map p58) One of Palma's most appealing boulevards, Passeig d'es Born is capped by **Plaça del Rei Joan Carles I** (named after

the present king and formerly after Pope Pius XII), a traffic roundabout locally known as Plaça de les Tortugues, because of the obelisk placed on four bronze turtles. On the east side of the avenue, on the corner of Carrer de Jovellanos, the distorted black face of a Moor, complete with white stone turban, is affixed high on a building.

Known as the **Cap del Moro** (Moor's Head), it represents a Muslim slave who is said to have killed his master, a chaplain, in October 1731. The slave was executed and his hand lopped off and reportedly attached to the wall of the house where the crime was committed. Chronicles claim the withered remains of the hand were still in place, behind a grille, in 1840. The Passeig was renamed in honour of Franco, but reverted to its original title after the dictator's death.

Casal Solleric　　　　　HISTORIC BUILDING
(Map p58; ☎ 971 72 96 04; Passeig d'es Born 27; ⏱ 11am-2pm & 3.30-8.30pm Tue-Sat, 11am-2.30pm Sun) **FREE** This grand 18th-century baroque mansion with the typical Palma courtyard of graceful broad arches and uneven stone paving is at once a cultural centre with temporary exhibitions, bookshop and tourist information office. Displays are usually free and found over a couple of floors. The part facing Passeig d'es Born was actually the rear of the original house, built in 1763. Archduke Ludwig Salvador thought its courtyard 'one of the most beautiful in Palma'.

Església de Santa Creu　　　　　CHURCH
(Map p58; Carrer de Sant Llorenç 4) Work on the original Gothic Church of the Holy Cross, one of Palma's original parish churches, began in 1335. The main entrance (Carrer de Santa Creu 7) is a baroque (18th-century) addition. What makes it particuarly interesting is the Cripta de Sant Llorenç (Crypt of St Lawrence), an early Gothic place of worship possibly dating to the late 13th century. Some paintings by Rafel Mòger and Francesc Comes are scattered about the interior.

⊙ **Passeig Marítim & Western Palma**

Castell de Bellver　　　　　CASTLE
(Bellver Castle; ☎ 971 73 50 65; http://castelldebellver.palma.cat; Carrer de Camilo José Cela; adult/child €4/2, free Sun; ⏱ 8.30am-1pm Mon, to 8pm Tue-Sat, 10am-8pm Sun) Straddling a wooded hillside, the Castell de Bellver is a 14th-century circular castle (with a unique

round tower), the only one of its kind in Spain. Jaume II ordered it built atop a hill known as Puig de Sa Mesquida in 1300 and it was largely completed within 10 years. Perhaps the highlight of any visit is the spectacular views over the woods to Palma, the Badia de Palma and out to sea.

The castle was conceived above all as a royal residence but seems to have been a white elephant, as only King Sanç (in 1314) and Aragón's Joan I (in 1395) moved in for any amount of time. In 1717 it became a military prison, and was subsequently used in both the Napoleonic and Spanish Civil Wars. Climb to the roof and check out the prisoners' graffiti, etched into the stonework.

The ground-floor **Museu d'Història de la Ciutat** (City History Museum) traces the development of the city from the prehistoric Talayotic civilisation to the present day. As well as Roman and Arabian ceramics there are explanatory panels, the classical statues of the Despuig Collection and other artefacts. Upstairs you can visit a series of largely empty chambers, including the kitchen.

About the nearest you can get to the castle by bus (3, 46 or 50) is Plaça de Gomila, from where you'll have to hoof it about 15 minutes (1km) up a steep hill. Instead, combine it with the Palma City Sightseeing open-top bus, which climbs to the castle as part of its circuit of the city.

🏃 **Activities**

Magic Catamarans　　　　　BOATING
(Map p54; ☎ 971 45 61 82; http://magic-catamarans.com/es; 1st fl, Passeig Marítim 8; adult/child €49/24.50; ⏱ 10am-3pm & 3.30-8.30pm) From April to October Magic puts on twice-daily, five-hour catamaran tours to either Cala Portals Vells or Cala Vella, just east of the Badia de Palma. The price includes food on board and snorkelling gear, and hotel pick-ups can be arranged (adult/child €10/5). Note that the 2½-hour tour to Ses Illetes is cheaper, at just €16/8 (without food and drink).

Cruceros Marco Polo　　　　　BOATING
(Map p54; ☎ 647 843667; www.crucerosmarcopolo.com; off Passeig Marítim; 1hr cruise €12; ⏱ hourly 11am-4pm Mon-Sat, 2-4pm Sun Mar-Oct) Marco Polo, one of the first tour operators in the Badia de Palma, offers a one-hour whiz around the bay, up to six times daily aboard the *Mar y Sol II*. There's a bar on board, and limitless opportunities to snap Palma's scenic attractions from the water.

Real Club Náutico BOATING

(Map p54; www.rcnp.es; Plaza de San Pedro 1) The most prestigious of Palma's yacht clubs has been around since 1948, and now organises more than 20 events during the year.

 Courses

Akzent LANGUAGE

(Map p58; ☑971 71 99 94; www.akzent-palma. com; Carrer del Carme 14; 2-week course €395; ◷9.30am-8.30pm Mon-Fri, 10am-2pm Sat) This bookshop offers well-regarded, two-week intensive Spanish courses. Each day's tuition lasts four hours, and classes are capped at 10 students.

Estudi Lul·lià de Mallorca LANGUAGE

(Map p58; ☑971 71 19 88; www.estudigeneral. com; Carrer de Sant Roc 4; €410) This institute has offered intensive summer courses in Spanish language and culture since its foundation, in 1951. Successful students receive a certificate in Spanish Language and Hispanic Studies from the University of Barcelona.

Die Akademie LANGUAGE

(Map p58; ☑971 71 82 90; www.dieakademie. com; Carrer d'en Morei 8; 1-week course €198; ◷9am-1.30pm & 5-7.30pm Mon-Fri) Housed in a 16th-century late-Gothic mansion, Die Akademie runs a variety of Spanish-language courses based on the 'Superlearning' method (which sounds impressive!). Standard classes run for four hours each morning, from 9.30am to 1.30pm.

Palma Sea School BOATING

(Map p54; ☑971 10 05 18; www.palmasea-school.com; Passeig Marítim 38; 2-day yachting courses from €500; ☀) Whether you're cutting your teeth or honing your skills, this Royal Yachting Association–affiliated school offers a wide range of courses in yachting, sailing, powerboating and jet-skiing.

 Tours

★**Mallorca Rutes** TOURS

(Map p58; ☑971 72 89 83; www.mallorcarutes. es; Carrer d'en Morei 7; per person €15-37) Mallorca Rutes runs a wide range of guided walking tours, which afford insight into different aspects of Palma. These range from basic city walking tours covering the main sights to themed walks, such as one exploring Palma's hidden courtyards and palaces. It also arranges tastings of wine and typical Mallorcan products. Book at Típika, next to Plaça de Santa Eulàlia.

Palma City Sightseeing BUS

(Map p58; ☑902 10 10 81; www.mallorca-tour.com; Avinguda d'Antoni Maura; adult/child bus €16/8.50, boat €12/6, bus & boat €25/15; ◷9.30am-10pm,reduced hours outside summer) Run by the *ajuntament* (town hall) this hop-on-hop-off bus departs from Avinguda d'Antoni Maura every 20 minutes, with commentary in various languages. It follows a circuit of the city centre, waterfront and the Castell de Bellver, and can be combined with a boat tour of the bay.

Festivals & Events

Cinema a la Fresca FILM

(◷Jul-Sep) Running each summer since 1986, Cinema a la Fresca has become something of a Palma institution, bringing free open-air cinema to the Parc de la Mar, beneath the Catedral. Most films start at 9.30pm or 10pm.

Copa del Rey SAILING

(www.regatacopadelrey.com; ◷Jul-Aug) The 'King's Cup', held over eight days in July and

---

PALMA WITH KIDS

With its beaches, parks, water activities and plentiful cafes and ice-cream shops, Palma is a wonderful city to visit with children. What kid doesn't love castles? **Castell de Bellver** (p67) and **Castell de Sant Carles** (www.museomilitarsancarlos.com; Carretera del Dic de l'Oest; ◷10am-2pm Tue-Sun) FREE have the right, imposing story-book dimensions, while you can combine art with fun on the ramparts at **Es Baluard** (p66). **Palma Aquarium** (p85) to the east is outstanding, and you could easily spend half a day there (kids can even spend a (possibly sleepless) Friday night at a monthly 'Shark Sleepover'). **Aqualand** (p86), the island's largest water park, is another sure-fire hit, with its slides, rides, pools and speedball flumes.

Playgrounds are scattered about town, for instance in Parc de les Estacions, behind the train and bus station, and Sa Feixina park near Es Baluard. There's a brilliant adventure playground further along near the walls just east of **Parc de la Mar** (p61).

August, is a high point in the sailing calendar. King Juan Carlos I and his son Felipe frequently race on competing boats.

TaPalma FOOD & DRINK
(www.tapalma.es; ⊙ late Oct) Nibble your way around Palma at this event celebrating the city's best tapas. Some 40 restaurants and bars take part and there are dedicated tapas trails to follow – see the website for a map.

Trofeo Ciutat de Palma SAILING
(www.trofeociutatdepalma.com; ⊙ Dec) Run by the Royal Nautical Club of Palma, the Ciutat de Palma-Regata is a huge event for smaller boats, held over four days.

Nit de Foc FIESTA
(⊙ 23 Jun) In Palma, the night before the midsummer feast of St John is celebrated with fiery abandon. The *correfoc* (fire running) begins in the Parc de la Mar, as costumed demons leap and dance in an infernal procession. To finish, the city's beaches host musical groups, bonfires and a crowd that parties until dawn.

Fiesta Sant Sebastià MUSIC
(⊙ 18-20 Jan) On the eve of the feast day of Palma's patron saint, concerts (from funk to folk) are staged in the city squares, along with flaming pyres and the *aiguafoc,* a fireworks display over the bay. It's a big (if chilly) night.

Nit de l'Art CULTURAL
(www.nitdelartpalma.com; ⊙ Sep) One Saturday night in September Palma's historic heart is given over to the arts, as the city's many galleries throw open their doors, and the streets are illuminated by installations, exhibitions and live performances.

Christmas Market CHRISTMAS MARKET
(Plaça Major; ⊙ 10am-9pm late Nov-early Jan) The Christmas market takes over Plaça Major, Plaça d'Espanya and La Ramblas. Expect handicraft stalls, music and multiple Santas.

Semana Santa RELIGIOUS
(Holy Week; ⊙ Mar-Apr) Processions dot the Easter week calendar, but the most impressive are those on Holy Thursday evening. In the Processó del Sant Crist de la Sang (Christ of the Blood), robed and hooded members of *confraries* (lay brotherhoods) parade with a *paso* (heavy sculpted image of Christ). The procession starts at 7pm, in the Església del Crist de la Sang.

Corpus Christi RELIGIOUS
(⊙ May-Jun) The feast of the Body of Christ (the Eucharist) falls on the Thursday of the ninth week after Easter, although the main procession from the cathedral takes place on the following Sunday, when carpets of flowers are laid out in front of the cathedral. Concert cycles (many held in the city's *patis*) add a celebratory note.

Sa Rueta & Sa Rua CARNIVAL
(⊙ Feb-Mar) Palma's version of Carnaval (celebrated in the last days before Lent starts) involves a procession for kids (Sa Rueta) followed later by a bigger one (Sa Rua) with floats and the like.

Eating

Palma's dining scene, starting from the already-strong base you'd expect in a major Spanish city, just keeps improving. As well as bold experiments with traditional Mallorcan dishes by innovative young chefs, you'll find excellent tapas and traditional Spanish food and, increasingly, very good renditions of many different world cuisines.

Mercado Gastronómico San Juan MARKET €
(St John Gastronomic Market; Map p54; ☏ 971 78 10 04; www.mercadosanjuanpalma.es; Carrer de l'Emperadriu Eugènia 6; ⊙ noon-midnight) This gastronomic market occupies a coral-pink Modernista building in the S'Escorxador cultural centre, once a slaughter house. With a bar, cafe, terrace and 17 stalls selling *fideuá* (like paella, but made with fine noodles), silky *croquetas,* top-grade acorn-fed *jamón, sobrassada* (paprika-flavoured cured pork sausages) and a galaxy of other Mallorcan and Spanish treats, it's a gourmand's dream.

Mercat de l'Olivar MARKET €
(Map p58; www.mercatolivar.com; Plaça de l'Olivar; ⊙ 7am-2.30pm Mon-Thu, to 8pm Fri & Sat) Palma's main retail produce market is a wonderland of Mallorcan (and Spanish) comestibles. Cheese, meat, fish, vegetables and prepared dishes are just some of the delights gathered under one roof. It's a place to linger, with cafes and tapas bars

Mercat de Santa Catalina MARKET €
(Map p54; www.mercatdesantacatalina.com; Plaça de la Navegació; ⊙ 7am-5pm Mon-Sat) Local produce markets like this are the lifeblood of Palma's neighbourhoods, and are always the best bet for fresh fruit and vegetables, seafood, charcuterie, bread and other

TO MARKET

Nosing around the colourful stalls of Palma's produce markets is a great way to take the flavour of the city. There's all you need to assemble your own picnic, from cheeses and cold meats to fruit and veg. The largest and best is the central Mercat de l'Olivar, where you'll find everything from plump olives to never-heard-of legumes, melons as big as footballs, strings of *sobrassada* (paprika-flavoured cured pork sausage), hunks of Serrano ham and enough fish to fill a small ocean. Make a morning of it and linger for lunch at the deli stalls for tapas or oyster shucking. Equally busy but with fewer tourists are the **Mercat de Santa Catalina** and **Mercat de Pere Garau** (Map p54; ☑ 971 24 46 74; https://mercatperegarau.es; Plaça de Pere Garau; ⊘ 7am-3pm Mon-Sat). Gourmets should head to the **Mercado Gastronómico San Juan** (p69), a hub of fine food housed in a redeveloped abbatoir in the northern part of the city.

staples. Inside, three tapas bars are placed at intervals convenient for refuelling.

🍴 Old Palma

Bar Bodega Morey   TAPAS €
(Map p58; ☑ 634 673351; Carrer d'en Morei 4; tapas €3; ⊘ 6am-5pm Mon-Fri) As Palma's food evolution races ahead, and the tourist dollars keep pouring in, it's reassuring to find places still giving the locals what they've long loved, at very decent prices. This white-washed, timber-floored hole-in-the-wall deals in classics – tortilla, *albondigas* (meatballs), *pulpo* (octopus) – but nails them. Great for a coffee or draught beer, too.

Forn del Santo Cristo   BAKERY €
(Map p58; www.hornosantocristo.com; Carrer de Paraires 2; ensaïmades from €1.30; ⊘ 8am-8.30pm Mon-Sat, 8.30am-1pm Sun) The 'Oven of Holy Christ' has been baking up *ensaïmades* (a light, spiral pastry emblematic of the island) since 1910, and also offers a range of other traditional goodies, including *cocas de patata* (sweet potato buns).

★ Can Cera Gastro-Bar   MEDITERRANEAN €€
(Map p58; ☑ 971 71 50 12; www.cancerahotel. com; Carrer del Convent de Sant Francesc 8; tapas €9-22; ⊘ 12.30-11pm) This restaurant spills onto a lovely inner patio at the Can Cera hotel, housed in a *palau* that dates originally to the 13th century. Dine by lantern light on tapas-sized dishes such as *frito mallorquín* (seafood fried with potato and herbs), Cantabrian anchovies, and pork ribs with honey and mustard. The vertical garden attracts plenty of attention from passers-by.

L'Ambigú   MODERN EUROPEAN €€
(Map p58; ☑ 971 57 21 51; http://elambigu-bar.com; Carrer de Carnisseria 1; mains €12-14;

⊘ noon-midnight Mon-Sat) Tucked in behind the Església de Santa Eulàlia, this irresistible little bar-restaurant specialises in modern Spanish takes on ceviche, pasta and other exogenous favourites. It does retain something of the vibe of the tapas bar it once was (plus some favourite tapas on the menu) and can get quite convivial (and noisy) on Fridays and Saturdays .

Las Olas   MEDITERRANEAN, VIETNAMESE €€
(Map p58; ☑ 971 21 49 05; www.lasolasbistro. com; Carrer de Can Fortuny 5; mains €14-17, tapas €2-9; ⊘ 12.30-4pm Wed-Mon, plus 8.30-11.30pm Wed-Sat; ⚑) Now here's something unusual. Run by an Irish-Cambodian couple, Las Olas divides the day into two: lunch is all about reinterpreted French Mediterranean flavours (perhaps cod with apples and soft garlic), while dinner is a Vietnamese-Cambodian affair, when fresh, herby dishes such as *bánh xèo* (Vietnamese crepe with chicken and prawns) come out to play.

La Taberna del Caracol   TAPAS €€
(Map p58; ☑ 971 71 49 08; www.tabernacaracol. com; Carrer de Sant Alonso 2; tapas €1.80-19, tapas tasting plate €16; ⊘ noon-3pm Mon-Sat, plus 7.30-11pm Tue-Sat) Descend three steps into this high-ceilinged Gothic basement to find traditional tapas, such as grilled artichokes, snails, *jamón* (cured ham) and anchovies. Through a broad sandstone arch at the back you can see what's cooking, and may be tempted by the tasting plate (four tapas for €16, two to three people) that's a meal in itself.

Fosh Kitchen   MODERN EUROPEAN €€€
(Map p58; ☑ 971 72 13 54; www.marcfosh.com; Carrer d'Orfila 4; mains €30-35; ⊘ 12.30-3.30pm & 7.30-10.30pm Tue-Sun; ☎) Expertly executed assemblies of top-notch ingredients are

the focus of the slick, contemporary Fosh Kitchen, the less-formal cousin of Michelin-starred Marc Fosh's flagship restaurant. Within the striking Modernista building once home to iconic Palman confectioner Confiteria Frasquet, you'll love dishes such as Iberian bacon with potatoes, mustard seeds and watercress, and Mallorcan-style sea bass.

Plaça Major & Around

Restaurant Celler Sa Premsa   MALLORCAN €
(Map p54; 971 72 35 29; www.cellersapremsa.com; Plaça del Bisbe Berenguer de Palou 8; mains €9-14, menús €14; 12.30-4pm & 7.30-11.30pm Mon-Sat Sep-Jun, Mon-Fri Jul & Aug) A visit to this local institution, going strong since 1958, is almost obligatory. It's a cavernous tavern filled with huge old wine barrels and faded bullfighting posters – you find plenty of these places in the Mallorcan interior but they're a dying breed here in Palma. Mallorcan specialities dominate the menu.

Come for the well-prepared roast lamb, *tumbet* (Mallorcan-style vegetable ratatouille), *frito mallorquín*, pork with cabbage, and rabbit with onion. Service is quietly excellent, but it's the atmosphere you'll remember.

Ca'n Joan de S'Aigo   BAKERY €
(Map p58; www.canjoandesaigo.webs-sites.com; Carrer de Can Sanç 10; pastries €1.30-3; 8am-9pm) Tempting with its sweet creations since 1700, this clattering, tiled cafe is *the* place for thick hot chocolate (€2) and pastries in gloriously atmospheric, antique-strewn surrounds. The house speciality is *quart*, a feather-soft sponge cake that children love, with almond-flavoured ice cream.

Horno San Antonio   BAKERY €
(Map p54; Plaça Sant Antoni 6; ensaïmades from €1.30; 8am-8pm Tue-Fri, to 2pm Sat & Sun) Considered by most Mallorcans to be the best of the best when it comes to *ensaïmades,* this wonderfully traditional old pastry shop does a roaring trade in all sizes and types, from plain to chocolate, with cream or apricot filling. You can get them nicely packed if you plan on taking one home.

Forn des Teatre   BAKERY €
(Map p58; www.forndesteatre.com; Plaça de Weyler 9; ensaïmades from €1.30; 8am-1am) This pastry shop does featherweight *ensaïmades* and, with its beautiful Modernist detailing, is a historic landmark. Larger *en-*

saïmades are prepared to order, but smaller, takeaway ones start from €1.30. Also on offer is a mean almond cake.

Bar España   SPANISH €€
(Map p58; 971 72 42 34; Carrer de Ca'n Escurrac 12; tapas menus €12-22; 6.30pm-midnight Mon-Fri, 12.30-4.30pm & 6.30pm-1am Sat) Happening upon this place in the evening when everything else in the vicinity is closed is like discovering a hidden secret. Hugely popular and deservedly so, it has stone walls and an agreeable hum of conversation accompanies the fine *pintxos* (Basque tapas).

Quina Creu   TAPAS €€
(Map p58; 971 71 17 72; www.quinacreu.com; Carrer de Cordería 24; mains €17-23, weekday lunch menú €13; noon-1am Mon-Sat) With its mishmash of vintage furniture, flickering haunted-house chandeliers and poster-plastered walls, Quina Creu nails bric-a-brac chic. Deep sofas, a tapas-lined bar and blackboards promising other delights – perhaps *sobrassada* with quail egg, or cod with *gambas* (prawns) and salsa verde – encourage lingering over aperitifs, and the overall atmosphere is one of relaxed cheer.

★ Marc Fosh   MODERN EUROPEAN €€€
(Map p58; 971 72 01 14; www.marcfosh.com; Carrer de la Missió 7A; menús €68-89, lunch menús €28-40; 1-4.30pm & 7.30pm-midnight) The flagship of Michelin-starred Fosh's burgeoning flotilla of Palma restaurants, this stylish gastronomic destination introduces novel twists to time-honoured Mediterranean

THE PERFECT ENSAÏMADA

Most Mallorcans and just about every Spanish visitor to the island has one culinary favourite above all others – the humble *ensaïmada*, a delicate, feather-light croissant-like pastry dusted with icing sugar, and sometimes filled with cream. Getting them to agree on where to buy the best is surprisingly simple. Having extensively researched the most highly regarded bakers, we've concluded these are the best you'll find in Palma, and possibly the entire island:

➤ **Horno San Antonio**

➤ **Ca'n Joan de S'Aigo**

➤ **Forn des Teatre**

➤ **Forn del Santo Cristo**

PALMA & THE BADIA DE PALMA EATING

dishes and ingredients, all within the converted refectory of a 17th-century convent. The weekly lunch *menú*, three/five courses for €28/40, is a very reasonable way to enjoy dishes such as foie gras and duck terrine, or truffled pasta with burrata.

Flavours are clean, bright and seasonal. You might begin with red prawn and scorpion fish tartar with plankton jelly and green tomato consommé, then proceed to wild sea bream with young almonds and squid ink. Reservations are essential.

La Bodeguilla SPANISH €€€
(Map p58; ☑971 71 82 74; www.la-bodeguilla.com; Carrer de Sant Jaume 3; mains €20-28; ☺noon-11pm) This proper foodie's restaurant reinterprets dishes from across Spain in a modern dining room lined with wine and hams. Try the *porc negre* (rare-breed pork) from Mallorca or the *lechazo* (young lamb, baked Córdoba-style in rosemary). Also on offer is an enticing range of tapas – the grilled octopus with potato foam is a perfectly cooked mouthful of the sea.

✖ Es Puig de Sant Pere

Bon Lloc VEGETARIAN €
(Map p58; ☑971 71 86 17; www.bonllocrestaurant.com; Carrer de Sant Feliu 7; mains €9-10, lunch menú €15; ☺1-4pm Mon-Sat, plus 8-11pm Thu-Sat; ☑) ✖ Long-standing favourite of the hip and health-conscious, this 100% vegetarian place does great work with organic produce. Palma's first veggie restaurant, it's light, open and airy with a casual but classy atmosphere. At lunchtime there's a four-course *menú* (juice or salad, entrée, main and dessert), while dinner is à la carte. It's always popular, so ring to reserve.

13% TAPAS €
(Map p58; ☑971 42 51 87; www.13porciento.com; Carrer de Sant Feliu 13A; tapas €5-9, lunch/tasting menú €11/20; ☺12.30-11.30pm Mon-Sat, from 6pm Sun; ☑) This L-shaped barn of a place is at once a wine and tapas bar, bistro and delicatessen. Most items are organic and there's plenty of choice for vegetarians. Alongside classics such as Galician octopus, you'll find more daring concoctions like *bacallà* (salt cod) with pea purée and black olive cream. There are also salads, carpaccios and pastas. The lunch *menú* is a choice selection of three tapas.

Forn de Sant Joan SPANISH €€
(Map p58; ☑971 72 84 22; www.forndesantjoan.com; Caller de Sant Joan 4; menú €18-22; ☺1-4pm & 7pm-midnight; ☎) Yet another example of Palma's forward-thinking food scene, 'Saint Joan's Oven' is all stripped-brick, perfectly mixed cocktails and Mallorcan/Mediterranean food taken to the next level. Expect local ingredients like mahi-mahi or lamb to be taken somewhere global: perhaps Morocco (tagine) or Peru (ceviche). The three-course lunch *menú* is an excellent introduction.

Bruselas INTERNATIONAL €€
(Map p58; ☑971 71 09 54; www.restaurantebruselas.com; Carrer d'Estanc 4; mains €13-20; ☺1-3.30pm & 8-11.30pm Mon-Sat) Bruselas basically provides red meat to aesthetes, with Argentine steaks – such as *solomillo con foie* (sirloin with foie gras) – gourmet hamburgers and kobe beef served in a stone-vaulted basement. There are some innovative tapas and non-meaty options, and all goes down well with a throaty Mallorcan red, such as Son Bordils Negre.

Opio FUSION €€
(Map p58; ☑971 28 28 72; www.purohotel.com; Puro Oasis Urbano, Carrer de Montenegro 12; mains €18-20; ☺restaurant 8-11.30pm Tue-Sun May-Sep, Wed-Sun Apr & Oct-Dec) Opio traces the Pacific Rim with dishes originating in Asia (prawn tempura) and South America (ceviche) alongside Iberican flavours and the inevitable burgers. Set within the Puro Hotel, it's a glam affair, so expect DJs, cocktails and the beautiful set to accompany your dinner. The attached bar stays open later than the restaurant, up to 4am in some cases.

Caballito de Mar SEAFOOD €€€
(Map p58; ☑971 72 10 74; www.caballitodemar.info; Passeig de Sagrera 5; mains €19-34; ☺1pm-midnight) One of Palma's dining beacons, the 'Little Seahorse' is a dependably top-notch seafood destination. There are monkfish medallions, *sobrassada* and *butifarrón* (blood sausage) wrapped in cabbage leaves in a nut sauce. Or you could go for something more traditional, such as turbot with confit vegetables or red shrimp from Sóller.

✖ Santa Catalina & Around

El Perrito SWEDISH €
(Map p54; ☑971 45 59 16; Carrer d'Anníbal 20; mains €8-11; ☺8am-5pm Mon-Sat) The 'little dog' takes its canine moniker from the black-

and-white photos of customers' pooches that hang on its walls. Run by Swedes, this cute-as-a-button cafe is a pleasantly bohemian haunt for bagels, homemade cakes, fresh juices and hearty specials, such as goulash, meatballs with lingonberries or 'Jansson's Temptation' (potatoes baked with anchovies and cream).

Japo Sushi Bar SUSHI €
(Map p54; ☑ 971 73 83 21; www.ilovejapo.com; Carrer de Sant Magí 25; sushi/sashimi €1.50/6; ☺ 1.30-4pm & 7-11.30pm) You can't miss the hot-pink decor and dangling Japonica of this funky Santa Catalina sushi bar. Paper lanterns hang in the whitewashed interior, where you can dig into winningly fresh sushi, maki, sashimi and nigiri. The two-course lunch, including hot choices such as gyoza and spring rolls, is a snip at €9.

Koh SOUTHEAST ASIAN €€
(Map p54; ☑ 971 28 70 39; Carrer de Servet 15; mains €13-15; ☺ 7-11pm Mon-Sat) This stylish, friendly Southeast Asian restaurant in Santa Catalina prepares (chiefly Thai) curries, soups and stir-fries with real panache. The flavours are punchy, whether you go for bouncy prawn and chive dumplings, or a perfectly balanced yellow seafood curry. Produce comes from neighbouring Santa Catalina market and there's a pretty patio to enjoy a ginger mojito in warm weather.

Trens MALLORCAN €€
(Map p54; ☑ 971 28 35 03; Carrer d'Anníbal 21; mains €18-20; ☺ 12.30-11.30pm Wed-Sat, to 4.30pm Tue & Sun) The model train delivering entrées and desserts is certainly fun, as are the train decor and other *ferrovial* touches, but this resturant is no one-gimmick pony. The traditional Mallorcan and Spanish food is superb, and not afraid to venture into the less-safe margins of the menu: liver, snails and other treats share space with paella, grilled fish and the like.

Nola CAJUN €€
(Map p54; ☑ 971 66 70 06; www.disfrutadenola. com; Carrer de Sant Magí 13; mains €15-18; ☺ 7.30-11pm Mon-Sat) Funky Santa Catalina is the logical neighbourhood for this dedicated Cajun-Creole restaurant, the first outpost of New Orleans cool in Palma. Bayou classics like jambalaya, gumbo and ribs are given some refinement (a slick of calvados jus here, a touch of truffle oil there) but basically the food and soundtrack stick close to the Louisiana originals.

Room CAFE €€
(Map p54; ☑ 971 28 15 36; www.theroom-catalina.com; Carrer de Cotoner 47; mains €10-12; ☺ 8am-5pm Mon-Sat; ▥) This slick, contemporary cafe is a much-loved breakfast and lunch spot, with its easygoing air and colouring books to amuse tots. The menu is strong on eggs, burgers, salads, pastas and sandwiches.

Hórreo Veinti3 MEDITERRANEAN €€€
(Map p54; ☑ 649 033806; http://horreoveinti3. jimdo.com; Carrer de Sa Fàbrica 23; mains €19-23; ☺ 1pm-12.30am Thu-Mon, 7pm-12.30am Tue & Wed) Transparent chairs, gleaming tiles and wicker lampshades set the scene at this modern, upbeat pick, with tables spilling out onto a pavement terrace. Dishes range from mussels in albariño to grilled tuna and chateaubriand.

La Baranda ITALIAN €€€
(Map p54; ☑ 971 45 45 25; www.labaranda. co.uk; Carrer de Sant Magí 29; pizza €11-14, mains €20-25; ☺ 6.30pm-midnight) An easygoing Italian with Tuscan affinities, La Baranda is a good choice for wood-fired pizzas, pasta dishes and homemade cakes. It's a pleasant place to linger over a meal, with exposed stone, warm-yellow-hued walls, simple timber furniture and art scattered about. If you can't decide on Italian or Spanish, there's also a tapas menu.

✖ Passeig Marítim & Western Palma

★ Toque INTERNATIONAL €€
(Map p54; ☑ 971 28 70 68; http://restaurante-toque.com; Carrer Federico García Lorca 6; mains €17-19, 3-course lunch menú €14.50; ☺ 1-4pm & 7-11pm Tue-Sat; ▥) A father-and-son team run this individual little place with real pride and warmth. The food is Belgian-meets-Med (perhaps cauliflower cream with *butifarrón* sausage, raisins and pine nuts, or pork cheeks with peach) and has generated a loyal following among *palmeros*. Wines are well chosen and modestly priced, and the €14.50 lunch *menú* is a dead-set bargain.

El Náutico SEAFOOD €€
(Map p54; ☑ 971 72 66 00; www.elnauticorestaurante.com; Real Club Náutico, Plaza de San Pedro 1; mains €18-22; ☺ 1pm-3am; ❄ ▥) One of Palma's standout seafood options in the Royal Sailing Club, 'The Nautical' does hake in a variety of ways (including 'Roman-style' – with vinegar and raisins), simply grilled

shellfish and other spanking-fresh marine delights. The space, with wraparound windows overlooking the marina and a decked terrace, is beautifully designed in a nautical theme.

Casa Jacinto MALLORCAN €€
(☑971 40 18 58; www.casajacintomallorca.com; Camí de la Tramvía 37; mains €14-20, menús €15-22; ⊙1-5pm & 7pm-12.30am) A classic since the 1980s, this huge and no-nonsense eatery attracts Mallorcans from far and wide for copious servings of mainland Spanish and local food, especially grilled meats, including game cuts such as venison and wild boar. It's situated in Gènova, 4km west of the town centre.

Ca'n Eduardo SEAFOOD €€€
(Map p54; ☑971 72 11 82; www.caneduardo. com; Es Mollet, 3rd fl, Travesía Contramuelle; mains €23-29; ⊙1-11pm; ⊕) What better place to sample fish than here, right above the fish market? Ca'n Eduardo, in business since the 1940s, is hardly cutting-edge, but makes the most of stunning harbour views and super-fresh ingredients. Black-vested waiters serve seafood and some fantastic rice dishes (minimum of two) – the *arroz bogavante* (lobster rice; €26 per person) is a favourite.

✖ Es Portixol & Es Molinar

Es Mollet SEAFOOD €€€
(Map p54; ☑971 24 71 09; www.restaurantees-mollet.com; Carrer de la Sirena 1; mains €18-40; ⊙1-3.30pm & 7.30-10.30pm Mon-Sat) This classic seafood joint is the ideal place to sample the delights of the deep, in the former fishing village of Portixol. The catch of the day (sold by weight: €45 to €60 per kg) begs with clear eyes to be picked, while squid with *sobrassada* and other super-fresh delights dance on the busy grill.

Portixol MEDITERRANEAN €€€
(Map p54; ☑971 27 18 00; www.portixol.com; Carrer de la Sirena 27; mains €23-27, 3-course lunch menú €19; ⊙7.30am-11pm; ⊕☑) The harbourside restaurant at Hotel Portixol, a bright and breezy affair, with sea views and a blue-white colour scheme, is a cut above the typical hotel restaurant. The menu is ingredient-driven, treating Med produce to the occasional international twist: perhaps a seafood laksa that uses rice rather than noodles, or grilled red tuna with green soy beans and wasabi mayonnaise.

Sa Roqueta SEAFOOD €€€
(Map p54; ☑971 24 94 10; www.restaurante-saroqueta.com; Carrer Sirena 11, Portixol; mains €20-24; ⊙noon-4pm & 8pm-midnight Mon-Sat) One of former-fishing-village Portixol's excellent seafood restaurants, Sa Roqueta has been doing as little as possible to the daily catch since 1987. Grilled fish, clams with artichokes, lobster rice and seafood *fideuà* (pasta) are all prepared simply and expertly.

Ola del Mar SEAFOOD €€€
(Map p54; ☑971 27 42 75; www.oladelmar.es; Carrer del Vicari Joaquim Fuster 1; mains €22-26; ⊙1-4.30pm & 7.30-11pm) A relative newcomer to Portixol's seafront dining scene (it opened in 2013), Ola del Mar keeps up the enclave's standards, with top-quality fresh fish and seafood and rice dishes. There are no surprises on the menu, but everything's executed with simple flair, and the terrace and switched-on service invite you to linger.

♟ Drinking & Nightlife

Palma's clubbing epicentre is around the Passeig Marítim and the Club de Mar.

Most clubs open around midnight, but don't get going until 2am. Things go strong until 5am, when the early-morning clubs (some around Plaça de Gomila) begin.

Admission costs €10 to €20, usually including your first drink, although if you're not dressed to impress you may be turned away no matter how much cash you're willing to spend.

Siente GAY
(Map p58; ☑971 77 39 33; www.sientespa.com; Carrer de Fray Luis de León 5; ⊙4-11pm Tue-Fri & Sun, 4pm-10am Sat) With a pool, Jacuzzi, wet and dry saunas and private rooms, Siente is the best-equipped and -recommended gay sauna in central Palma.

Bar Michel GAY
(Map p54; ☑971 90 02 84; Avinguda de Joan Miró 58; ⊙8am-2.30am Mon-Sat, 4pm-midnight Sun; ⊕) This friendly terraced bar in the heart of Palma's gay 'district' is a great place to kick-start your night. Very reasonable cocktails and tapas.

Nassau Beach BAR
(Map p54; ☑664 449053; www.nas-saubeach-palma.com; Passeig de Portitxol 5; ⊙9am-1am) This cruisy beach club – with DJs, driftwood decor, beach chairs for lounging, and spectacular views out to sea and

back along the bay to the cathedral – is one of the nicest places for a sundowner in Es Portixol. The restaurant (mains €18 to €27) isn't bad, either.

Anima Beach   BAR
(Map p54; ☎971 59 55 91; www.animabeach-palma.com; Platja de Can Pere Antoni; ☺10.30am-1.30am May-Oct, 11am-8pm Nov-Mar; ☎) Beachfront chill-out lounge and much-loved spot for a sundowner and tapas. DJs bring the beats Thursday to Sunday. You can reserve a sunbed for €25, and add a cocktail, water and fruit for €35.

Dark Cruising Bar   GAY
(Map p54; www.darkcruisingmallorca.com; Carrer de Ticià 22; ☺7pm-3am) For all your (male-only) dark room encounters, including naked and fetish parties, this is the place. Look for the small illuminated sign and the deep blue glow.

Nikki Beach   BAR
(☎971 12 39 62; www.nikkibeach.com; Avenida Notario Alemany 1; ☺11am-8pm late Apr-Sep) Sushi, champagne, plush white loungers, bronzed bods, DJ beats and summertime barbecues are what Magaluf-based Nikki Beach has to offer. There's also a yacht pick-up service, should you require one.

Guinness House   BAR
(Map p58; Parc de la Mar; ☺8am-1am) This otherwise unremarkable bar is blessed with a stunning location, between the cathedral and the sea. It's at its best for an early-morning coffee before the crowds arrive, or after dark.

Old Palma

La Vinya de Santa Clara   WINE BAR
(Map p58; ☎666 664330; www.lavinyadesantaclara.es; Carrer de Santa Clara 8A; ☺1-11.30pm Mon-Sat, 5-11pm Sun) With over 60 varieties by the glass, this convivial little cubby hole gives you every opportunity to get to grips with the wines of Mallorca (and beyond, if you choose). Basic tapas – cheese, *sobrassada,* empanadas and the like – keep you on your feet and socialising.

Gibson   BAR
(Map p58; ☎971 71 64 04; Plaça del Mercat 18; ☺8am-2am Sun-Thu, to 3am Fri & Sat) This chirpy cocktail bar with outside seating is still busy with (mostly local) punters on a weekday night when everything else around has pulled the shutters down.

Cappuccino   CAFE
(Map p58; www.grupocappuccino.com; Carrer del Conquistador 13; ☺8.30am-1am Sun-Wed, to midnight Thu-Sat; ☎) Part of a cafe chain (albeit a stylish one), it's Cappuccino's location in the lee of the Palau March that's the attraction here. Light meals, cakes and good (if overpriced) coffee are all perfectly fine, but it's the people-watching you'll appreciate.

Plaça Major & Around

Ca La Seu   BAR
(Map p58; Carrer de Cordería 17; ☺7pm-2am Mon-Sat) What was once a workshop for the cathedral is now one of Palma's most atmospheric bars, a 500-year-old room graced by marble tables and festooned with the wickerwork that was once its *raison d'être.* Creative tapas, craft beers and the agreeable buzz typical of the best places in Sa Gerreria round out a thoroughly convivial destination.

Bar Flexas   BAR
(Map p58; www.barflexas.com; Carrer de la Llotgeta 12; ☺noon-5pm & 7pm-1am Tue-Sat) A lively locals' bar with a hint of grunge, Bar Flexas took up residence long before the streets southeast of the Plaça Major became trendy and remains a great spot for a tipple far from the tourist haunts. Charmingly offbeat, it hosts art exhibitions and occasional live acts, serves good tapas and has just the right sort of attitude.

GAY & LESBIAN PALMA

The bulk of gay life on the island happens in and around Palma. The biggest concentration of gay bars is on Avinguda de Joan Miró, south of Plaça de Gomila. To get your night going, you could start with the following:

➡ **Dark Cruising Bar**

➡ **Siente**

➡ **Bar Michel**

Useful websites for plugging into Palma's gay community:

➡ www.mallorcagaymap.com (a paper version is available from some tourist offices)

➡ www.gay-mallorca.blogspot.com

BEACH-CLUB COOL

When the city turns up the heat in summer, many gravitate towards Palma's chill-out lounges to linger by the poolside, slurp cocktails and hang with a bronzed, beat-digging crowd. Here's our pick of the beachfront bunch:

➡ **Nikki Beach** Sushi, champagne, plush white loungers, bronzed bods, DJ beats and summertime barbecues are what Magaluf-based Nikki Beach has to offer.

➡ **Anima Beach** Beachfront chill-out lounge and much-loved spot for a sundowner and tapas.

➡ **Nassau Beach** Slick beach club in Es Portixol, with views out to sea and back along the bay to the cathedral.

Café L'Antiquari
BAR

(Map p58; ☑871 57 23 13; Carrer d'Arabi 5; ☺noon-1am Mon-Sat) This old antique shop has been transformed into one of the most original places in Palma to nurse a drink and nibble on tapas. Curios, prints and knick-knacks adorn every corner and inch of wall space, and even the tables and chairs belong to another age. Occasionally there's music or photo exhibitions, and always the coffee is excellent.

Es Puig de Sant Pere

Atlantico Café
BAR

(Map p58; ☑971 72 62 85; www.cafeatlantico.es; Carrer de Sant Feliu 12; ☺1pm-2am Mon-Sat, from 7pm Sun) Spangled with an upended cornucopia of bric-a-brac, blessed with welcoming, laid-back staff and capable of cranking the merriment up to 11, this is one of Palma's most charismatic bars. Ever-expanding swaths of graffiti testify to the numberless nights of bonhomie and cocktails downed since it opened in 1997.

Bodega Can Rigo
BAR

(Map p58; ☑971 41 60 07; www.bodegacanrigo.es; Carrer de Sant Feliu 16; ☺9.30am-3pm & 6-11.30pm Mon, Tue, Thu & Fri, from noon Sat, from 6pm Sun) The tapas and *pintxos* at this charismatic little place, which has been going strong since 1949, are rated as some of the best in Palma. As if the intimate vibe, profu-

sion of cosy nooks and great wine list weren't enough incitement to linger!

Café La Lonja
CAFE

(Map p58; ☑971 72 27 99; http://cafelalonja.es; Carrer de Sa Llotja 2; ☺10am-2am Mon-Sat, 11am-1am Sun) With its curved marble bar, tiled-chessboard floor, smattering of tables and padded benches and eclectic decor of old luggage and portraits, this place is as appealing for breakfast as it is for tapas and a *pomada* (Menorcan gin and lemon soft drink). Sit outside when the weather's warm, in the shadow of Sa Llotja.

Ginbo
BAR

(Map p58; ☑971 72 21 75; Passeig de Mallorca 14A; ☺4pm-3am Mon-Fri, from 6pm Sat & Sun) Not in the hippest neighbourhood, Ginbo nonetheless does the best G&T in Palma. Besides over 120 different kinds of gin, it mixes some superb cocktails, including the lip-smacking Tangerine (basically a gin sour made with rosemary syrup), which you can sip in the buzzy, stylishly urban, backlit bar or on the terrace.

Abaco
COCKTAIL BAR

(Map p58; ☑971 71 49 39; www.bar-abaco.es; Carrer de Sant Joan 1; ☺8pm-1am Sun-Thu, to 3am Fri & Sat) Behind a set of ancient timber doors is this extraordinary bar. Inhabiting the restored *pati* of an old Mallorcan house, Abaco hovers between extravagant and kitsch, with ornate candelabras, elaborate floral arrangements, cascading towers of fresh fruit, and bizarre artworks. Paying €15 and more for a cocktail is an outrage, but one might just be worth it here.

Santa Catalina & Around

Idem Café
BAR

(Map p54; Carrer de Sant Magí 15A; ☺7pm-2am, to 3am in summer; 🔊) Slink into this bordel-lo-chic cocoon of deep, dark-red velvet, chandeliers, baroque mirrors and risqué art. With a fabulously burlesque look and pre-clubbing vibe, Idem is a unique spot to sip a mojito or gin.

Hotel Hostal Cuba
BAR

(Map p54; ☑971 45 22 37; www.hotelhostalcuba.com; Carrer de Sant Magí 1; ☺8am-2am Sun-Thu, to 4am Fri & Sat) Inhabiting an early-20th-century Santa Catalina landmark for sailors passing through Palma, this place has been reborn as a watering hole of a more sophisticated kind. With a kitchen open from 9am to midnight, DJs on busy nights, and a roof-top Skybar with superb 27-degree views of central Palma and the Badia de Palma, it covers most bases.

Soho Bar
BAR

(Map p54; ☏ 971 45 47 19; www.sohobarpalma.com; Avinguda d'Argentina 5; ☺ 6pm-3am; ☏) This self-proclaimed 'urban vintage bar' has a green-lit beer fridge, vintage 1960s decor and a dedication to indie music. The laid-back crowd seems oblivious to the traffic pounding past the footpath tables, and there are old-school game consoles for the easi-ly distracted. Cocktails go for €7 – the bar prides itself on its mojito.

Passeig Marítim & Western Palma

Pacha
CLUB

(Map p54; www.pachamallorca.es; Passeig Marítim 42; ☺ 10pm-6am daily Jul-Aug, Thu-Sat rest of year) This glamour puss of a club brings a splash of Ibiza to Palma's late-night scene. Set away from the town centre, down by the port, it's a three-floor temple to hedonism, with regular fiestas, DJs pumping out dance music of all flavours and multiple chill-out terraces. Entry costs around €15.

Tito's
CLUB

(Map p54; www.titosmallorca.com; Passeig Marítim 33; admission €15-20; ☺ 11pm-6am daily Jun-Sep, Fri & Sat Oct-May) Ray Charles, Mar-lene Dietrich and Frank Sinatra once used to let their hair down at this clubbing classic, which has been going strong since the 1950s. Today DJs spin Euro-house and popular dance to a crowd that comes for the upbeat vibe, sweeping city views and the occasion-al sexy floor show. There's also an outdoor stage in warm weather.

Varadero
BAR

(Map p54; ☏ 971 72 64 28; www.varaderomal-lorca.com; Carní de l'Escullera; ☺ 8am-1am Mon-Thu & Sun, to 3am Fri & Sat) This minimalist, glass-fronted bar's splendid situation, jut-ting out into the Badia de Palma, makes it feel as though you've weighed anchor. The squawking of seagulls mixes with lounge sounds as you sip your favourite tipple and watch passenger jets rake low across the bay, or contemplate the majesty of the cathedral from the teak-timbered terrace.

⭐ Entertainment

From pop concerts to opera, movies to folk dancing, international regattas to football matches, there's always an entertaining di-version happening in Palma. Most events can be booked online through www.ticket-master.es, or through the department store El Corte Inglés (www.elcorteingles.es).

Go to http://ocio.diariodemallorca.es for up-to-date event listings.

Cinema

Palma has at least seven cinema complex-es, each with several screens, but only one shows films not dubbed into Spanish.

Cine Ciutat
CINEMA

(Map p54; ☏ 971 20 54 53; www.cineciutat.org; Carrer de Emperadriu Eugènia 6) About 2km north of central Palma, this cinema pro-grams art-house films, many in their orig-inal language with Spanish subtitles. On Mondays the ordinary ticket price of €7.50 drops to €5.

Theatre

Teatre Principal
THEATRE

(Map p58; ☏ box office 971 21 96 96; www.tea-treprincipal.com; Carrer de Sa Riera 2; ☺ box office 5-9pm Wed-Sat, 11am-2pm Fri & Sat) Built in 1854 on the site of a 17th-century predecessor, destroyed by fire in 1858, rebuilt in 1860 and again restored in 2007, this is the city's prestige theatre for drama, classical music, opera and ballet. The renovation recreated the theatre's neoclassical heyday and com-bined it with the latest technology, resulting in great acoustics.

Teatre Municipal
DANCE

(Map p58; ☏ 9am-2pm 971 73 91 48; Passeig de Mallorca 9; ☺ box office 1hr before show) Here you might see anything from contemporary dance to drama.

Live Music

Most of Palma's live acts perform on the stages of intimate bars around Sa Llotja. Concerts begin between 10pm and midnight and wrap up no later than 2am.

Jazz Voyeur Club
LIVE MUSIC

(Map p58; ☏ 971 72 07 80; www.jazzvoyeurfesti-val.com; Carrer dels Apuntadors 5; ☺ 8.30pm-1am Mon-Thu & Sun, to 3am Fri & Sat) Tiny, intimate Voyeur hosts live bands nightly for much of the year – jazz is the focus, but you'll also hear flamenco, blues, funk and the occa-sional jam session. Red candles burn on the

LA RUTA MARTIANA

The Sa Gerreria neighbourhood of Palma, southeast of the Plaça Major, has undergone an extraordinary makeover, from the no-go area of central Palma to one of its hottest nightlife districts. Part of the momentum is attributable to the inexplicably named **La Ruta Martiana** (The Martians' Route), where 25 bars clustered tightly around these streets offer a small morsel to eat (a tapa, or a *pintxo*) and a drink for €2 from 7.30pm to midnight on Tuesday and from 7.30pm to 2am on Wednesday. Apart from being great value and allowing you to go on a tapas and bar crawl without breaking the bank, it has breathed life into this long-neglected corner of town. Among the bars taking part are **L'Ambigú** (p70) and **Ca La Seu** (p75).

tables and photography (including a permanent exhibition by Gerardo Cañellas) graces the walls. In autumn it hosts a fine jazz festival.

Novo Café Lisboa　　　　LIVE MUSIC
(Map p54; ☑ 661 785667; Carrer de Sant Magí 33; ⊗ 9pm-3am Wed-Sun) One of Palma's best live music–DJ venues, the New Lisbon Cafe's curved wooden bar is thronged three-deep on the more popular nights. Expect jazz-funk, disco, electro, synthpop and much else besides. Most nights are free.

Auditòrium　　　　LIVE MUSIC
(Map p54; ☑ 971 73 47 35; www.auditoriumpalma.es; Passeig Marítim 18; ⊗ box office 10am-2pm & 4-9pm) This spacious, modern theatre is Palma's main stage for major performances, ranging from opera to light rock, ballet, musicals, tribute bands and gospel choirs. The Sala Mozart hosts part of the city's opera program (with the Teatre Principal), while the Orquestra Simfónica de Balears (Balearic Symphony Orchestra) are regulars from October to May.

Garito Cafe　　　　LIVE MUSIC
(Map p54; ☑ 971 73 69 12; www.garitocafe.com; Dàrsena de Can Barberà; ⊗ 8pm-4am, closed Sun-Wed Oct-May) DJs and live performers – slinging anything from nu jazz to disco classics and electro – get the Garito going from around 10pm Thursday to Saturday nights.

The food's quite funky, too: expect riffs on traditional classics, such as quinoa risotto or fried black ravioli. Admission is generally free, but you're expected to buy a drink.

Blue Jazz Club　　　　LIVE MUSIC
(Map p58; ☑ 971 72 72 40; www.bluejazz.es; 7th fl, Passeig de Mallorca 6; ⊗ 10pm-late Thu-Sat, 8.30pm-late Mon) Located on the 7th floor of the Hotel Saratoga, this sophisticated club with high-altitude views over Palma offers after-dinner jazz, soul and blues concerts from 11pm to 1am Thursday to Saturday, and a Monday-evening jam session from 9pm to 11pm. Admission is free; but you're expected to buy a drink.

Football
RCD Mallorca　　　　FOOTBALL
(☑ booking 971 22 15 35; www.rcdmallorca.es; Iberostar Estadi, Camí dels Reis, Polígon Industrial) Palma's RCD Mallorca, which plays at the Iberostar Estadi, is one of the better sides battling it out in La Liga. Never champions, they usually wind up achieving mid-table respectability. You can get tickets at the stadium or call the ticket booking number.

Iberostar Estadi　　　　STADIUM
(☑ booking 971 22 15 35; www.rcdmallorca.es; Camí dels Reis, Polígon Industrial; ☑ 6,8) The Iberostar Estadi is about 3km north of central Palma, and hosts football games, including those featuring Palma's top division RCD Mallorca. Tickets are available at the stadium or by phoning the booking number.

🛍 Shopping
Start browsing the chic boutiques around Passeig d'es Born. The Passeig itself is equal parts high street and highbrow, with chain stores like Massimo Dutti and Zara alongside elitist boutiques. In the maze of pedestrian streets west of the Passeig, you'll find some of Palma's most tempting (and expensive) stores. Another good shopping street is pedestrianised Carrer de Sant Miquel.

Old Palma
Colmado Santo Domingo　　　　FOOD
(Map p58; ☑ 971 71 48 87; www.colmadosantodomingo.com; Carrer de Sant Domingo 1; ⊗ 10am-8pm Mon-Sat) It's almost impossible to manoeuvre in this narrow little shop, so crowded are its shelves with local Mallorcan food products – cheeses, honey, olives, olive oil, pâté, fig bread, balsamic vinegar, Sóller

marmalade to name just a few – while *sobrassada* (from €10 per kilo) hangs from the ceiling.

Vidrierias Gordiola
GLASS

(Map p58; ☑971 66 50 46; www.gordiola.com; Carrer de la Victòria 2; ☺10.15am-1.45pm & 4.30-8pm Mon-Fri, 10.15am-1.45pm Sat) The Gordiola family can call on nearly 300 years of glass-making skill, everywhere evident in the fan-tastically shaped and coloured vases, lamps, stemware and other vitreous works of art.

Típika
ARTS & CRAFTS

(Map p58; ☑971 72 89 83; www.tipika.es; Carrer d'en Morei 7; ☺11am-8pm Mon-Sat, to 4pm Sun) This small shop is dedicated to promoting the craftsmanship and gastronomy of Mallorca. Here you'll find wines, olive oils, salts and liquors, as well as ceramics and other handicrafts from small family artisan businesses across the island. You can also book Mallorca Rutes (p68) walking tours of Palma here.

Chocolate Factory
CHOCOLATE

(Map p58; ☑971 22 94 93; www.chocolatfactory.com; Plaça des Mercat 9; ☺10.30am-8.30pm Mon-Sat, 11am-3pm Sun) The Chocolate Factory does precisely what it says on the tin. Besides irresistible pralines, macaroons and slabs of amazingly intense 100% cocoa chocolate, it also does a fine line in chocolate-filled *ensaïmadas,* chocolate fondues, cakes and ice cream.

Carmina
SHOES

(Map p58; www.carminashoemaker.com; Carrer de l'Unió 4; ☺11am-8.30pm Mon-Sat) A classic of traditional Mallorcan shoemaking, Carmina makes a virtue of dark tones, brogues and loafers that will set you back €340 to €500. If you want Cordoban leather, expect to pay €600 and more.

Fine Books
BOOKS

(Map p58; ☑971 72 37 97; Carrer d'en Morei 7; ☺10am-8pm Mon-Sat) This extraordinary collection of secondhand books, including some really valuable treasures, rambles over three floors. It's *the* place for secondhand, English-language books in Palma: if you can't find what you're looking for, Rodney will try to track it down for you.

Addaia
CLOTHING

(Map p58; ☑971 72 40 20; www.addaia.es; Plaça del Rosari 2; ☺10am-8pm Mon-Sat) This upmarket fashion retailer sells shoes, bags and more.

🏠 Plaça Major & Around

El Paladar
FOOD & DRINKS

(Map p54; ☑971 71 74 04; www.elpaladar.es; Carrer de Bonaire 21; ☺8am-9pm Mon-Sat, 9.30am-2pm Sun) 'The Palate' is a wonderland for *jamón* lovers. The flavour of air-cured pig scents the air, mingling with the cheese, *sobrassada* and other delights on display. There's plenty of other Mallorcan produce, including wines and canned fish, and you can perch on a stool to enjoy a glass and tasting plate.

El Corte Inglés
DEPARTMENT STORE

(Map p54; ☑971 77 01 77; www.elcorteingles.es; Avinguda d'Alexandre Rosselló 12-16; ☺9.30am-10pm Mon-Sat) This flagship branch of Palma's biggest department store sells clothes, cosmetics, homewares and accessories, and tickets to local shows and events.

Rosario P
CLOTHING

(Map p58; ☑971 72 35 86; www.rosariop.com; Carrer de Sant Jaume 20; ☺10.30am-1.30pm & 5-8pm Mon-Fri, 10.30am-1.30pm Sat) Local designer Rosario Pérez, a trained artist, sells her delicate hand-painted silk clothes, scarves and accessories from this boutique.

Bordados Valldemossa
ARTS & CRAFTS

(Map p58; ☑971 71 63 06; Carrer de Sant Miquel 26; ☺10am-8pm Mon-Sat) Embroidered linens, many made on the island, fill this shop.

Dialog
BOOKS

(Map p58; ☑971 66 63 31; www.dialog-palma.com; Carrer de Santa Magdalena 3; ☺11am-2pm &

MARKET WATCH

Flea markets, speciality markets and artisan markets abound in Palma. For handicrafts, head to the **Plaça Major Artisan Market** (Map p58; Plaça Major; ☺10am-2pm daily Jul-Sep, Mon, Tue, Fri & Sat Feb-Jun & Oct-Dec, Fri & Sat Jan & Feb) or **Plaça des Meravelles Artisan Market** (Map p58; Plaça des Meravelles; ☺8pm-midnight May-Oct). A sprawling **flea market** (Map p54; Avinguda de Gabriel Alomar & Avinguda de Villalonga; ☺8am-2pm Sat) takes over the *avingudes* east of the city centre (Avinguda de Gabriel Alomar and Avinguda de Villalonga) each Saturday. The Christmas market takes over the Plaça Major from 16 December to 5 January.

4.30-8pm Mon-Fri, 10am-2pm Sat) The selection of German- and English-language books here is small but very carefully chosen, with especially good sections on languages and books about Mallorca.

Es Puig de Sant Pere

Camper SHOES
(Map p58; ☑971 71 46 35; www.camper.com; Avinguda de Jaume III 5; ☺10am-8.30pm Mon-Sat, to 8pm Sun) Best known of Mallorca's famed shoe brands, funky, eco-chic Camper is now incredibly popular worldwide.

El Corte Inglés DEPARTMENT STORE
(Map p58; ☑971 77 01 77; www.elcorteingles.es; Avenida de Jaime III 15; ☺9.30am-9.30pm Mon-Sat, 11am-8.30pm Sun) This branch of the huge Spanish department store franchise is good for getting many things under one roof.

Santa Catalina & Around

B Connected Concept Store HOMEWARES
(Map p54; ☑971 28 21 95; www.bconnected-conceptstore.com; Carrer de Dameto 6; ☺10am-2.30pm & 5-9pm Mon-Fri, 10am-3pm Sat) Part of a local cluster of B Connected stores focusing on various facets of stylish living, this designer 'concept' store is very much at home in Santa Catalina. Dedicated to homewares and interior design, it sells all sorts of knick-knacks that you never knew you needed. The look is generally contemporary with the occasional retro touch.

Trading Place BOOKS
(Map p54; ☑871 94 13 50; www.mallorca-books.com; Carrer de Pou 35; ☺10am-1.30pm & 5-7.30pm Mon-Fri, 10am-1.30pm Sat) One of the largest dealers in secondhand books (mostly English, but some Spanish and German), it also sells furniture and serves as something of a meeting and information point for Palma's expat community.

ℹ️ Information

DANGERS & ANNOYANCES
In general, Palma is a safe city. The main concern is petty theft – pickpockets and bag snatchers.
➡ Some streets are best avoided at night, when the occasional dodgy character comes out to play; if you're alone after dark, perhaps avoid Plaça de Sant Antoni and nearby avenues, such as Avinguda de Villalonga and Avinguda d'Alexandre Rosselló. But really, the risks are very slight.

EMERGENCY

Ambulance	☑061
General EU Emergency Number	☑112
Policía Local	☑092 (emergency), ☑971 22 55 00
Policía Nacional	☑091 (emergency), ☑971 22 55 00

MEDIA
Foreign-language newspapers include the following:
➡ *Daily Bulletin* (www.majorcadailybulletin.es) English-language paper established in 1962.
➡ *Mallorca Magazin* (www.mallorcamagazin.net) A substantial German-language weekly.
➡ *Mallorca Zeitung* (www.mallorcazeitung.es) A German-language weekly.

For an idea of what's on, look for free printed listings in tourist offices and bars:
➡ *Youthing* (www.youthing.es) Published fortnightly.
➡ *Dígame* (www.digamemallorca.com) A monthly island-wide round-up of events, activities and up-to-date listings.
➡ See Mallorca (www.seemallorca.com) A useful online-only source of events and listings

Palma has a growing field of glossy mags and lifestyle websites, in English and German:
➡ *abcmallorca* (www.abc-mallorca.com) Free, with articles on the city and island.
➡ *Contemporary Balears* (http://amoyles.com/portfolio/contemporary-balears), Bimonthly arts and lifestyle magazine with interesting articles and listings – look for it in hotels and some restaurants, bars and galleries.
➡ Anglo Info (www.angloinfo.com) This website has a forum, events listings and a directory of English-speaking businesses.
➡ *Mallorca Geht Aus!* (www.mallorca-geht-aus.de) Published annually (€9.80) and also available in Germany, Austria, Switzerland and online, this glossy has more than 200 pages of stories and reviews of anything from *fincas* (rural estates) to clubs.

MEDICAL SERVICES
In the main newspapers (such as the *Diario de Mallorca*) you will find a list of pharmacies open late.
Farmácia Castañer-Buades (☑971 07 06 35; Plaça del Rei Joan Carles I 3; ☺8.30am-10.30pm)
Farmácia Salvà Saz (☑971 45 87 88; Carrer de Balanguera 15; ☺24hr)
Hospital Universitari Son Espases (☑871 20 50 00; www.hospitalsonespases.es; Carretera de Valldemossa 79) Situated 4km north of

town, this hospital is best reached with bus lines 20, 29, 33 and 34.

TOURIST INFORMATION

Airport Tourist Office (☑ 971 78 95 56; Aeroport de Palma; ⊘ 8am-8pm Mon-Sat, to 2pm Sun)

Ben Amics (Map p54; ☑ 871 96 54 66; www.benamics.com; Carrer del General Riera 3; ⊘ 9am-3pm) Ben Amics is the island's umbrella association for gays, lesbians and transsexuals. There's also a bookable advice service at the office.

Consell de Mallorca Tourist Office (Map p58; ☑ 971 17 39 90; www.infomallorca.net; Plaça de la Reina 2; ⊘ 8.30am-8pm Mon-Fri, to 3pm Sat; 🛜)

Conselleria de Medi Ambient (Map p54; ☑ 971 17 68 00; http://maap.caib.es/; Avinguda de Gabriel Alomar i Villalonga 33) Useful for guidelines for anchoring your yacht in open water to protect the sea floor.

Oficinas del Parque Nacional Marítimo y Terrestre de Cabrera (☑ 971 17 76 45; http://en.balearsnatura.com; Carrer Gremí de Corredors 10; ⊘ 11am-3pm) Can help with information and permits for visiting the Parc Nacional Marítim-Terrestre de l'Arxipèlag de Cabrera.

Parc de ses Estacions Tourist Office (Map p54; ☑ 902 102365; www.infomallorca.net; Plaça d'Espanya; ⊘ 9am-8pm)

USEFUL WEBSITES

City of Palma Tourist Site (www.imtur.es) The city's main tourist portal.

Empresa Municipal de Transports Urbans de Palma de Mallorca (www.emtpalma.es) Palma's public transport corporation.

Federación Empresarial Hotelera de Mallorca (www.fehm.info) Has hotel and general information for Palma de Mallorca.

ℹ Getting There & Away

AIR

Palma de Mallorca Airport lies 8km east of the city and receives an impressive level of traffic. Sometimes referred to as Son Sant Joan Airport, it's Spain's third largest, with direct services to 105 European and North African cities.

BOAT

Palma is the island's main port. There are numerous boat services to/from Mallorca from mainland Spain and the other islands of the Balearics.

BUS

All island buses to/from Palma depart from (or near) the Estació Intermodal de Palma on Plaça d'Espanya. Services head in all directions, including Valldemossa (€1.85, 30 minutes, up to 17 daily), Sóller (€2.65 to €3.90, 45 minutes, regular daily), Pollença (€5.35, 45 to 60 minutes, up to 14 daily) and Alcúdia (€5.30, one hour, up to 18 daily). All other significant coastal and inland centres are connected to Palma by usually frequent services (although some are served instead by one of the island's three train lines).

THE SLOW TRAIN TO SÓLLER

Welcome to one of the most rewarding excursions in Mallorca. Since 1912 a **narrow-gauge train** (p84) has trundled along the winding 27.3km route north to Sóller. The train, which originally replaced a stagecoach service, departs from Plaça de l'Estació seven times a day (five times from November to February) and takes about 1¼ hours, with between four and five return trains daily. The route passes through ever-changing countryside that becomes dramatic in the north as it crosses the 496m-high Serra de Alfàbia, via 13 tunnels (some over 2km long) and a series of bridges and viaducts.

The train initially rolls through the streets of Palma, but within 20 minutes you're in the countryside. At this stage the view is better to the left, towards the Serra de Tramuntana. The terrain starts to rise gently and to the left the eye sweeps over olive gardens, the occasional sandy-coloured house and the mountains beyond. Half an hour out of Palma you call in at Bunyola (an alternative boarding place that costs just €9/15 single/return from Palma or Sóller).

Shortly after Bunyola, as the mountains close in (at one point you can see Palma and the sea behind you), you reach the first of a series of tunnels. Some trains stop briefly at a marvellous lookout point, the **Mirador Pujol de'n Banya**, shortly after the **Túnel Major** (Main Tunnel; which is almost 3km long and took three years to carve out of the rock in 1907–10). The view stretches out over the entire Sóller valley. From there, the train rattles across a viaduct before entering another tunnel that makes a slow 180-degree turn on its descent into Sóller, whose station building is housed in an early-17th-century mansion. Return tickets are valid for two weeks.

CYCLING & SAILING AROUND PALMA

PALMA TO CAPOCORB VELL

START/END PALMA DE MALLORCA
DISTANCE 67KM
DIFFICULTY EASY TO MODERATE
BIKE ROAD OR TOURING BIKE

Bicycle is a great way to explore Palma and Badia de Palma: there's a coastal bike path between Palma's port and S'Arenal, and bike lanes in the city itself, where cyclists are an accepted fact of life. There are also plenty of operators who rent out city and mountain bikes

Covering a huge swath of the Badia de Palma, this circular ride follows an easygoing seafront cycle path, then heads slightly inland towards Cap Blanc on the island's south coast. The return journey winds through peaceful country lanes, before a deserved downhill reverses the route back to town.

Pick up the waterfront bike path in **Central Palma** and head southeast. Hugging the coast for most of the way, the path is a breezy sweep to **Pastilla**. From here follow the sea-front road to the end of the long sandy strip of **Platja de Palma** and its extension **S'Arenal** (although you'll have to mind the crowds that will wander onto the bike-only zone the whole way). Then follow the wooden signs for **Cap Blanc**. Although along a major road (the Ma6014), this 23km section cuts through pleasant countryside, and motorists are used to lycra-clad cyclists plying the route. The road rises to 150m, but the ascent is not too gruelling.

Follow the signs up a slight hill to reach the lighthouse at the cape, where you can take a breather to appreciate the sensational coastal views. Once back on the main road, continue northeast to a junction (with signs right to Cala Pi); bear left and watch out for signs to **Capocorb Vell**, whose entrance is on the left. There's a simple coffee bar at the ruins.

Exit the bar to the right and take the Camí de Betlem, a quiet country lane (also signed Carreró de Betlem). Follow this to the junction, and continue on to the Camí

Palma, with its tight tangle of galleries, palaces, ancient streets and good road infrastructure, is a great place for cycling, while the harbour and broad Badia de Palma is made for sailing.

Estabits de s'Àguila, surrounded by farmland. Turning sharp right, it becomes the Camí de s'Àguila. After 200m, a left turn will bring you onto the Camí de sa Caseta, shaded by overhanging trees and lined by dry-stone walls. The end of the lane is marked by a **windmill** and, to the left, a church. Turn left here, where a wooden sign points along tranquil Camí de sa Torre and onwards to S'Arenal. Take a right when you hit the Ma6014 and follow the wooden signs to Platja de Palma. From here, retrace your tracks back to the capital.

BIKE RENTAL

Palma on Bike (Map p58; ☑971 71 80 62; www.palmaonbike.com; Avinguda d'Antoni Maura 10; city/mountain/e-bike hire per day €14/22/24, per week €67/119/129; ⊘9am-8pm) has city bikes to get around Palma, as well as road bikes, rollerblades and kayaks. Rates include insurance and a helmet. It also runs Palma city tours (€25 per person; minimum two people), including tapas (€35) and bike-and-kayak tours (€49).

You'll find plenty of rental outlets along S'Arenal's beachfront but if you're after a decent road bike, try **Ciclos Quintana** (☑971 44 29 25; www.ciclosquintana.com; Carrer de San Cristóbal 32; aluminium/carbon bikes per day €20/25; ⊘noon-6pm Tue-Sat, plus 9.30pm-midnight Mon-Fri), just up from the main drag. Opening hours vary; see the website for details.

Palma Lock & Go (☑971 71 64 17; www.palmalockandgo.com; Estación Intermodal de Palma, Plaça d'Espanya; large bag per day €5.90; ⊘9am-8pm Apr-Oct, 9.30am-7pm Nov-Mar) is on the underground level of the train station; it's a handy place to leave your luggage.

SAILING IN PALMA

Sailing is a big deal in Palma and numerous regattas are held in the course of the year. In addition to those listed, the **Real Club Náutico** (p68), the most prestigious of Palma's yacht clubs, organises more than 20 events (some in collaboration with other clubs) throughout the year.

Copa del Rey (p68) The King's Cup is one of the summer highlights of Palma's regatta calendar.

PalmaVela (www.palmavela.com; ⊘late April/early May) Held in April, the PalmaVela has hundreds of yachts of all classes from around the world.

Trofeo SAR Princesa Sofía (www.trofeoprincesasofia.org; ⊘Mar/Apr) Held in April, this is one of six regattas composing the World Cup Series, attracting Olympic crews from all over the world.

Superyacht Cup (www.thesuperyachtcup.com; ⊘Jun) Held over three days in October, this is one of the major races for super yachts from 25m to 90m.

Trofeo Ciutat de Palma (p69) A huge event for smaller boats, held over four days in December.

CRUISES & COURSES

For boat tours and cruises try **Magic Catamarans** (p67), **Cruceros Marco Polo** (p67), or **Real Club Náutico** (p68).

Palma Sea School (Map p54; ☑971 10 05 18; www.palmaseaschool.com; Passeig Marítim 38; 2-day yachting courses from €500) offers a wide range of courses in yachting, sailing, powerboating and jet-skiing.

TRAIN

The **Ferrocarril de Sóller** (Sóller Railway; ☑ 971 75 20 51; www.trendesoller.com; Eusebio Estada 1; single/return €16/22; ⊙10.10am-7.30pm Apr-Oct; 10.30am-6pm Nov-Mar; [♿]) is a popular heritage railway (p81) running from the old station on Carrer Eusebio Estada (next to Palma's Estació Intermodal de Palma) to the northwestern town of Sóller, stopping en route at Bunyola. The Estació Intermodal itself is the terminus for Mallorca's three regular lines: the T1 (to Inca; €3.25, 25 to 40 minutes), the T2 (Sa Pobla; €4.10, 58 minutes) and the T3 (Manacor; €4.10, 66 minutes). Services start at 5.45am and finish at 10.10pm on weekdays.

Make sure your service isn't an express bypassing the station you want; look for the bike symbol that indicates a peak service on which you can't bring your bike; and be aware that some trains require you to transfer at Enllaç. The T1 to Inca doesn't run on weekends, as the T2 and T3 both stop there anyway.

❶ Getting Around

TO/FROM THE AIRPORT

Bus 1 runs every 15 minutes from the airport to Plaça d'Espanya/Estació Intermodal de Palma in central Palma (€5, 20 minutes) and on to the entrance of the ferry terminal. It makes several stops along the way, entering the heart of the city along Avinguda de Gabriel Alomar i Villalonga, skirting around the city centre and then running back to the coast along Passeig de Mallorca and Avinguda d'Argentina. It heads along Avinguda de Gabriel Roca (aka Passeig Marítim) to reach the Estació Marítima (Ferry Port) before turning around. Buy tickets from the driver.

Taxis are generally clean, honest and abundant (when not striking); the ride from the airport to central Palma will cost around €18 to €22.

TO/FROM THE FERRY PORT

Bus 1 (the airport bus) runs every 15 minutes from the Estació Marítima (Ferry Port) across town (via Plaça d'Espanya/Estació Intermodal de Palma) and on to the airport. A taxi from/to the city centre will cost around €10 to €12.

BUS

There are 29 local bus services around Palma and its bay suburbs run by **EMT** (☑ 971 21 44 44; www.emtpalma.es). These include line 1 between the airport and port (€5), and line 23 serving Palma–S'Arenal–Cala Blava via Aqualand. Single-trip tickets on lines other than those to the airport and port cost €1.50, or you can buy a 10-trip card for €10.

CAR & MOTORCYCLE

Parking in the city centre can be complicated. Some streets are for pedestrians only and most of the remainder, including the ring roads (the *avingudes*, or *avenidas*) around the centre, are either no-parking zones or metered parking. Metered areas are marked in blue and generally you can park for up to two hours (€2.50), although time limits and prices can vary. The meters generally operate from 9am to 2pm and 4.30pm to 8pm Monday to Friday, and 9am to 2pm on Saturday.

Rent one of Mallorca Vintage's Vespas or Ducatis to zip around town or across the island from **Mallorca Vintage Motors** (☑ 620 476285; www.mallorcavintage.com; Plaça Espanya; ⊙9am-7pm). A day's high-season rental is €42 for a scooter, and €48 for a Ducati, including two helmets and insurance. It's located on the underground level of the train station (luggage can be left at the affiliated Palma Lock & Go) and there's another **branch** (Plaza de Porta de Santa Catalina 5; ⊙9am-7pm) near Es Baluard museum.

METRO

Of limited use to most travellers, a metro line operates from Plaça d'Espanya to the Universidad de las Islas Baleares (UIB; the city's university). Single trips are €1.60.

TAXI

For a taxi, call ☑ 971 72 80 81. For special taxis for the disabled, call ☑ 971 70 35 29.

Taxis are metered, but for trips beyond the city fix the price in advance. A green light indicates a taxi is free to hail or you can head for one of the taxi stands in the city centre, such as those on Passeig d'es Born. Flagfall is €3.90, thereafter you pay €1 per kilometre (more on weekends and holidays). There's a minimum fare from the airport, and a supplement to visit Castell de Bellver.

BADIA DE PALMA

The broad Badia de Palma (Bay of Palma) stretches east and west away from the city centre. Some of the island's densest holiday development is to be found on both sides, but the beaches, especially to the west, are quite striking, in spite of the dense cement backdrop. The beaches themselves are mostly very pretty and clean, but get very crowded (with very different crowds) in peak periods. Further south the coast quietens before rounding Cap de Cala Figuera.

East of Palma

On the east side of the bay, vast neon *bier kellers* and German-language menus alert you to which Western European nation's young choose to let their hair down here. A couple of nearby escape hatches allow respite from the madding crowds.

Ca'n Pastilla

POP 5125

In the shadow of the airport, heavily built-up Ca'n Pastilla is where Palma's eastern package-holiday coast begins. The Platja de Ca'n Pastilla marks the western and windier end of the 4.5km stretch of beach known as **Platja de Palma** (the windsurfing here can be good). Just west of Ca'n Pastilla is the pleasant **Cala Estancia**, a placid inlet whose beach is perfect for families. The waterfront, with a broad pedestrian walkway traversed by bikes, tourist trains and the odd Segway, is backed by thick mid-rise developments of hotels, eateries, cafes and bars.

◉ Sights & Activities

Palma Aquarium   AQUARIUM

(☑ 902 70 29 02; www.palmaaquarium.com; Carrer de Manuela de los Herreros i Sorà 21; adult/child €24/14; ☺ 9.30am-6.30pm, last entry 5pm; 🛝) Marine-research, -conservation and -preservation programs offset any animal-welfare qualms you may have visiting the excellent Palma Aquarium. Five million litres of salt water fill the 55 tanks, home to sea critters from the Mediterranean (rays, sea horses, coral and more) and far-away oceans. The central tank, which you walk through via a transparent tunnel, is patrolled by 20 sleek sharks, with which you can dive for €175. You could spend half a day here.

In total some 8000 specimens are found here ranging across a number of marine environments, with some stirring exhibits covering the threat to world tuna stocks. Yes, you'll see Nemo and there are good information panels in English, French, German and Spanish. If the kids fancy spending the night, the monthly Friday shark sleepover will certainly crank up the fear factor for little nippers.

Attraction   BOATING

(☑ 971 74 61 01; www.attractioncatamarans.com; Carrer de Nanses; adult/child €49/25; ☺ mid-Apr–Sep) Attraction arranges five-hour trips on a 24m catamaran around the Badia de Palma, taking in caves and bathing spots and including a paella lunch. The boarding point in Ca'n Pastilla is Carrer Nanses, and either daytime or sunset cruises are on offer.

Segway Palma   TOURS

(☑ 971 49 19 15; www.segwaypalma.com; Carretera del Arenal 9; 1/2/3hr tours €35/65/90; ☺ 9.30am-6pm) See the city by Segway (zippy battery-powered two-wheel scooters), with one-hour beach tours, two-hour tours to Es Portixol and three-hour excursions that go to the cathedral and back to Platja de Palma.

❤ Drinking & Nightlife

A predominantly German crowd pours into Ca'n Pastilla for endless drinking and deafening music, a phenomenon known as Ballermann. The action centres on enormous beer gardens around Carrer del Pare Bartomeu Salvà (aka Schinkenstrasse) and about three-quarters of the way along the beach east towards S'Arenal.

Puro Beach   LOUNGE

(☑ 971 74 47 44; www.purobeach.com; ☺ 10am-10pm May-Aug, to sunset Mar, Oct & Nov; 🐾) The pure-white beach bar carries more than a hint of Ibiza with a tapering outdoor promontory over the water that's perfect for sunset cocktails, DJ sessions and open-air spa treatments. Most of the toned, bronzed bods here wear white to blend in with the slinky decor – it's that kind of place.

Our tip: go for a drink or two and skip the sky-high-priced fusion food. It is a two-minute walk east of Cala Estancia (itself just east of Ca'n Pastilla).

❶ Getting There & Away

Bus 23 runs from Plaça d'Espanya to Ca'n Pastilla and parallel to Platja de Palma through S'Arenal and on past La Porciúncula to Aqualand. Buses run every half-hour or so and once every two hours they continue on to Cala Blava. Bus 15 runs from Plaça de la Reina and passes through Plaça d'Espanya on its way to S'Arenal every 10 minutes. For the Aquarium, get off at 366 (Ses Fontanelles).

S'Arenal

POP 8918

S'Arenal has so long been a favourite destination of young sunseekers, especially German ones, that its portion of the lengthy, broad Platja de Palma has been entirely developed. The hotels, bars, souvenir shops and kebab joints now spread several blocks back from the shore, for kilometres in each direction. Of course, that means there's lots of fun to be had by the young and feckless, and only the most curmudgeonly would deny that this is one of Mallorca's liveliest spots.

◎ Sights & Activities

AEqualand AMUSEMENT PARK
(☑971 44 00 00; www.aqualand.es; Ma6014; adult/child €28/19; ☉10am-6pm Jul & Aug, to 5pm mid-May–Jun, Sep & Oct; ⊞; ☒23) With 12 rides and pools, Mallorca's largest water park has plenty of splashy fun, including dedicated pools for tots, rapids, flumes and thrill-a-minute slides with names like anaconda, harakiri and kamikaze that leave little to the imagination. Parking is €4, 'minis' (kids between three and 10) cost only €10 and return visits are €14.

❶ Getting There & Away

Buses 15 and 25 (express) run along Platja de Palma from Palma's Plaça de la Reina to S'Arenal; bus 21 runs between S'Arenal and the airport; and bus 23 links Cala Blava and S'Arenal with Plaça d'Espanya. A single trip is €1.50, unless it's to the airport, in which case it's €5.

Cala Blava

POP 264
Despite being within whistling distance of the beer gardens of the Platja de Palma, Cala Blava is altogether different: it's residential rather than nakedly touristic, and offers a few quiet coves (several rocky; one sandy) to test the waters. It's really absurdly close to the hubbub of S'Arenal – just a few kilometres south on the Ma6014, then a short side road to Cala Blava. Just beyond is Bella Vista: part of the coast here is protected, and off-limits, but you can still slip down to the Caló des Cap d'Alt for a swim in crystal-clear waters.

❶ Getting There & Away

Bus 23 from Plaça d'Espanya to S'Arenal continues on to Cala Blava, but only every two hours.

West of Palma

Cala Major

POP 5633
Cala Major, a once-fashionable resort about 4km southwest of the city centre, boasts a pretty, rock-sheltered beach, and is the first of the coves that spread south from Palma, down the western shore of the Badia. It's quiet and residential in comparison to what lies further down the Ma1, but there are still plenty of mid-rise hotels, cafes, restaurants and clubs packed in between the hills and the beach.

Aside from the beach, the main attraction here is the wonderful Fundació Pilar I Joan Miró, inland and uphill from the waterfront.

◎ Sights

★**Fundació Pilar i Joan Miró** MUSEUM
(☑971 70 14 20; http://miro.palma.cat; Carrer de Saridakis 29; adult/child €6/free; ☉10am-7pm Tue-Sat, to 3pm Sun) The Catalan artist Joan Miró lived and worked at this beautiful hilltop compound, now a major museum to his life and work. Miró's friend, the architect Josep Lluís Sert, designed the studio space (much of which is preserved as it was during his working life) while the major exhibition space was designed by top Spanish architect Rafael Moneo, in 1992. With more than 2500 works by Miró (including sculpture, sketches and 118 paintings), it's a major collection.

No doubt influenced by his Mallorcan wife and mother, Miró moved to Palma in 1956 and remained here until his death in 1983.

A selection of his works hangs in the Sala Estrella, an angular, jagged part of Moneo's creation that is the architect's take on the artist's work. The rest of the building's exhibition space is used for temporary shows. Miró sculptures are scattered about outside. Beyond the studio is Son Boter, an 18th-century farmhouse Miró bought to increase his privacy. Inside, giant scribblings on the whitewashed walls served as plans for some of his bronze sculptures.

✖ Eating

Avinguda de Joan Miró, the main coastal road, has the most options.

Il Paradiso EUROPEAN €€€
(☑971 10 33 79; www.ilparadiso.es; Avinguda de Joan Miró 243; mains €25-31; ☉12.30-4pm & 7.30pm-midnight) Priceless views across the Badia de Palma are not the only forte of this slick beachside restaurant. The long list of pastas, including penne with scampi in saffron sauce and spaghetti al pescatore, suggests an Italian hand in the kitchen, but it's the simple seafood, perhaps grilled red tuna, or hake with broccoli and new potatoes, that really shines.

ⓘ Getting There & Away

From Palma take bus 3 or 46 (from Plaça d'Espanya) or bus 20 (from Plaça del Mercat) to get here (all fares €1.50).

Gènova

POP 3962

Most visitors to Palma come up here, around 1km north of Cala Major, to visit the closest caves to the capital, the Coves de Gènova. Aside from views, and some good Mallorcan restaurants, there probably isn't much else to tempt travellers. If you have wheels, follow the signs to Na Burguesa off the main road from the centre of Gènova (a short way north of the Coves turn-off). About 1.5km of winding, poor road takes you past the walled-in pleasure domes of the rich to reach a rather ugly monument to the Virgin Mary, from where you have sweeping views over the city (this is about the only way to look down on the Castell de Bellver) and bay.

◉ Sights

Coves de Gènova   CAVE

(✍971 40 23 87; http://covesdegenova.com; Carrer d'es Barranc 45; adult/child €10/5; ⊙10am-5.45pm) Discovered in 1906, these caves are worth a visit, their chambers dripping with curlicued stalactites and studded with pinnacled stalagmites. You descend 36m, and see all sorts of fanciful, backlit shapes. The temperature is always around 20°C in the caves, where water has been dripping away for many millennia to create these natural 'sculptures'. Take bus 46 from Palma or Cala Major, alight at Camí dels Reis 19, and walk 300m.

✗ Eating

Mesón Ca'n Pedro   MALLORCAN €€

(✍971 70 21 62; www.canpedro.es; Carrer del Rector Vives 14; mains €18-20; ⊙12.30pm-12.30am) One of Gènova's best, hearty, traditional Mallorcan restaurants is Mesón Ca'n Pedro, famous for its *frit mallorquí* (a lamb, liver and vegetable hash) snails and *pa amb oli* (bread rubbed with oil, garlic and super-fresh tomato). Running since 1976, it's a local favourite, with a terrace that's packed with *palmeros* when it's warm.

ⓘ Getting There & Away

Bus 46 runs from Carrer del Sindicat, on the eastern edge of Old Palma, to Gènova (€1.50, every 20 to 40 minutes).

Ses Illetes & Portals Nous

POP SES ILLETES 3209; PORTALS NOUS 2356

Ses Illetes and Portals Nous lie between narrow, picturesque coves and steep pine-stubbled hills. Together they comprise an upmarket holiday-residential zone and perhaps the most appealing stretch of the Badia de Palma. The coast is high and drops quite abruptly to the turquoise coves, principally Platja de Ses Illetes and, a little less crowded, Platja de Sa Comtesa. Parking is a minor hassle.

Virtually part of Ses Illetes is **Bendinat** (which takes its name from a nearby, neo-Gothic reworking of a 13th-century castle original that can only be seen from the Ma1 motorway). Next up is Portals Nous, with its super marina for the super yachts of the super rich at restaurant-lined **Puerto Portals**. The beach that stretches north of the marina is longer and broader than that in Ses Illetes.

✗ Eating & Drinking

Restaurante Illetas Playa   MALLORCAN €€

(✍971 70 18 96; www.illetasplaya.es; Passeig d'Illetes 75; mains €16-18; ⊙7-11pm Wed-Mon, plus 1-3.30pm Sat & Sun) With a plumb spot, looking down on the beach at Ses Illetes, this slightly old-fashioned Mallorcan restaurant is a welcome alternative to the glitz that dominates this part of the bay. It's not humble, but it isn't exorbitantly fancy either: ideal if you fancy just-so grilled squid, or lamb shoulder roasted to tender perfection.

Virtual Club   COCKTAIL BAR

(✍971 70 32 35; www.virtualclub.es; Passeig d'Illetes 60; ⊙10am-1am Apr-Oct; ☜) This hipper-than-thou waterside chill-out space has a long list of cocktails, wicker sofas, hammocks, cabana chairs and the inevitable DJ soundtrack. There's also a cave-like bar that fills with strange strobe lighting at night. We suggest skipping the overpriced food and going for a drink.

ⓘ Getting There & Away

Local Palma bus 3 reaches Ses Illetes from central Palma (€1.50); you can pick it up on Passeig de la Rambla or Avinguda de Jaume III). Buses 103, 104, 106 and 111 from Palma's bus station call in at Portals Nous (€1.45, 30 to 50 minutes).

Palmanova & Magaluf

POP PALMANOVA 6577; MAGALUF 4288

About 2km southwest from Portals Nous' elite yacht harbour is a whole other world. Palmanova and Magaluf have merged to form what is the epitome of the sea, sand, sunburn, sangria and shagging resort that has unfairly coloured perceptions of Mallorca in general. But the real Wild West days are substantially over: civic investment and new public order laws have managed to rein in the worst of the bacchanalian behaviour.

If you crave peace, head south of Magaluf to explore a couple of pretty *calas* (coves). Cala Vinyes has placid water, and the sand stretches inland among residential buildings. The next cove, Cala de Cap Falcó, is an emerald lick of an inlet surrounded by tree-covered rocky coast. Unfortunately, developers are getting closer and closer. Follow signs south for Sol de Mallorca and then the signs for each of these locations. Bus 107 from Palma reaches Cala Vinyes via Magaluf.

◉ Sights & Activities

There is a reason for Palmanova's and Magaluf's popularity: the four main beaches between Palmanova and Magaluf are broad, beautiful and immaculately maintained. The lavish sweeps of fine white sand, in parts shaded by strategically planted pines and palms, are undeniably tempting. And, to be fair, the development behind them could be considerably worse.

Western Water Park   AMUSEMENT PARK
(☑ 971 13 12 03; www.westernpark.com; Carretera de Cala Figuera a Sa Porrasa, Magaluf; adult/child €27/18; ⊙ 10am-6pm Jul & Aug, to 5pm May, Jun, Sep & Oct) This is the bucking bronco of Magaluf water parks, with wave pools and slides such as the Tijuana Twins, the Boomerang and The Beast, with a near-vertical 30m drop. There are quieter rides and pools for kids and the less adrenaline-addicted. 'Minis' (three- to four-year-olds) are only charged €10 admission, and return visits are €14 for adults and older kids.

Big Blue Diving   DIVING
(☑ 971 68 16 86; www.bigbluediving-mallorca.net; Carrer de Martí Ros García 6, Palmanova; snorkelling per person €35, 1-/2-die package with equipment €62/89; ⊙ Apr-Oct) The first freediving outfit on Mallorca, this well-run dive centre right on Palmanova beach offers the whole array of PADI courses. Scuba- and open-

water-diver courses for beginners are €269 and €399 respectively.

Cruceros Costa de Calvià   BOATING
(☑ 971 13 12 11; www.cruceroscostadecalvia.com; Avinguda Magaluf 10, Magaluf; ⊙ 11am, 1pm & 3pm Mon-Fri, 11am & 3pm Sat & Sun May-Oct) This operator offers two-hour boat trips in a glass-bottomed boat with the chance of seeing dolphins (adult/child €20/10). Also running speed-boat trips (€25/15), waterborne Palma city tours (€28/16) and day-long sea cruises (€37/20), it departs from the main beach in Magaluf, calling at Palmanova 15 minutes later.

🍷 Drinking & Nightlife

While restless young Germans party at the Platja de Palma's beer gardens, their British equivalents cut loose in the nightspots of Magaluf. This is big stag- and hen-night territory and the drinking antics of the Brits in Magaluf have become legendary (for the wrong reasons). The action is concentrated around the north end of Carrer de Punta Ballena, where pubs, clubs and bars are piled on top of one another.

Sol House Trinidad   CLUB
(☑ 971 13 14 00; www.mallorcarocks.com; Carrer Blanc 8, Magaluf) For clubbers and concert-goers, one of the most exciting additions to the party scene in Magaluf (or Palma for that matter) is Sol House Trinidad, the younger sister of the legendary venue Ibiza Rocks. Spruced up in 2016 (despite only opening in 2010), the complex comprises a monster-sized hotel (656 rooms) gathered around pools with pulsating music.

Pool parties with celebrity DJs and nonstop house are held most nights in season. Entry is free for all, not just guests.

ℹ Information

For hotel information try www.palmanova-magaluf.com, run by the local hoteliers' association.

Magaluf Tourist Office (☑ 971 13 11 26; www.visitcalvia.com; Carrer de Pere Vacquer Ramis 1; ⊙ 9am-6pm) Open year-round.

Palmanova Tourist Office (☑ 971 68 23 65; Passeig de la Mar 13; ⊙ 9am-6pm Apr-Oct, to 2pm Nov-Mar)

ℹ Getting There & Away

Buses 104, 106 and 107 connect Palma with Palmanova/Magaluf (€3.10, 50 minutes).

Western Mallorca

Best Places to Eat

Top Sights

Why Go?

'A sky like turquoise, a sea like lapis lazuli, mountains like emerald, air like heaven', enthused Romantic composer Chopin of his new home Valldemossa in 1838. His words ring true almost two centuries later in western Mallorca.

The Serra de Tramuntana range ripples all along the west coast, surveying the Mediterranean from above. Skirted by olive groves and pine forest, its razorback limestone mountains plunge 1000m down to the sea like the ramparts of some epic island fortress. Whether you hike their highland trails, bike their serpentine roads and steep inclines, or breeze along the cliff-flanked coastline by boat, these mountains will sweep you off your feet with their beauty and drama.

When to Go

Spring and autumn are peak season for cyclists in the Tramuntana, but otherwise you'll have its gorgeous coves, trails and flower-flecked heights pretty much to yourself. Most hotels and restaurants open Easter to October. In summer, coastal resorts and villages are full to bursting point, but vast expanses of wilderness mean you can always find a quiet retreat, be it a *finca* (farmhouse), castle or monastery. The festival season gets into full swing as the heat rises: both Deià and Valldemossa host classical musical concerts in summer. True pilgrims walk through the night from Palma to Lluc in August.

Western Mallorca Highlights

1 Deià (p103) Relishing the poetic loveliness of the winner in Mallorca's hill-town beauty pageant.

2 Monestir de Lluc (p115) Driving the length of the coast from seaside Port d'Andratx to this peaceful monastery.

3 Valldemossa (p100) Listening to Chopin on your iPod as you wander through narrow lanes.

4 Biniaraix (p111) Treading through citrus, almond and olive groves to this cute-as-a-button town.

5 Sóller (p105) Finding vintage trains, Miró and Modernista flair in the island's zesty orange capital.

6 Sa Calobra (p114) Feeling your heart do somersaults as you drive the snaking road.

7 Castell d'Alaró (p114) Climbing to the impregnable fortress ruins.

8 Illa de Sa Dragonera (p93) Diving the transparent depths.

9 Sa Foradada (p100) Wandering the coast as the setting sun paints the Mediterranean in aquarelles.

10 Cala Llamp (p92) Savouring this stunning cove round the headland from Port d'Andratx.

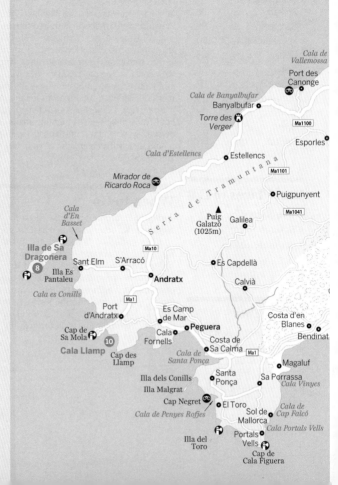

Puig Roig
(1002m) ▲

Serra de Tramuntana

Sa
Calobra **6**

Cala
Tuent

Torrent de Pareis

Escorca

Monestir
de Lluc **2**

Puig Tomir
(1103m) ▲

Ma10

Ma2130

Puig Major
(1445m)
▲

Son
Torella

Puig de
Massanella
(1365m) ▲

Binibona

Badia de
Sóller

Mirador de
Ses Barques

Caimari

Campanet

Cap Gros

Port de
Sóller

Fornalutx

Embassament
de Cúber

Moscari

Ma10

Biniaraix **4**

Refugi de Cúber

Selva

Mancor
de la Vall

Cala de
Deià

Sóller **5**

Puig de l'Ofre
(1093m) ▲

Ma13

Sa Foradada

Son
Marroig **9**

Lluc Alcari

Puig d'Alfàbia
(1069m) ▲

Castell
d'Alaró

Puig de
S'Alcadena
(815m) ▲

Biniamar

Puig de Santa
Magdalena
(307m) ▲

Miramar

Deià **1**

7

Lloseta

Inca

Puig des Teix
(1062m) ▲

Ma2100

Orient

Puig
d'Alaró
(822m) ▲

Port de
Valldemossa

Jardins
d'Alfàbia

Alaró

3

Valldemossa

Bunyola

Binissalem

Ma1110

Ma11

Consell

Costitx

S'Esgleieta

Santa Maria
del Camí

Ma13A

Biniali

Sencelles

Ma1040

Ses
Alqueries

Establiments

Ma13

Santa
Eugènia

Son
Sardina

Ma13

La Cabaneta

Ma13A

La Vileta

Ma20

Palma de
Mallorca

Son Ferriol

Ma15

Algaida

Gènova

Terreno

✈ Airport

Cala
Major

Cala Gamba
Ca'n Pastilla

Badia
de
Palma

Cala
Estancia

Las Maravillas

Randa

S'Arenal

▲
Puig de
Randa
(548m)

Cala Blava

Ma19

Llucmajor

Cap
Enderrocat

Ma19

Ma19

THE SOUTHWEST

Look beyond the occasional blip of tasteless development and you'll find a sprinkling of little-known treasures in Mallorca's southwest crook. Use Andratx, Port d'Andratx or Sant Elm as your springboard for day trips to the exquisite coves of Portals Vells or a boat trip over to Illa de Sa Dragonera. Activities on this stretch abound, with crystal-clear sea for all manner of water sports.

Andratx

POP 12,150

The largest town in southwest Mallorca, Andratx lies well inland (as a defensive measure against pirate attack), while its harbour, Port d'Andratx, is 4km away. Andratx has a low-key, untouristy vibe and makes a relaxed base for exploring the coast to the west and the mountains that spread to the northeast.

◉ Sights

Castell de Son Mas HISTORIC BUILDING
The 16th-century Castell de Son Mas, on the hill at the northern end of town, is an elegant defensive palace that now houses the *ajuntament* (town hall).

**Església de Santa Maria
d'Andratx** CHURCH
(Carrer de General Bernat Riera) This lovely church was built in the 18th century on the site of the original 1248 house of worship.

✗ Eating

Bar Restaurante Sa Societat MALLORCAN €€
(☑971 23 65 66; Avinguda Juan Carlos I 2; mains €11-19, 2-course menus €8.50-15.50; ☺1-4pm & 7.30-11pm Wed-Mon) For fine island fare in a time-warp atmosphere, Bar Restaurante Sa Societat has a courtyard out the back or you can sit inside beneath exposed beams for *trampó* (tomato, pepper and onion salad), followed by paella, suckling pig with crackling or cod in an aioli crust.

ⓘ Information

Tourist Office (☑971 62 80 19; Avinguda de la Curia; ☺10am-2pm Mon-Fri) Housed in the town hall at the top end of town.

ⓘ Getting There & Away

Bus 102 operates a roughly hourly service daily between Palma and Andratx (€4.60, 65 minutes).

Port d'Andratx

POP 3150

Port d'Andratx surrounds a fine, long natural bay that attracts yachting fans from far and wide and moves to an international beat rather than a Mallorcan one. Thick with art galleries, estate agents and restaurants, the town has an affluent air and a pleasant promenade for a walk and a waterfront meal.

◉ Sights & Activities

Cala Llamp BEACH
What a difference a bay makes. Located 2km south of Port d'Andratx, beautiful Cala Llamp is where locals gravitate for silence and sparkling, bottle-green water. There's no sand, but you can lie on a shelf of rock that tilts gently into the sea. The scenery is lovely too, with rugged, pine-cloaked cliffs rearing like an amphitheatre around the crescent-shaped cove. It's around a 30-minute walk, or you can drive by taking the Ma1020 from Port d'Andratx and following the signs over the ridge.

Cala Blanca BEACH
This very small cove, following a shallow curve down a dirt track from the car park above it, is all small pebbles, boulders and serene views. Pinched between the two jaws of the headland, it's only around 100m wide and sees few visitors, affording peace and quiet. Take the Ma1020 from Port d'Andratx towards Es Camp de Mar and look for the signs.

Museo Liedtke GALLERY
(☑971 67 36 35; www.liedtke-museum.com; Carrer de l'Olivera 35; ☺hr vary) FREE A synthetic meeting of landscape and architecture, the eccentric Museo Liedtke, 2km south of the port centre, was built between 1987 and 1993 into the cliffs near Cap de Sa Mola by German artist Dieter Walter Liedtke. Home to his art and temporary exhibitions, it's also a selling point for Liedtke's theories on life. The coastal views alone warrant the detour. Opening hours vary – it's worth calling ahead to check.

Llaüts BOATING
(☑971 67 20 94; www.llauts.com; Carrer de San Carlos 6A; half day/day €120/160; ☺Apr-Oct) A good place for boat rentals, Llaüts offers 4m crafts for those with no boat licence, with prices on request for more experienced boat

users. Rates leap by about 10% in August. You'll find it southwest of the main waterfront restaurant strip; opening hours are prone to change, so call ahead.

Diving Dragonera DIVING
(☑971 67 43 76; www.aqua-mallorca-diving.com; Avinguda de l'Almirante Riera Alemany 23; 6-/10-dive package €210/325; ⊗8am-7pm mid-Mar–Oct) If you fancy exploring the underwater caves and wrecks around Port d'Andratx and Sa Dragonera, you can take the plunge with this friendly and popular German-run dive shop. It offers the whole shebang of PADI and SSI courses.

✖ Eating

★**Trespaís** MEDITERRANEAN €€
(☑971 67 28 14; www.trespais-mallorca.com; Carrer Antonio Callafat 24; mains €16.50-32.50; ⊗6-11pm Tue-Sun) With its sleek monochrome interior and tree-rimmed patio all aglow with candles, Trespaís is a flicker of new-wave romance, and chef Domenico Curcio with his Michelin-starred background has made it the top table in town. Together with his wife, Jenny Terler, he assembles memorable dishes that play up integral flavours.

Restaurante El Coche SEAFOOD €€
(☑971 67 19 76; Avinguda de Mateu Bosch 13; mains €13.50-21; ⊗1-3.30pm & 7-10.30pm Wed-Mon) A slightly classier option than many along the waterfront, refurbished El Coche has been going strong since 1977, outlasting most of the competition in the process. Dishes are Mallorcan seafood classics with the occasional twist, such as the sea bream with garlic, vinegar and chilli.

◉ Drinking & Nightlife

Most of the harbourside restaurants morph into bars as the night wears on. Some reasonable choices can be found at the southwestern end of the strip, with the occasional DJ and live band.

Gran Folies Beach Club BAR
(www.granfolies.net; Carrer de Congre 2, Cala Llamp; ⊗10am-11.45pm May-Oct) This bar-restaurant sits right above the rocky cove of lovely Cala Llamp and offers use of a saltwater pool to cavort in between frozen margaritas. It also does breakfast, tapas and full meals and runs events from Mexican nights to G&T tastings. The views are fantastic and there's parking just up the road.

Tim's BAR
(Avinguda de l'Almirante Riera Alemany 7; ⊗10am-late) Overlooking the marina, this buzzing bar can stay open as late as 4am at the height of summer. It's a fine spot to sink a beer or toast the setting sun with a mojito. Live football is shown on the big screen, and there's live music on Friday and Saturday nights.

❶ Information

Tourist Office (☑971 67 13 00; Avinguda de Mateu Bosch; ⊗9am-4pm Tue-Sat, 9.30am-2.30pm Sun) Next to the bus stop.

❶ Getting There & Away

Most of the 102 buses from Palma continue from Andratx to the port (€1.50, 10 minutes). Bus 100 runs around six times a day between Andratx and Sant Elm (€2.10, 35 minutes), calling in at Port d'Andratx en route.

Sant Elm

POP 410
The narrow country Ma1030 road twists deep into pine forest from S'Arracó to emerge in Sant Elm. While it's by no means a secret, the relative remoteness of this beach resort has kept mass tourism at bay, and there's something magical about knowing that the tip of the Serra de Tramuntana lies just around the bend and spending an evening watching the sun drop behind the silhouetted Illa de Sa Dragonera.

◉ Sights & Activities

Illa de Sa Dragonera ISLAND
The uninhabited 4km-long **Illa de Sa Dragonera** is a ripple of an island that stretches out like a slumbering dragon to the west of Sant Elm. Constituted as a natural park (Parc Natural de Sa Dragonera), the island is accessible by ferry, which lands at a protected natural harbour on the east side of the island. From there you can follow trails to the capes at either end or ascend the **Na Pòpia peak** (Puig des Far Vell, 352m).

Platja Sant Elm BEACH
Sant Elm's main town beach is a pleasant sandy strand (no shade) that faces the gently lapping Mediterranean to the south. Within swimming distance for the moderately fit is **Illa Es Pantaleu**, a rocky islet that marks one of the boundaries of a marine reserve. To the south of Sant Elm's main beach is

Cala es Conills, a sandless but pretty inlet (follow Carrer de Cala es Conills).

A couple of nice walks head north from Plaça del Monsenyor Sebastià Grau, at the northeast end of town. One follows the GR221 long-distance route for about 1¼ hours or 4km to **La Trapa**, a ruined former monastery. A few hundred metres from the building is a wonderful lookout point. You can start on the same trail but branch off west about halfway (total walk of 2.5km and about 45 minutes) to reach **Cala d'En Basset**, a lovely bay with transparent water but not much of a beach.

Keida   ADVENTURE SPORTS
(🖉 971 23 91 24; www.keida.es; Plaça de na Caragola 3; ☺ hr vary) Keida offers a huge array of activities, from guided hikes (€38 to €60) to half-day boat excursions to Illa de Sa Dragonera (€42), three-hour horse-riding excursions (€60) and 1½-hour paddle-surfing courses (€45) and paddle-surf hire (full-day €45). You can also hire a bike (half-/full-day €10/15) or a kayak (half-/full-day €28/35) here.

Scuba Activa   DIVING, SNORKELLING
(🖉 971 23 91 02; www.scuba-activa.com; Plaça de Mossèn Sebastià Grau 7; dive incl equipment from €39, equipment per day €15-17; ☺ 9am-6pm Apr-Oct) This well-run dive centre takes you into the depths of the brilliantly clear waters around Illa de Sa Dragonera, among Mallorca's best for scuba diving, with equipment rental and a full range of courses. It also runs one-hour snorkelling trips (€29 to €38).

 **Eating & Drinking**

There is a large choice of restaurants, cafes and bars right down by the harbour and along Avinguda Jaume I.

⭐ **Es Molí**   MEDITERRANEAN €€
(🖉 971 23 92 02; http://esmoli.cat; Plaça de Mossèn Sebastià Grau 2; mains €14.50-21; ☺ 1-4pm & 6.30-10pm Apr-Oct; 🔊) Tucked away on a plaza close to the sea, this is without shadow of a doubt our favourite restaurant in town – and we'd love to take a ride in the baby-blue Seat 600 car parked outside. The decor is stripped-back minimalism, the team young and upbeat, and the food Mediterranean with distinct Italian overtones. Everything from salmon carpaccio with mango to home-made ravioli with wild mushrooms, truffle oil and Iberian ham hits the mark.

ℹ **Information**

Tourist Office (🖉 971 23 92 05; Avinguda de Jaume I 28B; ☺ 9am-4pm Mon-Sat & 9.30am-2pm Sun) A short walk from the beach.

ℹ **Getting There & Away**

The 100 bus runs six times a day from Andratx to Sant Elm (€2.10, 40 minutes) via S'Arracó. You can also take the boat between Sant Elm and Port d'Andratx (€8, 20 minutes, daily February to October). If you are driving, dodge the €3.50 beachfront parking fee by heading a little uphill to park.

Ferries to Illa de Sa Dragonera (return €13, 15 minutes, three to four daily February to November) operate from the small harbour north

---

WORTH A TRIP

SAILING FROM ANDRATX TO PORT DE SÓLLER

Driving, walking, cycling...whichever way you choose to explore the dramatic coast of the Serra de Tramuntana, you're in for some spectacular views. But there's also a different approach worth considering. Take a sailing route from **Port d'Andratx** in the southwest, around past **Sant Elm** and **Illa de Sa Dragonera** and northeast to **Port de Sóller**, a good, quiet port to overnight in. Places to stop during the day for a dip (they are no good for dropping anchor overnight) are Port des Canonge, Cala de Deià and Lluc Alcari. The inlets of Estellencs and Valldemossa are too shallow for most yachts. The next stage, tracking to Cap de Formentor and rounding it to find shelter in the Badia de Pollença, takes longer under equal conditions. Good daytime stops are Cala Tuent, Sa Calobra, Cala Sant Vicenç and Cala Figuera. The total trip is around 60 nautical miles.

One of the main factors to consider is weather. Wind is more of a rule than an exception, which means you can get your sails out. However, depending on conditions, it can also be uncomfortable. In winter it is often dangerous to sail along this coastline. It is possible to charter yachts in Port d'Andratx at **Llaüts** (p92), or ask at the tourist office. You can also charter yachts in Port de Sóller at **Mezzo Magic** (p110).

of Sant Elm's main beach. One of the main operators is **Cruceros Margarita** (☎ 639 617545; www.crucerosmargarita.com; €13); in peak season it is advisable to book tickets ahead.

Portals Vells & Cap de Cala Figuera

Take a short detour 20km south of Andratx to the Cap de Cala Figuera peninsula's eastern flank for one of the last remaining stretches of unspoilt coastline in this much-developed corner of the southwest. It feels light-years away from the crowds and bustle in nearby Magaluf.

Three dreamlike inlets, collectively known as Portals Vells, reside in blissful seclusion, backed by pine-clad sandstone cliffs and dazzlingly clear water.

◉ Sights

Cala Portals Vells   BEACH
(⚐) The fairest of the beaches known as Portals Vells is Cala Portals Vells. Turquoise waters lap the beach, whose sands stretch back beneath rows of straw umbrellas. To the south, a walking trail leads to **caves** that honeycomb the rock walls, one of them containing the rudiments of a chapel, where the altar has been hewn from the rock. According to local lore, Genoese sailors built it in the 15th century to give thanks for their lives being spared in a shipwreck.

Cala Mago   BEACH
Cala Mago is two narrow inlets: the one on the right has a restaurant and is frequented by nudists, while the longer inlet with the narrow, shady beach to the right is prettier.

❶ Getting There & Away

You'll need your own wheels to reach Portals Vells as there is no public transport. Take exit 14 off the Ma1 towards Portals Vells, passing the Western Park water park and golf club. About 2km through pine woods you reach a junction: turn left following signs to Cala Mago and park above the bay, or head 1.8km south to reach Cala Portals Vells.

SERRA DE TRAMUNTANA

Dominated by the splendid Serra de Tramuntana range, Mallorca's northwest coast and its hinterland are remarkably wild, ensnared by scarred limestone peaks and cliffs that loom over brilliant blue sea like ram-

parts. Gold-stone villages and ochre hamlets sit atop hillsides, their rhythms and hues providing tantalising insights into ancient Mallorca. The terraces that march up from the coast date back at least to the Moorish occupation, and walkers love the high, rugged interior for its pine forests, olive groves and wildflowers. The region's unique cultural and geographical features have been inscribed by Unesco on to its World Heritage List.

Andratx to Valldemossa Coast Road

Welcome to one of the Mediterranean's most exhilarating stretches of coastline, embraced by the Ma10 road, which climbs away from Andratx into the pine-clad hills marking the beginning of the majestic Serra de Tramuntana range. Pasted to cliff tops and hillsides, the hamlets and lookouts that dot this mostly lonely stretch of road have arresting views of raw coastal beauty.

Estellencs

POP 380 / ELEVATION 151M
Estellencs is an enticingly laid-back and very pretty village of warm-stone buildings scattered around the rolling hills below the **Puig Galatzò** (1025m); the views of the village are stunning, especially from the main road as you approach from the north.

◉ Sights & Activities

Cala d'Estellencs   BEACH
From Estellencs, a 1.5km road winds down through terraces of palm trees, citrus orchards, olives, almonds, cacti, pines and flowers to Cala d'Estellencs, a rocky cove with bottle-green water.

Puig Galatzò   WALKING
To ascend Puig Galatzò (1025m), a walking trail starts near the Km 97 milestone on the Ma10 road, about 2½ km west of Estellencs. It's not easy going, so you'll need good maps and plenty of water and food. Prepare for a five- to six-hour round trip. An alternative but easily confused trail leads back down into Estellencs.

✖ Eating

Cafeteria Vall-Hermós   CAFE €
(☎ 971 61 86 10; www.vallhermos.com; Carrer de Eusebio Pascual 6; mains €7.50-17.50; ☺10am-

11pm Thu-Tue) It's all about the sea view at this simple cafe on the main drag through town, particularly at sunset from one of the rattan chairs on the terrace. Go for a coffee and *bocadillo* (filled roll) by day or linger over a glass of red and some tapas by night. The pizzas are filling and reasonable value too.

★**Arandora**   INTERNATIONAL €€
(☑638 417595; Plaça de la Constitució 6; mains €14-18; ☺2pm-midnight Wed-Mon) Swedish-run Arandora, right opposite the church, is a delight. On summer evenings the terrace is great for watching the world go lazily by over a glass of cava with dishes like beetroot, goat's cheese and rocket salad, seafood soup and lamb burger on focaccia with feta and spicy sauce, rounded off with chocolate truffle.

Montimar   MALLORCAN €€
(☑971 61 85 76; Plaça de la Constitució 7; mains €16-30; ☺1-3.30pm & 7-10.30pm Tue-Sun) This is a bastion of traditional Mallorcan cooking. Dishes range from fish soup to fresh wild sea bass baked in salt, suckling pig or *sobrassada* (Mallorcan cured sausage) with honey, while local cheeses are the pick of the desserts.

🛍 **Shopping**

Estel@rt   FOOD, CRAFT
(Carrer de Sa Siquia; ☺10am-2pm & 5-8pm Mon & Wed-Sat, to 2pm Sun) At the northern end of town, this engaging little place sells primarily Mallorcan and Menorcan clothes, jewellery, ceramics, speciality foods and wine; the selection is small but well chosen. There's a two-room art gallery downstairs.

ℹ **Getting There & Away**

The 200 Palma–Estellencs bus (€3.90, 80 minutes, four to 11 times daily) passes through Banyalbufar (€3.10) and also goes through Esporles.

Banyalbufar

POP 560 / ELEVATION 112M

Pretty Banyalbufar finds itself in a cleft in the Serra de Tramuntana's seaward wall, high above the coast. It's a tight, steep rabbit warren of a town, with quiet pot-plant-lined lanes that wind down towards the sea and beckon strollers.

The village, 8km northeast of Estellencs, was founded by the Arabs in the 10th century; the name Banyalbufar means 'built next to the sea' in Arabic. All around the village are carved-out, centuries-old, stone-walled farming terraces, known as *ses marjades,* which form a series of steps down to the sea. They are kept moist by mountain well water that gurgles down open channels and is stored in cisterns. West of town along the coast road is the **Torre des Verger**, one of the most recognisable symbols of Mallorca.

◉ **Sights**

Torre des Verger   TOWER
(Torre de Ses Animes; Ma10) **FREE** One kilometre out of town on the road to Estellencs, the Torre des Verger is a 1579 *talayot* (watchtower), an image you'll see on postcards all over the island. It's one of the most crazily sited structures on Mallorca – one step further and it would plunge into the Mediterranean far below. Climb to the top, fighting off vertigo as you proceed, and scan the horizon for yachts in the waters where sentinels once warned of pirates.

Cala Banyalbufar   BEACH
A steep 1km walk downhill past terraced slopes from Banyalbufar brings you to this rugged shingle and pebble, seaweed-scattered cove, where you can swim or sip a cold one at the beach shack on the rocks and look out over the dark turquoise water; there's also a lovely waterfall nearby.

Bodega Son Vives   WINERY
(☑609 601904; www.sonvives.com; Ma10; ☺11am-7pm Thu-Sun May-Oct) High on the hill at the southern entrance to the village, this small winery has cellar-door tastings and sales in summer. It offers a number of fusion wines, but its best drop comes from the locally grown malvasia grape. Son Vives also produces olive oil.

🍴 **Eating**

With some very good restaurants in town, Banyalbufar is a worthy spot for lunch or dinner.

Pegasón y el Pajarito Enmascarado   MEDITERRANEAN €
(☑971 14 87 13; Carrer del Pont 2; mains €7-16; ☺12.30-4pm & 7.30-11pm Sat-Wed, 7.30-11pm Fri) Stone walls, checked tablecloths and cobbled-together vintage furnishings give this button-cute bistro a distinctly boho feel. It's tucked into the corner of a narrow backstreet just under the main road, with a plant-dotted patio for people-watching over everything from *tumbet* (Mallorcan ratatouille) with roast pork to lamb meatballs.

The bargain three-course €15.50 lunch includes water, wine and olives (Saturday to Tuesday).

Ca'n Paco
MALLORCAN €€

(☑ 971 61 81 48; Carrer de la Constitució 18; mains €11.50-17.50; ☺ 1-5pm & 7.30-11pm Tue-Sun) On the road leading down to Cala de Banyalbufar, this traditional haunt stays true to its Mallorcan roots with generous portions of *arroz negro* (black rice cooked in squid ink) and grilled fish. Its *gató con helado de almendra*, a moist sponge with almond ice cream, takes some beating, as do the terrace views as the sun sinks into the sea.

Son Tomás
MALLORCAN €€

(☑ 971 61 81 49; Carrer de Baronia 17; mains €14-22; ☺ 12.30-4pm & 7-10pm Wed-Mon; ☀) This classic place at the west end of the village draws cyclists seeking snacks to its streetside tables, while the upstairs restaurant is first class. Both the *lechona* (suckling pig; €16.90) and fish Mallorcan style are cracking.

🔒 Shopping

Malvasia de Banyalbufar
WINE

(☑ 971 14 85 05; www.malvasiadebanyalbufar.com; Carrer de Comte Sallent 5; ☺ 11am-2pm & 5-8pm Tue-Sat, to 2pm Sun Jun-Aug, shorter hr Sep-May) This shop run by a cooperative of local wineries was set up to promote the locally grown malvasia grape. As such, it's the perfect place to pick up a bottle of wine for a picnic or to take back home.

❶ Getting There & Away

The 200 Palma–Estellencs bus (€3.90, 80 minutes, four to 11 times daily) passes through Banyalbufar (€3.10) and also goes through Esporles.

Esporles

POP 4940

Cradled between the mountain folds in the foothills of the Tramuntana, this pretty village of ochre-stone town houses is set beside a generally dry stream and has a Saturday market. The pace is very laid-back in the cafe-lined alleys presided over by a neo-Gothic church, dedicated to St Peter. Esporles can be animated at night, as many folk from Palma have opted to live here and commute to the capital. Walk up the road alongside the church (keeping the church to your right) and up Carrer Costa de Sant Pere for the pleasant 2½-hour Camí des Correu walk to Banyalbufar, along the GR221.

⊙ Sights

La Granja
HISTORIC BUILDING

(www.lagranja.net; Carretera de Esporles-Banyalbufar; adult/child €15; ☺ 10am-7pm summer, 10am-6pm winter) This magnificent *possessió* (rural estate) has been turned into something of a kitsch Mallorca-land exhibit, with folks in traditional dress. The grand mansion is, however, well worth the visit, as are its extensive gardens. Some elements of the property date to the 10th century. You could spend hours exploring the period-furnished rooms, olive and wine presses, grand dining room, stables, workshops and some medieval instruments of torture in the cellars. The admission includes a wine tasting.

🡒 Courses

Mallorca Cuisine
COOKING

(☑ 971 61 67 19; www.mallorcacuisine.com; Sa Mola Gran 8, Galilea) Variety of courses from paella to tapas and Mallorca fusion cooking, as well as market visits.

🍴 Eating

Esporles is a delightful stop-off with several recommended restaurants, conveniently located near the heart of town.

El Mesón La Villa
MALLORCAN €€

(☑ 971 61 09 01; Carrer de Nou de Sant Pere 5; mains €15-25; ☺ 1-4pm Thu-Tue, 8-11pm Thu-Sat) Locals wax lyrical about the *asados* (roasts) at El Mesón La Villa, where a chef can usually be found shovelling lamb and suckling pig into a wood-fired clay oven to slow-bake to juicy perfection. The setting matches the rustic, hearty food, with its beams and farming implements, all of which assures it a faithful local following.

Es Brollador
SPANISH €€

(☑ 971 61 05 39; Passeig del Rei 10; mains €11.50-21.50; ☺ 10am-10pm) With its tiled floors, high ceilings and rear courtyard, Es Brollador makes a pleasant stop for anything from a morning coffee to lunch or dinner. The pork sirloin with a sauce made with *sobrassada* (cured pork sausage flavoured with paprika and spices) is good; lighter meals are also served. The outdoor tables under green parasols are perfect for people watching.

❶ Getting There & Away

The 200 Palma–Estellencs bus (€3.90, 80 minutes, four to 11 times daily) passes through Esporles (€2.15) and Banyalbufar.

ROAD TRIP: ANDRATX TO MONESTIR DE LLUC

• •

Western Mallorca's dramatic coastline, swelling uplands, hidden coves and scenic seaside villages are ripe for exploration from behind the wheel. To fully appreciate the sheer drama of this coastline, hire a car and drive this astonishing 140km route from Andratx in the south to the pilgrimage site of Monestir de Lluc in the north.

❶ Andratx

Start at the ancient inland town of **Andratx**, 4km north of harbourside Port d'Andratx and a relaxing inland base for exploring the coast and mountains. The road (Ma10, which forms the main artery for this trip) climbs steadily through pine forests before revealing the first glimpses of the Mediterranean below.

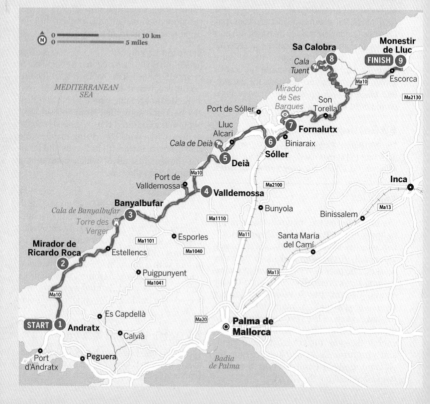

1 Day 140km

Great for... Outdoors, History & Culture

Best Time to Go: June to October

② Mirador de Ricardo Roca

About 14km from Andratx, pull into the parking lot opposite Restaurant El Grau and climb up to the Mirador de Ricardo Roca for some of the most extraordinary views anywhere along the west coast.

③ Banyalbufar

A further 4km on you pass through Estellencs, a pretty village with stunning views of 1025m Puig Galatzò. Continue 5km to the iconic Torre des Verger, one of the Mediterranean's most dramatically sited watchtowers. The tower lies on the outskirts of Banyalbufar, another charming clifftop coastal village, worth a stop for its attractive stone-walled farming terraces and local bodega. From here the road winds inland; at the road junction after 7km, take the narrow road north, which climbs through pine trees and boulders before crossing a high plateau.

④ Valldemossa

The main road heads towards Valldemossa, but before getting there take the turn-off west to Port de Valldemossa, an exhilarating 5.5km descent down to the water's edge and a solitary seafood restaurant. Back on the main road it's only a further 1.5km to Valldemossa, a worthwhile stopover at the halfway point of the route. The main attraction here is the striking Real Cartuja de Valldemossa monastery and a good supply of restaurants and bars.

⑤ Deià

It's another nine spectacular kilometres beyond the Valldemossa turn-off along the Ma10 to the romantic village of Deià, surrounded by hills and shadowed by 1062m Puig des Teix. Don't miss the brief 3km detour down off the main road to Cala de Deià, one of Mallorca's prettiest coves, with a lovely shingle surf beach and a popular bar-eatery. From the main road, the views of the tiny hamlet of Lluc Alcari, with its terracotta roofs and Mediterranean backdrop, are also exceptional.

⑥ Sóller

From Deià it's 10km to Sóller, a valley town with a fabulous location deep in the Serra de Tramuntana. Stop in for a ride on the vintage tram or visit two of Mallorca's best art galleries, before rolling on to two of Mallorca's loveliest villages, Biniaraix and Fornalutx.

⑦ Fornalutx

It's about 7km from Sóller to Fornalutx, but don't miss the detour off the main Ma10 to the charming hamlet of Biniaraix (only 2km from Sóller so you could walk it), where the lovely town square has a single cafe and the village church. Continue on to the larger but still sweet stone-built village of Fornalutx, with its postcard mountain views and photogenic town square. From Fornalutx, the Ma10 climbs sharply up to the viewpoint of Mirador de Ses Barques, passing high-altitude lakes in the shadow of Mallorca's highest mountains. The vistas down the coast from the lookout are superb. By the time you reach the turn-off to Sa Calobra, the mountains appear bare and otherworldly.

⑧ Sa Calobra

One of the most exhilarating parts of the route is following the hair-raising 12km of hairpin bends down to the popular white-pebble cove of Sa Calobra. On the way back, turn off and continue some 2km to the less-crowded but magical inlet of Cala Tuent. After enjoying some time on the beach, wind back up to the main road and continue north to Monestir de Lluc.

⑨ Monestir de Lluc

Magnificently nestled in a valley overlooked by the mountains, Monestir de Lluc, a huge monastery complex and place of pilgrimage, is the final stop on this road trip. Spend the afternoon exploring the cloistered gardens and museum before continuing on or heading south to Palma.

Valldemossa

POP 2027 / ELEVATION 425M

Crowned by the spire of its Carthusian monastery, which slowly lifts the gaze to the Tramuntana's wooded slopes, Valldemossa is one of the island's most eye-catching sights. Set on a gentle rise, the village insists on aimless wandering and chance discoveries along pinched lanes, as breathtaking vistas onto the surrounding valley and hills and pockets of almost indescribable charm await. The allure of Valldemossa's tree-lined, cobbled lanes, stout stone houses and impressive villas means there's no shortage of visitors, and that the bulk of the restaurants and bars serve average fare at inflated prices. But it's not hard to slip away from the crowds and find a part of Valldemossa for yourself and revel in its manifold beauty.

◉ Sights

Its rich ecclesiastical heritage, especially in the astonishing monastery that dominates the village and the settlement's celebrated connection with Frédéric Chopin and George Sand means there is no shortage of specific sights to explore beyond ambling around Valldemossa's beguiling lanes.

Around town you may notice that most houses bear a colourful tile depicting a nun and the words *'Santa Catalina Thomàs, pregau per nosaltres'* (St Catherine Thomas, pray for us). Yes, Valldemossa has its very own saint.

★ Real Cartuja de Valldemossa   MONASTERY

(www.cartujadevalldemossa.com; Plaça Cartoixa; adult/child €8.50/4; ◉9.30am-6.30pm Mon-Sat, 10am-1.30pm Sun) This grand old monastery and former royal residence has a chequered history. It was once home to kings, monks and a pair of 19th-century celebrities: composer Frédéric Chopin and George Sand. A series of cells now shows how the monks lived, bound by an oath of silence they could only break for half an hour per week in the library. Various items related to Sand's and Chopin's time here, including Chopin's pianos, are also displayed.

Sa Foradada   LANDMARK

While visiting Son Marroig, ask permission to wander down to Sa Foradada, the strange hole-in-the-wall rock formation by the water, which resembles an elephant from afar. It's a stunning 3km walk (one way) down through olive groves tinkling with sheep bells and along paths flanked by pine trees and caves. A soothing swim in the lee of this odd formation is the reward. Avoid the midday heat as there is little shade. The fiery sunsets here are riveting.

Miranda des Lledoners   VIEWPOINT

For an exquisite view embracing the ochre Valldemossa rooftops descending in steps down to the Església de Sant Bartomeu, the terraces below, the orchards, gardens, cypresses, palms, the occasional house through the mountains and the distant plains that lead to Palma, walk down Carrer de Jovellanos to Miranda des Lledoners.

Son Marroig   HISTORIC BUILDING

(www.sonmarroig.com; Carretera de Valldemossa-Deià; adult/child €4/free; ◉9.30am-6pm Mon-Sat May-Oct, shorter hr Nov-Apr) Seven kilometres from Valldemossa is another of Habsburg Archduke Ludwig Salvador's residences. This delightful, rambling mansion is jammed with furniture and period items, including many of the archduke's books. Above all, the views are the stuff of dreams. Son Marroig hosts the Festival Internacional de Deià (p104), a series of light-classical concerts on Thursday nights from June to September.

Miramar   HISTORIC BUILDING

(www.sonmarroig.com; Carretera de Valldemossa-Deià; adult/child €4/free; ◉10am-5.30pm Mon-Sat May-Oct, shorter hr Nov-Apr) With tremendous views, Miramar, 5km north of Valldemossa on the road to Deià, is one of Habsburg Archduke Luis Salvador's former residences. It's built on the site of a 13th-century monastery, founded by the evangelist and patron saint of Catalan literature, Ramon Llull. Here he wrote many of his works and trained brethren for the task of proselytising among the Muslims. Walk out the back and enjoy the stunning cliff-top view.

Casa Natal de Santa Catalina Thomàs   HISTORIC BUILDING

(Carrer de la Rectoria) The Casa Natal de Santa Catalina Thomàs, birthplace of St Catherine Thomas, is tucked off to the side of the parish church, the **Església de Sant Bartomeu**, at the east end of the town. It houses a simple chapel and a facsimile of Pope Pius VI's declaration beatifying the saint in 1792; she was canonised in 1930.

Valldemossa

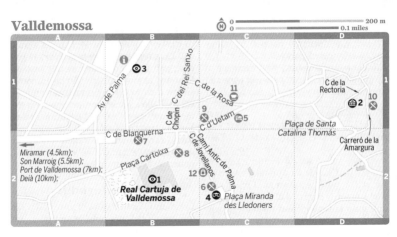

Valldemossa

Costa Nord   CULTURAL CENTRE
(📞971 61 24 25; www.costanord.es; Avinguda de Palma 6; adult/child €6/free; ⊙9am-5pm) The brainchild of part-time Valldemossa resident and Hollywood actor Michael Douglas, Costa Nord describes itself as a 'cultural centre' and begins well with a 15-minute portrayal of the history of Valldemossa, narrated by Douglas himself. The subsequent virtual trip aboard *Nixe*, the 19th-century yacht of Austrian Archduke Luis Salvador, who owned much of Western Mallorca, will be of less interest to most.

🎉 Festivals & Events

Sunday is market day in Valldemossa.

Festa de la Beata   RELIGIOUS
(⊙28 Jul) Valldemossa celebrates the life of Santa Catalina Thomàs with a donkey-drawn carriage parade and kids dressed in peasant garb throwing sweets to the crowds.

Festival Chopin   MUSIC
(www.festivalchopin.com; ⊙Aug) Classical-music performances are held in Valldemossa's Real Cartuja throughout August; most of the works are by Chopin, although music by other composers also features. Tickets go for between €20 and €30.

🍴 Eating

A sprinkling of cheerful and long-established eateries festoons the streets; many are clearly signposted. Few are of outstanding culinary significance, yet many are elegantly housed and often feature excellent views of the mountain, the valley or the tempting architecture of Valldemossa.

★QuitaPenas   TAPAS €
(📞675 993082; www.quitapenas-valldemossa. es; Carrer de la Amargura 1; tapas €3-15; ⊙noon-4pm) Descend cobbled steps to this tiny deli for tapas prepared with care and first-class seasonal ingredients. Grab one of the few

seats and minute tables for highly appetising takes on *pa amb oli* (bread with olive oil and vine-ripened tomatoes) or tangy *sobrassada* (cured pork sausage flavoured with paprika and spices) with caramelised fig. Couple with chilled Mallorcan wine and magical mountain views.

★**Casa de Sa Miranda**　FUSION €€
(☑ 971 61 22 96; Plaça Miranda des Lledoners 3; tapas €8-10, mains €14-24; ⊙ 7-10pm Mon, 1-3.30pm & 7-10pm Tue-Sat) What a view! The entire town and valley spread picturesquely before you at Casa de Sa Miranda, where an innovative stamp is put on local produce in bright, expertly prepared dishes like octopus with miso sauce and pear ravioli with gorgonzola and strawberries – all big on flavour and delivered with flair. The tapas are excellent, too.

Gelatimossa　ICE CREAM €
(www.gelatimossa.com; Plaça de Cartoixa 18; ice cream per scoop €1.90; ⊙ 11am-10pm Jun-Sep, shorter hr Oct-May) Pistachio, Mallorcan almond, lemon, peach, watermelon, banana, coffee and yoghurt...how ever will you choose? It's all home-made and delicious at this friendly *gelateria*. Grab a cone, or a tub, and head to the garden behind the Real Cartuja (50m away).

Forn Ca'n Molinas　BAKERY €
(Carrer de Blanquerna 15; coca de patata/ensaïmada €1.20/1.25; ⊙ 7.30am-8pm; 🏴) This place along the main pedestrian drag has been baking up the local speciality of *coca de patata* (a bready, sugar-dusted pastry) and the island-favourite *ensaïmades* (light pastry spirals dusted with icing sugar) since 1920. It stays open later in the height of summer.

Hostal Ca'n Marió　MALLORCAN €
(☑ 971 61 21 22; http://hostalcanmario.net; Carrer d'Uetam 8; mains €8.50-14; ⊙ 1.30-3.30pm & 8-10.30pm Wed-Mon, shorter hr in winter) If you can, grab a window table at this homely, light and airy upstairs restaurant for views almost clear to Palma (as long as staff have cut back those horse chestnut trees). On the menu are good honest Mallorcan dishes, such as *lomo com col* (pork loin with cabbage), *cargols* (snails), stuffed aubergines and *tumbet,* a garlicky aubergine, tomato, potato and courgette bake.

🍷 Drinking & Nightlife

Cafe/bars litter the centre of town and while few are particularly notable and many are over-visited by tourists, finding a chilled beer is not hard.

Aromas　CAFE
(Carrer de la Rosa 25; ⊙ 11am-9pm; 🏴) With chequerboard floor, warm terracotta walls and jazzy music, this sedate and arty cafe is a relaxed spot to sip speciality teas or thick hot chocolate. It's a tempting alternative to the tourist-stuffed cafes and out back there's a fragrant garden.

🛍 Shopping

Es Carreró　ARTS & CRAFTS
(Carrer de Jovellanos 6B; ⊙ 11am-9pm Jun-Sep, shorter hr Oct-May) Vicky Vidal's artistic eye rarely misses anything. The homewares, jewellery and accessories at this petite boutique are mostly either handmade or recycled by her – from button rings to wooden sunglasses, pewter bookmarks, notebooks from recycled paper, dishes crafted from newspaper cuttings and origami fish and birds.

CHOPIN'S WINTER OF DISCONTENT

Valldemossa owes much of its fame to the fact that the ailing composer Frédéric Chopin and his domineering writer/lover George Sand spent their 'winter of discontent' here in 1838–39. Their stay in the town – at the grand **Real Cartuja de Valldemossa** (p100) no less – wasn't an entirely happy experience and Sand later wrote *Un hiver à Majorque* (A Winter in Mallorca), which, if nothing else, made her perennially unpopular with Mallorquins. Chopin's poor health, the constant rain and damp, and the not-always-warm welcome from the villagers, who found these foreigners rather too eccentric, turned a planned idyllic escape from the pressure cooker of social life in Paris into a nightmare. But time is a great healer and Valldemossa makes great mileage from its discontented former guests, with a music festival in Chopin's name and references to the couple visible all over town.

DRIVING THE INLAND CIRCUIT

Offering a change of perspective and fewer tourist numbers, a worthwhile drive peels away from the coast to head inland. A few hundred metres beyond the Port des Canonge turn-off as you drive east along the Ma10, hang a left onto the Ma1100 southward towards Esporles. After 1km you reach a road junction and the mansion **La Granja**.

From La Granja, follow the Ma1101 south, which plunges through thick woods and slithers down a series of hairpin bends to reach **Puigpunyent**. This typical inland town offers few sights but the luxury, rose-hued hilltop Gran Hotel Son Net is reason enough to detour here if money is no object.

From Puigpunyent, make a dash for **Galilea**, a high-mountain hamlet a serpentine 4km south. Climb to the town's church square for views across the valleys and a drink in the bar next door, or head even higher up this straggling place for a greater sense of altitude.

Back in Puigpunyent, take the Ma1101 to Esporles.

ⓘ Information

Tourist Office (☑ 971 61 20 19; www.ajvall-demossa.net; Avinguda de Palma 7; ⊘10am-6.30pm Mon-Fri, to 2pm Sat & Sun) On the main road running through town, about two minutes' walk from the main bus stop.

ⓘ Getting There & Away

The 210 bus from Palma to Valldemossa (€1.85, 30 minutes) runs four to nine times a day. Three to four of these continue to Port de Sóller (€2.55, one hour) via Deià.

Port de Valldemossa

About 1.5km west from Valldemossa on the road to Banyalbufar, a spectacular mountain road (the Ma1113) clings to cliffs for 5.5km all the way down to Port de Valldemossa. The giddying sea and cliff views are breathtaking and the descent is akin to traversing a precipice, with a village glimpsed through the trees a very long way down below; drivers shouldn't take their eye off the road and there's only one place to pull over for photos. At journey's end, a shingle and algae 'beach' awaits, backed by low red cliffs and a cluster of a dozen or so houses, one of which is home to the justifiably popular Restaurant Es Port.

✕ Eating

The sole restaurant in Port de Valldemossa, **Restaurant Es Port** (☑971 61 61 94; www.restaurantesport.es; Carrer Ponent 5; mains €9.50-24.80; ⊘10am-10pm Jun-Aug, shorter hr Sep-May), enjoys both a splendid monopoly and a fantastic setting.

ⓘ Getting There & Away

There is no public transport down to the port, but it's a lovely drive down.

Deià

POP 768 / ELEVATION 222M

When the late afternoon sun warms Deià's honey-coloured houses, which clamber breathlessly up a conical hillside, and the sea deepens to darkest blue on the horizon, it's enough to send even the most prosaic of souls into romantic raptures. This eyrie of a village in the Tramuntana is flanked by steep hillsides terraced with vegetable gardens, citrus orchards, almond and olive trees and even the occasional vineyard – all set against the mountain backdrop of the Puig des Teix (1062m).

Deià was once a second home to writers, actors and musicians, the best known of whom (to Anglo-Saxons at any rate) was the English poet Robert Graves.

⊙ Sights

Climbing up from the main road, the steep cobbled lanes, with their well-kept stone houses, overflowing bougainvillea and extraordinary views over the sea, farm terraces and mountains, make it easy to understand why artists and other bohemians have loved this place since Catalan artists 'discovered' it in the early 20th century.

★**Casa Robert Graves**　HISTORIC BUILDING
(Ca N'Alluny; www.lacasaderobertgraves.com; Carretera Deià-Sóller; adult/child €7/3.50; ⊘10am-5pm Mon-Fri, to 3pm Sat) Casa Robert Graves is a fascinating tribute to the British writer

and poet who moved to Deià in 1929 and had his house built here three years later. It's a well-presented and rewarding insight into his life and a tribute to his work; on show you'll find period furnishings, a detailed film on his life, love-life and writings, and sundry books, pictures and everyday objects that belonged to Graves himself.

Cala de Deià   BEACH

A 3km drive from Deià (take the road towards Sóller), or a slightly shorter walk, is Cala de Deià, one of the most bewitching of the Serra de Tramuntana's coastal inlets. The enclosed arc of the bay is backed by a handful of houses and the small shingle beach is lapped by crystal-clear water crested with white surf. Competition for a parking spot a few hundred metres back up the road can be intense; get here early.

Es Puig   VIEWPOINT

From Es Puig, the hill at the heart of Deià, you peer across the rooftops of the higgledy-piggledy village and take in the full sweep of the valley to the glinting Mediterranean beyond. At the top is the modest parish church, the **Església de Sant Joan Baptista** (whose Museu Parroquial, with a collection of local religious paraphernalia, rarely opens). Opposite is the small town **cemetery**. Here lies 'Robert Graves, Poeta, 24-4-1895 – 7-12-1985 E.P.D' (*en paz descanse*, meaning 'may he rest in peace').

★★ Festivals & Events

Festival Internacional de Deià   MUSIC

(☑ 678 989536; www.dimf.com; €20; ⊙ Thu Apr-Sep) Outside Deià on the Serra de Tramuntana coast, the Son Marroig (p100) mansion hosts the Festival Internacional de Deià, a series of light-classical concerts.

✗ Eating

The Ma10 passes though the town centre, where it becomes the main street and is lined with bars, restaurants and shops, particularly at the village's eastern end. Quality varies, but there are some high-quality mainstays sprinkled among the others, which come and go with the years.

Village Cafe   INTERNATIONAL €€

(☑ 971 63 91 99; www.thevillagecafedeia.com; Carrer de Felipe Bauzà 1; mains €10-13; ⊙ noon-11pm Wed-Sun Mar-Oct; ⓘ) Swathed in flowers and vines, the terrace at this stone-walled cafe has broad views of the Tramuntana. The gourmet burgers are a fine pick, as are the salads, *bocadillos* (filled rolls) and pizzas. As the ceramic lanterns flick on and the cicadas chirp at dusk, it's a highly atmospheric spot for a G&T, fresh lemonade and tapas.

WORTH A TRIP

AN ARCHDUKE'S ROMANTIC ABODES

Head northeast of Valldemossa on the spectacular coastal road that twists to Deià and you will come across two of the most remarkable residences on the island, both of which belonged to Habsburg Archduke Ludwig Salvador (1847–1915), a hopeless romantic who found his idea of heaven right here.

The first is **Miramar** (p100). This splendid sea-facing mansion, 5km north of Valldemossa, is built on the site of a 13th-century monastery and has a *tàfona* (olive-oil press), a cloister and landscaped gardens to explore. Ramon Llull, the evangelist and patron saint of Catalan literature, founded the monastery, where he wrote many of his works and trained brethren for the task of proselytising among the Muslims. Walk out the back and enjoy the cliff-top views.

About 7km from Valldemossa is another of Habsburg Archduke Ludwig Salvador's residences, **Son Marroig** (p100). It's a delightful, rambling mansion jammed with furniture and period items, including many of the archduke's books. But above all, the views are the stuff of dreams.

Ask permission to wander down to **Sa Foradada** (p100), the strange hole-in-the-wall rock formation by the water, which resembles an elephant from afar. It's a stunning 3km walk (one way) down through olive groves tinkling with sheep bells and along paths flanked by pine trees and caves. A soothing swim in the lee of this odd formation is the reward. Avoid the midday heat as there is little shade. The fiery sunsets here are riveting stuff.

Sa Vinya
MEDITERRANEAN €€

(🖊 971 63 95 00; www.restaurant-savinya.com; Carrer de Sa Vinya Vella 4; mains €12-26; ⊗ 1-11pm Tue-Sun Feb-Nov; 🐾) Cobbled steps trail up to Sa Vinya and its subtly lit terrace, overlooking citrus groves and the Tramuntana's wooded peaks. It's a truly magical spot for dinner, and freshness shines through in sunny Mediterranean flavours like melon gazpacho with tarragon, hake with saffron risotto and monkfish saltimbocca with gnocchi and sage. BBQ nights are popular and the friendly service is unfaltering.

Ca's Patró March
SPANISH €€

(🖊 971 63 91 37; Cala de Deià; mains €10-25; ⊗ 10am-11pm Jun-Aug, shorter hr Sep-May) This is probably the pick of the two places overlooking the water for its slightly elevated views, but it's a close-run thing. It has a wide range of grilled meat and fish dishes – the star of which seems to be the Sóller *gambas*. It's run by the third generation of a local fishing family.

Can Lluc
SEAFOOD €€

(🖊 649 198618; Cala de Deià; mains €10-20; ⊗ 10.30am-7pm May-Oct) If you can't bear to drag yourself too far from your towel, this simple bar-eatery side-on to Cala de Deià couldn't be more convenient. Cold drinks, grilled sardines and calamari with just a squirt of lemon on a lazy summer's afternoon – bliss. It's a useful alternative when the other Cala de Deià restaurant is full, which is often the case. Service is rather harried.

★ Es Racó d'es Teix
FUSION €€€

(🖊 971 63 95 01; www.esracodesteix.es; Carrer de Sa Vinya Vella 6; mains €36-38, 3-course lunch menu €37, with wine €52, 4-/6-course tasting menu €72/100; ⊗ 1-3pm & 7-10pm Feb-Oct) An island legend, Josef Sauerschell has one Michelin star and it is well deserved. He tends to concentrate on elaborate but hearty meat dishes – anything from braised veal shoulder in sherry-vinegar sauce with marrow to Mallorcan suckling pig, trotters with foie gras and rack of lamb with olive crust.

Sebastian
MEDITERRANEAN €€€

(🖊 971 63 94 17; http://restaurantesebastian.com; Carrer de Felipe Bauzà 2; mains €26-30; ⊗ 7.30-10.30pm) In a former stable, with bare stone walls and crisp white linen, Sebastian is a refined experience. The short, sweet menu offers three fish and three meat mains, each enhanced with a delicate sauce or purée.

What's available depends on the season, but you can expect dishes such as lobster ravioli and green asparagus, and there's always a vegetarian choice.

🛈 Getting There & Away

Deià is 15 minutes up the winding road from Valldemossa on the 210 bus route between Palma (€2.85, 45 to 60 minutes) and Port de Sóller (€1.60, 30 to 40 minutes). As Deià is so visited, parking can be tricky (even though paid parking spaces are provided, they can be often full). But you may be able to find a spot to park alongside the Ma10 roadside just east of town.

Sóller
POP 14,150

The ochre town of Sóller lies in a valley surrounded by the grey-green hills of the Serra de Tramuntana. The Arabs saw the potential of the valley, known as the Vall d'Or (Golden Valley), and accounts of orange and lemon groves, watered from sources in the hills, date to the 13th century. The citrus-fruit export market laid the foundations for the great wealth of the town, reflected in its railway line to Palma (1912), tram line to the Port de Sóller (1913) and the grand merchant houses that throng the town, such as those strung out along Gran Via and Carrer de Sa Lluna.

Worth visiting in its own right, with its vintage train and tram rides, graceful modernist architecture and galleries showcasing Picasso and Miró, Sóller is also a wonderful base for exploring the west coast and the Tramuntana. It is also the trailhead for some stirring mountain hikes.

⊙ Sights & Activities

Simply wandering Sóller's peaceful, often cobbled, streets is a pleasure. In any direction, within a few minutes you exchange tight, winding lanes bordered with smooth limestone pavements and lined with tall and grand wooden doors for country roads bordered by stone walls, behind which flourish amply irrigated orange and lemon groves.

★ Sala Picasso & Sala Miró
GALLERY

(Plaça d'Espanya 6, Estación de Tren; ⊗ 10.30am-6.30pm) FREE In two rooms at street level in Sóller's station are two fascinating, introspective and contemplative art exhibitions: the Sala Picasso and Sala Miró. Few train

Sóller

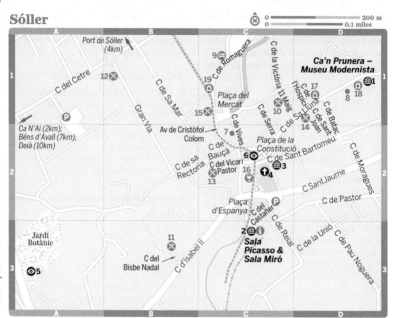

Sóller

stations boast such a splendid artistic legacy. The Sala Picasso contains more than 50 gently illuminated ceramics from the hands of Picasso from 1948 to 1971, many bearing the artist's trademark subjects: dancers, women, bullfighting. The Sala Miró is beautiful, home to playful, mysterious and beguiling prints from the Catalan master; Miró's maternal grandfather was from Sóller.

★ **Ca'n Prunera – Museu Modernista** GALLERY
(☎ 971 63 89 73; http://canprunera.com; Carrer de Sa Lluna 86-90; adult/child €5/free; ⊙ 10.30am-6.30pm Mar-Oct, closed Mon Nov-Feb) One of Mallorca's standout galleries, Ca'n Prunera occupies a landmark modernist mansion along Carrer de Sa Lluna. The list of luminaries here is astonishing – works by Joan Miró, along with single drawings by Toulouse-Lautrec, Picasso, Gauguin, Klimt, Kan-

dinsky, Klee, Man Ray and Cézanne. Also part of the permanent collection is a gallery devoted to Juli Ramis (1909–90), a Sóller native and world-renowned painter who had his studio in the neighbouring village of Biniaraix, plus works by Miquel Barceló, Antoni Tapiès and Eduardo Chillida.

Plaça de la Constitució
SQUARE
(Town Centre) Besieged with tables and seats from the cafes on its northern, eastern and western perimeters, the lovely main square, Plaça de la Constitució, is 100m from the train station. The tram line bends its way across the square, conveying the loaded and tooting tram to the beaches of Soller Port. Filled with children playing in the evenings, stuffed with panama-wearing visitors and home to the *ajuntament* (town hall), the square is Sóller's vibrant heart and soul.

Església de Sant Bartomeu
CHURCH
(Plaça de la Constitució; ⊙ 11am-1.15pm & 3-5.15pm Mon-Thu, 11am-1.15pm Fri & Sat, noon-1pm Sun) FREE A disciple of architect Antoni Gaudí, Joan Rubió landed some big commissions in Sóller. The town didn't want to miss the wave of modernity and so Rubió set to work in 1904 on the renovation of the 16th-century Església de Sant Bartomeu. The largely baroque church (built 1688–1723) preserved elements of its earlier Gothic interior, but Rubió gave it a beautiful if unusual modernist facade.

Jardí Botànic & Museu Balear de Ciències Naturals
GARDENS, MUSEUM
(www.jardibotanicdesoller.org; Carretera Palma-Port de Sóller; adult/child €8/free; ⊙ 10am-6pm Mon-Sat) A short stroll 600m west from Sóller's town centre onto the busy road to Soller Port brings you to the peaceful Jardí Botànic, with collections of flowers and other plants native to the Balearic Islands – from holm oaks to magnolias, myrtle to the endangered caraway pine – alongside other Mediterranean samples. The same ticket includes the **Museu Balear de Ciències Naturals** (Natural Science Museum) and its elementary insights into the flora and fauna of the Balearics; the fossil collection is of particular note.

Banco de Sóller
HISTORIC BUILDING
(Plaça de la Constitució) Joan Rubió i Bellver, a Catalonian student of Antoni Gaudí, designed the strikingly modernist frontage of the 1912 Banco de Sóller (nowadays Banco de Santander), which is separated by a narrow road from the Església de Sant Bartomeu (the facade of which he also created). The bank is an imposing and roughly hewn stone building, with two large, circular galleries, windows framed within lacy wrought-iron grilles and a carved lion gazing ferociously out over the square from the edifice's corner.

Lenguas Sóller
LANGUAGE
(☑ 674 216677; http://lenguas-soller.es; Carrer de Vives 5; ⊙ 11am-1pm & 5-8pm Mon-Fri) This central language school runs intensive Spanish-language courses, costing €18 per person (one to one) per hour, or €15 per hour (for two students). The school is a very short walk from the Plaça de la Constitució.

☞ Tours

Tramuntana Tours
ADVENTURE
(☑ 971 63 24 23; www.tramuntanatours.com; Carrer de Sa Lluna 72; bicycle rental per day €12-75; ⊙ 9am-1.30pm & 3-7.30pm Mon-Fri, 9am-1.30pm Sat) This experienced operator organises a range of activities-based guided excursions, including canyoning (from €59), sea kayaking (€50), hiking (from €25) and mountain biking (from €24, without bike rental) in the Serra de Tramuntana, as well as renting out as-new bikes. It also has a gear shop. If it's not open, try the sister shop in Port de Sóller, which has longer opening hours.

☆☆ Festivals & Events

Es Firó
FIESTA
(⊙ early May) Around the second weekend of May, Sóller is invaded by a motley crew of Muslim pirates. Known as Es Firó, this conflict (involving about 1200 townsfolk) between *pagesos* (town and country folk) and Moros (Moors) is full of good-humoured drama and copious drinking. It re-enacts an assault on the town that was repulsed on 11 May 1561.

✗ Eating

A large and much-visited town, Sóller has a fine choice of restaurants, cafes and bakeries, serving a tantalising choice of Mallorcan and Mediterranean food. For picturesque views, head to Béns d'Avall (p108) on the winding road to Deià.

Cafe Scholl
CAFE €
(☑ 971 63 23 98; Carrer de la Victòria 11 Maig 9; light bites & mains €5-15; ⊙ 9am-8pm Mon-Fri,

JARDINS DE ALFÀBIA

The **Jardins de Alfàbia** (☑971 61 31 23; www.jardinesdealfabia.com; Carretera de Sóller Km 17; adult/child €6.50/free, adult Nov & Mar €5.50; ☺9.30am-6.30pm Mon-Sat Apr-Oct, to 5.30pm Mon-Fri, to 1pm Sat Nov) reside in the shadow of the rugged Serra d'Alfàbia mountain range stretching east of Sóller. Here an endearingly faded *finca* with a baroque facade, which looks like it was stripped from a Florentine basilica, is surrounded by gardens, citrus groves, palm trees and a handful of farmyard animals. The murmur of water gurgling along irrigation canals hints at the place's past as the residence of an Arab Wāli (viceroy).

Little remains of the original Arab house, except for the extraordinary polychromatic coffered ceiling, fashioned from pine and ilex, immediately inside the building's entrance. It is bordered by inscriptions in Arabic and is thought to have been made around 1170. To the right of the inner courtyard is the *tafona* (large oil press), a mix of Gothic, Renaissance and baroque styles. The rambling house is laden with period furniture and a 1200-volume library. Within the library is the original *Llibre de les Franqueses* (Book of Franchise), written by King Jaume I as the basis for all rights in Mallorca after the Christian conquest.

9am-5pm Sat) With its chandeliers, brass mirrors and pretty open-air courtyard out back with a rectangle of sky above, this elegant boho-retro cafe is a relaxing spot. Pull up an art nouveau chair for breakfast with crumbly croissants and fresh orange juice, a light lunch or coffee with a slice of moist orange-almond cake.

Sa Fàbrica de Gelats   ICE CREAM €
(Avinguda de Cristòfol Colom 13; ice cream per scoop €1.30; ☺9am-10pm Jul & Aug, shorter hr Sep-Jun) Legendary ice cream. Among the 40 or so trays of locally made flavours, those concocted from fresh orange or lemon juice are outstanding. There's a small patio with a handful of tables.

Luna 36   MALLORCAN €€
(www.luna36.es; Carrer de Sa Lluna 36; mains €14-24; ☺12.30-3pm & 6.30-10pm Mon-Sat) This excellent restaurant is a burst of colour on Carrer de Sa Lluna. The staff likewise radiate positivity. Aim for a seat in the lovely courtyard garden at the back, where the bougainvillea spills down in dark pink bundles. There's also upstairs seating for dinner.

Casa Alvaro   TAPAS €€
(☑871 709315; www.casalvaro.com; Carrer del Vicari Pastor 17; tapas €4.50-7, mains €16-24.50; ☺noon-4pm & 7pm-midnight Wed-Mon, 1.30-4.30pm & 7.30pm-midnight Sun) Scoot down a cobbled lane off the main plaza to find this delightful nook, which pulls off the minimalist-traditional bodega look with little effort. Sample superb tapas under the beams brought to your table by upbeat and welcoming staff: crispy calamari, tender rabbit, artichoke hearts and the like. Pair with a decent bottle of Mallorcan wine and enjoy!

Ca'n Boqueta   MEDITERRANEAN €€
(☑971 63 83 98; Gran Via 43; 3-course menu €15, 5-course menu €31; ☺1-3.15pm & 7.45-10.15pm Tue-Sat, 1-3.15pm Sun) A tastefully converted townhouse bistro, with art on the walls, beamed ceilings and a garden patio, Ca'n Boqueta offers creative cooking with a seasonal touch. Starters like cherry gazpacho and scallops with white zucchini cream are a delicious lead to mains like Mallorcan black pork with tangy orange sauce.

★Béns d'Avall   SEAFOOD €€€
(☑971 63 23 81; www.bensdavall.com; Urbanització Costa Deià, off Carretera Sóller-Deià; tasting menus €64-94; ☺1-3.30pm Tue-Sun & 7-9.30pm Wed-Sat) From its cliff-top perch overlooking the sea, this restaurant's terrace is pop-the-question-at-sunset romantic. Not only that, it's the home turf of Benet Vicens, one of Mallorca's foremost chefs. The nouvelle Balearic-style tasting menu follows the seasons, with dishes like lobster ravioli with rabbit loin and sorrel sauce, fruit-filled suckling pig slow-cooked to crackling perfection or Tramuntana lamb with eggplant confiture.

Ca'l Bisbe   MALLORCAN €€€
(☑971 63 12 28; www.hotelcalbisbe.com/restaurante; Carrer del Bisbe Nadal 10; menus €29.50-38.50; ☺8-10.30pm Mar-Oct) Converted from an old olive mill, Ca'l Bisbe has heavy wood beams in the lantern-lit dining room or al fresco seating on the poolside terrace. The

menu is a cut above the norm, with refined dishes like slow-cooked cod with calamari noodles and black-olive crusted lamb with basil risotto, expertly matched with local wines. Watching the sun set over the Tramuntana lends a romantic mood.

🍷 Drinking & Nightlife

Sóller's Plaça de la Constitució, right at the heart of town, is strewn with cafes and bars. A drink here is the ideal way to people-watch and measure the town's comings and goings.

Sa Butigueta BAR

(Avinguda de Jeroni Estades 9; 📶) Free of tourist trimmings and paraphernalia, this down-to-earth Mallorcan bar/cafe/restaurant serves affordable drinks and tapas. Also acting as a club for locals, this is the place to come to for a clutter-free, authentic vibe, where locals deal cards and chat, quaffing the best-priced booze in town. Take a seat on Avinguda des Born, facing the church, and watch the tram grind by.

🛍 Shopping

Arte Artesanía JEWELLERY

(📳971 63 17 32; www.arteartesania.com; Carrer de Sa Lluna 43; ⊙10.30am-8pm Mon-Fri, to 3pm Sat) A dynamic and inspiring artistic space that's simply bursting with ideas, Arte Artesanía is at once classy and avant-garde, with its designer jewellery and small range of paintings, ceramics and sculpture. It's the work of Spanish and international artisan-designers, and exhibitions are often hosted upstairs and also in the small basement room.

Fet a Sóller FOOD

(www.fetasoller.com; Carrer de Romaguera 12; ⊙10am-7.30pm May-Oct, to 6pm Nov-Apr) Fet a Sóller is an altogether different culinary experience. Mallorcan products, primarily from Sóller, line the shelves: olive oils, wines, almonds, jams, preserves, figs in cognac, charcuterie, balsamic vinegar made from Sóller oranges, and ceramics.

Ben Calçat SHOES

(📳971 63 28 74; www.bencalcat.es; Carrer de Sa Lluna 74; ⊙9.30am-8.30pm Mon-Fri, to 1.30pm Sat) The place for authentic Mallorcan handcrafted *porqueras,* shoes made from recycled car tyres. The funky bowling-shoe designs in rainbow-bright colours won't appeal to everyone, but this is very Mallorca. Prices start at around €55.

ℹ Information

Tourist Office (📳971 63 80 08; www.visitsoller.com; Plaça d'Espanya 15; ⊙10am-4.30pm Mon-Fri, 9am-1pm Sat) Sóller's tourist office is in an old train carriage beside the station.

ℹ Getting There & Away

BUS

Bus 211 shoots up the Ma11 from Palma to Sóller (€2.65, 30 minutes, up to five daily). Bus 210 takes the long way to/from Palma (€3.90) via Valldemossa (€2.15, 40 to 50 minutes) and Deià (€1.55). A local service connects Sóller with Fornalutx (€1.50, 15 minutes, two to four daily) via Biniaraix.

CAR & MOTORCYCLE

When coming from Palma, you have the option of taking the tunnel (€4.95 toll per car and €2 per motorbike, no bicycles) or adding 7km to the trip and taking the mountainous switchbacks up to the pass, with some great views back down towards Palma on the way. If you aim to do that, take the last turn-off for Sóller before the tunnel. For other magnificent views down to Sóller and its splendid valley, take the mountain road from Fornalutx to the Sóller-Port de Sóller road. If taking the tunnel, make sure you get into the right lane if you want to pay with cash. There are handy petrol stations on either side of the road just before the tunnel on the Palma side.

TRAIN

The train journey from Palma to Sóller is a highlight. From April to October, trains (€16; www.trendesoller.com) run from Palma to Sóller six times a day from 10.10am to 7.30pm and five times in the other direction from 9am to 6.30pm. There is a reduced service in November, December, February and March, with four trains per day in each direction.

TRAM

Sóller's antique open-sided **trams** (Tranvías; 1-way €6; ⊙ every 30 or 60min 8am-8.30pm) run to Port de Sóller on the coast and back. They depart from outside the train station but also stop at the northwest corner of Plaça de la Constitució on the way to the Port. Generally, they run from Sóller to Port de Sóller every 30 minutes from 8am to 8.30pm and in the other direction from 8.30am to 9pm (pick up a timetable from the tourist office or visit the station).

Port de Sóller

POP 2909

Sóller's outlet to the sea is a quintessential Mallorcan fishing and yachting harbour, arrayed around an almost perfectly enclosed bay. Around a decade ago, millions of euros were poured into sprucing up the port but, as with all such places, the atmosphere wavers between classy and crass. The architecture reflects French and even Puerto Rican influences, as these were the two main destination countries of many Mallorcan emigrants, some of whom returned with cash and imported tastes.

The sunsets can be stunning, especially in mid-summer, when – from the right vantage point – the sun dips into the sea precisely between the jaws of the port's two headlands.

⊙ Sights & Activities

The bay is shaped something like a jellyfish and shadowed by a pleasant, pedestrianised and restaurant-lined esplanade. It makes for pleasant strolling, especially around the northern end where the heart of the original town is gathered together.

The beaches are OK, although hardly the island's best. The pick of the crop is **Platja d'en Repic** at the southern end of the bay, not least because it's nicely removed from the streams of passers-by. Keep walking in the same direction around the rocky headland for even more peace and quiet and some fantastic perches for jumping into the sea. The same can't be said for **Platja d'es Port**, which is alongside the marina.

★**Mezzo Magic** BOATING
(🖉664 679875; www.mezzomagic.co.uk; Carrer de L'Església; per person half-/whole-day from €75/100; yacht half-/whole-day from €450/650) Mezzo Magic provides stirring chartered yacht voyages up and down the coastline to Cala Deià, Sa Calobra, Cala Tuent and Sa Foradada. It also sails the boat further afield (even to Ibiza, Formentera and Menorca) for an entirely different perspective on the island and the Mediterranean, with all the drama of a yachting expedition. Sunset tours are also on the menu.

Octopus Dive Centre DIVING
(🖉971 63 31 33; www.octopus-mallorca.com; Carrer del Canonge Oliver 13; 1 dive with/without own equipment €39/49, 2 dives €67/88; ⊙8.30am-7pm mid-May–Oct) Dive with Octopus Dive Centre, a five-star English-run PADI centre with first-rate equipment, courses (including the Bubblemaker for kids), and dives that range from beginner to expert and depart from shore or off a boat. It operates boat dives at about 30 sites along the Serra de Tramuntana coast.

Nàutic Sóller BOATING
(🖉609 354132; www.nauticsoller.com; Platja d'en Repic; 1-person sea kayak per hr/half day/ day €10/30/50, 2-person €15/45/75) This place rents out sea kayaks and can also arrange motorboat rental (half-/whole-day €120/170). Skippers can be provided for excursions.

☞ Tours

Tramuntana Tours ADVENTURE
(🖉971 63 27 99; www.tramuntanatours.com; Passeig Es Través 12; bicycle rental per day €12-75, 3hr sea-kayaking excursion €50; ⊙9am-7.30pm Mar-Oct) This excellent gear shop and activity-tours operator right on the waterfront is the place to come for sea kayaking and bicycle hire. It can also arrange guided hikes into the Serra de Tramuntana, canyoning, mountain biking, boat charters and deep-sea fishing. There's another office in Sóller (p107).

Barcos Azules BOATING
(🖉971 63 01 70; www.barcosazules.com; Passeig Es Través 3; adult/child 1-way €20/10, return €30/15; ⊙hr vary) Tour boats do trips to Sa Calobra (up to four times daily) and Cala Tuent (up to once a day Monday to Friday, minimum seven people) and Sa Foradada (up to once every day, minimum seven people). Get tickets at a booth on the dock, next to the tourist office.

✗ Eating

Port de Sóller waterfront is lined with eateries. Most serve fish and seafood and quality varies wildly, but there are a few quite outstanding places.

★**Kingfisher** SEAFOOD €€
(🖉971 63 88 56; www.kingfishersoller.com; Carrer San Ramon de Penyafort 25; mains €17-24; ⊙noon-late Tue-Sat) Sit out beneath one of the vast white parasols and enjoy as the breeze lifts from the port waters. Kingfisher has it all: friendly and warm service, a fine setting, soothing jazzy music and astonishingly fine fare. The fish and chips is all chunky, juicy cod, a smear of the smoothest of smooth mushy peas, gorgeous potatoes and gherkins, served on a slate plate.

Randemar INTERNATIONAL €€
(🖉971 63 45 78; www.randemar.com; Passeig Es Través 16; mains €13.50-23; ⊙12.30pm-midnight mid-Mar–early Nov) You almost feel like you're turning up to a *Great Gatsby*-style

party in this pseudo-waterfront mansion, but few make it that far, preferring to linger over cocktails on the candlelit terrace to the backbeat of mellow music. The menu trots the globe from Thai curry to sushi, pizza to Peruvian *ceviche*.

Es Passeig MEDITERRANEAN €€€
(☑ 971 63 02 17; www.espasseig.com; Passeig de Sa Platja 8; mains €17-27; ⊘ 1-3.30pm & 6.30-10pm Wed-Sun, 6-10pm Tue Mar-Oct) Grab one of the sea-facing terrace tables or aim for one by the window at this artfully understated, yet triumphant restaurant. The bright, creative dishes are richly inflected by the seasons and presented with a razor-sharp eye for detail – no coincidence given chef Marcel Battenberg's Michelin-star credentials. Families are welcome – there's a good kids' menu.

❶ Information

Tourist Office (☑ 971 63 30 42; Carrer del Canonge Oliver 10; ⊘ 9am-3.15pm Mon-Fri Apr-Oct) Right in the heart of the town, near the bus terminus.

❶ Getting There & Away

Most buses to Sóller terminate in Port de Sóller. If driving, you must choose between going to the centre (take the tunnel) or the Platja d'en Repic side (follow the signs). The trams *(tranvías)* to Sóller run along the waterfront. Several car and scooter-rental offices line Passeig Es Través.

If you want to look good on Mallorca's roads, snappy **Bullimoto Vespa** (☑ 971 63 26 96; www.bullimoto.com; per day from €25) rents three types of Vespa (two automatic, one manual), all in white and fancy, sparkling condition. Bullimoto also runs Vespa tours of the island.

Biniaraix

From either Fornalutx or Sóller, it's a pleasant 2km drive, pedal or stroll to the sweet hamlet of Biniaraix, with the brooding Tramuntana peering over its shoulder. Sights are few – hence the reason most people continue on to neighbouring Fornalutx - but there's something special about pausing, however briefly, in a place where most visitors arrive on foot, or along narrow country lanes lined with drystone walls.

⊙ Sights & Activities

The village started life as an Arab *alquería* or farmstead and has a pleasant central square, Plaça de Sa Concepció.

To go for a sublime ramble, walk up Carrer de Sant Josep from the church to the turning at the top of the road, where the old wash house stands (women of Biniaraix would scrub their clothes here) and turn right where a sign says 'Barranc de Biniaraix Cúber'; this walk will take you into a splendid gorge. The walking trail to Biniaraix is well signposted from the centre of Sóller. You can also walk from Fornalutx, either by following the winding road down from the plaça towards Sóller, or by taking the far more attractive path alongside the Fornalutx Cemetery and past the terraced fields on the edge of the village, via the small settlement of Binibassí.

Plaça de Sa Concepció SQUARE
The very small, but utterly charming, central square is the focal point of the village, home to an inviting little bodega, a tall solitary plane tree that affords shade to walkers seeking a breather and the Església de la Immaculada Concepció.

Església de la Immaculada Concepció CHURCH
(Plaça de la Concepció) The sweet Church of the Immaculate Conception just up the steps from the plaça at the heart of Biniaraix dates from the late 16th century. Topped with a bell tower (added in the 19th century), the church interior has a barrel-vaulted ceiling and a graceful array of round arches.

✖ Eating

The very cute Bar Bodega Biniaraix in Plaça de Sa Concepció is the natural point of gravitation for snackers, although it has a rather limited menu. For a fuller meal, proceed to Fornalutx or Sóller.

Bar Bodega Biniaraix CAFE €
(Plaça de Sa Concepció; snacks from €5; ⊘ 9am-9.30pm Apr-Oct, 10.45am-9.30pm Nov-Mar) This charmer of a bar/cafe sits alone on the square in Biniaraix, with a host of tables out front. It's a lovely spot for a *cafe con leche* with lashings of peace and quiet, a glass of Mallorcan wine, fresh orange juice and perhaps some *pa amb-oli* or a slice of cake.

❶ Getting There & Away

A local service (€1.50, 15 minutes, two to four daily) connects Sóller with Biniaraix, before continuing to Fornalutx (€1.50). Alternatively, the walk from Sóller is a pleasant way to arrive and you can continue on foot to Fornalutx.

WESTERN MALLORCA BINIARAIX

Fornalutx

POP 704

On foot, there are three ways to reach Fornalutx (the name means 'oven light'), one of Mallorca's most adorable stone-built villages. The first is along a narrow, scenic route from Biniaraix, passing through the minute hamlet of Binibassi and then terraced groves crowded with orange and lemon trees. Another is the road that drops down off the Ma10, with aerial views of the village's stone houses and terracotta roofs. The more prosaic route is along the winding vehicular road from Sóller.

Whichever way you choose, the mountainous backdrop means Fornalutx is postcard pretty, and the effect is heightened as you draw near, with green shuttered windows, flower boxes, well-kept gardens and flourishing citrus groves. Many of the houses are owned by expats (Germans and British in the main), but it's a far cry from the comparative bustle of Sóller. Like Biniaraix, Fornalutx is believed to have its origins as an Arab *alquería*.

◎ Sights

Fornalutx rewards those who simply wander. Begin with the lanes around the central Plaça d'Espanya at the top of the road and pop into the ajuntament with its cool courtyard dominated by a palm tree. Outside, water gurgles cheerfully along one of several irrigation channels. You can follow the course of the town stream east past fine houses and thick greenery, or climb the stairs heading north out of the town from the Església de la Nativitat de Nostra Senyora. Keep heading up the steps, and if you take a left fork on Carrer de Tramuntana, you will eventually make it to a dead end and the last house in the village; keep going straight up and you can head off up into the hills.

Plaça d'Espanya
SQUARE

The communal heart of the village, this gorgeous square is flanked on one side by the magnificent steps up to the church, the side wall of which occupies another flank; the steps continue on up to the top of the village and beyond, forming a delightful clamber for visitors. On a further side of the square, a cafe occupies pole position on the square, alongside a local supermarket. Opposite the supermarket stands the principal village fountain, supplying fresh, potable water.

Mirador de Ses Barques
VIEWPOINT

The viewpoint of Mirador de Ses Barques, about 6km above Fornalutx, has phenomenal views all the way down to Port de Sóller; the cafe here serves great freshly squeezed orange juice, as well as snacks. Parking is plentiful out front, or across the road at the bend. You can also walk down from here on an engaging hike to Fornalutx below, or indeed clamber up from the village.

Església de la Nativitat de Nostra Senyora
CHURCH

The lovely church of Fornalutx presides over the square, the sound of its sonorous bell marking the hours and quarter hours (it stops at around 10pm so residents can get some shut eye), travelling over the terracotta tiles of the village before being swallowed up by the hills.

Ajuntament
HISTORIC BUILDING

(Town Hall; Carrer de Vicari Solivellas 1) A minute's walk from the square, pop into the old town hall with its cool courtyard dominated by a palm tree. Outside, water gurgles cheerfully along one of several irrigation channels, leading down to the old wash house, where local women used to scrub clothes. If you keep going down the steps, you will see the fabulous torrent that runs down from the hills and gushes onward to Sóller during the rains.

✖ Eating

The village is liberally scattered with restaurants and cafes, most of which are located around the central plaça or occupy shady roadside terraces (with panoramic views) about 500m out of the centre on the Ma2121 road leading northeast out of town.

Ca N'Antuna
MALLORCAN €€

(☑ 971 63 30 68; Carrer Arbona-Colom 6; mains from €12.50; ◷ 12.30-4pm & 7.30-11pm) With tables facing the stupendous view of the mountains from its outdoor terrace, this long-standing restaurant has an appetising focus on wholesome Mallorcan fare, and doesn't skimp on portions. The *lechona* (roast suckling pig) is ample and succulent, while the roast lamb is worth coming back for. Reserve ahead for a table with a view; otherwise you get a seat roadside.

Es Turó
MALLORCAN €€

(☑ 971 63 08 08; www.restaurante-esturo-fornalutx.com; Carrer Arbona-Colom 12; mains €7-21.50; ◷ noon-10.30pm Fri-Wed) The views over the village to the Tramuntana peaks at sunset are glorious. The menu is solidly Mallorcan, from *pa amb oli* (rye bread rubbed with olive oil and garlic, topped with chopped tomatoes) to *arros brut* ('dirty' rice) and crisp, although dry, *lechona* (roast suckling pig). Be sure to try the zingy juice, freshly squeezed from local oranges.

❶ Getting There & Away

A local service connects Fornalutx with Sóller (€1.50, 15 minutes, two to four daily), via Biniaraix.

Bunyola
POP 6662

This drowsy town, known for olive oil and its *palo* (herbal liquor) distillery, resides at the foot of lush terraced hillsides and the wild grey peaks of the Tramuntana. The rickety wooden train that trundles between Palma and Sóller stops here. It's a fabulous base for rock climbing and – back at ground level – for observing Mallorcan village life in the central square, Sa Plaça, which hosts a small Saturday morning market.

◎ Sights & Activities

Església de Sant Mateu CHURCH
(Carrer de l'Església 2; ⊙ mass) Next to the main square in the heart of town, the Església de Sant Mateu was built in 1230 but largely redone in 1756. You'll only be allowed to peek inside during mass.

Sa Gubia CLIMBING
Just west of Bunyola, where the foothills of the Tramuntana thin to the flatlands around Palma, rises this magnificent rock amphitheatre – a holy grail to climbers, who come to play on 125 multi-pitch routes graded 4 to 8, including some excellent, fully bolted long climbs. The Cara Oeste (West Face) ranks as one of Europe's most impressive limestone walls.

✗ Eating

Bunyola does not have an excellent range of restaurants in town, but Orient and Alaró are not far away, both provided with good dining options. Alternatively, Sóller has an excellent selection of restaurants.

Ca'n Topa MALLORCAN €
(☑971 14 84 67; www.cantopa.com; Careterra Palma a Soller Km 22.1; snacks €5-10; ⊙ hr vary) Its high-on-a-hill location on the windy mountain road to Sóller makes Ca'n Topa a much-loved pit stop of cyclists and hikers, who love its languid rhythm, poolside deck, snacks (pizzas, *bocadillos*, cakes and the like) and ice-cold drinks after exploring the Tramuntana.

❶ Getting There & Away

Buses and trains running between Palma and Sóller stop at Bunyola (the bus stop is at Sa Plaça, and the train station a short walk west of the centre). Local bus 221 runs twice a day east to Orient (€2, 30 minutes). This is a microbus service and you need to book a seat in advance by calling 617 365365.

To drive through the tunnel to Sóller costs €4.95. Alternatively, hit the hairpin bends up the cross-mountain road and down into the Sóller valley.

Orient
POP 35

With its huddle of ochre houses clustered on a slight rise, pretty Orient is one of the loveliest little hamlets on the island. A few houses on the north side of the road seem set to slide off, as if they're an afterthought.

✗ Activities

The 9km road (the Ma2100) that wends northeast from Bunyola to Orient attracts swarms of lithe, lycra-clad cyclists. The first 5km is a promenade along a valley brushed with olive and cypress trees that slowly crests a plain and the **Coll d'Honor** (550m) before tumbling over the other side of a forested ridge. The next 2km of serried switchbacks flatten out on the run into Orient. All the way, the **Serra d'Alfàbia** is in sight to the north.

✗ Eating

Orient is not a large village, so its selection of restaurants is limited, but the excellent **Mandala** (☑971 61 52 85; Carrer Nou 1; mains €17-25; ⊙8.30-10.30pm Tue-Sun Jun–mid-Sep, shorter hr rest of yr & closed Dec-Feb; ☷) is a standout choice and worthy of a visit in itself.

❶ Getting There & Away

The 221 bus runs from Bunyola to Orient (€2) twice a day, but must be reserved the day before (call ☑ 617 36 53 65).

Alaró

POP 5227 / ELEVATION 252M

Topped by castle ruins, Alaró is pleasantly sleepy and rewards those who linger. Head for Plaça de la Vila, flanked by the Casa de la Vila (town hall), the parish church and a couple of cafes. The square springs to life at its Saturday morning market. Cafes also congregate around Carrer Petit and Carrer de Jaume Rosselló.

☉ Sights

★ Castell d'Alaró CASTLE

(off Carretera Alaró-Bunyola) Perched at an improbable, almost comical angle on a gigantic fist of rock, Castell d'Alaró is one of the most rewarding castle climbs on the island. The ruins are all that remain of the last redoubt of Christian warriors who could only be starved out by Muslim conquerors around 911, eight years after the Moors invaded Mallorca. The astonishing views, from Palma to Badia de Alcúdia, are something special. If the two-hour walk up doesn't appeal, you can cover most of the ascent by car.

✕ Eating

★ Es Verger SPANISH €€

(📞 971 18 21 26; Camí des Castell; mains €8-16; ⊙ 9am-9pm Tue-Sun) On the zigzagging road up to Castell d'Alaró, this gloriously rustic haunt is well worth the trek, bike ride or gear-crunching ascent. The sheep hanging out in the car park are a menu give-away. In

---

DON'T MISS

THE ROAD TO ALARÓ

One of the most scenic ways to approach Alaró is on the Ma2100 from Orient, which takes you through bucolic scenery of cypresses and orchards of fig, olive and almond. The road meanders about 4km northeast before taking a leisurely turn around the outriders of the mighty rock plug, **Puig d'Alaró** (822m), which thrusts up from the valley floor. Its identical twin to the east is **Puig de S'Alcadena** (815m). Ripped apart by a geological fault millions of years ago, these twin peaks are one of Mallorca's most distinctive images. To the south you can make out the flat interior of **Es Pla** (the Plain).

---

his *Mediterranean Escapes* series of books, UK-based chef Rick Stein praises the lamb (*cordero*) as the moistest he has ever tasted – and right he is.

Traffic MALLORCAN €€

(📞 971 87 91 17; www.canxim.com; Plaça de la Vila 8, Hotel Can Xim; mains €12-22; ⊙ 12.15-5.15pm & 8-11.30pm Mon & Thu-Sun, 8-11pm Wed) The pick of the places on Plaça de la Vila, this countrified restaurant at the Hotel Can Xim rolls out Mallorcan specialities with a few innovative twists. Meats such as rabbit and suckling pig are definitely the strong point, but the cod with *sobrassada* (cured pork sausage flavoured with paprika and spices) and honey is terrific, too. Choose between the terrace and the beamed, tiled interior.

❶ Getting There & Away

The Palma–Inca train calls at the Consell-Alaró train station (20 to 30 minutes), where it connects with local bus 320 for Alaró (€1.50, 15 minutes).

Cala de Sa Calobra & Cala Tuent

The hairpin-riddled 12km helter-skelter of a road down to Sa Calobra and Cala Tuent is one of Mallorca's top experiences. Whether you're swooning over the giddy ravine views, gulping as a coach squeezes through an impossibly narrow cleft in the rock, or aping Tour de France winner Bradley Wiggins with a thigh-burning pedal to the top (he does it in 26 minutes, for the record), this spectacularly serpentine road, which branches north off the Ma10, is pure drama. Carved through the rock and skirting narrow ridges as it unfurls to the coast, it is the feat of Italian engineer Antonio Paretti, who built it in 1932; its twists and turns were inspired by tying a tie, some say (explaining the section of road that turns round before threading under itself).

☉ Sights

If you come in summer, you won't be alone. Legions of buses and fleets of pleasure boats disgorge battalions of tourists. It's a different world to Sa Calobra on a quiet, bright midwinter morning. From the northern end of the road a short trail leads around the coast to a rocky river gorge, the Torrent de Pareis, and a small white-pebble cove with fabulous (but usually crowded) swimming spots.

Cala Tuent
BEACH

To skip the Sa Calobra crowds, follow a turn-off west, some 2km before Sa Calobra, to reach Cala Tuent, a tranquil emerald-green inlet in the shadow of Puig Major, with a single tall pine tree right by the beach. The broad pebble and shingle beach is backed by a couple of houses and a great, green bowl of vegetation that climbs up the mountain flanks. Cars park alongside the road near the beach, but things can get tight.

Sa Calobra
BEACH

After the turning to Cala Tuent, the road continues to wind down to this small and undeniably attractive white-pebble cove, but it's a coach-fest during the summer crush, when carloads of visitors also descend. There is parking at the end of the road, but you will need to pay. A short trail and walk-way leads around the coast to a rocky river gorge, the **Torrent de Pareis**, the dramatic conclusion to the torrent's descent from Escorca.

Puig Major
MOUNTAIN

Mallorca's tallest peak (1445m) can be seen from all round these parts. It's topped with a globular radar station, built by the US.

✖ Eating

Before getting behind the wheel to take on the wriggling bends back to the Ma10, have a seat booked for a meal in the old *finca* (farmhouse) of Es Vergeret, which looks out on to awesome views. Alternatively, you can find a few rather average restaurants in Sa Calobra.

Es Vergeret
MALLORCAN €€

(📞971 51 71 05; Camí de Sa Figuera Vial 21; mains €15-20; ⊙12.30am-4.30pm Mar-Oct) A narrow country lane forking from the road to Cala Tuent on the dramatic drive down passes sheep farms and olive groves before reaching this glorious old *finca,* where astonishing views take in the full sweep of the bay below and the mountains. The terrace is a cracking spot for a lazy lunch of paella, grilled fish or lamb chops.

ℹ️ Getting There & Away

One bus a day (bus 355, Monday to Saturday, May to October) comes from Ca'n Picafort (9.30am) via Alcúdia, Cala Sant Vicenç, Pollença and the Monestir de Lluc. It returns at 3pm. The whole trip takes just under four hours to Sa Calobra (with a one-hour stop at the Monestir de Lluc) and 2½ hours on the return leg. From Ca'n Picafort, you pay €9.15 one way. Boats make excursions to Sa Calobra and Cala Tuent from Port de Sóller.

Monestir de Lluc

The site's sacred nature is heavily embroidered with ancient lore. Back in the 13th century, a local shepherd saw an image of the Virgin Mary in the sky. Later, a similar image appeared on a rock. Others say it was an Arab shepherd boy who discovered an image of a beautiful woman in 1238 and, returning with a monk from Escorca, saw a holy crown suspended over the spot. Another story relates how a statuette of the Virgin was found here and taken to Escorca. The next day it was back where it had been found. Three times it was taken to Escorca and three times it returned. A chapel was built near the site to commemorate the miracle, possibly around 1268. The religious sanctuary came afterwards. Since then thousands of pilgrims have come every year to pay homage to the 14th-century (and thus not the original) **Statue of the Virgin of Lluc.**

⊙ Sights

★Monestir de Lluc
MONASTERY

(www.lluc.net; Plaça dels Peregrins; monastery & gardens free, museum adult/child €2/free, Lluc ticket €3; ⊙10am-5pm) Entered via a cloistered garden, the monastery is a huge complex, dating mostly from the 17th to 18th centuries. Off the imposing central courtyard rises up the **grand façade** of the late-Renaissance basilica, behind which is a rather gloomy interior and a fine altarpiece by Jaume Blanquer; the **Virgin Mary and Infant Jesus statuette** is contained in a room behind the altar. The church received an ornate, baroque-style revamp in the early 20th century, based on plans drawn up by Gaudí.

Camí dels Misteris del Rosari
SACRED SITE

FREE An old stone trail, partly shaded by holm oaks, leads up the Pujol des Misteris (Hill of the Mysteries), which rises behind the monastery complex. The path recounts the mysteries of the rosaries, with monuments and three bronze reliefs. A place for peaceful contemplation, it also offers stirring views on the way up, especially into the valley behind. From the austere cross

THE PATHS OF PILGRIMS

Like so many before him, Antoni Gaudí made the pilgrimage to the Monestir de Lluc in April 1908, leaving a donation of 25 pesetas. In October that same year he returned, this time with his protégé Joan Rubió. He redesigned the church in the same baroque style as the chancel and oversaw the creation of the stone monuments that grace the **Pujol des Misteris** (Hill of the Mysteries), which rises behind the monastery complex.

An old stone trail, partly shaded by holm oaks, leads up this hill, which recounts the mysteries of the rosaries. Taking in monuments and three bronze reliefs, hidden in the twilight of a rock overhang, the trail is a place for peaceful contemplation; there are also stirring views on the way up, especially into the valley behind. From the austere cross (fenced off with barbed wire) at the top, linger for grandstand views and the boulder-strewn peaks of the Tramuntana. The walk takes around 20 minutes to complete.

Numerous walking routes leave from the monastery. One is a challenging 11km, five-hour circuit of **Puig de Massanella** (1365m), Mallorca's second highest peak, with sensational vistas from its summit. Another is a 9km, 3½-hour circuit of **Puig Tomir** (1103m), a stiff, rocky ascent into the lonely heights of the Tramuntana, where you may sight vultures and falcons. Another route is a four- to five-hour hike around **Puig Roig** (1102m), to the northwest of the monastery; this route should only be done on Sundays as some of the route traverses private land. Lluc is also a stop on the long-distance GR221 between Sant Elm and Pollença.

For the true spirit of blister-footed pilgrimage, join thousands of Mallorcans on the **Marxa des Güell a Lluc a Peu**, a 42km all-night march from the Plaça Güell in Palma to the Monestir de Lluc, taking in farmland, hill towns and the Serra de Tramuntana by torchlight.

(fenced off with barbed wire) at the top, linger for grandstand views and the boulder-strewn peaks of the Tramuntana.

Centre d'Informació Serra de Tramuntana
MUSEUM

(⏀971 51 70 83; www.serradetramuntana.net; adult/child €2/free; ⏀9am-4.30pm) Opposite the monastery complex, this interpretation centre has audiovisual displays and a small museum providing background on the Serra de Tramuntana. Here you can brush up on regional flora and fauna, including bird species such as the Eleonora's falcon and Balearic shearwater, and learn about farming in the mountains. The centre has a stock of multilingual leaflets detailing walks in the area, and the friendly staff can arrange camping in the grounds of Lluc for €5 per night.

✷ Festivals & Events

Marxa des Güell a Lluc a Peu RELIGIOUS
(http://desguellallucapeu.es; ⏀1st Sat Aug) Annual 42km walk from Palma to Lluc held on the first Saturday of August.

✖ Eating

Sa Fonda SPANISH €€
(⏀971 51 70 22; Plaça del Lledoner; mains €9-18.50; ⏀8-10.30am & 1-11pm) Housed in the expanded pilgrims' refectory at the monastery, this rambling restaurant is a historic spot for breakfast, lunch or dinner at a varnished table below marble arches and wood beams. The all-Mallorcan menu stars dishes such as *frito mallorquín* (a tasty lamb offal and vegetable fry-up), suckling pig from the oven (€15.50) and grilled sole (€16).

ⓘ Getting There & Away

Up to two buses a day (May to October) run from Ca'n Picafort to the Monestir de Lluc (€6.45, 1¾ hours) on their way to Sóller and Port de Sóller. From Palma, two all-stops buses (€4.70; buses 330 and 354) to Inca continue to Lluc via Caimari from Monday to Saturday (one on Sunday).

Northern Mallorca

Best Places to Eat

➜ Mirador de La Victòria
(p134)

➜ Restaurante Jardín
(p133)

➜ Manzanas y Peras (p121)

➜ Ca'n Cuarassa (p126)

➜ S'Arc (p129)

Top Sights

➜ Parc Natural de S'Albufera
(p135)

➜ Pollèntia (p128)

➜ Platja des Coll Baix (p134)

➜ Calvari (p120)

➜ Església de la Mare de Deu
dels Àngels (p120)

Why Go?

Northern Mallorca is the island's heart and soul, bundling coastal drama, cultured towns with spirited fiestas, a twin-set of white-sand bays and an exciting portfolio of adventure sports into one enticing package.

The Serra de Tramuntana is at its most fabulous where the range culminates on the Cap de Formentor, flicking out into the Med like a dragon's tail. The road that wraps around its cliff tops elicits gasps of wonder from drivers and cyclists. Across the water, the pine-forested peninsula of Cap des Pinar is hiking heaven. Elsewhere, kitesurfers, cliff jumpers, scuba divers, cavers and paragliders harness its unique coastscapes and steady breezes.

Resorts here have a low-key, kid-friendly vibe. Inland, towns have retained an authentic Mallorcan air: from medieval-walled Alcúdia to Pollença, with its cafe-rimmed plazas, pilgrim trails and live-to-party summer festivals.

When to Go

Some of the beach resorts barely have a pulse until May or after October (Cala Sant Vicenç, for instance), and the best beach weather is from June to August. Pollença is one big fiesta in August. Yet our favourite time to visit is spring and autumn – migrating birds flock to the Parc Natural de S'Albufera, the roads are quieter (especially out along the Cap de Formentor), Pollença's Good Friday celebration is captivating, and Alcúdia hosts a terrific market in early October. Cooler weather is better for hitting the walking trails, too.

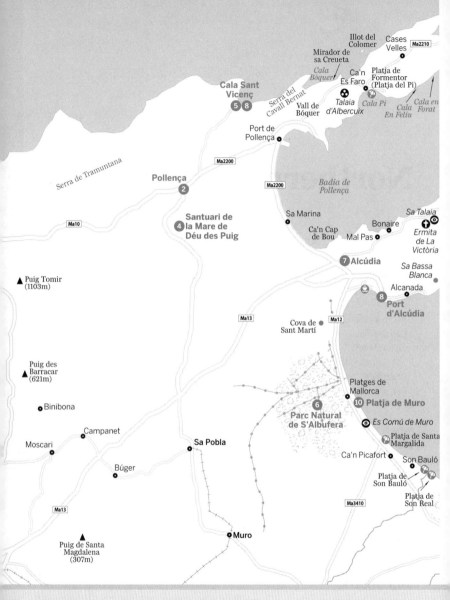

Illot del Colomer

Cases Velles

Ma2210

Mirador de sa Creueta

Cala Bóquer

Ca'n Es Faro

Platja de Formentor (Platja del Pi)

Cala Sant Vicenç

5 8

Serra del Cavall Bernat

Vall de Bóquer

Talaia d'Albercuix

Cala Pi

Cala En Feliu

Cala en Forat

Port de Pollença

Ma2200

Pollença

2

Ma2200

Badia de Pollença

Ma10

Santuari de la Mare de Déu des Puig

4

Sa Marina

Ca'n Cap de Bou

Mal Pas

Bonaire

Sa Talaia

Ermita de La Victòria

▲ Puig Tomir (1103m)

7 **Alcúdia**

Sa Bassa Blanca

Alcanada

8 **Port d'Alcúdia**

Ma13

Cova de Sant Martí

Ma12

Puig des Barracar (621m) ▲

● Binibona

Platges de Mallorca

10 **Platja de Muro**

Campanet

Moscari

Sa Pobla

Parc Natural de S'Albufera

6

Es Comú de Muro

Platja de Santa Margalida

Ca'n Picafort

Son Bauló

Búger

Platja de Son Bauló

Ma3410

Platja de Son Real

Ma13

▲ Puig de Santa Magdalena (307m)

●**Muro**

Northern Mallorca Highlights

1 Cap de Formentor (p127) Feeling your jaw drop as low as the cliffs on this coastal thriller.

2 Pollença (p120) Counting your blessings

pilgrim-style on the the 365-step Calvari.

3 Penya Rotja (p130) Hiking to see the north coast reduced to postcard format.

4 Santuari de la Mare de Déu des Puig (p120) Lifting your spirits with sensational views.

5 Cala Sant Vicenç (p124) Snorkelling in

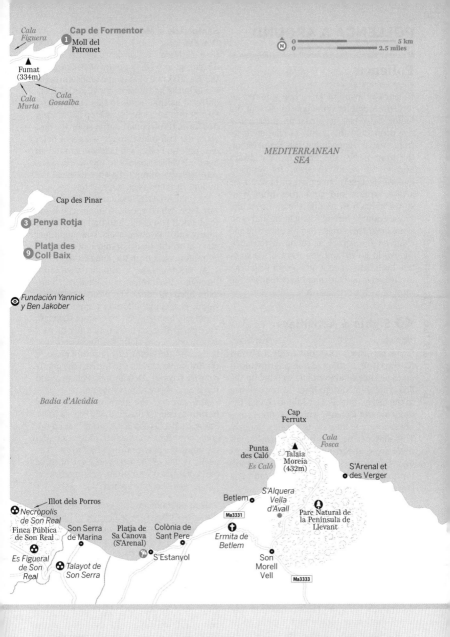

Cala
Figuera

Cap de Formentor
1 Moll del
Patronet

▲
Fumat
(334m)

Cala   Cala
Murta   Gossalba

☊ N   0 _____ 5 km
       0 _____ 2.5 miles

*MEDITERRANEAN
SEA*

Cap des Pinar

3 **Penya Rotja**

9 **Platja des
Coll Baix**

◉ *Fundación Yannick
y Ben Jakober*

Badia d'Alcúdia

Cap
Ferrutx
                                                    *Cala
                                                    Fosca*
                        Punta
                        des Caló   ▲
                        Es Caló   Talaia
                                    Moreia
                                    (432m)   S'Arenal et
                                                  ● des Verger
            Betlem ●   S'Alquera
                        Vella
✪ *Illot dels Porros*   d'Avall
✪ *Necròpolis   ✪
de Son Real*   Parc Natural de
Finca Pública Son Serra   Platja de   Colònia de   la Península de
de Son Real   de Marina   Sa Canova   Sant Pere   Llevant
✪   ●   (S'Arenal) ⊕
*Es Figueral   ✪ ●   *Ermita de*
de Son   S'Estanyol   *Betlem*
Real*   ✪ *Talayot de   Son
             Son Serra*   Morell
                                                    Vell   Ma3333
Ma3331

translucent water and eating
just-caught seafood.

6 **Parc Natural de
S'Albufera** (p135) Bird-
spotting in the rushes.

7 **Alcúdia** (p127) Winging

back to Roman and medieval
times.

8 **Port d'Alcúdia** (p132)
Marvelling at Mallorca's finest
seascapes on a boat trip to
Cala Sant Vicenç.

9 **Platja des Coll Baix**
(p134) Descending to this
gorgeously remote beach.

10 **Platja de Muro** (p135)
Stretching out on the fine
sands.

POLLENÇA & AROUND

Pollença

POP 16,088 / ELEV 41M

Pollença is beautiful. On a late summer afternoon, when its stone houses glow in the fading light, cicadas strike up their tentative drone and the burble of chatter floats from cafe terraces lining the Plaça Major, the town is like the Mallorca you always hoped you would discover. Its postcard looks and vaguely bohemian air have drawn artists, writers and luminaries from Winston Churchill to Agatha Christie over the years. Saunter through its gallery and boutique-lined backstreets or pull up a ringside chair on the square at sundown to watch the world go by and you too will be smitten. Even better, check into one of Pollença's lovely hotels and overnight here to make the most of its historic charm.

◉ Sights & Activities

★ Calvari   CHRISTIAN SITE

(Carrer del Calvari) They don't call it Calvari (Calvary) for nothing. Some pilgrims do it on their knees, but even just walking up the 365 cypress-lined steps from the town centre to the lovely 18th-century hilltop chapel, the **Església del Calvari**, with its simple, spartan and serene interior, is penance enough. This may not be a stairway to heaven, but there are soul-stirring views to savour back over the town's mosaic of terracotta rooftops and church spires to the Tramuntana beyond.

★ Església de la Mare de
Déu dels Àngels   CHURCH

(Plaça Major; ⊙ 11am-1pm & 3-5pm Jun-Aug, shorter hours rest of year) A church was first raised on this site in Gothic style shortly after the conquest in 1229, but was given a complete makeover in the 18th century, so what you see today overlooking the Plaça Major is predominantly baroque. The unusually simple rough-sandstone facade is a superb backdrop to the square. Lit by a rose window, the interior has an unusual and barrel-vaulted ceiling with extravagant ceiling frescoes (some restored with a heavy hand) and a magnificent, bombastic altarpiece.

Santuari de la Mare de
Déu des Puig   MONASTERY

(Puig de Maria; ⊙ 9am-6pm Oct-Mar, 8.30am-8.30pm Apr-Sep) FREE South of Pollença, off the Ma2200, one of Mallorca's most tortuous roads bucks and weaves up 1.5km of gasp-out-loud hairpin bends to this 14th-century former nunnery, which sits atop 333m **Puig de Maria**. If you come pilgrim style (the best way), the stiff hike through woods of holm oak, pine and olive will take you around an hour – Pollença shrinks to toytown scale as you near the summit. Be sure to avoid the midday heat and pack some water.

No taxi driver is foolhardy enough venture here, which speaks volumes about the road, but if you crank into first gear, take it steady and say your prayers, you might just make it to the final parking bay, around a 20-minute walk from the refuge.

At the top, take a contemplative stroll through the refectory, kitchen, heirloom-filled corridors, and incense-perfumed Gothic chapel of the former nunnery. That's if you can tear yourself away from the view. Though modest in height, this fist of rock commands one of Mallorca's finest outlooks: to the west the hauntingly beautiful peaks of the Tramuntana range, to the east the gently curving bays of Alcúdia and Pollença and the jagged Formentor peninsula.

You can stay the night in a **converted hermit's cell** (🖉 971 18 41 32; Puig de Maria, Pollença; s/d/t €14/22/30; 🐾) to rise at an ungodly hour for a spectacular sunrise, or simply enjoy the silence over a bite to eat. The paella is one of the best you'll get in these parts, but place your order well in advance. Life moves slooowly up here.

Museu de Pollença   MUSEUM

(Carrer de Guillem Cifre de Colonya; ⊙ 10am-1pm & 5.30-8.30pm Tue-Sat Jun-Sep, shorter hours rest of year) FREE This museum's star attraction is the 17th-century baroque cloister of the Convent de Sant Domingo, in which the museum is housed, which is a picture of tranquillity and poise. At the entrance is a small collection of pottery, while upstairs is a fantastic collection of modern and contemporary art, where you can also find a bright Buddhist Kalachakra mandala created from coloured grains of sand, donated by the Dalai Lama to the town in 1990.

An explanation in English explains how the mandala was painstakingly created. Other exhibits include archaeological finds from the surrounding area and some Gothic altarpieces, housed in a separate room. Also part of the museum is the Església de la Mare de Déu del Roser.

Església de la Mare de Déu del Roser
CHURCH

(Carrer de Guillem Cifre de Colonya) Part of the Museu de Pollença, the Església de la Mere de Déu del Roser is a marvellous old and now-empty church that is used for art exhibitions and contemporary art installations.

Pont Romà
BRIDGE

(Carrer del Pont Romà) On the northern outskirts of town, this two-arched bridge originally dates to Roman days, although it was much restored in medieval times.

Església de Monti-Sion
CHURCH

(Carrer de Jesús) This attractive baroque church, located near the base of the steps up Calvari, was built by the Jesuits in the late 17th century. The church's convent is today the home of the Town Hall.

Casa-Museu Dionís Bennàssar
MUSEUM

(📋 971 53 09 97; www.museudionisbennassar.com; Carrer de Roca 14; adult/child €3/free; ⊙ 10am-2pm Tue-Sun mid-Mar–Oct) This museum, the former home of local artist Dionís Bennàssar (1904–67), hosts a permanent collection of his works. Downstairs are early etchings, watercolours and oils, depicting mostly local scenes. Works on the other floors range from a series on fish that is strangely reminiscent of Miquel Barceló's efforts in Palma's cathedral, to a series of nudes and portraits of dancing girls.

Museu Martí Vicenç
MUSEUM

(📋 971 53 28 67; www.martivicens.org; Carrer del Calvari 10; ⊙ 10.30am-2pm & 5-8pm Mon & Wed-Sat, 10.30am-2pm Sun) FREE A short way up the Calvari steps is the Museu Martí Vicenç. The weaver and artist Martí Vicenç Alemany (1926–95) bought this property, once part of a giant Franciscan monastery that also included the nearby former Església de Monti-Sion, in the 1950s. His works, mostly canvases and textiles, are strewn around several rooms.

Oratori de Sant Jordi
CHURCH

(Carrer Sant Jordi) Dedicated to St George, this lovely church dates to 1532 and contains a fine interior with a baroque altarpiece.

Món d'Aventura
ADVENTURE SPORTS

(📋 971 53 52 48; http://mondaventura.com; Plaça Vella 8; canyoning €50-55; ⊙ 10am-2pm & 4.30-8.30pm Mon-Fri, 10am-2pm Sat & Sun) Sports and adventure activities provider Món d'Aventura has canyoning, caving, kayaking, climbing, coasteering and hiking all covered. This is one of the most reputable adventure sports operators on the north coast.

✦ Festivals & Events

Davallament
RELIGIOUS

(⊙ Good Friday) At this haunting re-enactment of the Passion Play, the body of Christ is solemnly paraded down the 365 steps of Calvari during Davallament ('Lowering') by torchlight. It is one of the island's most moving and evocative Easter celebrations.

Festes de la Patrona
CULTURAL

(⊙ late Jul-early Aug) Dress up as a swashbuckling pirate or all in white and throw yourself into the crowd to celebrate the big and boisterous Festes de la Patrona, with mock battles between the Moros i Cristians (Moors and Christians) to mark the siege and attack by Saracen pirates in 1550, led by the infamous Turkish pirate Dragut (1500–65). A famous victory for the townsfolk, the 'battle' is the highpoint of the festival.

La Fira
FOOD & DRINK

(⊙ 2nd Sun in Nov) A massive market held in the Convent de Sant Domingo and elsewhere around town.

Festival de Pollença
CULTURAL

(📋 971 53 40 11; www.festivalpollenca.com; ⊙ late Jul-Aug) Orchestras, exhibitions and film screenings come to the atmospheric Sant Domingo cloister for this summer arts festival, running since 1962.

✖ Eating

Plaça Major is encircled by good-natured eateries and cafe-bars where tables are scattered about, providing sustenance to legions of diners morning, noon and night; some of the better options are only a short walk away, tucked down the side streets.

★ Manzanas y Peras
TAPAS €

(📋 971 53 22 92; www.manzanasyperas.eu; Carrer del Martell 6; tapas tasting menu €29.50; ⊙ 10am-10pm Mon-Fri, 10am-4pm Sun; 🛜 📋 ⊞) Tiny but brilliant, Manzanas y Peras (apples and pears) is a friendly oasis next to the Calvari steps, with tables set under trees lit by fairy lights. The evening tapas menu is a real feast, with taste sensations like crostini topped

NORTHERN MALLORCA POLLENÇA

Pollença

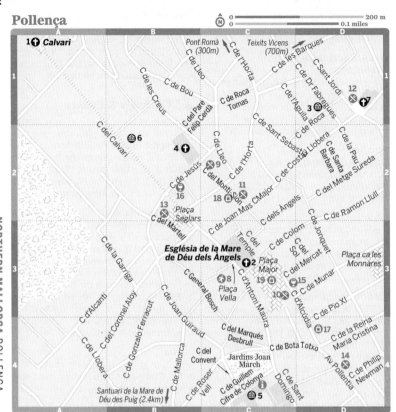

with Provençale tuna păté, goat's cheese cream cheese, blueberry jelly and walnuts, and chicken cooked in Moroccan spices with dates. Vegetarians are catered for.

Restaurant Clivia   MALLORCAN €€
(📞971 53 36 35; Avinguda Pollentia 7; mains €12-23; ☺1-3pm & 7-10.30pm Thu-Tue) More contemporary than most and superb in every respect, Clivia gathers around an inner courtyard, where a mosaic of pine panels and bell-shaped lights create an abstract artwork. The food (especially the fish) is prepared with panache. Prawn carpaccio with sweet red pepper is a delicious lead to the house speciality: wild sea bass steamed in malvasia wine.

Cantonet   MEDITERRANEAN €€
(📞971 53 04 29; Carrer del Monti-Sion 20; mains €12-20; ☺12.30-3pm & 7-11pm) As day slides into dusk, this restaurant terrace in front of the Esglésias de Monti-Sion is an en-

trancing choice, with views reaching across the old town rooftops to the Puig de Maria beyond. The food has Italian undertones: mussels in oregano sauce, gilthead bream in a Sardinian wine sauce and lamb cutlets grilled with honey and thyme. They do a mean tiramisu, too.

Il Giardino   ITALIAN €€
(📞971 53 43 02; www.giardinopollensa.com; Plaça Major 11; mains €17-24, set meals €14-19; ☺9.30am-3pm & 7-10.30pm Mar-Oct; 🚼) For our money, this is the pick of the restaurants on Plaça Major, with a fine terrace and friendly service. The menu whispers longingly of *bella Italia,* with mains like wild mushroom ravioli and king prawn with saffron and coriander sauce hitting the mark. Its adjacent patisserie and chocolate shop is a delectable post-dinner detour. Children are well provided for.

Pollença

La Placeta   SPANISH €€
(☑ 971 53 12 18; Carrer Sant Jordi 29; mains €13.50-16; ⊙ 12.30-3pm & 7.30-11pm Tue-Sun; 🖪) Everyone raves about La Placeta at Hotel Sant Jordi, whether for its pretty alfresco setting on the square, child-friendly waiters or no-nonsense home cooking. Dishes as simple as prawns sautéed with artichokes and lamb roasted in its own juices, and Madeira wine reveal true depth of flavour.

La Font del Gall   MALLORCAN €€
(☑ 971 53 03 96; Carrer del Monti-Sion 4; mains €7.50-22, set menus €25-35; ⊙ 6.30-11pm daily, plus noon-3pm Mon, Thu, Fri & Sun; 🖋) You'll be lucky to bag a spot on the pavement terrace here in summer. The chef keeps it simple, with spot-on Mallorcan dishes like crisp, slow-roasted suckling pig with grilled vegetables and jacket potato and seafood paella. There's a range of vegetarian starters and mains, too. Our only gripe is that portions can be modest.

🍷 Drinking & Nightlife

With several fine cocktail bars and cafe-bars of note in its historic centre, Pollença is an excellent place for an evening drink, preferably coupled with a chance to stay in town.

Club Pollença   BAR
(Plaça Major 10; ⊙ 7am-midnight) Observe Pollença life in all its guises over drinks and tapas on the terrace of this rambling colonial-flavoured cafe on Plaça Major, which first opened its doors in 1910. Grab a front-row seat and enjoy the spectacle.

U Gallet   BAR
(☑ 691 54 36 51; Carrer de Jesús 40; ⊙ 7pm-2am Sun-Thu, to 4am Fri & Sat) Known also to locals as the 'Gallito' (cockerel) and full of enticingly cosy nooks, this drinking hole is a very welcome choice on Carrer de Jesús. British owner and bartender Neil mixes great cocktails and G&Ts. The vibe is chilled, the music upbeat.

🛍 Shopping

Pollença is filled with engaging and creative little boutiques and its shopping is the best on the island outside Palma.

★Hito   ARTS & CRAFTS
(www.hitohome.com; Carrer del Calvari 10; ⊙ 10.30am-2pm & 5-8pm Mon & Wed-Sat, 10.30am-2pm Sun) A gallery, designer homeware store and artist-in-residence project rolled into one, Hito is run by New York expat jewellers Gillian Conroy and Danica Wilcox. On display are eye-catching, one-of-a-kind local crafts and accessories, from Teixits Vincens' fine *robes de llengües* (Mallorcan striped fabrics) to sheepskin baby booties and faux hunting trophies made of felt.

There are rotating art exhibitions upstairs, many of which have a contemporary slant, and downstairs you'll find the Museu Martí Vicenç (p121).

La Merceria   ARTS & CRAFTS
(Carrer del Monti-Sion 3; ⊙ 10am-2pm & 5-9.30pm Tue-Fri, 10am-2pm Sat & Sun) This gloriously retro emporium merges vintage style with contemporary design. Among the unique trinkets and gifts are nostalgic sepia post-

cards of old Pollença, Barcelona fashion, handmade straw boaters for a dash of Gatsby glamour, funky lampshades, gorgeous ceramics, cool glassware, creative candles, ace photos, art, jewellery and uplifting designs. Out back there's a fab collection of kids' books and clothing.

Sunday Market   MARKET
(Plaça Major; ⊙8.30am-1pm Sun) Held year-round, Pollença's Sunday market is one of the largest and liveliest in Mallorca. Fruit, veg, cheese, wine, herbs and spices are concentrated in the Plaça Major, with handicrafts and other stalls taking over an ever-widening arc of surrounding streets.

Enseñat   FOOD & DRINKS
(www.ensenyat.com; Carrer d'Alcúdia 5; ⊙8.30am-3pm & 4.30-8.30pm Mon-Sat, 8.30am-2pm Sun) A full-on savoury and pungent aroma of wholesome food fills your nostrils as you walk into Enseñat. Pick up salts, preserves, cheeses, meats, including homemade *sobrassada* (paprika-flavoured cured pork sausage), and Sóller marmalade at this gourmet deli, in business since the 1940s. There's also a superb range of Mallorcan wines.

Teixits Vicens   ARTS & CRAFTS
(www.teixitsvicens.com; Ronda Can Berenguer; ⊙9am-8pm Mon-Fri, 10am-2pm & 4-8pm Sat Apr-Sep, shorter hours rest of year) Artisans have been making the striped Mallorcan fabrics known as *robes de llengües* here at this family-run business since 1854, and the contemporary fabrics they turn out are faithful to traditional designs. Some of their works are on display at Hito.

ⓘ Information

Tourist Office (☑971 53 50 77; www.pollensa. com; Carrer de Guillem Cifre de Colonya; ⊙8.30am-1.30pm & 2-4pm Mon-Fri, 10am-1pm Sun May-Oct, shorter hours rest of year) Right by the Museu de Pollença, this tourist office is a mine of information on the town and its surrounds, with helpful staff and loads of literature.

ⓘ Getting There & Away

From Palma, bus 340 heads nonstop for Pollença (€5.35, 45 minutes, up to 12 daily). It then continues on to Port de Pollença (€1.50, 20 minutes, up to 30 daily). Bus 345 runs from Pollença to Cala Sant Vicenç (€1.50, 20 minutes, frequent).

Cala Sant Vicenç
POP 285

One of the loveliest little corners of the northern Mallorcan coast, Cala Sant Vicenç is arrayed around four jewel-like *cales* (coves) in a breach in the Serra de Tramuntana, with fine views across stunning turquoise waters northwest towards the sheer limestone cliffs of Cap de Formentor. The village is really only open for business from May to October, then largely shuts up shop.

🏊 Beaches

It doesn't take more than 20 minutes to walk the entire distance between Cala Sant Vicenç's four beaches: **Cala Barques**, **Cala Clara**, **Cala Molins** and **Cala Carbó**.

If you walk for 15 minutes along Carrer Temporal from behind Cala Clara and then down Carrer de Dionís Bennàssar, you'll hit a rise with park benches and the **Coves de L'Alzineret**, seven funerary caves dug in pre-Talayotic times (c 1600 BC).

🏃 Activities

atemrausch   ADVENTURE SPORTS
(☑622 12 21 45; www.atemrausch.com; Carre Temporal 9; kids/trekking/mountain/road bikes per day from €8/15/25/25; ⊙9.30am-1pm & 4-7pm Mon-Sat May-Oct) This German-run one-stop shop specialises in adventure sports, from kayaking and snorkelling, to mountain biking and scuba diving. They rent out all kinds of bicycles, including kid-sized ones; rates fall the longer you rent the bike. Bike insurance is €2 per day.

🍴 Eating

The best restaurants overlook Cala Barques, and serve an appetising variety of fresh seafood.

Bar-Restaurant Cala Barques MALLORCAN €€
(☑971 53 06 91; Cala Barques; mains €13-26; ⊙12.30-3.30pm & 7.30-10.30pm Tue-Sun May-Oct) The location, on a perch overlooking Cala Barques, is excellent. Pair it with grilled fish, squid and other seafood, or appetising steaks and roasts, and you've an excellent combo.

Cal Patró   SEAFOOD €€
(☑971 53 38 99; Cala Barques; mains €15-22; ⊙12.30-3.30pm & 7.30-10.30pm Jul & Aug, shorter hours rest of year) On the steps down towards

the beach, this breezy fisher's shack has views of the sea from its blue-clothed tables and serves up the freshest catch of the day. You might want to plump for the lovely cuttlefish Mallorcan-style (cooked in a rich casserole), followed by a rice dish or lobster stew.

ℹ Information

Tourist Office (971 53 32 64; Plaça de Cala Sant Vicenç; 9am-4pm Mon-Fri, 10am-1pm Sat May-Oct) A short walk away from Cala Barques.

ℹ Getting There & Away

Cala Sant Vicenç is 6.5km northeast of Pollença, off the road towards Port de Pollença. The 345 bus runs to Cala Sant Vicenç (€1.50, 20 minutes, up to six times daily) from Pollença and from Port de Pollença.

Port de Pollença

POP 6596

This low-key resort at the northern cusp of the Badia de Pollença has entrancing views over to the jagged formations of the Formentor peninsula. Yes, tourism is quite full-on, but the marina, cafe-lined promenade and long arc of sand still makes an appealing base for families and water-sports enthusiasts.

🏖 Beaches

The beaches immediately south of the main port area are broad, sandy and gentle. Tufts of beach are sprinkled all the way along the shady promenade stretching north of town – these rank among Port de Pollença's prettiest corners. South along the bay towards Alcúdia, the beaches are a grey gravel mix, frequently awash with poseidon grass. At the tail end of this less than winsome stretch, the stiff breezes on **Ca'n Cap de Bou** and **Sa Marina** (just before entering Alcúdia) are among the best on the island for wind- and kitesurfing.

🤾 Activities

Some of the island's finest diving is in the Badia de Pollença. There's plenty of wall and cave action, reasonable marine life (rays, octopuses, barracuda and more) along the southern flank of the Formentor peninsula and the southern end of the bay leading to Cap des Pinar.

★ **Bike & Kite** ADVENTURE SPORTS
(971 09 53 13; www.bikeandkite.com; Carrer Temple H Fielding 3; guided cycling tour incl rental from €75, 1hr kitesurfing lesson €45; 9am-1pm & 4-7pm Mon-Fri, 4-7pm Sun) Kai and Julia know the Serra de Tramuntana inside out and take you to its most exceptional places on their guided tours, which range from mountain-bike excursions to Lluc monastery and Cap de Formentor to hikes up to the Talaia d'Alcudia and through the Torrent de Pareis. This is also the place for kitesurfing lessons.

Rich Strutt HIKING
(668 54 22 74; www.mallorcanwalkingtours.puertopollensa.com) An English-speaking guide with more than 20 years' experience. Rich is based in Port de Pollença and offers a huge number of day hikes (or longer treks) for groups of four or more.

Boat Trips BOATING
(http://lanchaslagaviota.com; Marina; May-Sep) At the small ticket booth alongside the car park entrance at Port de Pollença's marina, you can buy tickets for regular return departures to Platja de Formentor (adult/child €13.50/6.75, up to five daily departures in summer, 11am to 4pm), Cap de Formentor (adult/child €25/12.50, three days per week at 10.30am) and Cala Sant Vicenç (adult/child €30/15, Thursdays at 10.30am).

Rent March CYCLING
(971 86 47 84; www.rentmarch.com; Carrer de Joan XXIII 89; bike rental per day €8-27; 9am-1pm & 3.30-8pm) Rent March hires out all sorts of bikes, from basic bicycles to mountain, electro, tandem, lightweight racer bikes and children's bikes. It also rents out scooters and motorbikes.

Sail & Surf Pollença SAILING, WINDSURFING
(971 86 53 46; www.sailsurf.eu; Passeig de Saralegui 134; beginner windsurfing/sailing courses €124/136; 9am-6pm Mon-Sat Apr-Oct, shorter hours rest of year) Come here for two- to three-day courses in sailing and windsurfing. Those with experience can also rent equipment.

Scuba Mallorca DIVING
(971 86 80 87; www.scubamallorca.com; Carrer d'Elcano 23; 2-dive package €80, equipment extra €20; 9.30am-7pm Mon-Thu, 9.30am-6.30pm Fri & Sat, 9am-6pm Sun Jun-Sep, shorter hours rest of year;) Scuba Mallorca is a PADI five-star outfit offering some 20 different diving courses, including the Bubblemaker for kids.

Kayak Mallorca KAYAKING

(☑971 91 91 52; www.piraguasgm.com/kayakmallorca; La Gola; 3hr trip incl transport per person from €40, rental per hr/half-day/full-day from €10/20/30; ⊙10am-1pm Mon-Wed & Sat, 10am-1pm & 5-8pm Thu-Fri) On the beach south of the marina, Kayak Mallorca organises trips for all levels, whether you fancy paddling around the coast to Cap des Pinar or via caves to Formentor. It also rents out kayaks and runs kayaking courses.

✖ Eating

There's a market every Wednesday on Plaça Miguel Capllonch, two blocks inland, northwest of the marina. The port is well-supplied with a tempting range of restaurants, some very appealing.

Bellaverd INTERNATIONAL €

(☑971 86 46 00; www.pensionbellavista.com; Carrer Monges 14; lunch menu €6-12, mains €9.50-22.50; ⊙8.30am-midnight Tue-Sun; ☑⍾) Sit in a gorgeous setting under the canopy of an old fig tree in the courtyard garden of this arty enclave, which hosts the occasional sculpture workshop. The kitchen rustles up healthy, mostly vegetarian dishes, from creative salads to pumpkin, leek and walnut filo parcels, goat's cheese lasagne or simple spaghetti with pesto. Kids are catered for, too.

Celler La Parra MALLORCAN €

(☑971 86 50 41; Carrer de Joan XXIII 84; mains €10-16.50; ⊙1-3pm & 7-11pm; ⍾) In business since the 1960s, this atmospheric, rustic and old-style Mallorcan restaurant is something of a rarity in these parts. It serves up genuine island fare, from fresh fish to *frito mallorquín* (sautéed lamb offal), *lechona* (roast lamb) and *tumbet* (Mallorcan ratatouille). Throw in a wood-fired oven, wine-cellar decor and nary a pizza in sight, and you'll soon see why we like it.

★ Ca'n Cuarassa SPANISH, MALLORCAN €€

(☑971 86 42 66; www.cancuarassa.com; Carretera Port de Pollença-Alcúdia; mains €15-30, 3-course menu €33.80; ⊙noon-3.30pm & 7-11pm; ⍾) With tantalising sea views and a tranquil garden terrace fringed by palm and tamarind trees, this genteel villa is an excellent choice. Homemade bread and tapas are a delicious intro to dishes like fillet of hake with saffron sauce and charcoal-grilled meats. There's a play area for kids. Ca'n Cuarassa sits 3km south of Port de Pollença.

La Llonja MEDITERRANEAN €€€

(☑971 86 59 04; www.restaurantlallonja.com; Carrer del Moll Vell; mains €16-30; ⊙12.30-4pm & 7.30-11pm Apr-Oct) Upstairs overlooking the water, La Llonja does seriously good seafood, meat dishes and rice dishes such as lobster paella with the occasional dash of creativity (like the lemonfish carpaccio) and bold flavours (the salmon fillet with red curry sauce). Downstairs La Cantina (10am to 11pm April to October) is far easier on the pocket for breakfast, snacks and sandwiches.

Stay INTERNATIONAL €€€

(☑971 86 40 13; www.stayrestaurant.com; Moll Nou; mains €15-42, 3-course menu incl wine & coffee €34.40; ⊙9am-11pm) A slick slice of seaside

---

PORT DE POLLENÇA TO CAP DE FORMENTOR BY ROAD

The stirring journey from Port de Pollença to the Cap de Formentor is a highlight of the region and a memorable expedition either by car or on two wheels.

The road quickly climbs away from Port de Pollença, affording splendid views of the bay, and whips its way towards the blustery cape. The traffic moves at a snail's pace here in summer, owing to a succession of **lookouts** with ranging views, such as the **Mirador de Sa Creueta**, 3km northeast of Port de Pollença. Look out to the east and spot the small islet of **Illot del Colomer**. From the same spot you can climb a couple of kilometres up a side road to the **Talaia d'Albercuix**, an 18th-century watchtower. Constructed to warn of pirates, the location was selected for its far-ranging 360-degree views. Time your journey to climb up for sunset, if you can.

From here, the Ma2210 sinks down through the woods some 4km to **Platja de Formentor**, a slender beach with soft sand and inviting waters. The road then slithers another 11km from Hotel Formentor out to the cape and its 19th-century **Cap de Formentor Lighthouse**, where the views look south to Cap Ferrutx at the far side of the Badia d'Alcúdia. The short walking track (the **Camí del Moll del Patronet**) leads south to another supreme **viewpoint**.

chic, with an extensive outdoor dining area out on the pier, this is the place for yachties and their ilk. Seafood is the name of the game, from simply grilled shrimp to local hake cooked in saffron sauce, but there's a tasty range of meat dishes too. It's classy but casual, pricey but almost always worth it.

ℹ️ Information

Tourist Office (☎ 971 86 54 67; www.puertopollensa.com; 1 Passeig Saralegui; ⊙ 9am-8pm Mon-Fri, 9am-4pm Sat May-Sep, shorter hours rest of year) On the waterfront in front of the marina.

ℹ️ Getting There & Away

The 340 bus from Palma to Pollença continues to Port de Pollença (€1.50, 20 minutes direct or 30 minutes via Cala Sant Vicenç). Bus 352 makes the run between Port de Pollença and Ca'n Picafort (€2.60, one hour), stopping at Alcúdia (€1.80, 15 minutes) and Port d'Alcúdia (€1.60, 25 minutes) along the way. The 353 runs to Formentor (€1.55, 20 minutes).

Cap de Formentor

The most dramatic stretch of Mallorca's coast, Cap de Formentor is an otherworldly domain of razor-edge cliffs and wind-buckled limestone peaks jutting far out to sea; from a distance, it looks like an epic line of waves about to break.

⦿ Sights

Talaia d'Albercuix   TOWER
You can climb a couple of kilometres up a side road from the Mirador de Sa Creueta to the Talaia d'Albercuix watchtower (380m), built to warn of pirates and you can see why; the views extend far out to sea. When the cliffs glow at sunset, it's the perfect photo op.

Cap de Formentor Lighthouse   LIGHTHOUSE
At the end of the road on the cape rises this 19th-century lighthouse, with fine views from Cap Ferrutx to the south and a short walking track (the **Camí del Moll del Patronet**) south to another viewpoint.

Mirador de Sa Creueta   VIEWPOINT
Popular lookout 3km northeast of Port de Pollença, with dizzying views along the ragged north coast.

Platja de Formentor   BEACH
(Platja del Pi) A fine ribbon of pale, pine-fringed sand, with crystal-clear water. Parking costs €10 for the day.

Illot del Colomer   ISLAND
Rocky islet off the Formentor peninsula.

🍴 Eating

The **Hotel Barceló Formentor** (☎ 971 89 91 00; www.barcelo.com; Platja de Formentor 3, Cap de Formentor; d €225-525, ste €575-900; ⊙ mid-Apr–Oct; P ❋ @ 🛜 🛝) on the Platja de Formentor has three restaurants, including a fine one right on the beachfront, but there are some excellent choices in Port de Pollença, further west along the coast.

ℹ️ Getting There & Away

The 18km stretch from Port de Pollença (via the Ma2210) is best done with your own vehicle, bicycle or feet, although the 353 bus runs from Port de Pollença to Platja de Formentor (€1.55, 20 minutes, four daily Monday to Saturday).

BADIA D'ALCÚDIA

Alcúdia

POP 19,768

Just a few kilometres inland from the coast, Alcúdia is a town of quiet charm and character, ringed by mighty medieval walls that enclose a maze of narrow lanes, historic mansions, cafe-rimmed plazas and warm-stone houses. On the fringes of town are the captivating remains of Pollèntia, once the island's prime Roman settlement.

⦿ Sights

⭐**Medieval Walls**   LANDMARK
Although largely rebuilt, Alcúdia's fine city walls are impressive. Those on the north side are largely the medieval originals while near the **Porta Roja** (Red Gate) are remnants of an 18th-century bridge. From the bridge, you can climb up and walk around 250m atop the walls, as far as Carrer del Progres, with fine views over town and towards the distant hills. Beyond the bridge to the northeast, the Plaça de Toros (bullring) has been built into a Renaissance-era fortified bastion.

Alcúdia

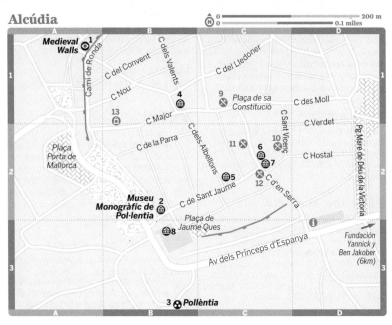

Alcúdia

★ **Pol·lèntia** ARCHAEOLOGICAL SITE
(www.pollentia.net; Avinguda dels Prínceps d'Espanya; adult/child incl Museu Monogràfic €3/2; ⊙9.30am-8.30pm Tue-Sat, 10am-2pm Sun May-Sep, shorter hours rest of year) Ranging over a sizeable (but walkable) area, the fascinating ruins of the Roman town of Pol·lentia lie just outside Alcúdia's walls. Founded around 70 BC, it was Rome's principal city in Mallorca and is the most important archaeological site on the island. Pol·lèntia reached its apogee in the 1st and 2nd centuries AD and covered up to 20 hectares – its sheer geographical spread (most of it not excavated) suggest it was a city of some scale and substance.

In the northwest corner of the site is the **Sa Portella** residential area – with the foundations, broken pillars and remains of the walls of houses (*domus*) separated by two streets. The best-preserved of the houses is the **Casa dels Dos Tresors** (House of the Two Treasures), a typical Roman house, centred on an atrium, which stood from the 1st to the 5th centuries AD. The 14.4cm bronze head of a young girl was found in the **Casa del Cap de Bronze** (House of the Bronze Head) nearby. A short stroll away are the remnants of the **Forum**, which boasted three temples and rows of *tabernae* (shops). Finally, you can walk another few hundred metres to reach the fascinating 1st-century-AD **Teatre Romà** (Roman Theatre), which seems to be returning into the rock from which it was hewn. The semi-circular *orchestra* at the front and the *cavea* (where spectators were seated) still survive. It wasn't until the late 19th century that the remains were identified as being a theatre. The theatre alone, with a diameter of 75m and a former capacity of around 1000 spectators, is worth the entrance fee. Visitors are free to wander among the ruins.

★ **Museu Monogràfic**
de Pollèntia MUSEUM

(www.pollentia.net; Carrer de Sant Jaume 30; adult/child incl Pollèntia €3/2; ⏱9.30am-8.30pm Tue-Sat, 10am-2pm Sun May-Sep, shorter hours rest of year) This one-room museum has a fascinating but limited collection of statue fragments, coins, jewellery, household figurines of divinities, scale models of the Casa dels Dos Tresors and Theatre and other remains excavated from the ruins of the Roman town of Pollèntia. It's well presented but labels are only in Catalan, so ask for the 'English guidebook' pamphlet from the helpful receptionist.

Ca'n Canta HISTORIC BUILDING

(Carrer Major 18) A fine old home with stunning carvings around its 1st-floor windows, just west of Plaça de sa Constitució, opposite the entrance to Carrer dels Albellons.

Ca'n Fondo HISTORIC BUILDING

(Carrer d'en Serra 13) This stolid and imposing building with classical carvings around its 1st-floor windows is a short walk north of the turning with Carrer de Sant Jaume.

Ca'n Domènech HISTORIC BUILDING

(Carrer dels Albellons 7) One of Alcúdia's finest, this large, grand and noble building has a largely unadorned facade.

Ca'n Torró HISTORIC BUILDING

(Carrer d'En Serra 15) This grand old building is next door to Ca'n Fondo.

Fundación Yannick y Ben Jakober GALLERY

(📞tours 971 54 98 80; www.fundacionjakober. org; Camí de Coll Baix; admission Tue free, guided tours €9-15; ⏱9.30am-12.30pm & 2.30-5.30pm Tue, 10am-noon Thu, prebooked guided tours 11am & 3pm Mon & Wed-Sat) Around 6km east of Alcúdia, in a Hispano-Moorish style house, this eclectic cultural institution concentrates on children's portraits from the 16th to 19th centuries. It also has exhibition space devoted to contemporary artists, a sculpture garden featuring works by the British artist couple Ben Jakober and Yannick Vu, and the Espacio SoKraTES, showcasing art from the likes of Mallorcan painter Miquel Barceló and a 10,000-crystal curtain by Swarovski.

Spring, when the rose garden is in full bloom, is a fine time to visit. To reach the gallery, follow the signs to Fundació and Bonaire. At Bodega del Sol restaurant, turn right and follow the road, which turns into a potholed track. The foundation is on the right.

Museu de Sant Jaume MUSEUM

(Plaça de Jaume Ques; adult/child €1/free; ⏱10am-1pm Tue-Sat) This museum, housed in the large eponymous Gothic church, contains a collection of priestly vestments, paintings and religious items.

★ **Festivals & Events**

Tuesday and Sunday are market days, held on and around Passeig de la Victòria.

Fira d'Alcúdia CULTURAL

(⏱1st weekend in Oct) The big annual market event is the Fira d'Alcúdia, which sees a produce market come together with traditional dances, music and parades.

✕ Eating

Alcúdia is well-served with restaurants, largely catering to the sizeable influx of day trippers. Several are notable for their attractive side-street, traditional settings and standout Mallorcan and international menus, while there's no shortage of choices with alfresco seating for avid people-watchers.

★ **S'Arc** INTERNATIONAL €€

(📞971 54 87 18; www.restaurantsarc.com; Carrer d'en Serra 22; mains €15-25; ⏱noon-3.30pm & 6.30-11.30pm; 🍴) Part of the Petit Hotel Ca'n Simó, this old-town charmer has a pretty inner courtyard, exposed stone walls and Mediterranean cuisine with some inventive twists, such as Iberian pork with lemon couscous and tuna tataki with mango

---

ALCÚDIA'S HISTORIC MANSIONS

Alcúdia's old town is dotted with grand, handsome and impressive mansions, within a short walk of each other. Among the finest examples are **Ca'n Canta**, **Ca'n Domènech**, **Ca'n Fondo** and **Ca'n Torró**.

HIKING THE COAST OF NORTHERN MALLORCA

HIKING TOUR: THREE COASTAL PEAKS

START ERMITA DE LA VICTÒRIA
FINISH PENYA ROTJA
LENGTH 6KM; 2½ TO THREE HOURS

One of Mallorca's most dramatic and exciting coastal walks, this medium-level hike takes you along precipitous ridges and cliff tops to three crags, perched like eyries above the Cap des Pinar peninsula. Look out for the Mallorcan wild goat (*Capra ageagrus hircus*) that inhabits these rocky heights. It's wise to avoid the midday heat and take a map and plenty of water. Make sure you wear sturdy shoes, too.

From the **Ermita de la Victòria** (☑ 971 54 99 12; www.lavictoriahotel.com; Carretera Cap des Pinar; s/d €50/60, breakfast €8) hermitage, head up the hill along the wide path through the pine forest, passing the signposted **Ses Tres Creus** (p134) – three crosses among the trees, overlooking the Badia de Pollença. Turn left after around 15 minutes, following signs to Penya Rotja and Penya des Migdia, onto a narrow footpath (don't follow the signs for **Talaia d'Alcúdia** (p134), which is another hike), which wends uphill through woods, then gently downhill (watch out for roots across the way that can trip you up). Pause for sensational Badia de Pollença and Formentor views to the west. Sheer cliffs now rise above you and the sea glints far below. Pass overhanging cliffs and at a fork in the path, veer right and follow cairns uphill to crest **Puig des Romaní** (387m) after 1½ hours, where a superb panorama awaits.

From the summit, return to the main trail, which descends gradually along a ridge as it skirts a bluff, with the cliffs to your left falling away sharply. Squeeze through a vertiginous tunnel that burrows through the rock. Entering old coastal fortifications with gun emplacements, follow the path that skirts the knife-edge cliff face, using the fixed rope to negotiate the steepest parts, to reach the top of **Penya Rotja** (354m) after 1½ hours.

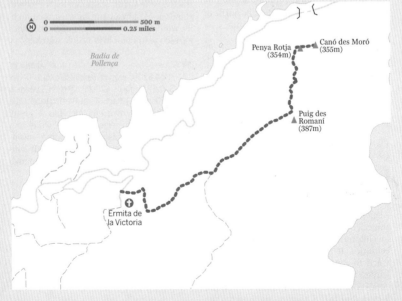

The rocky, pine-swaddled coastline of the Cap des Pinar, thrusting into the blue Mediterranean, is one of Mallorca's most rewarding hiking destinations.

Topped by a cannon, the 360-degree lookout takes in the full sweep of Mallorca's north coast, reaching across Cap des Pinar to the Badia d'Alcúdia, Pollença and Formentor.

An optional boulder-strewn scramble takes you up to the cannon atop **Canó des Moró** (355m), where you'll most probably be alone with the goats, wild rosemary and striking views across the peninsula to the cobalt waters pummelling Platja des Coll Baix far below. Retrace your steps along the same path back to Ermita de La Victòria.

WALKING TRAILS ON THE CAP DE FORMENTOR

The peninsula has various trails that lead down to pebbly beaches and inlets. The walk from **Port de Pollença** to crescent-shaped **Cala Bóquer** is signposted off a roundabout on the main road to Cap de Formentor. This valley walk, with the rocky Serra del Cavall Bernat walling off the western flank, is an easy 3km hike.

About 11km along the peninsula from Port de Pollença, trails lead off left and right from the road (there is some rough parking here) to **Cala Figuera** on the north flank and **Cala Murta** on the south. The former walk is down a bare gully to a narrow shingle beach, where the water's colours are mesmerising. The latter is through mostly wooded land to a stony beach. Each takes about 40 minutes down.

Near Cala Murta is quiet **Cala Gossalba**, reached via a shady 30-minute walk (try to park at the bay just before Km 15 and descend the trail opposite). From here you can head right to traverse cliffs to the next cove. This is the trailhead for Formentor's most memorable hike. Ascend the boulder-speck-led gully behind the cove and then follow the serpentine old military path up to the summit of 334m **Fumat** (around 1½ hours from the cove). The crag has knockout 360-degree views of the cape to the east and the Badia de Pollença to the south, with the peaks of the Tramuntana rising like shark fins to the west. From here, retrace your steps and veer left onto a trail that leads back to the road and the parking bay.

A couple of other small inlets to check out along the coast are **Cala des Caló** and **Cala En Feliu**. Walkers can also hike to or from the cape along the Camí Vell del Far, a poorly defined track that criss-crosses and at times follows the main road. At Port de Pollença you can link with the GR221 trail that runs the length of the Serra de Tramuntana.

The Pollença and Port de Pollença tourist offices can give you booklets that contain approximate trail maps, which for these walks should be sufficient.

CLIFF JUMPING IN CALA SANT VICENÇ

Jumping off a cliff may sound suicidal, but it's a thrilling summer pursuit around the ragged cliffs of Cala Sant Vicenç, where locals diving from giddy heights make it look like a piece of cake. If you plan to take the plunge, however, we highly recommend getting a guide.

Experience Mallorca (p135) guides know the rocks like the back of their hands. You'll jump off cliffs between 3m and 12m in height, which sounds easy-peasy, but don't be fooled – the moment when you leap and plunge is every bit as nerve-shattering as it is exhilarating.

vinaigrette. World flavours also shine here, from Peruvian ceviche to Thai red curry.

Ca'n Costa
MALLORCAN €€

(☑ 971 54 53 94; Carrer Sant Vicenç 14; mains €12-19; ⊙ 12.30-4pm & 7.30-11pm Wed-Mon; 🖼) It feels little has changed at this grand old house since it was built in 1594, with its beams and oil paintings still intact. There's alfresco seating for balmy days and a menu packed with Catalan and Mallorcan classics like *suquet,* a rich fish casserole, cod with *sobrassada* and roast suckling pig.

Bistro 1909
TAPAS €€

(☑ 971 53 91 92; Carrer Major 6; mains €10-19; ⊙ 11am-11pm Sun-Fri, 4.30-11pm Sat Apr-Oct) Opposite the opening to Carrer de la Cisterna, this sweet yet busy bistro with outside people-watching seating serves up fine food ferried to tables by chipper staff; expect paellas, tapas (a mixed platter for two costs €12.50), big full-on burgers, fat chips and more.

Ca'n Pere
MEDITERRANEAN €€

(☑ 971 54 52 43; www.hotelcanpere.com; Carrer d'en Serra 12; mains €8.50-22; ⊙ noon-4pm & 6-10.30pm) Another attractive stone-walled courtyard restaurant, Ca'n Pere, in the hotel of the same name, serves up fresh Mediterranean dishes such as black ravioli filled with prawns and salmon. Service can be slow when things are busy.

🛍 Shopping

Flor de Sal d'es Trenc
FOOD

(www.flordesaldestrenc.com; Carrer Major 30; ⊙ 10.30am-8pm Mon-Sat, 10am-3pm Sun) No time to go south? Taste and buy Es Trenc's famous hand-harvested sea salt here in many flavours, from rose to orange and chilli, tomato, black olive and hibiscus. The shop also stocks extra virgin olive oils, tangy organic jams from Sóller and herbal liqueurs, as well as its own wines.

ℹ Information

Tourist Office (☑ 971 54 90 22; Avinguda dels Príncep d'Espanya; ⊙ 9.30am-5pm Mon-Sat May-Oct, shorter hours rest of year) This helpful tourist office has maps, leaflets and stacks of info on Alcúdia and its surrounds.

ℹ Getting There & Away

The 351 bus from Palma to Platja de Muro calls at Alcúdia (€5.30, 45 minutes, up to 16 daily). Bus 352 connects Ca'n Picafort (€1.80, 45 minutes) with Alcúdia as often as every 15

minutes from May to October. Local service 356 connects Alcúdia with Port d'Alcúdia and Platja d'Alcúdia (€1.55, 15 minutes, every 15 minutes from May to October).

Port d'Alcúdia

POP 4850

Draped along the northeastern corner of the Badia d'Alcúdia, Port d'Alcúdia is a very busy beach-holiday centre with a more appealing waterfront, marina and fishing harbour. Dotted with palms, its gently sloping, fine-sand beach has shallow water and plenty of activities geared towards families.

◉ Sights

Cova de Sant Martí
CAVE

An otherworldly religious shrine and grotto in a 20m-deep hollow, Cova de Sant Martí dates back to the 13th century. Find it at the foot of Puig de Sant Martí crag (behind the BelleVue Club hotel); the tourist office can point you in the right direction. A pilgrimage leads to the cave on the Sunday after Easter.

Hidropark
AMUSEMENT PARK

(☑ 971 89 16 72; www.hidroparkalcudia.com; Avinguda del Tucá; adult/child 3-11yr/under 3yr €22.90/16.90/free; ⊙ 10am-5pm May-Jun & Sep-Oct, 10am-6pm Jul & Aug) Amuse the kids at this water park with slides, wave pool and infant splash area. It's about 600m inland from the beach. It's slightly cheaper to book online.

🏃 Activities

Alcudiamar Sports & Nature
WATER SPORTS

(☑ 871 57 70 17; www.sportsandnaturealcudia-mar.com; Port Turistic i Esportiu; 🖼) This water-sports specialist offers a full range of PADI courses, from day baptism courses to Advanced Open Water Diver certificates. It also arranges kayak rental and tours, sailing and windsurfing courses and boat trips to sea caves.

Tandem Mallorca
PARAGLIDING

(☑ 616 17 34 02; www.mallorcaparapente.es; tandem flight €85-150; ⊙ May-Oct) Tandem Mallorca takes you paragliding, with tandem flights for beginners. Most flights launch from 230m Puig de San Martí. There is a free pick-up service in the Alcúdia area.

Wind & Friends WATER SPORTS
(☑971 54 98 35, 661 745 414; www.windfriends.
com; Carrer de Neptú; ☺Apr-Oct) On the waterfront, next to the Hotel Sunwing, this
outfit organises sailing, windsurfing and
kitesurfing. A five-day beginners' course in
windsurfing costs €240. Boat, kayak and
stand-up paddle board rental (from €10) is
also available. A basic five-day sailing course
is €260 (children €190).

Transportes Marítimos Brisa BOATING
(☑971 54 58 11; www.tmbrisa.com; Passeig
Marítim; ☺May-Oct) Transportes Marítimos
Brisa offers catamaran trips (adult/child
€57/28.50, five hours), excursions to Platja
de Formentor (adult/child €25/12.50, four
hours) and coasts, coves and caves of east
Mallorca (adult/child €35/17.50, three hours)
plus trips to see dolphins and the sunrise
(adult/child €49/38, two hours).

Easy Rider SCOOTER HIRE
(☑606 543099, 971 54 50 57; www.easyridermobil-
ityhire.com; Playa de Muro)

🎉 Festivals & Events

Festival de Sant Pere FIESTA
(☺29 Jun) This festival celebrates the port's
patron saint. The week leading up to this
day is a time of concerts, kids shows and activities and on the big day a statue of Sant
Pere is paraded on land and sea.

🍴 Eating

The emphasis in Port d'Alcúdia is pretty
much on quantity rather than quality, but
there are a few places of real culinary worth
and certainly no shortage of restaurant options, reaching all the way down to the Platja de Muro.

Willy's Hamburger FAST FOOD €
(Carrer Juià 5; snacks & light meals €4-8; ☺8am-
2.30am; 🐕) This *snackeria* in Platja de Muro
is a hit with locals for its ultra-fresh, homemade fast food. Despite being as busy as a
beehive in summer, Juan is always ready
with a smile. Burgers are good, as is the
pepito de lomo (pork loin in a bap with garlicky aioli).

Como en Casa SPANISH €€
(☑971 54 90 33; www.restaurantcomoencasa.com;
Carrer dels Pins 4; mains €7-16; ☺6pm-midnight
Tue-Sun; 🚗🐕) Tucked down a side street
near the marina, Como en Casa always has
a good buzz and warm welcome. Snag a ta-

ble on the terrace for dishes rich in local ingredients and home-grown veg. We like the
zingy flavours in seared tuna on kiwi-mango
salad and the smoked tofu lasagne with vegetable bolognese. Tasty kids' menu too.

Miramar SEAFOOD €€
(☑971 54 52 93; www.restaurantmiramar.es; Passeig Marítim 2; mains €13-30; ☺1-3.30pm & 7-11pm
Mar-Dec; 🐕) Grab a seat on the ample terrace of this waterfront classic (there's been
a restaurant here since 1871) for one of a
broad selection of paellas or *fideuá* (a pael-
la-like noodle dish). Well-executed standard
fish dishes (sole, bream etc) are dependably
tasty, while the groaning seafood platter is
epic in scale and price (€66.50 per person).

⭐Restaurante Jardín MEDITERRANEAN €€€
(☑971 89 23 91; www.restaurantejardin.com; Carrer dels Tritons; menú degustación €85; ☺hours
vary, consult website) Chef Macarena de Castro
walks the culinary high wire at this Michelin-starred restaurant, its smart interior out
of sync with its nondescript villa facade.
Inspired by the seasons, the 11-course tasting menu brings nouvelle twists to essential
Med products, from mussels with orange
and sage to white prawn with sea meringue
– all exquisitely presented. Book ahead.

ℹ️ Information

Tourist Office (☑971 54 72 57; www.alcudia-
mallorca.com; Passeig Marítim; ☺8am-8.30pm
Mon-Fri, 8.30am-3.30pm Sat & Sun Mar-Oct) In
a booth behind the marina.

ℹ️ Getting There & Away

Boats leave for Ciutadella on the island of
Menorca from the ferry port.
   Regular buses run from here to Alcúdia (€1.55,
15 minutes) and Port de Pollença (€1.55, 25
minutes).

Cap des Pinar

From Alcúdia and Port d'Alcúdia, the phenomenally beautiful Cap des Pinar thrusts
eastward into the deep blue and, together
with Cap de Formentor away to the north,
encloses the Badia de Pollença within its
embrace. The cape bristles with Aleppo pine
woods at its eastern end as it rises to precipitous cliffs. Its walking trails are hands down
some of the most spectacular on the island.
The headland is military land and off-limits,
but the rest is well worth it.

From Alcúdia, head northeast through residential Mal Pas and Bonaire to a scenic route that stretches to Cap des Pinar. After 1.5km of winding coastal road east of Bonaire you reach the beach.

◉ Sights

★ Platja des Coll Baix   BEACH
It's a fantastic ramble to Platja des Coll Baix – and what a bay! Snug below sheer, wooded cliffs, this shimmering crescent of pale pebbles and translucent water is soul-stirring stuff. The catch: it's only accessible on foot or by boat. Come in the early morning or evening to see it at its peaceful best. From Alcúdia, it's about 8km to an open spot in the woods where you can park. Follow the purple road signs for the Fundación Yannick y Ben Jakober and keep on for another 2km.

From this spot, you could climb the south trail to Talaia d'Alcúdia, then follow the signs to Coll Baix, a fairly easy half-hour descent. The main trail will lead you to the rocks south of the beach, from where you have to scramble back around to reach Platja des Coll Baix.

Talaia d'Alcúdia   MOUNTAIN
This lovely walk is a relatively undemanding 30- to 40-minute hike through the pine trees to this astonishing viewpoint with 360-degree wide-angle views over the surrounding sea. From the Ermita de La Victòria, take the road up in to the pines behind the Mirador de la Victòria and follow the signs. The Talai d'Alcúdia – a 16th-century lookout tower – is a final scramble up some boulders at the top, where the views are simply awesome.

Ses Tres Creus   VIEWPOINT
On the way up to the Talaia d'Alcúdia or the Puig de Romani and around five minutes from Ermita de La Victòria, keep an eye out for Ses Tres Creus, three crosses among the trees that overlook the Badia de Pollença.

Platja s'Illot   BEACH
A curtain of pines rises behind Platja s'Illot, a pretty cove beloved of locals where crystal-clear water and an islet makes it great for a spot of snorkelling. You'll need to bring a towel to lay on as there are no sunbeds, but there is a cafe for beachside snacking and the views ranging across to Cap de Formentor are something else. Just don't expect to have them all to yourself on a summer's day.

✕ Eating

With such beautiful panoramas out to sea, it's hardly surprising there's a particularly fine option for a meal on Cap des Pinar.

★ Mirador de La Victòria   MALLORCAN €€
(☑971 54 71 73; www.miradordelavictoria.com; Carretera Cap des Pinar; mains €7.50-25.50; ☺1-3.30pm & 7pm-midnight Tue-Sun May-Oct, shorter hours rest of year; P ⊕) Climb the steps through pine forest past the Ermita de La Victòria to reach this gorgeous rustic restaurant, with no-nonsense home cooking and amazing views out over the treetops towards Cap de Formentor. Besides local dishes like *caracoles* (snails) and *lomo con col* (pork loin wrapped in cabbage), the grilled fish and rice dishes are also good.

The restaurant makes one of the best *ali olis* (garlic mayonnaise) on the island. You can drive here as well, just head up the winding road till you can go no further.

ⓘ Getting There & Away

The 356B bus (€1.55) runs from Alcúdia to Bonaire three times a day, but no further than that. By far the best way to reach the Ermita de La Victòria and the start of the walk is to drive up the winding road to the top.

SOUTH OF ALCÚDIA

Ca'n Picafort

Ca'n Picafort, and its southern extension, Son Bauló, is a package-tour frontier town, somewhat raw and raggedy. But the beaches are pretty good and some interesting archaeological sites dot the surrounding terrain. The main resort backs on to Platja de Santa Margalida, a crowded shallow beach with turquoise water.

For a wilder feel, swing southwest of town to Platja de Son Real. This almost 5km stretch of coast, with snippets of sandy strands in among the rock points, is backed only by low dunes, scrub and bushland dense with Aleppo pines.

◉ Sights & Activities

★ Finca Pública de Son Real   FARM
(adult/child under 12yr €3/free; ☺10am-5pm) Much of the area between the coast and the Ma12 has been converted into the Finca Pública de Son Real. Its main entrance is just

south of the Km 18 milestone on the Ma12, and the former farm buildings host an information office for those who wish to walk the property's several coastal trails. There's also a museum zooming in on traditional Mallorcan rural life.

Parc Natural de S'Albufera   PARK
(☑971 892 250; www.mallorcaweb.net/salbufera; ☺visitor centre 9am-6pm Apr-Sep, 9am-5pm Oct-Mar) FREE The 688-hectare Parc Natural de S'Albufera, west of the Ma12 between Port d'Alcúdia and Ca'n Picafort, is prime birdwatching territory, with 303 recorded species (more than 80% of recorded Balearic species), 64 of which breed within the park's boundaries. More than 10,000 birds overwinter here, among them both residents and migrants. Entrance to the park is free, but permits must be obtained from the visitor centre, which is a 1km walk from the entrance gates on the main road.

The so-called **Gran Canal** at the heart of the park was designed to channel the water out to sea. The five-arched Pont de Sa Roca bridge was built over it in the late 19th century to ease travel between Santa Margalida and Alcúdia. The park is considered a Ramsar Wetland of National Importance and, in addition to the bird species, around 400 plant species have been catalogued here. In spring, wildflowers bloom, bringing vibrant splashes of colour.

The visitor centre can provide information on the park and its birdlife, and is the trailhead for several walks through the protected wetlands. From here, 14km of signposted trails fan out across the park. There are four marked itineraries, from short 725m (30 minutes) routes to 11.5km (3½ hours) trails, two of which can be covered by bike. Of the six timber birdwatching observatories, or *aguaits* – come inside and watch in silence – some are better than others. You'll see lots of wading birds in action from the Bishop I and II *aguaits* on the north side of the Gran Canal.

Buses between Ca'n Picafort and Alcúdia stop by a car park near the park entrance.

Platja de Muro   BEACH
Around 5km south of Port d'Alcúdia (on the bus line to Ca'n Picafort), Platja de Muro is a long and attractive stretch of sand, with terrific views of the Badia d'Alcúdia. The setting, with pale, soft sand backed by pines and the dunes of the Parc Natural de S'Albufera, is a winner. The water is shallow and azure, but the crowds can be intense. The beach is named after the delightful hilltop town of Muro, around 8km off to the west.

Necròpolis de Son Real   ARCHAEOLOGICAL SITE
On the sea about 10 minutes' walk southeast of Platja de Son Bauló, this impressive necropolis appears to have been a Talayotic cemetery with 110 tombs (in which the remains of more than 300 people were found). The tombs have the shape of mini-*talayots* (ancient watchtowers) and date as far back as the 7th century BC. Some suggest this was a commoners graveyard.

Illot dels Porros   ARCHAEOLOGICAL SITE
Not far from Necròpolis de Son Real, the island called Illot dels Porros also contains remains of an ancient necropolis. It's a fairly easy swim for the moderately fit.

Es Figueral de Son Real   ARCHAEOLOGICAL SITE
From the Finca Pública de Son Real, one trail leads through a largely abandoned fig plantation to the overgrown Talayotic ruins of Es Figueral de Son Real. This settlement dates at least to 1000 BC and consists of several buildings that you'll need considerable imagination to decipher.

Experience Mallorca   ADVENTURE SPORTS
(☑687 35 89 22; www.experience-mallorca.com; Avinguda Josep Trias 1, Vent-i-Mar Apts; activities €45-75; ☺Mar-Nov) If you want to crank up the thrill factor a notch or two, head for this adventure specialist, who will raise your pulse with activities such as canyoning, cliff jumping, coasteering, caving, abseiling, trekking and rock climbing.

ⓘ Information

Tourist Office (☑971 85 07 58; Plaça Cervantes; ☺8.30am-1.30pm & 5-7.30pm Mon-Fri Easter-Oct) This helpful tourist office is located close to the beach.

ⓘ Getting There & Away

Bus 390 runs from Palma to Ca'n Picafort (€6.50, 1¾ hours, four to seven daily). Bus 352 is the main service between Ca'n Picafort and Port de Pollença (€2.60, 1¼ hours), via Port d'Alcúdia (€1.60, 45 minutes).

Son Serra de Marina
POP 500

Spreading 5km east along the coast from Son Bauló, Son Serra de Marina keeps the mood low-key and relaxed. On its southeast edge starts the long Platja de Sa Canova, a 2km stretch of quiet beach, backed by dunes and pine trees, which attracts the odd nudist and stretches to S'Estanyol. The stiff breezes and waves lure kite- and windsurfers.

Some buses on the Palma–Ca'n Picafort route continue to Son Serra de Marina.

Colònia de Sant Pere

Named after the patron saint of fishers (St Peter), this peaceful former farming village is an antidote to the tourist resorts to the west, but there's limited history to explore. The huddle of houses has expanded beyond the central square and church to accommodate a small populace that seems to be on permanent vacation.

In the centre of town you'll find the **Platja de la Colònia de Sant Pere**. Nearby is the small marina and fishing port. About 2.5km west, you'll reach **Platja de Sa Canova**, a fine and tranquil sweep of sand that reaches all the way to Son Serra de Marina. From the village of S'Estanyol the only way to Sa Canova is on foot, but it's not a long walk as S'Estanyol is almost on the beach's edge.

✖ Eating

With long vistas out to sea and a regular stream of visitors, there's no shortage of restaurants running along the water's edge on Passeig Marítim.

Sa Xarxa   SEAFOOD €€
(📞 971 58 92 51; www.sa-xarxa.com; Passeig; mains €12-20; ☺ noon-11pm Tue-Sun Mar-Oct) Along the waterfront you'll find tables set under the tamarind trees, with incredible sea and sunset views. Seafood is the big deal, especially the catch of the day, done simply in a salty crust. Everything, such as the carpaccio of angler fish with lime-yoghurt, gets the delicate touch. Inside, it's largely wood, with model ships, walls crammed with pictures and panama hats hanging from pegs.

Look out for the bright blue Renault 4 with Sa Xarxa livery on the waterfront.

ⓘ Getting There & Away

Bus 481 runs from Colònia de Sant Pere to Artà (€2, 25 minutes) three or four times a day from Monday to Friday.

Betlem

If you head 3km northeast on the Ma3331 along the coast from Colònia de Sant Pere, you run into dozy Betlem. Though not much goes on here and there's little history in the (largely villa) settlement, it's an entry point to several hikes and a trail to Cap Ferrutx at the tip.

⊙ Sights

Ermita de Betlem   CHURCH
At the top of a steep climb and approached through a row of cypresses, this charming small church of stone dates to the early 19th century and contains a magnificent painted vault. The true appeal of the church lies in the splendid hike that is required to reach it.

ⓘ Getting There & Away

The L481 bus runs from Betlem to Colònia de Sant Pere four times a day between Monday and Friday. The service requires reservation by telephone the day before travel by calling 📞 617 36 53 65.

The Interior

Best Places to Eat

➡ Celler Es Grop (p145)

➡ Ca Na Toneta (p143)

➡ Joan Marc Restaurant (p142)

➡ Es Celler (p148)

➡ Celler Ca'n Amer (p142)

Top Sights

➡ Els Calderers (p147)

➡ Coves de Campanet (p144)

➡ Ermita de Santa Magdalena (p142)

➡ Museu Arqueològic de Son Fornés (p147)

Why Go?

Mallorca's serene interior is the alter ego to the island's coastal buzz. Although the beaches are rarely more than an hour's drive, the interior feels light years away, with its vineyards, hilltop monasteries and meadows stippled with olive, almond and carob trees. It's here that the island's rural heart beats strongly in church-topped villages, where locals fiercely guard their traditions – and throw some of Mallorca's most spirited fiestas (festivals).

When to Go

Unlike the coast, inland Mallorca tends to remain open for business year-round: Palma folk like nothing better than escaping from city life in the depths of winter (shallow as they are) and finding a rural retreat for a heartwarming meal or a quiet night's sleep. The last third of the year is the rainiest (although there hasn't been much of that in recent years) and average lows only drop to 8°C or 9°C in January. High summer, on the other hand, is reliably sweltering.

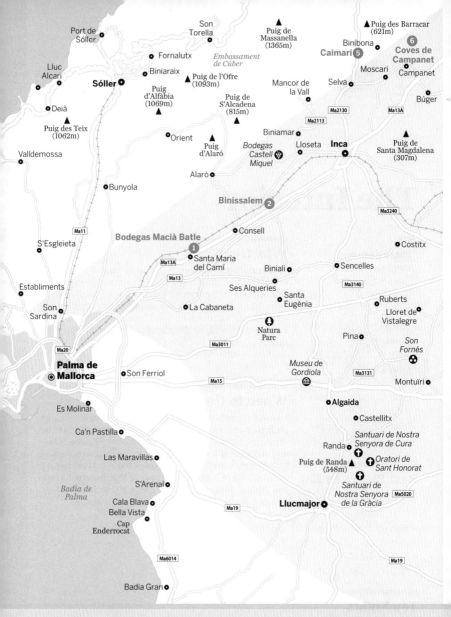

The Interior Highlights

1 Bodegas Macià Batle
(p140) Touring the vineyards
and finishing with a glass at
this much-lauded winery.

2 Festes de la Verema
(p141) Throwing grapes

and cavorting with devils at
Binissalem's annual harvest
festival.

**3 Santuari de Sant
Salvador** (p149) Taking

divine inspiration from the
views at this hilltop hermitage.

4 Els Calderers (p147)
Seeing how the rural señors
lorded over the land at this
mansion-museum.

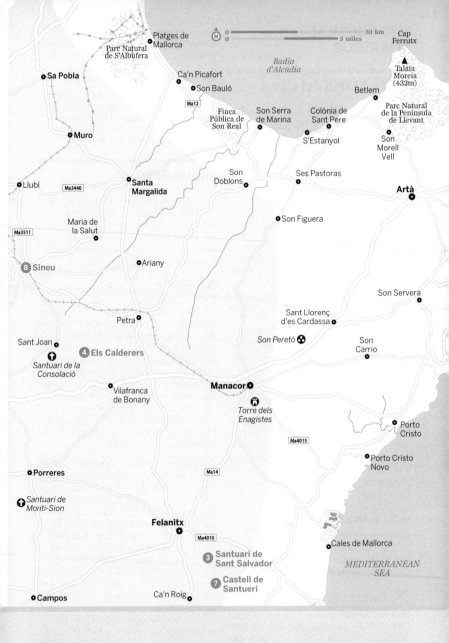

THE CENTRAL CORRIDOR

Santa Maria del Camí

POP 6685

Santa Maria del Camí is an attractive little town, with a couple of pretty squares, but it's not exactly exciting. If coming from Palma, as you roll into town the Ma13a widens to become bar-lined Plaça dels Hostals, often populated by flocks of refuelling cyclists.

◉ Sights

Bodegas Macià Batle   WINERY
(☑971 14 00 14; www.maciabatle.com; Camí de Coanegra; ☉9am-6.30pm Mon-Sat; ℗) One of Mallorca's biggest names in wine, having used the area's 300 annual days of sun to produce great grapes since 1858, Bodegas Macià Batle is based just outside of central Santa Maria. Tastings are free, or you can arrange a one-hour tour of the vineyard and production facilities, finishing with four wines and nibbles (€10, five per day March to October; fewer in quiet months). You can also admire their labels, all designed by renowned contemporary artists.

Convent de Nostra Senyora de la Soledat   CONVENT
(Plaça dels Hostals 30) The centrepiece of Plaça dels Hostals is the 17th-century Convent de Nostra Senyora de la Soledat, aka Can Conrado. If the main doors happen to be swung open, you can peer into the magnificent front courtyard, while a peek into the rear gardens can be had around the corner from Carrer Llarg.

✦ Festivals & Events

Festes de Santa Margalida   FIESTA
(☉Jul) Held over almost three weeks in July, though the key day is 20 July; concerts, traditional dances and communal meals.

✖ Eating

Moli des Torrent   MALLORCAN €€€
(☑971 14 05 03; www.molidestorrent.de; Carretera de Bunyola 75; mains €20-26; ☉1-3pm & 7.30-10.30pm Fri-Tue; ℗) The area's most atmospheric restaurant, set in a stone windmill on the country road leading north of Santa Maria to Bunyola. Sit in the vaulted interior or on the pretty patio for delightful home cooking that makes the most of the seasons, from

Mallorcan *gambas* with *tumbet* (essentially prawns with ratatouille) to veal and sweetbreads with chanterelle risotto. Book ahead.

ⓘ Getting There & Away

Santa Maria is around halfway along the Palma–Inca train line, a stop on all three island lines. Fares in either direction cost €2.25, journey times range between 18 and 23 minutes, and there are frequent services every day.

Binissalem

POP 7850

The Romans brought their winemaking nous to Binissalem some 2000 years ago and this handsome little town at the foot of the Tramuntana, its long streets lined with stone buildings and orange trees, has been wedded to the grape ever since.

◉ Sights

Celler Tianna Negre   WINERY
(☑971 88 68 26; www.tiannanegre.com; Camí des Mitjans; ☉cellar door 9am-6pm Mon-Fri Mar-Oct, to 4pm Nov-Feb, tours by prior arrangement; ℗) ⚲ With 20 hectares of biological plantings, architect-designed buildings and sincere commitments to sustainability, Tianna Negre is at the bleeding edge of winemaking. Happily the results – made from manto negro, prensal blanc and other varieties – are excellent. Tours and tastings start at €6 for a sample of three wines, and run to €40 for three hours, tapas and premium wines.

Casa-Museu Llorenç Villalonga   MUSEUM
(☑971 88 60 14; www.fundaciocasamuseu.cat; Carrer de Bonaire 25; ☉10am-2pm Mon-Fri plus 4-8pm Tue & Sat) FREE Binissalem's prosperity as a wine making town was reflected in the construction of several notable 18th- and 19th-century mansions. One that has been well preserved is Can Sabater, a country residence for the Catalan writer Llorenç Villalonga and now the Casa-Museu Llorenç Villalonga. Inside, note the 18th-century wine vats and room set aside for the crushing of grapes underfoot, and the many artefacts of the author's life, including his Civil War diary. Summer concerts are held in the garden.

Ca'n Novell   WINERY
(☑971 51 13 10; Carrer de Bonaire 17; ☉8am-1pm & 3-8pm Mon-Fri, 8.30am-2pm Sat) Locals fill their own bottles (€1.5 to €3 per litre) from huge, 18th-century vats at this delightfully old-school winery. Made of olive wood and held

together by sturdy rings of oak, these grand old barrels were a standard feature of cellars and mansions across much of this part of the island. They also bottle extra-virgin olive oil and hold 'micro-theatre' and other cultural events in the evocative space, heady with vinous fumes.

José Luis Ferrer WINERY
(☑971 51 10 50; www.vinosferrer.com; Carrer del Conquistador 103; guided tours from €10; ⊙10am-7pm Mon-Fri, 10am-6pm Sat, 10am-2pm Sun Apr-Oct, closed Sun Nov-Mar) One of Mallorca's largest and most celebrated wineries, José Luis Ferrer, was launched in 1931. To get a better insight into the wine making process, hook onto one of the 45-minute guided tours, which start at 11am bin and 4.30pm most days, and include a three-wine tasting. More extensive (and expensive) tours are offered; call ahead to book.

★ Festivals & Events

Festes de la Verema FIESTA
(⊙September; 🎉) This vintage festival, renowned for its climactic grape fight, is actually a week-long bash of wine tastings, concerts, readings, exhibitions and a wild nighttime *correfoc* (fire run), with fire-breathing devils dashing through the streets to the crashing of firework displays. But of course it's the grape fight that gets most people's juices flowing.

✕ Eating

The restaurants and bars dotted around the Plaça Església are fine places to sample the local wine over a few tapas.

Singló MEDITERRANEAN €€
(☑971 87 05 99; Plaça de l'Església 5; mains €11-15; ⊙1-4pm & 8pm-midnight) Overlook the slight cafeteria feel: you can eat well at Singló. It offers some enticing Mallorcan dishes, such as *porcella rostida* (roast suckling pig, in winter) and *bacallà a la mallorquina* (cod prepared with tomato and potato). It also has an extensive wine list and Italian dishes such as *pasta alla arrabiata*.

ℹ Getting There & Away

Binissalem is on all three train lines between Palma (€2.15, 20 to 30 minutes) and Inca (€2.15, eight minutes) with frequent services in both directions every day. Be aware that morning T1 express services from Palma don't stop here.

Santa Eugènia

POP 1638

Amid the quiet back roads south of Binissalem is the pretty, steeply layered town of Santa Eugènia, home to three picturesque 18th-century windmills, and lovely views from the hilltop on which it's perched.

◉ Sights

Natura Parc ZOO
(☑971 14 40 78; www.naturaparc.net; Carretera de Sineu Km 15.4; adult/child 3-12yr/child under 3yr €15/9/free; ⊙10am-3pm; 🅿) Kids will love the Natura Parc, a zoo and sanctuary with everything from kangaroos and Himalayan takins to flamingos and black panthers prancing around. You can enter the bat cave, and get up close to the adorable lemurs.

✕ Eating

A few cosy local bars and restaurants are the extent of the choice in the town proper, but *finca* (farm) restaurants in the farming land below extend your options.

★ Sa Torre Restaurant SPANISH €€€
(☑971 14 40 11; www.sa-torre.com; 4-course tasting menu €40; ⊙8-10.30pm Tue-Sat; 🅿) Run by the fabulously hospitable López Pinto Ivars family, this wonderful country *restaurante* makes great use of a high-vaulted 15th-century cellar, complete with stone columns and giant wine casks. The four-course tasting menu changes weekly, but expect such well-prepared dishes as cod gratin with aioli and chicken filled with plums and spinach.

ℹ Getting There & Away

Ideally you'll have your own transport to explore this quiet pocket of Mallorca. If not, the 311 bus connects Santa Eugènia with Santa Maria del Cami (€1.50, 15 minutes, up to nine daily), which is on all three of the island's train services.

Inca

POP 30,651

There are two main reasons for coming to Inca, Mallorca's third city – it has some of the finest traditional *celler* restaurants on the island, and it's at the heart of the Mallorcan leather industry: globally coveted Spanish shoe brands Camper and Farrutx took their first baby steps here. Otherwise, it offers only modest attractions to the traveller.

◉ Sights

★ **Ermita de Santa Magdalena** VIEWPOINT
(☑ 971 50 40 08; Puig Santa Magdalena; ⊙ church 11.30am-7pm May-Oct, to 4pm rest of year) FREE
For extraordinary views, make the pilgrimage to this hermitage with 13th-century origins, which sits astride the **Puig de Santa Magdalena** (307m). From the little chapel, your gaze will take in the full sweep of the plains to the Serra de Tramuntana and the Alcúdia and Pollença bays. It's a terrific starting point for hikes, providing you've brought sturdy footwear. Pilgrims ascend to the chapel in numbers on Diumenge de l'Àngel (Angel Sunday, a week after Easter Sunday).

Claustre de Sant Domingo CONVENT
(☑ 871 91 45 00; Plaça de Sant Domingo; ⊙ 8am-3pm & 4-8pm Mon-Fri, 10am-1.30pm Sat) FREE
The last Dominican convent to be founded in Mallorca, Claustre de Sant Domingo is notable for its baroque architecture. Attached to the 17th-century convent-church of the same name, it was built in 1730, used as a prison in the Spanish Civil War, and is now a cultural centre, hosting musical and dramatic performances, exhibitions and the like.

Església de Santa Maria Major CHURCH
(Plaça de Santa Maria Major; ⊙ 10.30am-1pm Thu, May-Oct) Inca's baroque church stands proud on Plaça de Santa Maria Major. Its greatest treasure is a Gothic retable of Santa Maria d'Inca, painted in 1373 by the early Mallorcan artists Joan Daurer.

★彡 Festivals & Events

Dijous Bo CULTURAL
(Holy Thursday; ⊙ 3rd Thurs in Nov) This is the town's biggest shindig, with processions, livestock competitions, sports and concerts.

✕ Eating

A peculiarity of Inca is its *cellers*, basement restaurants in some of the oldest buildings in the town centre.

★ **Celler Ca'n Amer** MALLORCAN €
(☑ 971 50 12 61; www.celler-canamer.es; Carrer de la Pau 139; mains €16-18, lunch menu €24; ⊙ 1-4pm & 7.30-11pm Mon-Sat, 1-4pm Sun; P)
Refinements to Mallorcan classics are the hallmark of Tomeu Torrens, who slings the pans at this lively *celler*, rustically charming with its wooden beams and huge wine

barrels. The house speciality is lamb shoulder stuffed with eggplant and *sobrassada* (paprika-spiced cured pork sausage), but the suckling pig with spot-on crackling, and seafood options such as stuffed courgette are equally delicious.

Joan Marc Restaurant MEDITERRANEAN €€
(☑ 971 50 08 04; www.joanmarcrestaurant.com; Plaça del Blanquer 10; mains/menús €12-16/32-50; ⊙ 1-3.30pm Tue-Sun & 8-10.30pm Tue-Sat; closed Jan; ✔) A total contrast to Inca's dark and traditional *cellers* is this light, imaginative restaurant. The minimalist decor is softened by nature-themed design touches like tree trunk coat hangers and almond shells. Sunny, herby flavours shine in Joan Marc's deft cooking: perhaps wild *corvina* (fish) with garlic soup, ham and olives, or roasted aubergine with house-made *sobrassada* and Mahon cheese.

Celler Ca'n Ripoll MALLORCAN €€
(☑ 971 50 00 24; www.restaurantcanripoll.com; Carrer de Jaume Armengol 4; mains €14-18; ⊙ noon-4pm & 7.30-11.30pm Mon-Sat, noon-4pm Sun) Delve down to this enormous, cathedral-like 18th-century *celler*, with a high-beamed ceiling resting on a series of stone arches. On the menu are hearty island specialities like roast suckling pig and cod with *sobrassada*. It's not quite valet parking, but they can arrange a place to park your bike.

Celler Sa Travessa MALLORCAN €€
(☑ 971 50 00 49; Carrer de Murta 16; mains €15-17; ⊙ 10am-11pm Sat-Thu) With a chattering indoor fountain, and every nook crammed with Mallorcan rural emphemera, this *celler* is big on old-school atmosphere, as you'd expect from a place in business since 1878. The menu is all Mallorcan standards, from rabbit with onion to *llengua amb tàperes* (tongue with capers), suckling kid and a good variety of Mediterranean fish, including red mullet and swordfish.

🔒 Shopping

ReCamper SHOES
(☑ 971 88 82 33; www.camper.com; Carrer Cuartel 91, Polígon Industrial; ⊙ 10am-8pm Mon-Sat) Snag a bargain at this factory outlet, which does a brisk trade in seconds and end of lines.

Mercat d'Inca MARKET
(⊙ 8am-1.30pm Thu) Sprawling over most of the town centre, Inca's Thursday market is one of the biggest on the island, with

hundreds of stalls doing a brisk trade in everything from honey and herbs to ceramics, flowers, fabrics and fruit and veg. Local leather is wheeled out in massive fashion in the shape of jackets, bags and shoes.

Barrats SHOES
(☑ 971 50 42 07; www.barrats1890.com; Avinguda del General Luque 480; ⊙10am-8pm Mon-Fri, 10am-2pm Sat) Barrats has been making shoes since the days of Queen Victoria. Its flagship store also sells jackets and luggage.

ⓘ Getting There & Away

If you're not driving down the Ma13 motorway from Palma, get the train along the same route (€3.25, 30 minutes, frequent services).

Lloseta
POP 5639
Perfectly poised between the foothills of the Tramuntana and the open country of the interior, Lloseta is a sweet, ochre-hued town, with one of the top wineries on the island. It's at its photogenic best from late January to early March, when the almond trees burst into puffballs of pinkish white blossom. In early June it stages a fair in Plaça d'Espanya with local shoe manufacturers.

◉ Sights

Bodegas Castell Miquel WINERY
(☑ 971 51 06 98; www.castellmiquel.com; Carretera Alaró-Lloseta Km 8.7; wine tasting €5, 2hr winery tour & tasting €15; ⊙noon-7pm Mon-Fri & 11am-2pm Sat Apr-Oct, shorter hours rest of year) About 1.5km west of Lloseta on the road to Alaró is the German-owned and prize-winning Bodegas Castell Miquel. You can't miss the place – it looks like a little white castle. Besides wines like the 'Stairway to Heaven' cabernet sauvignon and 'Pearls of an Angel' cava, the German pharmaceutical professor who runs it, Dr Michael Popp, has also developed a red-wine pill, Resveroxan, that supposedly contributes to a longer and healthier life. Tours and tastings must be booked ahead.

✖ Eating

Celler Ca'n Carrossa MALLORCAN €€
(☑ 971 51 40 23; Carrer Nou 28; 5-course tasting menu €32; ⊙1-3.30pm & 7-11pm) Sit inside by the exposed stone walls or opt for the garden at this converted 18th-century house. What's on the five-course tasting menu depends on

the whim of the chef, Joan Abrines, but the food, which draws on old recipes and over a century of the one family's hospitality, is superb.

ⓘ Getting There & Away

Lloseta is on all three of Mallorca's train lines, lying between Palma (€3.05, 25 minutes, frequent) and Inca (€1.60, five minutes, frequent). Do be careful your morning train from Palma isn't a T1 express, which shoots past Lloseta.

Caimari
POP 747
Where fields of almonds, olives and carob yield to the foothills of the Serra de Tramuntana, and sheep-bells ring to the munching of wind-fallen figs, this gorgeous little town quietly goes about its business. Travellers are increasingly switching on to Caimari's manifest charms, but the locals seem to take it in their stride, and the rhythm of their lives doesn't seem to have changed much.

✖ Eating

★**Ca Na Toneta** MALLORCAN €€€
(☑ 971 51 52 26; www.canatoneta.com; Carrer Horitzó 21; menu €45; ⊙8-11pm in summer, 8.30-11pm Fri-Sun plus 1.30-4pm Sat & Sun in winter) Making loving use of the fruits of local producers, and what they grow themselves, Ca Na Toneta is an exceptional country restaurant that invites diners to linger over six courses – whatever the chef has created for the day's degustation.

🍷 Drinking & Nightlife

Sa Ruta Verda CAFE
(☑ 636 681091; www.ruta-verda.com; Carrer Nuestra Senora Virgen del Lluc 62; ⊙9am-6pm Feb-Nov; 🐾) Beloved of the many cyclists that pedal through this part of the island, gearing themselves up for the climb through the Tramuntana, Sa Ruta Verda pumps out coffee, juices, *pa amb oli* (bread with oil) and homemade energy bars with enthusiasm.

ⓘ Getting There & Away

It's nice to travel under your own steam if you want to fully explore these quieter parts of the islandIf you're reliant on buses, the 330 connects Caimari with Palma (€3.65, one hour, two daily) while the 332 goes to Inca (€1.50, 15 minutes, up to five daily).

Campanet

POP 2524

Set above a beautiful stretch of little-visited countryside quilted with orchards and sheep-grazed meadows, Campanet is an appealing village, worth a brief detour. The town's central square, Plaça Major, is dominated by a looming Gothic church, but the surrounding cafes always seem busier than the ill-attended Mass.

⊙ Sights

Coves de Campanet　　　　　　CAVE
(www.covesdecampanet.com; Camí de ses Coves; adult/child 5-10 yr/under 5yr €13.50/7/free; ⊙10am-6.30pm) An eerie forest of wax-like stalactites and stalagmites, the Coves de Campanet aren't as flashy as some of Mallorca's other cave systems, and are perhaps more authentic for it. There are guided tours every 45 minutes and visits last just under an hour. Scientists find these caves especially interesting as they're home to a local species of blind, flesh-eating beetles. Find them 3km north of town, and if driving on the Palma-Sa Pobla motorway, take exit 37.

✖ Eating

A handful of welcoming, good-value cafes and restaurants clusters around Plaça Major and along Carrer Llorenç Riber.

Ca'n Calco　　　　　MALLORCAN €€
(☑971 51 52 60; www.cancalco.com; Carrer Campanet 1, Moscari; mains €16, menús €15-32; ⊙7-10pm late-Jan–early Nov) Sitting 3km southwest of Campanet is the restaurant of Hotel Ca'n Calco, where dinner is an intimate affair on a poolside terrace. Alongside *pa amb oli* (bread with oil) and hefty meat plates, the emphasis is on seafood and, with its own boat in Badia d'Alcúdia, the catch couldn't be fresher.

❶ Getting There & Away

Ideally you need your own transport to reach the best of what Campanet and surrounds have to offer. Otherwise, the 333 bus links Campanet with Inca (€2.70, 20 minutes, nine per day).

Sineu

POP 3612

Once a centre of kingly power, now a quietly grand stone settlement mounting a prominence in the central Mallorcan plain, Sineu is one of the most engaging of the island's inland towns. It's also one of the oldest – a local legend traces the town's origins back to Roman Sinium, while the link to the Islamic settlement of Sixneu is less tenuous. Less ambiguous is the antiquity of its two traditional rural fairs, one weekly, one annual, both dating to the early 14th century.

⊙ Sights

Església de Santa Maria　　　CHURCH
(Plaça Sant Marc) Rebuilt after a calamitous fire in 1505, this sombre Gothic church, with its detached campanile, is Sineu's most significant, and the heart of the town. It houses a small museum of medieval pottery that opens when the weekly market takes over Sa Plaça, every Wednesday morning.

Sa Plaça　　　　　　SQUARE
At Sineu's heart is Sa Plaça, a busy square fronted by several bars and restaurants, plus the crumbling sandstone, late-Gothic facade of the 16th-century Església de Santa Maria.

Convent de la Concepció　　CONVENT
(Carrer del Palau 17) Between 1309 and 1349, this was the site of the Mallorcan kings' second palace (after Palma), making Sineu the de facto capital of rural Mallorca. In 1583 it was given to the Order of the Immaculate Conception, who rebuilt extensively in the 17th century, and still live here today. A two-minute stroll southwest of Sa Plaça, the convent has a *torno,* a small revolving door through which you can receive pastries made by the nuns, in return for a few euros.

Plaça des Fossar　　　　SQUARE
On Plaça des Fossar, a statue honours Francisco Alomar, a Sineu-born professional cyclist who died in 1955; it has something of a cult status among visiting cyclists.

Convent dels Mínims　　　CONVENT
(Ajuntament; Carrer de Sant Francesc) The town hall is housed in this 17th-century baroque convent, confiscated from the Minims in the 19th century. You can generally wander in any time to admire the somewhat neglected cloister. One block west is a beautiful example of a waymarking cross, the 1585 Renaissance **Creu dels Morts** (Cross of the Dead).

✦ Festivals & Events

Sa Fira　　　　　FAIR
(Plaça des Fossar; ⊙1st Sun May) Sineu's annual Sa Fira is a major agricultural spring fair

held on the first Sunday of every May, and dating to 1318.

Festa del Siurell   FIESTA
(Llubí) The little town of Llubí is worth visiting on the Saturday before the Tuesday of Carnaval. The Festa del Siurell involves townsfolk dressing up as *siurells*, traditional Mallorcan ceramic whistles. That night, a big *siurell* is burned in effigy in Plaça de l'Església, dominated by the outsized Església de Sant Feliu.

Fira de Sant Tomás   CULTURAL
(🕙 2nd Sun Dec) In the depths of winter, the Fira de Sant Tomás features the annual *matanza* (pig slaughter). It's one for the sausage-fanciers, not for the faint-hearted.

✖ Eating

Beyond the more generic tapas bars in the main squares, Sineu has some excellent Mallorcan restaurants, worth seeking out.

Celler Es Grop   MALLORCAN €€
(🖉 971 52 01 87; Carrer Major 18; mains €14-18; 🕙 9.30am-4pm & 7-11pm Tue-Sun) Watch your step as you descend into this cheerful, white-washed 18th-century cellar, lined with huge old wine vats and other historical ephemera. Galician cuisine vies with Mallorcan favourites on the meat-heavy menu – the roast spring lamb and rice dishes can be fervently recommended. It's around 100m northeast of Sa Plaça.

Sa Fàbrica   MALLORCAN €€
(🖉 971 52 06 21; Carrer Estació 1; mains €11-18; 🕙 noon-4pm & 7-11pm Wed-Mon; 🅿) Most come for the seafood, steaks and brochettes of Mallorcan pork, served sizzling hot from the grill at this convivial restaurant, housed in a former carpet factory. The lamb shoulder and rice dishes are also top-notch. Pep the owner keeps everything ticking over, and there's a pleasant terrace for summer dining.

🛍 Shopping

Sineu Market   MARKET
(🕙 8am-1pm Wed) One of rural Mallorca's most venerable traditions, Sineu's weekly market has taken over the town centre every Wednesday morning since 1306. Spreading out from Sa Plaça and down to the Plaça des Fossar, it sells livestock, leathergoods, ceramics, food and much more from all over the island, while the surrounding bars and cafes do a merry trade.

ℹ Getting There & Away

T3-line trains call at Sineu from Palma (€3.15, 45 minutes, regular) and Manacor (€2.25, 20 minutes, regular). The station is about 100m east of Plaça des Fossar.

Sa Pobla & Muro

Sa Pobla, a grid-street rural centre and the end of the (railway) line from Palma, is in Mallorca's agricultural heartland. It has only a few attractions, but gets a shot of cultural adrenaline during several lively festivals, and the weekly Sunday market. Five kilometres south across the potato flats, Muro is a dignified hilltop town with a handsome church at its apex.

⊙ Sights

Bodegas Crestatx   WINERY
(🖉 971 54 07 41; Carrer de Joan Sindic 49; 🕙 9am-1pm Mon-Fri) FREE One of the longest-standing winemakers on the island (going strong since 1898) Bodegas Crestatx is well worth a visit. Not only are the wines excellent, but presses, wine-pumps and other machinery from the 19th century are on display.

Can Planes   MUSEUM
(Carrer d'Antoni Maura 6; adult/child €2/free; 🕙 10am-2pm Tue-Sun & 4-8pm Tue-Sat) The handsome manor house Can Planes contains the **Museu d'Art Contemporani**, a changing display of works by Mallorcan and foreign artists residing on the island. Upstairs, the **Museu de Sa Jugueta Antiga** is a touching collection of old toys, some with a bullfighting theme.

Església de Sant Joan Baptista   CHURCH
(🖉 971 53 70 22; Carrer Bisbe Ramon de Torrella 1) Muro boasts an outsized parish church, a brooding, early-17th-century Gothic sandstone creation reminiscent of Sineu's main church. Its detached campanile is the town's most prominent landmark, and can be seen for miles across the plain.

⭐ Festivals & Events

Festes de Sant Antoni Abat   CULTURAL
(🕙 16-17 Jan) This festival has a little bit of everything with processions, fireworks, folk music, dancing, costumed devils and blessings for work animals. Pre-festival activities run for a week, but the night of the 16th is the liveliest.

Mallorca Jazz Festival MUSIC

(☉Aug) Jazz comes to Sa Pobla every August for the Mallorca Jazz Festival. Shows kick off in the Sala Es Cavallets, on Plaça Major Sa Pobla, at 10.30pm, and cost €5.

❶ Getting There & Away

From Palma you can take the T2 (Tren Sa Pobla) to both Sa Pobla and Muro (€4.10, around one hour, up to 17 services per day); the same service connects both towns with Inca (€2.15, 15 to 20 minutes).

THE SOUTHEAST

Algaida

POP 5410 / ELEV 201M

A typically sober and dignified central Mallorcan town, Algaida has few sights beyond the gothic **Església de Sant Pere i Sant Pau** and nearby **Església de la Mare de Déu de la Pau de Castellitx**. Its greatest attractions are the Festes de Sant Honorat (16 January) and the Festa de Sant Jaume (25 July). On both occasions, *cossiers* dance for an appreciative local audience. The origins of the *cossiers* and their dances are disputed, but always a group of dancers, six men and one woman, plus the devil, perform various pieces that end in defeat for the fiend.

◉ Sights

Museu de Gordiola MUSEUM

(☎971 66 50 46; www.gordiola.com; Carretera Palma-Manacor Km 19; ☉9am-7pm Mon-Sat, to 1.30pm Sun) **FREE** The Museu de Gordiola glassworks and museum, set in a mock-Gothic palace and named for a family that's made glass since 1719, has a factory area on the ground floor where you can observe the glassmakers working from 9am to 1.30pm. Upstairs, the museum has a curious collection of glass items from around the world. The on-site shop contains some lovely pieces amid the tack. The museum lies 2.5km west of town on the Ma15.

Santuari de Nostra Senyora de Cura MONASTERY

(☎971 12 02 60; www.santuaridecura.com; Puig de Randa; ☉cafe 8am-7pm daily Apr-Oct, 9am-5pm Mon-Fri Nov-Mar) This gracious monastery stands atop the 548m hill of Puig de Randa. Like most monasteries, it was built partly for defensive purposes, though supposedly the monks enjoyed the heavenly views, too.

Ramon Llull lived here as a hermit, praying in a cave (now closed to visitors), and in the 16th century the Estudi General (university) in Palma created the Collegi de Gramàtica here. Now it's possible to follow in their scholarly footsteps, and stay the night here (single/double from €38/51).

✕ Eating

Seek Mallorcan tradition, not modish sophistication, and you can eat happily here.

Ca'l Dimoni MALLORCAN €

(☎971 66 50 35; Carretera Vella de Manacor Km 21; mains €12-15; ☉8am-11pm Thu-Tue) On Algaida's northern fringes, Ca'l Dimoni is rustic Mallorca through and through, with wood beams, chunky tables, cured sausages hanging from the rafters and an open fire where chefs sizzle up meaty mains. There's always a good local buzz here, as well as heart-warming dishes like *frit Mallorquín* (fried lamb innards), *cargols* (snails) and *arros brut* ('dirty' rice).

❶ Getting There & Away

The 490 bus stops in Algaida on its way from Palma to Portocolom (€2.35, 30 minutes, up to 10 daily), and the 454 runs from Algaida to Cala Millor (€6.90, 80 minutes, once daily, Monday to Saturday). In summer, seasonal buses also connect Algaida with the east-coast resorts.

Montuïri

POP 2850

Riding a ridge above spreading farmland, solid, undemonstrative Montuïri is one of Mallorca's oldest towns, dating back to the Moorish dominion. Known for its apricots, it's appropriately apricot that its handsome stone buildings glow, when lit by the morning sun. The sandstone **Església de Sant Bartomeu** dominates central Plaça Major, through which runs Carrer Major, graced by the occasional mansion and bar.

◉ Sights

Mesquida Mora WINERY

(☎687 971 457; http://en.mesquidamora.com; Camí de Sant Joan, Porreres; ☉9am-5.30pm Mon-Fri) 🌿 With a range of whites, reds and rosés, a commitment to sustainable and biodynamic production and a winemaking history traceable to the current owners' 16th-century ancestors, this 'newcomer' on Mallorca's winemaking scene is well worth visiting. To get here from Montuïri, take the MA3210 and MA5030/MA5030A south into Porreres, then the Carrer del Pont to Camí de Sant Joan.

Museu Arqueològic de
Son Fornés
MUSEUM

(www.sonfornes.mallorca.museum; Carrer d'Emili Pou, Molí d'en Fraret; adult/child €3.50/free; ⊙10am-5pm Mar-Oct; 10am-2pm Mon-Fri Nov-Feb) Housed in an 18th-century mill on the northwest edge of town, this enthusiastic, well-curated little museum explores the prehistoric talayotic civilisation of Mallorca. Many exhibits are from the nearby Son Fornés *talayot* (watchtower), inhabited from around 900 BC to the 4th century AD. One of Mallorca's most important, the *talayot* is easy enough to visit: head 2.5km northwest out of Montuïri on the Ma3200 towards Pina and you'll see it to the right (east) of the road.

Sa Font
ARCHAEOLOGICAL SITE

FREE Sa Font is one of the few reminders of the Arab presence on the island. This complex *qanawat* (well and water distribution structure) is difficult to date but was taken over by the Muslims' Christian successors after 1229. It lies in Pina, 5.5km northwest of Montuïri, just 50m south of the Església de Sants Cosme i Damià, on the road to Lloret de Vistalegre.

⚜ Festivals & Events

Festa de Sant Bartomeu   CULTURAL
(⊙Aug) The main event of this celebration in honour of Montuïri's patron saint is the dance of the *cossiers* (a group of dancers, six men and one woman, plus the devil), both on the eve and the 24th.

S'Encuentro   RELIGIOUS
(⊙Easter Sun) On Easter Sunday, a figure of Christ resurrected is met in a parade by a figure of the Virgin Mary, who does some excited hops to show her joy at the resurrection of her son.

🍷 Drinking & Nightlife

Montuïri has a few very pleasant bars spilling out onto the Carrer de Palma, running through its heart.

S'Hostal   BAR
(📞971 64 60 49; Carrer Constitució 58; ⊙1pm-midnight) Renowned for taking the ubiquitous Mallorcan bar snack *pa amb oli* ('bread with oil') to the limits of its potential, this greenery-draped roadside bar downhill

from central Montuïri is one of those 'local secrets' travellers delight in uncovering. There's a terrace for warm weather, a cheering fireplace for cold – and at all times, the welcome is sincere.

❶ Getting There & Away

The 411 connects Palma and Montuïri (€3.90, 30 minutes, up to six daily). It stops outside the bar S'Hostal, down the hill to the south of the centre of town.

Petra
POP 2816

The birthplace of Catholic saint and missionary Juníper Serra, Petra is a quiet, comely midland town, its former prominence demonstrated by long streets of solid stone houses, and two impressive churches, dating to the 16th and 17th centuries. With an in-town winery, a couple of very nice places to eat and an intriguing museum, it's an undemonstrative place that rewards exploration.

◎ Sights

Petra's principal claim to historical fame is its favourite son, Juníper Serra, born here in 1713. A Franciscan missionary and one of the founders of what is now the US state of California, he could have had no inkling of his destiny as he grew up in this rural centre. Colourful majolica tiles depicting his missionary exploits enliven an already-handsome town.

Els Calderers   HISTORIC BUILDING
(📞971 52 60 69; www.elscalderers.com; adult/child €8/4; ⊙10am-6pm Apr-Oct, to 5pm Nov-Mar; 🅿) On a pretty country back road between Montuïri and Manacor, this stout rural mansion has been converted into a period museum. Els Calderers was built around 1750, on the site of an estate granted to the eponymous Calderers family in 1285. Sold to the Verí family in the 18th century, its grand dimensions, extensive grounds and outbuildings, and well-preserved collection of antique Mallorcan furnishings strongly evoke a vanished world of aristocratic privilege.

Museu Fra Juníper Serra   MUSEUM
(www.spiritualmallorca.com; Carrer des Barracar 6, 8, 10; €5 incl access to 5 other sites; ⊙10am-1.30pm Mon-Fri) The Museu Fra Juníper Serra contains mementos of Juníper Serra's missionary life. Next door is the house in which he was born, while all over the streets in this

part of town are ceramic depictions of his eventful life. Entry is via the Spiritual Mallorca ticket (€5), which also gets you into five other important religious sites.

Bodegas Miquel Oliver   WINERY
(☑971 56 11 17; www.miqueloliver.com; Carretera Petra-Santa Margalida Km 1.8; ☺10am-6pm Mon-Fri & 11am-1.30pm Sat; ℗) Going strong since 1912, Bodegas Miquel Oliver is one of the island's most respected winemakers. You can pick up a decent bottle of red at the cellar door for under €10.

**Ermita de la Mare
de Déu de Bonany**   MONASTERY
(Carrer de Bonany) Four kilometres southwest of Petra on a wooded hill stands this hermitage, where Juníper Serra gave his last sermon in Mallorca before heading for the New World. Elements of the present church date to the 18th century, but the place was overhauled in 1925. The views over the plains are magnificent, and picnic tables are provided for lingering.

✖ Eating

They're unobtrusive, but a handful of very good traditional Mallorcan restaurants can be found in Petra's long, quiet streets.

Es Celler   MALLORCAN €€
(☑971 56 10 56; Carrer de l'Hospital 46; mains €12-15; ☺noon-11pm) Step down off the street and into this wonderfully cavernous cellar restaurant with soaring ceilings and old wine barrels. Its specialities are barbecued meats, roast lamb and roast suckling pig, but it also rustles up Mallorcan classics like *arros brut*.

Ca n'Oms   MALLORCAN €
(☑971 56 19 20; www.canoms.com; Carrer de Caparrot de Ca n'Oms 7; mains €12-15; ☺9am-4pm & 6.30-11pm, shorter hours in winter; ♿) Vaulted stone ceilings and a general air of solidity attest to the 18th-century origins of this restaurant, a lovely place to eat fine variations on *pa amb oli* (local bread with tomato), including with cuttlefish. It's also a smartly designed chill-out space with occasional live music in the evenings and a shady garden that's perfect on warm evenings.

ℹ Getting There & Away

Petra is one stop short of Manacor (€1.60, nine minutes) on the Palma–Manacor (T3) train line and gets at least one service an hour in both directions. From Palma, the trip takes just under an hour and costs €4.10.

Manacor

POP 40,170

Manacor, Mallorca's second-largest city, is perhaps best known as the birthplace of tennis great Rafael Nadal and as a centre of furniture manufacturing. There are definitely more compelling attractions to be found elsewhere, but don't discount this place entirely: it does have a striking church at its centre, and there's some fine shopping to be had on its outskirts – from wineries to Mallorca's world-famous pearls.

◎ Sights

Vins Toni Gelabert   WINERY
(☑971 55 24 09; www.vinstonigelabert.com; Camí dels Horts de Llodrà Km 1.3; ☺10am-1pm & 3.30-6.30pm, by appointment) The family-run winery of Toni Gelabert produces some superb wines from callet, cabernet sauvignon and other dark grapes, as well as macabeu, chardonnay and white varieties. Visitors are welcome to pop by to see the bodega and sample the wine. Organised tastings, including three red/white wines and appetisers, cost €25 per person and must be booked in advance..

**Església de Nostra Senyora
Verge dels Dolors**   CHURCH
(Plaça del General Weyler; ☺8.30am-12.45pm & 5.30-8pm) The massive Església de Nostra Senyora Verge dels Dolors lords it impressively over the Manacor skyline. It was raised on the site of the town's former mosque and has a hybrid Gothic/neo-Gothic style, which reflects the fact that construction began in the 14th century and wasn't completed until the 19th century.

Torre de Ses Puntes   HISTORIC BUILDING
(Plaça de Gabriel Fuster Historiador; ☺6.30-8.30pm) Once part of the city's defences, this 14th-century tower has received some mostly-sensitive modern, plate-glass additions, and is now used for the odd exhibition.

✖ Eating

Ca'n March   MALLORCAN €€
(☑971 55 00 02; www.canmarch.com; Carrer de València 7; mains €16-18, menus €12-30; ☺1-3.30pm Tue-Sun plus 8.30-11pm Sat & Sun) Fish prepared with a minimum of fuss using salt from Es Trenc and Mallorcan olive oil is a strong point at this warm, traditional haunt, which has been knocking out the plates

Manacor

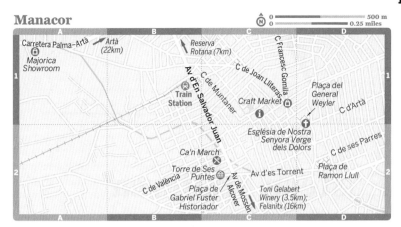

since 1925. Or you can opt for rice dishes like paella with rabbit and snails.

Reserva Rotana   MEDITERRANEAN €€€
(☑ 971 84 56 85; www.reservarotana.com; Camí de Bendris Km 3; mains €24-32; ⊗ 7-11pm Mar-Oct) A slice of rural luxury, this tucked-away *finca* (estate) offers genteel ambience and polished service in its beamed dining room and flower-draped garden.

🛍 Shopping

Most visitors come to Manacor for the manufactured pearls.

Majorica Showroom   JEWELLERY
(www.majorica.com; Carretera Palma–Artà Km 47; ⊗ 9am-7pm Jun-Sep, to 5pm Nov-Feb, to 6pm Mar-May & Oct) This company, the best-known Manacor pearl manufacturer, was founded by German Eduard Heusch in 1902 and now has its two-storey showroom on the edge of town on the road to Palma.

Craft Market   MARKET
(Plaça Sa Bassa; ⊗ 9am-1pm Sat) Stalls selling local handicrafts (and some trinkets) set up in this square every Saturday morning.

ℹ Information

Tourist Office (☑ 662 350891; www.visitmanacor.com; Plaça del Convent 3; ⊗ 9am-2pm Mon-Fri)

ℹ Getting There & Away

The T3 train connects Manacor and Palma (€3.55, 70 minutes, hourly between 6am and 10pm). Plenty of buses on cross-island routes

call in, terminating in front of the train station, a 10-minute walk from Plaça del General Weyler.

Felanitx

POP 17,412
Felanitx is an important regional centre with a reputation for ceramics, white wine and capers (of the culinary variety). A handsome if unspectacular town, it's perhaps most visited as the gateway to two stunning hilltop sites nearby.

◎ Sights

Santuari de Sant Salvador   MONASTERY
(www.santsalvadorhotel.com; ⊗ church 8am-11pm) One of inland Mallorca's most spectacular viewpoints, the hermitage Santuari de Sant Salvador crowns a hilltop 5km southeast of Felanitx and 509m above sea level. Built in 1348, the year of the Black Death, it's plausible that the hermits were safe here.

Castell de Santueri   CASTLE
(☑ 691 223679; http://santueri.org; €4; ⊗ 10am-6.30pm Mar-Oct) This clifftop castle, whose proud walls rise seamlessly from a craggy natural peak, offers spectacular views, extending southeast far out to sea. The castle was built by the Moors, and not taken until 1231, two years after the rest of the island had fallen. To get here from Felanitx, take the Ma14 for 2km, then follow the signs to the left (east).

ℹ Getting There & Away

From Palma the 490 (and 491 express) connect with Felanitx (€5.20, one hour, up to 12 daily).

Eastern Mallorca

Best Places to Eat

➡ Forn Nou (p153)

➡ Cases de Son Barbassa (p155)

➡ Andreu Genestra (p155)

➡ Es Coll d'Os (p158)

➡ Restaurant Sa Llotja (p164)

➡ Sa Sal (p163)

Top Sights

➡ Coves del Drac (p162)

➡ Ses Països (p152)

➡ Sa Torre Cega (p156)

➡ Castell de Capdepera (p155)

➡ Cala Mesquida (p158)

Why Go?

There's a reason tourists arrive in Eastern Mallorca in their hundreds of thousands on their annual sun pilgrimage: this is one of the prettiest coasts on an island of many. Yes, there are sections that seem to combine all that's abhorrent about Mediterranean coastal tourism, but Mallorca's rocky eastern walls also conceal perfectly formed caves, coves and inlets, some of which are accessible only on foot, and can never really be developed. And, to the north, you'll find wild stretches of natural park and stunning medieval towns.

When to Go

You could be forgiven for thinking that Eastern Mallorca hibernates throughout winter, rumbling into life only from April to October. There's an element of truth in this: many restaurants, hotels and other businesses only open in these months (although an increasing number are extending from February to November). Winters are relatively mild and the beauty of Eastern Mallorca's coast and hill towns has a special allure without the crowds. Most towns and villages celebrate Sant Antoni with great gusto in mid-January.

Eastern Mallorca Highlights

1 Artà (p152) Getting a grasp on medieval Mallorca by roaming the castle ramparts and backstreets.

2 Parc Natural de la Península de Llevant (p154) Hiking the wind-buckled hills to reach pristine coves.

3 Portocolom (p164) Diving by day and dining by night in this unspoilt fishing town.

4 Coves North of Cala Ratjada (p158) Escaping the summer hordes at a string of quiet, unspoilt beaches.

5 Coves del Drac (p162) Delving into the bowels of the earth at Mallorca's most spectacular caves.

6 Castell de Capdepera (p155) Feeling Mallorca ripple out from beneath you atop this fortified hill town.

7 Ses Països (p152) Wandering through the remains of Mallorca's enigmatic Talayotic prehistory.

8 Sa Torre Cega (p156) Escaping Cala Ratjada's din to wander beautiful sculpture gardens.

THE NORTHEAST

There's great hiking, swimming, horse riding and birdwatching in the northeast, yet its attractions aren't solely natural. The medieval hill towns of Artà and Capdepera retain countless antique treasures, while the raucous resort town of Cala Ratjada is a reminder of what much of Mallorca's eastern coast has become.

Artà

POP 7630

The antithesis of Cala Ratjada's buzzing resort culture just a few kilometres away, the quiet inland town of Artà beckons with its maze of narrow streets, appealing cafes and medieval architecture. An impressive 14th-century hilltop fortress dominates the town centre.

◎ Sights

★ **Ses Païsses**   ARCHAEOLOGICAL SITE
(off Carretera Artà–Capdepera; adult/child €2/free; ⊙10am-5pm Mon-Fri, 10am-2pm Sat) Just beyond Artà proper lies the remains of a 3000-year-old Bronze Age settlement, the largest and most important Talayotic site on the island's eastern flank. The site's looming stone gateway, composed of rough, 8-tonne slabs, is an impressive transition into the mystery-shrouded world of prehistoric Mallorca. You can traverse the tree-shaded site in under 30 minutes, but may appreciate a longer visit. From the large roundabout east of Artà's tourist office, follow the signs towards Ses Païsses.

Cala Matzoc   BEACH
Eleven kilometres from Artà, or a 20-minute trek along the coast from Cala Estreta, Cala Matzoc comes into view. A quiet cove of sand and stone, it backs onto a hill where the ruins of a prehistoric *talayot* (watchtower) still stand.

ℹ ARTÀ CARD

If you're planning on doing a fair bit of sightseeing, buy the Artà Card (€3) at the **tourist office** (p154). It gets you entry to the major sights, including the Museu Regional d'Artà, the Transfiguració del Senyor and Ses Païsses, plus discounts elsewhere.

Museu Regional d'Artà   MUSEUM
(☑971 82 97 78; www.museuarta.com; Carrer de l'Estel 4; adult/child €2/free; ⊙10am-6pm Tue-Fri, 10am-2pm Sat & Sun) This little museum opens a window on Artà's fascinating past. There's a natural history section, and another tracing the development of the city through time, with Bronze Age, Talayotic, Punic, Roman and Moorish artefacts, including ceramics, jewellery, bronzes and funerary gifts. There's also space for rotating exhibitions, such as a recent one showcasing local art and traditions.

Santuari de Sant Salvador   CASTLE
(Carrer del Castellet; ⊙8am-8pm Apr-Oct, shorter hours rest of year) FREE Rising high and mighty above Artà, this walled fortress was built atop an earlier Moorish enclave and encloses a small church. The 4000-sq-metre complex, extensively restored in the 1960s, reveals all the hallmarks of a medieval fortress, down to the stone turrets ringing the top and the metre-thick walls. The views from here sweep over the rooftops of the medina-like old town and beyond to the bald, bumpy peaks of the Serra de Llevant.

Transfiguració del Senyor   CHURCH
(Carrer del Mal Lloc; adult/child €2/free; ⊙10am-5pm Mon-Sat) This church, built atop the foundations of a Moorish mosque, was begun soon after the Christian reconquest, although the facade – restored in 2016 – dates to the 16th century. Inside, note the large rose window, the ornately carved mahogany pulpit and the 14 chapels in the nave. There's also a small museum exhibiting artefacts such as precious altarpieces and a silver cross bearing a sliver of Palma Cathedral's relic of the True Cross (brought here in 1512).

🏃 Activities

Manacor–Artà Greenway   CYCLING
(www.viasverdes.com) This easy cycle route between the two eponymous cities follows a disused railway over 29km of packed-earth and gravel pathway. Occasional sea glimpses and a quieter perspective on the rural northeast are your rewards.

🎊 Festivals & Events

Festes de Sant Antoni Abat   CULTURAL
(⊙16-17 Jan) During this curious festival, everyone dresses in traditional costume and heads to the Santuari de Sant Salvador for dancing, music and an odd display of backward-facing equestrians swinging sticks.

Artà

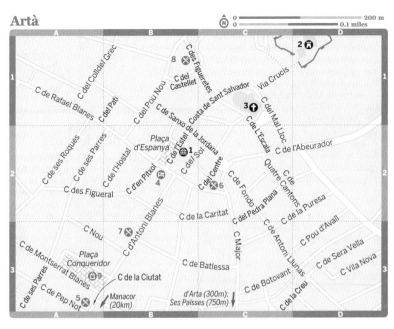

Eating

Artà has some brilliantly atmospheric restaurants and cafes, many with a boho vibe and sidewalk seating.

★**Forn Nou**   MEDITERRANEAN €€
(☑971 82 92 46; www.fornnou-arta.com; Carrer del Centre 7; 3-course dinner menu €26; ⏱6.30-11pm; 🛜) Forn Nou's terrace perches high above Artà's medieval maze and peers across the rooftops to the church and fortress. The season-driven menu changes twice monthly, but you can expect clean, bright Mediterranean flavours, along the lines of Atlantic anchovies with roasted peppers and paprika, or lobster risotto. The wine cellar is visible through the lobby's glass floor.

Mar de Vins   INTERNATIONAL €€
(☑971 59 64 10; Carrer d'Antoni Blanes 34; mains €12-16; ⏱10am-10pm Mon-Fri, to 2pm Sat; 🛜🖊🚲) Our favourite hangout to linger over coffee and a good book, this cafe conceals one of Artà's loveliest garden patios. The interior is cosy, with its cobbled floor, paintings and marble-topped tables, and there are plenty of vegetarian options to complement carnivorous Spanish favourites, such as chicken *croquetas* and meltingly tender *albóndigas* (meatballs).

Artà

◉ Sights
1 Museu Regional d'Artà	B2
2 Santuari de Sant Salvador	D1
3 Transfiguració del Senyor	C1

🛏 Sleeping
4 Hotel Casal d'Artà	B2

🍽 Eating
5 Cafe Parisien	A3
6 Forn Nou	C2
7 Mar de Vins	B3
8 Salvador Gaudí	B1

🛍 Shopping
9 Market	A3

Cafe Parisien   MEDITERRANEAN €€
(☑971 83 54 40; Carrer de la Ciutat 18; mains €15-18; ⏱10am-12.30am Mon-Sat; 🛜) White wrought-iron chairs, modern art and swing music give this boho cafe a dash of Parisian class. Swathed in jasmine and vines, the courtyard is a beautiful spot on a balmy day.

Salvador Gaudí   MEDITERRANEAN €€€
(☑971 82 95 55; www.santsalvador.com; Carrer del Pou Nou 26; mains €19-25; ⏱1-3pm & 7-10pm) Gathered around an inner courtyard lit by tealights and purportedly designed by

CYCLING AROUND ARTÀ

The tourist office hands out an excellent brochure called Bike Tours that includes a dozen route maps and descriptions through the area that you can complete on foot or by bike. Particularly recommended is the 7km route from Artà to the **Ermita de Betlem** hermitage (the last section of which is relentlessly steep). If you prefer things flat and car free, the **Manacor–Artà Greenway** (p152) follows a disused railway between the two cities.

Antoni Gaudí, this is a fabulously intimate setting for lunch or dinner. Dishes such as sole *meunière* with Sòller oranges, ham and artichokes, or the intriguing-sounding blanquette of monkfish with squid and 'his things', indicate an ambitious kitchen. Live music accompanies the tapas on Tuesday.

🛍 Shopping

d'Artà   ARTS & CRAFTS
(☑ 971 83 69 81; http://darta.es; Avinguda de Costa i Llobera 7; ☉ 9am-8pm, reduced hours in winter) Housed in Artà's handsome, disused train station and incorporating the tourist office, this collective venture displays the wares of local, traditional artisans for sale. Beautiful leatherwork, handsome ceramics and handmade clothes are sold alongside herbal liquors, organic smallgoods made from Mallorcan black pigs, single-flower honeys, dried fruit and other lip-smacking bounty. Upstairs you'll find exhibitions of local art.

Market   MARKET
(Plaça Conqueridor; ☉ 9am-1pm Tue) Artà's bustling traditional market comes to the centre of town each Tuesday, with stalls selling local produce and handicrafts.

ℹ Information

Tourist Office (☑ 971 83 69 81; http://darta. es; Avinguda de Costa i Llobera 7; ☉ 9am-8pm, reduced hours in winter) Artà's new local craft and cultural centre incorporates a helpful tourist office with plenty of info and maps of the area. It also sells the Artà Card (€3), which gives you entry to the Museu Regional d'Artà and Ses Païsses, and reduced entry to the Caves of Artà (near Canyamel), and the church and museum of Transfiguració del Senyor.

ℹ Getting There & Away

Bus services to/from Artà's Avinguda de Costa i Llobera include bus 411 to Palma (€9.60, 90 minutes, four to five daily) via Manacor (€2.85, 25 minutes), and bus 446 to Alcúdia (€5.65, one hour, six daily Monday to Saturday) and Port de Pollença (€6.60, 70 minutes).

Parc Natural de la Península de Llevant

This beautiful nature park, 5km north of Artà, is one of the most rewarding corners of Mallorca's east. It's dominated by the **Serra de Llevant**, a low mountain range of wind-sculpted limestone, cloaked in Mauritanian grass broken by holm oak, Aleppo pine and fan palms, and culminates in the **Cap Ferrutx**, a dramatic nature reserve (off-limits to the public) that drops vertiginously into the Mediterranean from Mallorca's northern and eastern coasts.

Although parts of the park are accessible by car, it's hugely popular with hikers, cyclists and binocular-wielding birdwatchers; the latter drawn by the prevalence of cormorants, Audouin's gulls, peregrine falcons and booted eagles. The remote nature of the park means that coves like **Cala Fosca** and **Platja de Sa Font Celada** are quiet and pristine, with flour-soft sand and crystal-clear sea. They're inaccessible (and inside the protected area) but the adjoining, accessible parts of the park are stunning, too.

◎ Sights

Ermita de Betlem   CHRISTIAN SITE
Founded in 1805, Ermita de Betlem is still home to hermits who live a life of seclusion and self-sufficiency. The alluring views over country and wind-whipped coast make the steep up-and-down road to this hermitage worthwhile. There is a small church with irregular opening hours – its lovely stone-built exterior stands in contrast to the modern whitewashed interior, ceiling frescoes and cave nativity scene, complete with stalactites and stalagmites. Stroll up the neighbouring hilltops to see all the way to Menorca.

ℹ Information

Parc Natural de la Península de Llevant Information Office (☑ 606 096830; http:// ibanat.caib.es; S'Alqueria Vella de Baix; ☉ 9am-4pm) The park office can help with itinerary maps and organises guided walks, generally in Catalan and Spanish.

ⓘ Getting There & Away

You'll need your own wheels: buses can only get you as close as Artà or Betlem.

Capdepera

POP 11,420

More of a fortified town than a town with a castle, Capdepera's stirring medieval fortress is visible from across the plains of northeastern Mallorca, its magnitude a reminder of the centuries in which it was the only protection from the degradations of pirates. The remainder of the village that clusters below its walls is pleasant, in parts beautiful, but the castle is the still main attraction.

⊙ Sights

★**Castell de Capdepera**   CASTLE
(☑971 81 87 46; www.castellcapdepera.com; Carrer Castell; adult/child under 12yr €3/free; ⊙9am-8pm mid-Mar–mid-Oct, to 5pm rest of year) Lording it over Capdepera is this early-14th-century fortress. A walled complex built on the ruins of a Moorish fortress, the castle is one of the best preserved on the island. Constructed as a self-contained fortified town by Jaume II (son of the conquering Jaume I), it was a bastion of safety (from pirate attacks) and royal power in this part of the island. Within the walls, a stone church contains a valuable wooden crucifix dating to the 14th century.

La Antigua Farmacia Melis Cursach   MUSEUM
(☑971 55 64 79; Carrer des Centre 9; ⊙11am Wed) The former home and workplace of Antònia Melis Cursach, bequeathed to the city on her death, is now a museum, preserved to look just as an 18th-century pharmacy-dwelling might. It's also an occasional exhibition space. Visits are allowed Wednesday mornings, and should be arranged through the tourist office on the ground floor.

🏃 Activities

Capdepera Golf   GOLF
(☑971 81 85 00; www.golfcapdepera.com; Carretera Artá–Capdepera, Km 3.5; 9 holes €39-49, 18 holes €59-89; ⊙8am-7pm) Designed by Dan Maples, this 18-hole course is highly regarded.

🎉 Festivals & Events

Mercat Medieval   CULTURAL
(⊙3rd weekend May) Commemorating the foundation of the town by Jaume II in 1300, this fair sees Capdepera given over to medieval costumes, events and food stalls.

Festa de Sant Antoni   RELIGIOUS
(St Anthony's Feast Day; ⊙16-17 Jan) Adapted from a pre-existing pagan festival, this archaic Balearic celebration of a 3rd-century Egyptian saint is ushered in by bonfires and masked dances.

Festa de Sant Bartomeu   CULTURAL
(⊙3rd week Aug) A week of exhibits, concerts, parades and fireworks.

🍴 Eating

Several upscale hotels in the surrounding countryside have excellent restaurants.

★**Cases de Son Barbassa**   MEDITERRANEAN €€
(☑971 56 57 76; www.sonbarbassa.com; Camí de Son Barbassa; mains €16-24, menu €28; ⊙12.30-3pm & 7-10pm) Follow a narrow lane to this blissfully secluded *finca,* which notches up the romance with its lantern-lit terrace and sweeping country views. Set among olive, almond and carob trees, it makes plenty of garden and market produce in dishes likes turbot in champagne with clam and oysters, and suckling pig cooked to crackling perfection – prepared with home-grown olive oil.

★**Andreu Genestra**   MODERN EUROPEAN €€€
(☑608 578198; http://andreugenestra.com; Carretera Cala Mesquida, Km 1; 5/8/10 courses €58/74/105; ⊙1.30-4pm Thu-Sun, plus 7-11pm Wed-Mon; 🅿✹📶) Michelin-starred Mallorcan chef Genestra runs this wonderful rural restaurant, attached to (but independent from) the Predi Son Jaumell hotel, and nestled among his own olive groves and vineyards. Shades of his experience at Mugaritz and El Bulli shine through his fixed-price menus, yet Mallorcan ingredients such as *cocarroi* (pastry) and local *butifarra* sausage are given due respect.

ⓘ Information

Tourist Office (☑971 55 64 79; Carrer des Centre 9; ⊙8.30am-2.30pm Mon-Fri).

ⓘ Getting There & Away

Bus 411 links Capdepera to Palma (€11, 1½ hours, up to five daily), via Artà (€1.50, 15 minutes) and Manacor (€3.90, 40 minutes). Bus 441 runs along the east coast, stopping at all the major resorts, including Porto Cristo (€3.25, 55 minutes, up to eight daily) and Cala d'Or (€9.20, 1¾ hours); a change may be necessary.

Cala Ratjada

POP 6098

Cala Ratjada is the Jekyll and Hyde of Mallorca's eastern resorts. Wander along the promenade that skirts the contours of the coast and plump for one of the quieter bays and it can be pretty or even peaceful. It's also a terrific base for water-borne activities. But come high season, the resort adopts a second persona as the Costa del Bavaria, with rollicking beer gardens attracting a tanked-up 18-to-30 crowd, doing a brisk trade in currywurst and other German grub. You'll need to push beyond its centre to find Mallorca again.

⦿ Sights

★ Sa Torre Cega   HISTORIC BUILDING

(☑971 81 94 67; www.fundacionbmarch.es; off Carrer d'Elionor Servera; adult/child €4.50/free; ⊙tours 10.30am-noon Wed-Fri & 11am-6pm Sat & Sun May-Nov, Wed, Fri & Sat mornings only Feb-Apr) Named for the 15th-century 'blind tower' (unsighted by similar watchtowers) at its centre, this coastal estate was built in the early 20th century by the noted architect Guillem Reynés Font. The beautiful Mediterranean garden is home to a collection of over 40 works by noted Spanish, Catalan and Latin American sculptors, such as Eusebio Sempere, Juan de Ávalos, Xavier Corberó and Agustín Cárdenas. All guided visits must be booked in advance through the tourist office.

Far de Capdepera   LIGHTHOUSE

This lighthouse on Mallorca's easternmost tip is the endpoint of a lovely drive, walk or cycle through pine forests, around 1.5km east of Sa Torre Cega. Sitting 76m above the sea, it began operating in 1861, and the views from here (all the way to Menorca on a clear day) are wonderful.

Font de Sa Cala   BEACH

(Font de Sa Cala) South of Cala Ratjada is Font de Sa Cala, where the crystalline waters are perfect for snorkelling. The serene, 100m-long beach is surrounded by a harshly beautiful rocky coast, swaddled in pines.

Platja de Son Moll   BEACH

Cala Ratjada's most accessible beach is the busy 200m strip of the Platja de Son Moll, just in front of Passeig Marítim, in the centre of town.

🏃 Activities

Skualo Adventure Sports   DIVING

(☑971 56 43 03; www.mallorcadiving.com; Carrer Lepanto 1; 2-day scuba course €290, 2hr snorkelling €45; 🚗) This reputable dive centre has an array of PADI courses and snorkelling excursions, many to the pristine waters around the Parc Natural de la Península de Llevant. It also arrange other activities, including speedboating (€45, 50 minutes) and cave tours (with swimming in saltwater and freshwater caves; €65, three hours).

Illa Balear   BOATING

(☑971 81 06 00; www.illabalear.com; adult/child round trip from €22/10; ⊙Apr-Oct) Round-trip and one-way excursions in glass-bottom catamarans to Porto Cristo, Sa Coma, Cala Millor, Cala Bona and other east-coast destinations. The 'Sea Adventure' takes five hours, while the 'Sea Odyssey' is 2½ to three hours, and there are generally three departures per day.

Rancho Bonanza   HORSE RIDING

(☑619 680688; www.ranchobonanza.com; Carrer de Ca'n Patilla; 1hr/2hr rides €20/35, full-day excursion per person €63; 🚗) The best of a few options on the pine-shaded outskirts of town, Bonanza runs excursions daily to quiet bays and along rural lanes. One-hour pony rides (€10) are available for kids six years and under, as are riding lessons (€20).

M Bike   CYCLING

(☑639 417796; www.m-bike.com; Carrer de l'Agulla 93; bike rental per day €10-32, per week €60-180, 1-/3-/4-day cycle tours €53/150/200; ⊙9am-noon & 5-7pm Mar-Oct) M Bike rents out quality mountain, racing and trekking bikes. From March to October, it also runs daily cycle tours along coastal trails and to the Ermita de Betlem – all tours start at 10am.

Segpark   OUTDOORS

(☑634 317266; www.segpark.es; Carrer de l'Agulla 85D; 90min Segway tour adult/child €44/34, e-bike tour 1hr/day €7/22; ⊙10am-8pm; 🚗) If you fancy a whiz around an obstacle course on a nifty two-wheeled, self-balancing scooter, this is the place to come. A taster session costs €5, a 15-minute circuit €10. It also runs 90-minute tours of Cala Ratjada.

Illes Balears Ballooning   BALLOONING

(☑607 64 76 47; www.ibballooning.net; Joan Moll 49, Cala Rajada) Balloons for charter, located in Cala Ratjada in the far east of the island.

Cala Ratjada

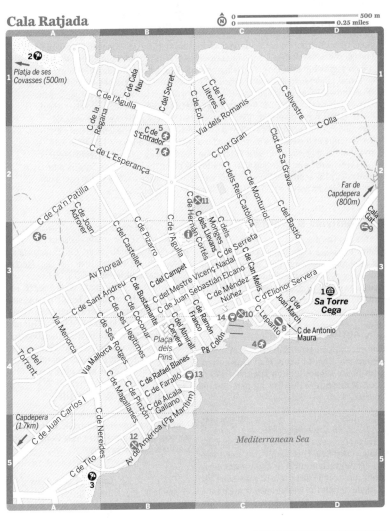

EASTERN MALLORCA CALA RATJADA

Cala Ratjada

TRANQUIL COVES AROUND CALA RATJADA

Heading north from Cala Ratjada, you'll find a wonderfully undeveloped stretch of coast-line flecked with beaches. Long-time favourites of nudists, these out-of-the-way coves are no secret, but their lack of development has kept them calm and pristine.

Broad, family-friendly **Cala Mesquida**, surrounded by sand dunes and a small housing development, is the most accessible, with free parking, a few beach bars in season and a regular bus service (bus 471) from Cala Ratjada (€1.85, 25 minutes, up to eight daily).

It requires more determination to access the undeveloped coves due west. Of-ten-windy **Cala Torta**, tiny, sheltered **Cala Mitjana** and the beachless **Cala Estreta** are all found at the end of a narrow road that ventures through the hills from Artà, yet a more interesting way to arrive is via the one-hour walking path from Cala Mesquida.

Further west, and following a 20-minute trek along the coast from Cala Estreta, **Cala Matzoc** (p152) comes into view. Often empty, the spacious sandy beach backs onto a hill where you'll find the ruins of a prehistoric *talayot* (watchtower).

★☆ Festivals & Events

Festes del Carme   RELIGIOUS

(☉mid-Jul) FREE Cala Ratjada's main festi-val celebrates the Verge del Carme, the holy patroness of fishers. It includes an elaborate maritime procession, fireworks and a host of cultural events.

✗ Eating

The pickings in Cala Ratjada are more in-ternational than in many Mallorcan towns, with pizza, kebabs and currywurst. There's good Mallorcan seafood to be had, too, of course.

★ Es Coll d'Os   MEDITERRANEAN €€

(☎971 56 48 55; www.escolldos.com; Carrer de Verge de l'Esperança 5; 3-course menu €31; ☉6.30-10.30pm Mon-Sat) This family-run *finca* (ru-ral estate) restaurant feels light years away from some of the tacky tourist places in Cala Ratjada. Sit on the vine-draped terrace for a meal that tastes profoundly of the seasons, creatively prepared with organic, home-grown herbs and vegetables, lamb reared on the estate and fish drawn from local waters.

Ca'n Maya   SEAFOOD €€

(☎971 56 40 35; www.canmaya.com; Carrer d'El-ionor Servera 80; mains €14-24; ☉noon-4pm & 7pm-midnight Tue-Sun Apr-Nov) This central, long-running restaurant (established 1938) is perhaps the most authentic and low-key of Cala Ratjada's seafood joints. Its glassed-in harbourside terrace is ideal for lingering over fried squid, razor clams, grilled monk-fish, spider-crab rice, Norwegian lobster and many other marine delicacies.

Restaurante del Mar   INTERNATIONAL €€€

(☎680 133381; www.mallorca-delmar.com; Avin-guda de América 31; mains €18-25, degustation menu €39; ☉11.30am-11pm Tue-Sun Apr-Jun, 5.30pm-midnight Tue-Sun Jul-Oct) A Swiss cou-ple run this restaurant, with breezy sea views from the terrace. The big deal is sea-food, including a superb *parrillada* (bar-becue), with five kinds of fish, shellfish and grilled vegetables. Otherwise the food has an international slant, where Thai curries rub shoulders with Wiener schnitzel and Zurich-style veal stew with rösti.

🍷 Drinking & Nightlife

Cala Ratjada is one place in northeastern Mallorca where you can really go hog-wild, especially around Carrer des Coconar and Carrer d'Elionor Servera.

Royal   BAR

(☎971 81 82 22; Carrer d'Elionor Servera 74; ☉9am-1am; 🛜) A much-loved sunset spot, the Royal has a classy terrace overlooking the narrow end of the harbour. There's live music from 8pm on Thursday (DJs), Friday (flamenco) and Saturday (jazz) and the kitchen pumps out a high standard of sea-food, salads and food from the grill, includ-ing a very good-value lunch menu (€10).

Café Noah's   BAR

(☎971 81 81 25; www.cafenoahs.com; Avinguda de América 2; ☉9am-2am) The sea views are entrancing from the terrace of this slick lounge bar: straddling the waterfront prom-enade, it's a prime spot for people watching and cocktail sipping. Inside there are comfy leather sofas and DJs to get the crowd on their feet Friday to Sunday nights.

ℹ️ Information

Tourist Office (📞 971 81 94 67; www.ajcapdep-era.net; Centre Cap Vermell, Carrer de l'Agulla 50; ⊙ 9am-1pm & 4-8pm Mon-Fri) Located in the white town hall building; free wi-fi in the plaza out the front. Visit in the morning for English-speaking service.

ℹ️ Getting There & Away

Bus 411 links Palma de Mallorca and Cala Rat-jada, via Artá, with up to five runs daily in each direction (€11, two hours). From May to October, a daily bus trundles frequently to nearby beaches and sights like Cala Mesquida, Cala Agulla and Coves d'Artà (all €1.85).

From the port, there's a daily hydrofoil to Ciutadella (Menorca).

Canyamel

POP 315

Little Canyamel is naturally more peaceful than the bigger resorts along the eastern seaboard, although it does have its share of medium-rise development, and the attractive Platja de Canyamel can get very crowded. The well-heeled inhabitants whose expensive houses cling to the southern slopes above the town keep well clear of all that. Inland, there's a fine medieval tower-turned cultural centre and a majestic cave complex that sees far fewer visitors than similar sites along this pitted coast.

◉ Sights & Activities

Coves d'Artà   CAVE
(📞 971 84 12 93; www.cuevasdearta.com; Carrer de Coves de s'Ermita; adult/child 7-12yr/child under 7yr €14/7/free; ⊙ 10am-6pm Apr-Jun & Oct, to 7pm Jul-Sep, to 5pm Nov-Mar) Head 1km north of Canyamel and pass through an unassuming fissure in the rock wall that buffers the coast and you'll find yourself in a stunning warren of limestone caves – the possible inspiration for Jules Verne's *Journey to the Centre of the Earth*. First up is a soaring vestibule, home to the 22m-tall stalagmite known as the 'Queen of Columns', while subsequent rooms include the 'Chamber of Purgatory' and 'Chamber of Hell'. Guided tours leave every 30 minutes.

Torre de Canyamel   CASTLE
(📞 971 84 11 34; www.torredecanyamel.com; Carretera Artà–Canyamel, Km5; adult/child under 13yr €3/free; ⊙ 10am-3pm Tue-Sun, plus 5-8pm Tue-Sat) Just 3km inland from Canyamel and signposted off the main coast road, the

striking Torre de Canyamel – a 23m-high, 13th-century defensive tower of golden stone, named for the sugar cane once grown in the district – is a rewarding detour. There's a restaurant, event space and a permanent exhibition tracing 700 years of development in the area, through artefacts from the Morell Ethnographic Collection.

Canyamel Golf   GOLF
(📞 971 84 13 13; www.canyamelgolf.com; Avinguda d'es Cap Vermell; 9/18 holes €59/98; ⊙ 7.45am-9pm Jun-Aug, shorter hours rest of year) Making sensitive (and challenging) use of some lovely terrain, this 18-hole course is one the island's most scenic. It's also home to turtles, so be careful near the water hazards.

Pula Golf   GOLF
(📞 971 81 70 34; www.pulagolf.com; Carretera Son Servera–Capdepera, Km 3; 9 holes €39-49, 18 holes €67-84; ⊙ 8am-7pm) Designed by José María Olazabal, this PGA Tour 18-hole course is Mallorca's longest. There's also a hotel and country club, housed in a handsome 16th-century rural villa.

🍴 Eating

★ Porxada de Sa Torre   MALLORCAN €€
(📞 971 84 13 10; www.restauranteporxadadesa-torre.com; Carretera Artà–Canyamel, Km5; mains €17-20; ⊙ 7-11pm daily, plus 1-3.30pm Tue-Sun) Opening onto a garden terrace, Porxada de Sa Torre is a beacon of Mallorcan cooking, serving *tumbet,* perfectly roasted rabbit with onions, and widely famed *lechona* (suckling pig, roasted over holm oak). You're welcome in the kitchen to see how the dishes are prepared, while stone-and-wood architecture, old farming implements, an ancient olive press and friendly service complete a charming package.

ℹ️ Getting There & Away

Bus 441 connects Canyamel with Cala Ratjada (€1.85, 25 minutes, frequent service). Other services only run to Canyamel in summer: bus 473 heads to Artà (€1.85, 20 minutes, up to five daily Monday to Saturday) and Cala Ratjada (€1.85, 25 minutes, two to nine daily).

CALA MILLOR TO PORTOCOLOM

For the millions of tourists who descend every year on its sandy beaches, splash in its gentle waves and stay in all-inclusive

HIKING MALLORCA'S EASTERN COAST

FOUR COVES HIKE

START FINCA CAN ROIG
END FINCA CAN ROIG
LENGTH 13KM; THREE TO 3½ HOURS

Just north of Cales de Mallorca the chaos of the resorts falls away and nature takes over. Over the 6km between Cales de Mallorca and Cala Romántica, there's only pine-specked rocky coves, pitted cliff faces and the aquamarine of the Mediterranean.

The walk begins at **Finca Can Roig**, a rural estate. To get here, take the Carretera Porto Cristo–Portocolom (Ma4014) and at Km 6 turn east towards Cales de Mallorca. Continue 2.2km and veer left; after 200m you'll reach the entrance to Can Roig.

Leave your car here and strike out along the wide, rocky track that parallels the coast. After about 15 minutes, take a slightly narrower path turns off to the right. Follow it alongside a small gully and through patches of trees to reach **Cala Bota**, a sheltered cove with a small sandy beach. A steep trail meanders around and above the cove, giving a bird's-eye view of its beauty.

From Cala Bota, retrace your steps and take the second right towards the next cove, **Cala Virgili**. The track brings you to a smaller trail that heads off right down to this narrow, cliff-flanked cove, with limpid water for a refreshing dip. (The walk down takes about 10 minutes.)

Return to the main trail and follow it. You'll pass a small trail on your right, but keep straight until you come upon a second path. Take it towards the **Cala Pilota**, a lovely cove backed by cave-pocked cliffs. The water is brilliantly turquoise.

Head back to the main trail and continue. Ignore the first right and instead take the second, which rolls down to the final cove, **Cala Magraner**, the grandest of the bunch both in size and beauty. The trail is wide at first but stops in a clearing; another, narrower trail leads you for the last few minutes. After splashing in the crystalline waters and

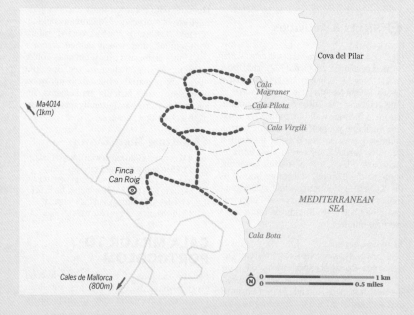

Cova del Pilar

Cala Magraner

Cala Pilota

Ma4014
(1km)

Cala Virgili

Finca
Can Roig

MEDITERRANEAN
SEA

Cala Bota

Cales de Mallorca
(800m)

0 _____ 1 km
0 _____ 0.5 miles

The dented coastline and pure azure waters of the eastern Mallorcan coast – approaching their most beautiful and least developed condition between Cales de Mallorca and Cala Romantica – are superb for hiking.

Hiker at Cala Matzoc, Artà (p152)

exploring the small caves that dot the rock, walk the main trail back to Finca Can Roig.

HIKING IN THE PARC NATURAL DE LLEVANT

Hikers are in their element in the Parc Natural de la Península de Llevant. The information office at **S'Alquera Vella de Baix** – where you can park – supplies a map highlighting 13 trails totalling 25km through the park. A classic walk leads from here to the coast and down to the little beach at **S'Arenalet des Verger**, where you can overnight (at a **campsite** (✍ reservations 9am-4pm Mon-Fri 971 17 76 52; www.caib.es; S'Arenalet des Verger; per person per night €5) or **refuge** (✍ reservations 9am-4pm Mon-Fri 971 17 76 52; www.caib.es; S'Arenalet des Verger; r €40-60)) if you've booked ahead. Reckon on two hours' walking time.

To reach the same point from the east along the coast, you could start at **Cala Estreta** (where you can leave your car, as it's outside the park proper). This walk follows the coast to **Cala Matzoc**, on past the 18th-century watchtower **Torre d'Albarca** and west. It takes another hour to reach S'Arenalet des Verger, inside the park and on the cusp of the nature reserve.

To reach S'Alquera Vella de Baix take the Ma3333 north of Artà in the direction of the Ermita de Betlem and follow the signposted turn-off right at Km 4.7, from where it's a further 600m to the car park.

COASTAL HIKES IN CALA RATJADA

Give the crowds in Cala Ratjada the slip by taking the **walking trail** that leaves from the far northern end of Cala Agulla and head through the pines of a protected natural area towards the pristine **Cala Mesquida**, a beach backed with dunes. The round trip is 10km. Along the way, a smaller trail veers off to the right at the signpost for the '*torre*', the **Talaia de Son Jaume II** watchtower. The trail (7km round trip from Cala Agulla) is marked with red dots, and the reward at the end is a spectacular panoramic view.

resorts, the coast from Cala Millor to Porto-colom is paradise. But for those who mourn the loss of Mallorca's once-pristine coastline, the overdevelopment is nothing short of a catastrophe. But the crowd-weary shouldn't be put off entirely. Head inland to cosy rural hotels and drive, cycle or hike to off-the-beaten-path beaches, such as Cala Romántica or Cala Varques.

Cala Millor

POP 5100

From humble beginnings in the 1930s, Cala Millor has grown to be a beast of a resort – the largest on Mallorca's eastern coast. Along the waterfront at twilight, wandering a 1800m-long beach reclining under the ceaseless caress of the Mediterranean, you can just about glimpse how it might have been, predevelopment. Of course, fun, sun, sand and sangria are just what many are after, and Cala Millor doesn't disappoint. If you do want to escape the crowds, set off for the challenging hike to the **Castell de n'Amer**, which overlooks the sea.

⊙ Sights

Safari-Zoo   ZOO
(☑971 81 09 09; www.safari-zoo.com; Carretera Portocristo–Son Servera, Km5; adult/child €19/12; ⊙9am-6.30pm Jun-Sep, 10am-4pm rest of year) Beyond Cala Millor's sprawl is Safari-Zoo, where you can see more than 600 animals (including rhinos, hippos, zebras, giraffes, baboons, wildebeest and numerous antelope species) from the comfort of your car or an open-sided tourist train (which skirts the reserve nine times daily). The animals have plenty of space to roam, unlike those in the depressing enclosures in the more traditional zoo that makes up the rest of the park.

ℹ Information

Tourist Office (☑971 58 58 64; www.visit-calamillor.com; Plaça Eureka; ⊙9am-5pm Mon-Fri, to 1pm Sat May-Oct, 9am-3pm Mon-Fri Nov-Apr)

ℹ Getting There & Away

Bus 441 runs up and down the east coast, linking Cala Millor with resorts such as Cala d'Or (€8.10, 1¼ hours, up to five daily), Porto Cristo (€1.85, 30 minutes, up to five daily) and Portocolom (€5.95, 1¼ hours), while bus 447 also gets you to Porto Cristo (€1.85, 30 minutes, twice daily). Bus 412 heads to Palma (€9.70, 1¾ hours, up to 15 daily).

Porto Cristo

POP 7287

Mallorca's grandest caves, the otherworldly Coves del Drac, ensure Porto Cristo is a perennially popular day-trip destination, attracting civilian spelunkers by the busload. It's true that as a resort it lacks some of the bang of glitzier destinations elsewhere on the coast, but that's no bad thing – what Porto Cristo lacks in glamour it makes up for in quiet charm.

⊙ Sights

★**Coves del Drac**   CAVE
(Dragon's Caves; ☑971 82 07 53; www.cuevasdel-drach.com; Carretera Cuevas; adult/child €15/8; ⊙10am-5pm Mar-Oct, 10.45am-3.30pm Nov-early Mar) Over-visited, probably overpriced, the Coves del Drac are by no means overrated. Of all Mallorca's accessible cave complexes, this is the least forgettable. A 1.2km shuffle with the inevitable crowd, accompanied by a multilingual commentary, leads through chamber after chamber of impossible shapes, colours and dimensions. The one-hour tour (leaving on each hour) finishes at a vast amphitheatre and lake, where you'll enjoy a brief classical music recital.

Passeig de la Sirena   BEACH
(🏖) Most of the town's activity crowds alongside the Passeig de la Sirena and the harbour, where a small crowded beach provides the perfect place to observe the comings and goings of fishing boats and yachts in the marina, perhaps over an ice cream or aperitif. Riddling the honey-coloured cliffs bordering the beach you'll find the modest Coves Blanques, a handful of small caves that were inhabited during the Talayotic period and were later used by fishers for shelter.

Coves dels Hams   CAVE
(www.cuevas-hams.com; Carretera Ma4020 Manacor–Portocristo, Km 11; adult/child €9/free; ⊙10am-5pm Mar-Oct, to 4pm Nov-Feb) On the northern side of town on the road to Manacor, this underground labyrinth has some fine stalactite formations and an open-roofed cave rich with plants and birds. The main cave, with its 12 galleries, is the setting for the *Sea of Venice* musical performance. Be aware that the massive signs all over town to the 'caves' lead here, not to the more famous (and crowded) Coves del Drac.

SECLUDED COVES SOUTH OF PORTO CRISTO

The coast running south of Porto Cristo is textured with a series of beautiful, unspoilt coves, many of them signposted from the Ma4014 highway linking Porto Cristo and Portocolom. The largest and most developed of the bunch is **Cala Romántica** (S'Estany d'en Mas; P), a 160m-long wedge of pale golden sand flanked by cliffs and calm turquoise shallows. A few hotels form a serene resorts and a rough promenade has been hewn out of the rock face by the sea.

Further south of Cala Romántica is a string of beautiful spots, such as **Cala Varques** (Cala Barques) (known for the cave on the cliff above the cove), **Cala Sequer, Cova del Pilar** or **Cala Magraner**, a wild and secluded cove at the foot of a gorge and some weather-pitted cliffs, popular with climbers. None has direct car access (in fact, some would be more easily reached by boat): plan on walking at least the last few minutes.

Activities

Skualo Adventure Sports & Dive Centre DIVING
(971 81 50 94; www.mallorcadiving.com; Passeig del Cap d'Es Toll 11; 2 dives with/without equipment €72/96; ⊙9am-6pm Mon-Sat Easter-Oct) This first-rate dive centre offers scuba 'baptisms' (€90) for novices, plus a wide array of other PADI courses. It also offers snorkelling (€45) and two-hour sea-kayaking excursions (€45), as well as a three-hour sea cave excursion, with the chance to swim. There are eight notable dive sites within reach, offering varied topography and lots of sea life.

Illa Balear BOATING
(971 81 06 00; www.illabalear.com; Carrer de Mestral 12; adult/child 2hr round trip €22/10, one way to Cala Ratjada €15/10; ⊙8.30am-5.30pm;) Runs boat excursions (most in glass-bottomed catamarans) between Porto Cristo and other east-coast resorts, such as Cala Ratjada, Cala Romántica and Cala Millor. Up to nine times daily in summer.

Festivals & Events

Festa de Sant Antoni RELIGIOUS
(⊙16 & 17 Jan) Porto Cristo goes all out with a bonfire and 'dance of the devils' for the eve of Sant Antoni, the traditional blessing of animals.

Verge del Carme RELIGIOUS
(⊙16 Jul) The feast day of the patroness of fisherfolk is celebrated with great cheer along the coast. In Porto Cristo, a statue of the lady is carried in procession to a specially decorated boat.

Eating

La Magrana CAFE €€
(971 55 69 74; Plaça de Déu del Carme 15; mains €15-16; ⊙9am-4pm Tue-Sat, 10am-2pm Sun;) Uphill from town, on a quiet church square, this cute cafe cultivates a boho vibe, with its appealing jumble of vintage knick-knacks, pot plants, wicker chairs, art and bold colours. Take a seat in the garden terrace for fresh juices, ice creams and light bites like *pa amb oli* (bread with oil) with Serrano ham and cannelloni with fresh salad.

Sa Sal MEDITERRANEAN €€€
(971 82 20 49; www.restaurantesasal.com; Carrer de la Tramuntana 11; mains €25-26; ⊙6.30-11.30pm Wed-Sun) In a surprisingly scruffy neighbourhood, Sa Sal stands head and shoulders above most restaurants in town, with its refined service, inventive menu and candlelit patio. The interior brings a modern aesthetic to the Mallorcan house's original beams and stone. Follow imaginative entrees, like ceviche with black garlic ice cream, with mains such as super-fresh fish, stewed with lentils and saffron.

Information

Tourist Office (971 84 91 26, 662 350882; www.visitmanacor.com; Plaça de l'Aljub; ⊙9am-3pm Mon-Fri) At the end of the wharf.

Getting There & Away

Eight bus lines serve Porto Cristo, among them bus 412 to Palma (€8.50, 1½ hours, up to 10 daily) via Manacor (€1.90, 30 minutes); buses 441, 445 and 448 connect to other east-coast resorts, including Cala Ratjada (varied prices, scores of buses).

Portocolom

POP 4294

A relatively sleepy place as far as east-coast holiday resorts go, Portocolom has resisted the tourist onslaught with dignity. Claimed rather dubiously as the birthplace of Christopher Columbus, by those who dispute his Genoese origins, it's a thoroughly maritime town based on a large, handsome natural harbour (one of the few on the island). Fishing boats, sailing boats and the odd luxury yacht bob in the calm waters of its large horseshoe-shaped bay, while divers are drawn to some of the island's best sites.

Beaches

Within reach of Portocolom are some fine beaches, such as the immaculate little cove of **Cala Marçal** and, at the northern end of town, scenic and gentle **Cala s'Arenal**, the locals' preferred beach. On the eastern headland at the mouth of the bay, there's the mid-19th-century lighthouse, **Far de sa Punta de ses Crestes**, with good views back towards the town.

Activities

Starfish   BOATING
(http://starfishboat.com;   May-Oct;   ) A glass-bottomed tour is a great way to explore the coastline south of Portocolom. Boarding at Portocolom Marina, or Cala Marçal just to the south, Starfish runs several daily trips to Cala d'Or (adult/child €22/12) and Cala Figuera (€30/14), calling at stunning coves and beaches on the way.

East Coast Divers Mallorca   DIVING
(971 82 52 80; www.bahia-azul.de; Ronda Miquel Massuti Alzamora 77; Apr-Oct) Founded in 1971, the former Bahia Azul dive centre has a new name, but is still German-owned, and still takes divers to 15 nearby sites filled with caves, cliffs, wrecks and critters. 'Discover' scuba packs, in the pool and sea, cost €79, while courses start from €210; two dives in the protected Illa Cabrera costs €159.

Skualo Adventure Sports Centre   DIVING
(971 83 41 97; www.mallorcadiving.com; Ronda del Creuer Balear 53; introductory dive €90; 8.30am-8pm Mon-Sat Apr-Oct) A well-respected dive centre, with snorkelling (€45) and sea-kayaking (two- to three-hour excursion €45). It's also branched out into stand-up paddleboarding, speedboating and, of course, dive-certification courses.

Eating

Portocolom's reputation as a relaxed holiday spot attracts a slightly older, wealthier crowd than some other east-coast resorts. Accordingly, the dining options are good!

★ Restaurant Sa Llotja   SPANISH €€
(971 82 51 65; www.restaurantsallotjaportocolom.com; Carrer dels Pescadors; mains €27-33, menus €37-50; 1-3.30pm & 7-10.30pm Tue-Sun;) A slick, glass-fronted restaurant with a wonderful terrace overlooking the harbour, Sa Llotja does delicious renditions of established dishes with slightly conservative restraint. Starters might be grilled Mallorcan octopus or red-tuna tartare, while mains include confited lamb shoulder and local sole *meunière*. The terrific-value three-course menu includes wine, water and coffee.

Restaurante HPC   INTERNATIONAL €€
(971 82 53 23; www.restaurantehpc.com; Carrer de Cristòfol Colom 5; mains €16-25; 9am-4pm & 6.30-11pm;) Draped in white, with the occasional lick of red or grey, HPC's dining room opens invitingly onto the street, suggesting everything from breakfast to a tapas lunch or afternoon aperitif. Beyond the slightly globetrotting tapas (hummus with crumbled oxtail, or tempura prawns) there's grilled fish and meat, pasta and pizzas.

Celler Sa Sinia   SEAFOOD €€€
(971 82 43 23; www.cellersasinia.com; Carrer dels Pescadors 25; mains €20-23; 1-3.30pm & 8-11pm Tue-Sun) With menus designed by artist Miquel Barceló and chairs marked with plaques bearing the names of famous people who have sat there, this vaulted maritime eatery has bags of character. Fresh fish (perhaps monkfish with onion, or turbot in mousseline), paellas and homemade desserts are as much the house specialities as the warm, old-fashioned service.

Information

Tourist Office (971 82 60 84; www.visitfelanitx.es; Avinguda de Cala Marçal 15; 9am-4pm Mon-Fri & 6-9pm Tue-Fri, 9am-1pm Sat & Sun) At the southern end of town, on the road to Cala Marçal.

Getting There & Away

Eight bus lines service Portocolom, including the coastal routes 441, 448 and 449 (dozens daily). Buses 490 and 491 (express) go to/from Palma (€6.95, 1¾ hours, up to seven daily).

Southern Mallorca

Why Go?

The forbidding geography of the coast between the Badia de Palma (Bay of Palma) and Colònia de Sant Jordi has preserved this area as one of Mallorca's least developed. Much of the shoreline is ringed by high, impenetrable cliffs lashed endlessly by the waters of the Mediterranean. They may not always be very accessible, but their untamed, raw beauty is hypnotising.

Beyond the cliffs are intimate coves and long swathes of fine sand, true marvels of nature. Whether tightly encircled by rock, or fading into rough scrub of pine and juniper, here are some of Mallorca's best beaches. This part of the island, inaccessible or devoted to agriculture and conservation, has been spared the worst excesses of overdevelopment that have scarred parts of Mallorca. It's a glimpse of how all of the island's coast must once have looked.

Best Places to Eat

➡ Restaurante Petite Iglesia (p174)

➡ Sal de Coco (p168)

➡ Casa Manolo (p169)

➡ Aventura (p175)

➡ Port Petit (p176)

When to Go

Mallorca's southern beaches live for the summer, to the extent that you won't find much going on if you arrive before Easter or after October. November to March, when the island is at its quietest and coolest, can still be a good time to visit. If you do, you're likely to have the place to yourself, including some eerily quiet resort towns with just a handful of restaurants, hotels and shops open. Summer is undoubtedly the peak season; if crowds turn you off, just seek out one of many resort-free stretches of coastline.

Top Sights

➡ Cala Pi (p166)

➡ Centro de Visitantes Ses Salines (p168)

➡ Parc Nacional Maritim-Terrestre de l'Arxipèlag de Cabrera (p172)

➡ Cap de Ses Salines (p169)

➡ Capocorb Vell (p166)

Cala Pi

POP 412

An intimate, geographically blessed and very likeable resort, Cala Pi overlooks a gorgeous white-sand, pine-flanked slither of a beach. On the coast, a circular 17th-century defence tower stands testament to the Mallorca of centuries past, when the threat from North African pirates was constant.

◉ Sights

Cala Pi   BEACH

Reached via a steep staircase (follow the signs along Cami de la Cala Pi), the beach is only 50m wide but it is a beauty, stretching more than 100m inland and flanked on either side by craggy cliffs that ensure the startlingly turquoise water in the inlet stays as still as bath water. There are no facilities at beach level so bring any provisions you're likely to need.

Capocorb Vell   ARCHAEOLOGICAL SITE

(🖉971 18 01 55; www.talaiotscapocorbvell.com; Carretera Arenal–Cap Blanc, Km 23; €2; ⊙10am-5pm Fri-Wed; ℗) At this sprawling prehistoric village, you can wander along stony pathways and beside rough stone structures that date to 1000 BC. The site, which includes 28 dwellings and five *talayots* (square and round stone towers made with – in the case of Capocorb Vell – no mortar). First excavated in the early 1900s, it gives a great sense of the scope and layout of the mysterious settlement.

✕ Eating

Typical Mallorcan restaurants, with local as well as foreign tourists in their sights, make up the perfectly pleasant suite of options. Summer terraces, paella, suckling lamb shoulder – all the classic ingredients recur.

Restaurante Miguel   SPANISH €€

(🖉971 12 30 00; Carrer de la Torre 13; mains €18-22; ⊙11am-11pm Tue-Sun Mar-Oct) Set back from the ruddy headland that sustains Cala Pi's highly photogenic 16th-century 'fire tower', Restaurante Miguel is a Mallorcan-style 'farmhouse' with a huge, inviting patio. Miguel cooks up excellent seafood dishes like paella, mussels in marinara sauce and grouper with lemon sauce, as well as heartier Mallorcan specialities like rabbit with mushrooms. There's a snack menu for grazers, too.

❶ Getting There & Away

Bus 525 links Cala Pi and Palma once in the morning and once in the evening (€5.55, 70 minutes).

Sa Ràpita

POP 10,000

The main settlement along this stretch of coast, Sa Ràpita is a sleepy seaside village whose rocky shoreline, harangued by waves, provides a scenic diversion from a largely nondescript town, as does the profile of nearby Illa de Cabrera. Neighbouring Vallgornera has the longest cave on the island.

◉ Sights

Platja de Ses Covetes   BEACH

This 200m sweep of pale, silky sand and gin-clear water forms part of the **Reserva Marina del Migjorn de Mallorca** (a protected marine reserve), so no buildings mar its backdrop of dunes and pines. It's unspoilt but not uncrowded. Walking east along the shore, you'll come upon Platja des Trenc. Platja de Ses Covetes is past Sa Ràpita and off the Ma6030 highway. You can park in Sa Rapita.

✕ Eating

Most of the places along the waterfront Avinguda de Miramar – in other words, most of the places in Sa Ràpita – hedge their bets between Mallorcan favourites and pizza and pasta. You can eat perfectly well, if unmemorably.

Xaloc   MALLORCAN €€

(🖉971 64 06 35; Carrer del Xaloc 36; mains €18-22; ⊙12.30-3.30pm Tue-Sun, 7.30-11pm Tue-Sat; 🖅) This little back-street Mallorcan joint comes highly recommended by locals, for its paellas, grilled fish and other simple Balearic favourites.

❶ Getting There & Away

From Palma, bus 515 heads to Sa Ràpita (€5.35, one hour, up to five daily).

Colònia de Sant Jordi

POP 2734

A once-sleepy fishing village that was 'discovered' by tourism in the 1950s, Colònia de Sant Jordi's popularity with *palmero* vacationers has made it the biggest beach resort

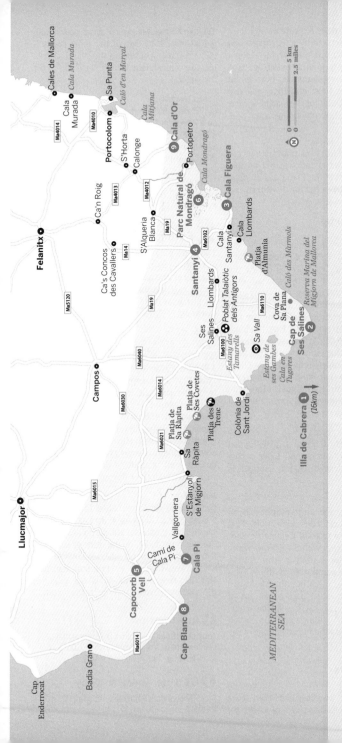

Southern Mallorca Highlights

1 Illa de Cabrera (p172) Boating to Mallorca's only national park.

2 Cap de Ses Salines (p169) Hiking to the coves that dot this island.

3 Cala Figuera (p174) Dining on the day's catch at this fishing village.

4 Santanyí (p173) Pottering through the handsome stone streets.

5 Capocorb Vell (p166) Wandering the relics of the prehistoric Talayotic people.

6 Parc Natural de Mondragó (p175) Swimming, exploring and birdwatching among the dunes and wetlands.

7 Cala Pi (p166) Clambering down the steep walls of this narrow cove, to sprawl on the soft sand below.

8 Cap Blanc (p171) Tracing the coast's contours from the lighthouse.

9 Cala d'Or (p176) Escaping the glamour and finding a quiet cove to kayak in.

of the southern coast. A prim town whose well-laid-out streets form a chequerboard across a gently rolling landscape, the Colònia is family friendly and surrounded by some of the best and least-developed beaches on Mallorca. Perhaps most enticingly, it's also the embarkation point for the marine wilderness of the Illa de Cabrera archipelago.

◎ Sights

Colònia de Sant Jordi's main attractions are its wonderful beaches and seafront promenade. Best known is the Platja des Trenc, a 20-minute walk from the northwestern end of town.

Centro de Visitantes
Ses Salines AQUARIUM
(☑ 971 65 62 82; www.balearsnatura.com; cnr Carrer Gabriel Roca & Plaça del Dolç; ◎10am-2am & 3-6pm, closed Dec & Jan) FREE At the northeastern end of town, watched over by a whale-skeleton sentry, this stone-and-glass swirl of a building is part aquarium and part interpretation centre for the offshore marine environs of the Parc Nacional Marítim-Terrestre de l'Arxipèlag de Cabrera. Free and fascinating, your visit to 18 aquariums and over 70 species ends with a climb up a spiral ramp that wraps around an extraordinary mural by Miguel Mansanet, based on 16th-century Mallorcan maps of the Mediterranean.

Platja de Ses Roquetes BEACH
This broad stretch of white sand is lapped by clear, shallow waters, and looks across to a scattering of small islands. Nudism is allowed.

Platja des Trenc BEACH
Platja des Trenc, the largest undeveloped beach on Mallorca, runs 2km northwest from the southern edge of Colònia de Sant Jordi. With long stretches of frost-white sand, azure water and a restful setting among pine trees and rolling dunes, des Trenc proves just how pretty the Mallorcan coast was before development got out of hand. Officially a nudist beach, des Trenc draws a mixed clothed and unclothed crowd, many of whom take advantage of the sun loungers for hire.

🏃 Activities

Piraguas Mix KAYAKING
(☑ 660 470723; www.piraguasmixkayaks.com; Cami de Alcaria Rotja, Campos; sea kayaks per

day from €30, guided excursions per person €30; ◎8.30am-8.30pm) One of the most respected sea-kayaking outfits on the island. Call to meet in central Sant Jordi if you'd like to hit the water.

Team Double J CYCLING
(☑ 971 65 57 65; www.teamdoublej.com; Avinguda de la Primavera 7A; carbon road bike per day/week €30/130; ◎9.30am-1.30pm & 3-7pm Mon-Fri, from 5pm Sat & Sun Feb-Oct) This outfit rents good-quality bikes, if you're tackling rough terrain or serious road distance, and can also provide maps and information on area routes. Call or email to arrange rental outside standard opening months.

✗ Eating

There are plenty of *pa amb oli* (bread with oil) and tapas places lining the Carrer Gabriel Roca (the part-pedestrianised harbourfront road), but finding the few places offering anything more adventurous will require research.

Sal de Coco MEDITERRANEAN €€
(☑ 971 65 52 25; www.restaurantsaldecoco.com; Moll de Pescadors; mains €15-20, menús €28; ◎1-3.30pm & 7.30am-11pm Wed-Mon Mar-Nov; 🛜) This slick, art-strewn bistro takes its name from the sea salt gathered on the rocks around Colònia de Sant Jordi. Marta Rosselló puts an original take on Mediterranean flavours in dishes like homemade fish and spinach ravioli with shrimp sauce, cuttlefish and mushroom risotto and just-right steak tartare – all beautifully presented and revealing true depth of flavour.

Marisol INTERNATIONAL €€
(☑ 971 65 50 70; Carrer Gabriel Roca 63; mains €16-20; ◎12.30-10.30pm; 🛜♿) Logically for a seaside joint, fish is a strong point here: try the salt-crust hake, or the dory or scorpion fish (when it's super-fresh), sold by the kilo. Or you could opt for pasta, pizza, fish and shellfish, rice dishes or stews at a table on the spacious covered terrace by the water.

ℹ Information

Tourist Office (☑ 971 65 60 73; www.mallorcainfo.com; Carrer Gabriel Roca; ◎10am-2pm & 5-9pm May-Sep, 4-6pm Oct-Apr)

ℹ Getting There & Away

Bus 502 connects Palma to Sant Jordi (€6.40, 1¼ hours, up to six daily).

Ses Salines

POP 10,288

Used as a source of salt since the days of the Romans, Ses Salines (Salt Pans) is a beautifully preserved agricultural centre that's quickly gaining recognition as one of inland Mallorca's most attractive towns. With quality bars, restaurants and hotels, plus grocers selling the local wines, salt and other produce that some travellers crave, it's transformed itself from a rural waystation to a destination in its own right. Plus, it's surrounded by some lovely rural landscape, crisscrossed by walking and cycling trails within whiffing distance of the salty sea.

◉ Sights

The town's attractions are quite spread out and you'll need a car (or bike) to reach them.

Cap de Ses Salines   LIGHTHOUSE

(Carretera de Cap de Ses Salines) Follow the Ma6110 highway 9km south of Llombards to reach the Cap de Ses Salines, a beautiful bluff on Mallorca's southernmost tip with a lighthouse dating back to 1863. There's not much here, but stretching out along either side are unspoilt beaches protected by the Reserva Marina del Migjorn de Mallorca.

Botanicactus   GARDENS

(☑971 64 94 94; www.botanicactus.com; Carretera Ses Salines–Santanyí, Km 1; adult/child €9.50/4.50; ⊙9am-7pm Mar-Oct, 10.30am-4.30pm Nov-Feb; Ⓟ) Just outside Ses Salines is Botanicactus, Mallorca's largest botanical garden. Not just given over to cacti, its 15 hectares bristle with palms, bamboo groves, cypress, carob, orange trees and (naturally) plants with prickles. A wander among its 1600-plus species of Mediterranean, exotic and wetland plants is pleasant in fine weather.

Artestruz Mallorca   FARM

(☑639 721735; www.artestruzmallorca.com; Ma6014, Km 14; adult/child €12/7; ⊙10am-8pm, consult website as times vary; 🐾) The main attraction at this ostrich farm is the chance to see, stroke and feed the birds, which kids will love; they're also active at night. Meals (featuring ostrich meat, eggs and Mallorcan wine) are available with advance notice, and there's also a shop on-site, selling a variety of ostrich-leather products, including bags and fine shoes. If you fancy a challenge, order an ostrich Scotch egg: they weigh 1.3kg even before the casing is added.

Poblat Talaiòtic dels
Antigors   ARCHAEOLOGICAL SITE

FREE About 1km south of Ses Salines (follow the signposts off the road to Colònia de Sant Jordi) is this neglected archaeological site. There's no visitors' centre, the gate is always open and only virtually illegible plaques remain, so use your imagination to see how these low stone walls would have once constituted a prehistoric settlement.

☞ Tours

Salines des Trenc   TOURS

(☑971 65 53 06; www.salinasdelevante.com; Carretera Colònia de Sant Jordi–Campos, Km 8.5; ⊙visits staggered 11am-6pm) If you fancy getting the inside scoop on des Trenc's famous *flor de sal* (hand-harvested sea salt), you can join a 45-minute tour of the salt pans, available in Spanish, English and German. The tours explore the salt production process and its history, as well as the life and times of the 170-plus bird species living in the surrounding wetlands.

✕ Eating

Ses Salines punches well above its weight in the eating department, with at least four establishments (pretty much most of them in town) you'd be delighted to dine at.

★ Casa Manolo   MALLORCAN €€

(☑971 64 91 30; www.bodegabarahona.com; Plaça Sant Bartomeu 2; mains €17-23; ⊙11am-4pm & 7-11pm Tue-Sun) With its photo-plastered walls and ceilings strung with Serrano hams, this corner bar looks much as it did when it opened in 1945. While the aged, Josper-grilled meat is fantastic, the real secret to its staying power lies in the rice, seafood and fish dishes. Try lobster stew or *arròs notari*, a rice dish overflowing with seafood and a rich squid-ink sauce.

Asador es Teatre   MALLORCAN €€

(☑971 64 95 40; www.asadoresteatre.com; Plaça Sant Bartomeu 4; mains €17-21; ⊙noon-11pm Thu-Tue) Asador Es Teatre specialises in roast lamb, T-bone steaks and other fine cuts of aged meat, all seared to perfection on the Josper (grill-oven). The building – which has been used as a barbershop, dentist and even a ballroom – dates to the 19th century; but the outdoor terrace, commanding a fine view of all the town's comings and goings, is the place to be.

HIKING IN SOUTHERN MALLORCA

CAP DE SES SALINES TO COLÒNIA DE SANT JORDI

START CAP DE SES SALINES
END COLÒNIA DE SANT JORDI
DURATION/DISTANCE 9KM; 3 HOURS

The coastal trail between Cap de Ses Salines and Colònia de Sant Jordi is a flat but rocky trek across battered rock outcrops and secluded sandy beaches, perfect for swimming. Be sure to take plenty of water – there are no freshwater sources and very little shade along the way. Plants you'll see on the trail include wild asparagus and leafy *azucena de mar* (sea purslane), whose fragrant white flowers appear in July and August.

Leave your car on the shoulder of the road at **Cap de Ses Salines**, which is signposted from the main highway. From here, head towards the sea and turn right (west). You'll see the Mediterranean glistening to your left, the Illa de Cabrera in the distance and the private Sa Vall estate, owned by the March family, bordering the walk on your right.

After 30 minutes of a fairly flat walk over the ruddy-coloured rocks that dominate the coast here (the same that give Palma's Catedral its striking colour), you'll come upon the first 'virgin' beach of the walk, Platja des Cargol, which is protected by a natural rock pier. In summer it can get quite crowded on land and at sea.

Continue along the coast for further coves and beaches, like Cala en Tugores (which you should reach in an hour's walk), Platja de Ses Roquetes and Platja des Carbó (after 2¼ hours) and finally Platja des Dolç (the full three hours). The beaches, with their fine-as-flour sand and gentle gradient (and thus waves) are simply gorgeous. Even with summer crowds, an idyllic backdrop of juniper trees and squawking seagulls ensures that it always feels like an escape.

At the western end of Platja des Carbó is Colònia de Sant Jordi, the end of the walk.

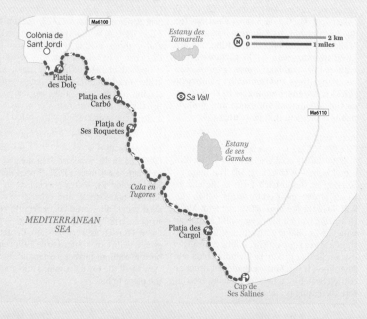

Pristine coastline can be hard to come by in Mallorca, but the walk from Cap de Ses Salines to Colònia de Sant Jordi has it in abundance.

TOLO BALAGUER/AGEFOTOSTOCK ©

Colònia de Sant Jordi (p166)

CAP BLANC

If you're travelling the coast road from Palma to Capocorb Vell and Cala Pi, take the short detour to this wind-torn, atmospheric headland. If you're on the Ma6014 highway south from S'Arenal, turn right at the sign pointing to 'Cap Blanc'. You'll soon come across a lighthouse and a desolate-seeming military compound, where you can park.

You can't get right up to the lighthouse, but can wander around its outbuildings to the sheer cliff it surmounts. From here, the views along the ruddy cliff-face, with Palma and the western mountains in one direction, the Illa de Cabrera in the other, and seabirds circling the Mediterranean sky overhead, are nothing short of breathtaking. If the wind isn't too fierce, this makes a fabulous picnic spot. But be careful with kids or dogs – there's no fence and the drop is abrupt, and almost certainly fatal.

HIKING THE ILLA DE CABRERA

The best-known walking route heads up to a restored 14th-century **castle**, a fortress once used to keep pirates off the island. The 30-minute walk to the castle meanders along the northern side of the island before taking you to the 80m-high bluff where the castle looms.

Guides also sometimes lead the 20-minute walk to **Es Celler**, a farmhouse-turned-museum once home to the Feliu family, which owned the entire island in the early 20th century. Nearby stands a monument to the French prisoners who died on Cabrera.

Other possible routes lead to the **N'Ensiola lighthouse** (four hours, permission required), the southern sierra of **Serra de Ses Figueres** (2½ hours, permission required), or the highest point of the island, the 172m **Picamosques** (three hours, permission required).

Cassai   INTERNATIONAL €€
(☑971 64 97 21; http://cassai.es; Carrer de Sitjar 5; mains €17-21; ☺11am-11pm; 🐾) The stone-flagged courtyard of this 300-year-old build-ing, graced with creeping ivy, potted shrubs and artfully weathered timber, is a lovely place to linger over an aperitif, tapas or something more substantial. Dishes include *lomo de bacalao* (cod loin) with *tumbet* (Mallorcan ratatouille), red tuna curry, and there's a well-priced express lunch (€8.50).

🍷 Drinking & Nightlife

★**Mon de Vins**   WINE BAR
(☑971 64 97 73; www.llumdesal.es; Carrer Bur-guera Mut 14; ☺11am-midnight) A wonderful place to sample the wines of Mallorca (and further afield), this latest outpost of Robert Chaves' burgeoning Llum de Sal empire is strewn with tempting bottles and opens onto an inviting courtyard. Take a bottle away, stay and wash down quality tapas with a few sympathetic glasses, or do both: the choice is yours.

🛍 Shopping

Bodega Llum de Sal   FOOD & DRINKS
(☑971 64 97 73; www.llumdesal.es; Carrer Bur-guera Mut 14; ☺9am-midnight, 10am-9pm in win-ter) Artworks jazz up the walls of this stone-and-wood, split-level gourmet food store on the main drag – one of the loveliest in this corner of the island. As well as doing great coffee, it sells gourmet food products, in-cluding local salt and ready-made herb com-binations for fish, meats and wok cooking.

Flor de Sal d'Es Trenc   FOOD & DRINKS
(☑971 64 28 61; http://flordesaldestrenc. com; Plaça Sant Bartomeu 9; ☺10am-1.15pm & 5-9.30pm) The official sales point for the sea salt you'll see for sale all over Mallorca, this shop sells the natural variety, as well as those scented with Mediterranean herbs, boletus mushrooms, black olives and other

SNORKELLING OFF THE ILLA DE CABRERA

The island is a wonderful place for snor-kelling. While you need special permis-sion to dive here, you can snorkel off the beach. Or, in July and August, sign up for the guided snorkelling excursions offered by park rangers.

additions (€8.95 for 150g to 250g). It also sells wines, olive oils and other local goodies.

ℹ Getting There & Away

The easiest way to arrive is with your own wheels, and you'll need them to explore the surrounding attractions. If you're reliant on public transport, bus 502 runs to Palma (€7.30, 80 minutes, up to 10 daily), Santanyí (€1.50, 10 minutes), Campos (€2.35, 25 minutes) and Colònia de Sant Jordi (€1.50, 10 minutes).

Illa de Cabrera

Nineteen uninhabited islands and is-lets make up the only national park in the Balearic Islands, the **Parc Nacion-al Marítim-Terrestre de l'Arxipèlag de Cabrera** (☑971 72 50 10; ☺Easter-Oct), an ar-chipelago whose dry, hilly islands are known for their birdlife, rich marine environment and abundant lizard populations. The Illa de Cabrera, the largest of the archipelago and the only one you can visit, sits 16km off the coast of Colònia de Sant Jordi. Other islands are used for wildlife research. Only 200 peo-ple per day (300 in August) are allowed to visit this highly protected natural area, so reserve your place at least a day ahead. The main **park authority** (☑971 17 76 45; http:// en.balearsnatura.com; Carrer Gremí de Corredors 10; ☺11am-3pm) is in Palma.

◉ Sights & Activities

Many enjoy the wonderfully calm beaches, **Sa Plageta** and **S'Espalmador**. The park has an extremely fragile ecosystem and there are few hiking trails open to the pub-lic – for most of them you'll either need to tag along with a guide or request permission from the park information office on Cabrera.

Castillo de Cabrera   CASTLE
(☑630 982363; www.balearsnatura.com; Illa de Cabrera) Attacked, damaged and rebuilt re-peatedly since its 14th-century origin, this squat hexagonal tower guards Cabrera's eastern harbour. At one point it was con-verted into a prison for French soldiers, more than 5000 of whom died after being abandoned in 1809 towards the end of the Peninsular War. It now enjoys peaceful re-tirement, watching tourists and not pirates disembarking below.

Es Celler MUSEUM
(☎630 982363; adult/child €2/free; ⊙11.30am-
1pm & 4-6pm) This restored farmhouse contains an ethnographic and natural history
collection. Outside is a botanic garden where
you can see many endemic Balearic species.

Mar Cabrera BOATING
(☎971 65 64 03; www.marcabrera.com; Carrer
Gabriel Roca 20; adult/child from €40/25; ⊙8am-
10pm, closed Dec & Jan) Mar Cabrera operates
a speedboat service and tours of the Illa de
Cabrera and coves of the southern coast.

Excursions a Cabrera BOATING
(☎971 64 90 34; www.excursionsacabrera.es;
Carrer Dofí 1l; adult/child boat €40/25, speedboat
€45/29; ⊙8am-10pm high season, to 4pm low
season, closed Nov-Feb; 🚤) Round-trip tours by
speedboat or slower boats from Colònia de
Sant Jordi to the marine- and birdlife-rich
Parc Nacional Marítim-Terrestre de l'Arxipèlag de Cabrera..

ℹ Information

Park Information Office (☎630 982363;
http://en.balearsnatura.com; Port of Cabrera;
⊙8am-2pm & 4-8pm) Advice and permits for
hikes and other things to do on the island.

ℹ Getting There & Away

Although private boats can come to Cabrera
if they've requested navigation and anchoring
permits in advance from the park authority,
nearly all visitors arrive on the organised tours.
Excursions a Cabrera runs both slow boats and
speedboats from Colònia de Sant Jordi; **Mar
Cabrera** operates a speedboat service.

On the cruise back to Colònia de Sant Jordi,
the boat stops in **Sa Cova Blava** (Blue Cave),
a gorgeous cave with crystalline waters where
passengers can take a dip.

Santanyí

POP 11,316

Wedged between the Parc Natural de Mondragó and Ses Salines, Santanyí has been
well and truly discovered. Travellers are
flocking to this handsome inland town,
where honey-coloured churches shelter a
fine array of bars, boutiques, ceramic shops
and restaurants. Such is its popularity with
well-heeled German tourists in particular
that every second shop now seems to be an
estate agent or art gallery.

**WILDLIFE WATCHING ON THE
ILLA DE CABRERA**

This is prime territory for bird-watching: marine birds, birds of prey and
migrating birds all call Cabrera home at
least part of the year. Common species
include the fisher eagle, the endangered
Balearic shearwater, Audouin's gull,
Cory's shearwater, shags, ospreys, Eleonora's falcon and peregrine falcons.

Terrestrial wildlife is also abundant.
The small Balearic lizard is the best-
known species on Cabrera. It has few
enemies on the archipelago and 80% of
the species population lives on Cabrera.

Most of the action spirals around the
church-dominated Plaça Major, especially on market days (Wednesdays and Saturdays) when stalls selling local produce,
leather goods and trinkets fill every available central street. Once they pack up, the
square is given over anew to laid-back cafes
and bars that subtly entice you to linger over
tapas and drinks, long into the evening.

◎ Sights

Cala Llombards BEACH
A petite cove defined by rough rock walls
topped with pines, Cala Llombards is a truly beautiful place. A beach-hut bar and sun
loungers shaded by palm-leaf umbrellas
constitute the extent of human interven-
tion. The view is soul-satisfying – turquoise
waters, a sandy beach and the reddish rocks
of the cliffs that lead like a promenade towards the sea. To reach Cala Llombards,
follow the sign off the Ma6102 down a
stone-walled road bordered by meadows of
grazing sheep.

Cala Santanyí BEACH
Cala Santanyí's popular but not overcrowded beach is the star in a scenic show that
also includes a gorgeous, cliff-lined cove
and impossibly cobalt-coloured waters. The
beach sits at the bottom of a ravine of sorts
where there is a car park (it's a stiff walk or
cycle ride back to the resort centre). A small
path leads along the coast, where the natural rock arch El Pontàs rises out of the surf.
This is a popular spot to snorkel.

✗ Eating

Diners are spoilt in Santanyí – every second door hides a tapas bar or restaurant, although prices are inflated.

Alchemy   EUROPEAN €€
(☑ 971 65 39 57; www.alchemysantanyi.com; Plaça Major 9; mains €18-21; ⊙ 9am-11pm) Despite the name, Alchemy has nothing to do with molecular gastronomy or other culinary excesses. With its pretty courtyard, slick bistro interior and warm welcome, it keeps its look, feel and food refreshingly simple. You might begin with, say, duck confit with pear chutney, salt cod with roasted peppers, or simply grilled meat and seafood.

Es Molí de Santanyí   TAPAS €€
(☑ 971 65 36 29; Carrer Consolació 19; tapas €7-13; ⊙ 1-11pm mid-Feb–mid-Nov) On the road leading east from Santanyí you'll find the windmill, a sprawling stone-built restaurant with a lovely garden terrace shaded by palms and rubber trees, and serving a great line in tapas. On the menu are imaginative, well-executed morsels for assembling your own little feast, from tuna sashimi to pork loin with *sobrassada* (spicy cured sausage) custard and roasted quail with lentils.

ⓘ Information

There's no tourist office, but the **Parc Natural de Mondragò Office** (☑ 971 64 20 67; http://en.balearsnatura.com; Carrer de Can Llaneres 8; ⊙ 8am-3pm Mon-Fri) can advise on visits to this nearby natural park.

ⓘ Getting There & Away

Bus connections with Palma are plentiful: take bus 501 (€6.55, 1¼ hours, up to 10 daily) or bus 502 (€6.55, 1¾ hours, up to 10 daily).

Cala Figuera

POP 627

A twisting fissure in the coastal slab of southern Mallorca forms the impossibly picturesque harbour town of Cala Figuera. Steep scrubby escarpments rise up on all sides from the glassy water, leaving little space for the few houses, bars and restaurants to cling to. Despite its great charm, and proximity to some of Mallorca's busiest resorts, it remains the fishing village it has always been. While a few yachts line up beside the smaller working boats, local fishermen still make their way down the winding

inlet before dawn, returning in the evening to mend their nets. Many of their houses have no street access, only private slipways.

☞ Tours

Red Star Tours   BOATING
(☑ 664 243464; www.redstartours.com; Carrer de Virgen del Carmen 52; ⊙ 10am-1pm & 3-5pm) Hop aboard for a 45-minute tour of the surrounding bays including Cala Santanyí (adult/child €20/14), or a 75-minute nature tour (€27/19) taking in a string of little-known coves. Red Star also rents kayaks (€20 for three hours) and rigid inflatable boats (€85 for two hours).

✗ Eating

★ La Petite Iglesia   FRENCH €€
(☑ 971 64 50 09; Carrer de la Marina 11; mains €17-19, menú €20; ⊙ 6-11pm daily, 9am-1.30pm Mon-Sat; 🖫) Inhabiting the shell of a little sandstone church, with outdoor tables under the trees, this atmospheric place serves up terrific French home cooking. Everything is spanking fresh, from the house-baked bread to whatever fish was hauled up to the harbour that day, with special mention going to the lip-smacking terrines and slow-cooked dishes, such as *boeuf bourguignon*.

L'Arcada   MALLORCAN €€
(☑ 971 645 032; Carrer de Virgen del Carmen 80; mains €15-20; ⊙ noon-10.30pm Apr-Oct) Watch the boats blink in the port at this laid-back hillside restaurant. The seafood – from grilled calamari to Mallorcan prawns – is good, naturally, but don't overlook island-wide faves such as paella, pork loin with *tumbet* and rabbit with onions.

Restaurante Mistral   MEDITERRANEAN €€
(☑ 971 64 51 18; Carrer de Virgen del Carmen 42; mains €18; ⊙ 6.30-11pm mid-Apr–Oct; 🖫) Choose between tasty, typical tapas or more elaborate dishes, such as grilled sole with fresh parsley paste, or *tumbet* with meat or fish at this stylish spot, just up from the port.

♟ Drinking & Nightlife

Bon Bar   BAR
(☑ 691 389867; www.bonbar.es; Carrer Virgen de Carmen 27; ⊙ 10am-midnight, to 10pm in winter) Views – that's what this place is all about. High above the main body of the inlet and with uninterrupted vistas, this is the place to nurse a cocktail, or a *pa amb oli*, or ice cream if it's too early for you.

Getting There & Away

Bus 503 connects Cala Figuera with Palma (€7.05, 1½ hours, four daily Monday to Saturday, with transfer at Santanyí) and Santanyí (€1.50, 20 minutes).

Portopetro

There's something in the air in Portopetro. This intimate fishing port's quiet appeal is immediately apparent as you stroll its steep, shady streets and look out over the protected natural inlet that originally made this town such a hit with fishers. It doesn't have a beach in the town centre, which may be a problem for some, but explains why it's escaped the development rampant in Cala d'Or, just to the north.

Activities

Petro Divers   DIVING
(☑ 971 65 98 46; www.petro-divers.eu; Es Calo d'es Moix 8; ☺ 8.30am-6.30pm Mar-Nov; 🚻) This diving outlet offers the full array of PADI and SSI courses, from intro and children's dives to Open Water Diving certifications. A single dive will set an already-certified diver back €40; the more you book, the cheaper it gets. Petro rents gear and runs up to four trips per day when things are busy.

Eating

A string of good Mallorcan restaurants – nothing fancy, but all worth their salt and all with waterside terraces for good weather – lines the marina.

Aventura   MALLORCAN €€
(☑ 971 65 71 67; Carrer de Sa Punta Mitjana 11; mains €17-22; ☺ noon-3.30pm & 6-11pm Apr-Oct) Breezy harbour views, friendly service and freshly caught fish make Aventura the pick of Portopetro's waterfront bunch. Go for mixed tapas for two (€25) with a bottle of *blanco*, or spot-on mains like hake with clams or grilled John Dory.

Restaurante Marítimo   MALLORCAN €€
(☑ 971 65 80 50; Caló d'en Moix; mains €15-22, lunch menú €14; ☺ noon-4pm & 7-11.30pm Tue-Sun Feb-Oct; 🚻) Next to Petro Divers, this friendly, unpretentious restaurant has a bougainvillea-draped terrace from which you can look out across the harbour. Unsurprisingly, fish is its forte, with everything from grilled monkfish to crustacean-studded paellas.

La Caracola   MALLORCAN €€
(☑ 971 65 70 13; Carrer Passeig d'es Port 40; mains €12-17, lunch menú €9; ☺ 8am-11pm; 🚻) Besides the usual paella and pasta, this enduringly popular place has been pleasing diners with plates of *calamares rellenos* (stuffed squid) *lechona* (suckling pig) and *tumbet* (Mallorcan ratatouille) for over 20 years. Not the flashiest place in town but it's often the most crowded.

Getting There & Away

Bus 501 connects Portopetro with Palma (€8.45, 1¾ hours, up to 10 daily) and Cala d'Or (€1.50, 10 minutes).

Parc Natural de Mondragó

A natural park encompassing beaches, dunes, wetlands, coastal cliffs and inland agricultural land, the 766-hectare Parc Natural de Mondragó is a beautiful area for swimming or hiking, but is best known as a birdwatching destination. Only 95 hectares of the park are publicly owned: much of the remainder is still divided into small drystone-walled fields known as *rotes*, bearing almonds, figs, carob and olives.

Sights & Activities

Most people who head this way come to take a dip in the lovely **Cala Mondragó**, one of the most attractive coves on the east coast. Sheltered by large rocky outcrops and fringed by pine trees, it's formed by a string of three protected sandy beaches connected by rocky footpaths.

Information

The small **park office** (☑ 971 18 10 22; http://en.balearsnatura.com; Carretera de Cala Mondragó; ☺ 9am-4pm) by the Ses Fonts de n'Alis car park (cars/motorbikes/caravans €5/2/9) has maps with walking suggestions. There's also a **park office** in Santanyí.

Getting There & Away

Cala Mondragó is 2km south of Portopetro. High-season bus 507 links Cala Mondragó with Cala d'Or (€1.85, 45 minutes, up to five daily Monday to Saturday, summer only) and a few other seaside resorts.

Cala d'Or

POP 3622

Although the pretty cove beaches and calm, azure waters are still here, they can be hard to find amid the endless bustle of this flashy, overgrown resort. Cala d'Or's five small calas each have their own main drag, where pubs, restaurants and souvenir shops flourish, making it difficult to get a handle on the place.

🏃 Activities & Tours

Xplore Mallorca   OUTDOORS
(📞971 65 90 07; www.xploremallorca.com; Carrer s'Alga; ⊙May-Oct) Xplore offers mountain-biking (€18), hiking (€15), cycling (€19), quad-biking (€42) and sea-kayaking (€18) excursions of varying duration. Children under 10 years pay half.

Sea Riders   BOATING
(📞615 998732; www.searidersweb.com; Cala Llonga; tours adult €22-42, child €17-33; ⊙May-Oct) Sea Riders, in Cala Llonga, offers a kid-friendly boat ride as well as a faster 'adrenaline' ride (reaching speeds of over 80km/h) with up to three departures daily in July and August.

Cooking Holidays Mallorca   COOKING
(📞971 64 82 02; www.cookingholidaysmallorca. com; Cala d'Or Yacht Club, Avinguda de Cala Llonga) Cala d'Or's beautifully sited yacht club is the venue for these English-language courses teaching the fundamentals of Mallorcan, Spanish and Italian cookery. Day-long courses cost €105 to €140, or you could upgrade to a luxurious four- to six-night 'gourmet break', including bed and board at the Club.

Moto Sprint   MOTORBIKE HIRE
(📞971 65 90 07; www.moto-sprint.com; Carrer d'en Perico Pomar 5; carbon bike/500CC motorbike hire per day €19/69, per week €102/382; ⊙8am-8pm Mar–mid-Nov) Moto Sprint rents bikes ranging from sturdy commuters to sleek carbon-framed road bikes, and motorbikes from 50CC scooters to powerful 750CC machines. Helmets and locks are included.

🍴 Eating

Aquarius   SPANISH €€
(📞971 65 98 76; Port Petit 308; mains €17-21; ⊙10am-midnight Mar-Nov) A cracking location overlooking the yacht port, chilled music and friendly service makes Aquarius stand out. Snag a spot on the terrace for seafood, such as sea bass with a brick-red *romesco* sauce or a mean *frit Mallorquí* (Mallorcan-style fried lamb, liver and vegetables).

Port Petit   MEDITERRANEAN €€€
(📞971 64 30 39; www.portpetit.com; Avinguda de Cala Llonga; mains €24-28, menús €20-70; ⊙1-3.30pm & 7-11pm Wed-Mon Apr-Oct) One of Cala d'Or's top tables, Port Petit puts an innovative spin on local seafood and produce, served on a covered terrace whose dazzling whiteness matches the yachts below. Service is attentive and dishes like fresh lobster sautéed in lime butter, squid with sepia rice or lamb slow-roasted in its own juices are cooked with aplomb.

Yacht Club Cala d'Or   MEDITERRANEAN €€€
(📞971 64 82 03; www.yccalador.com; Avinguda de Cala Llonga; mains €20-25; ⊙9am-10pm Mar-Oct; 🔊) You don't need to be a millionaire yachtie to eat in style at this glass-fronted harbour restaurant, where tables overlook a tantalising infinity pool. The menu is best described as Mallorcan with plenty of international flourishes, as seen in simple dishes such as wild turbot in sage butter, or tagliolini made with truffled eggs.

ℹ️ Information

There are two tourist offices in town: **one** (📞971 65 74 63; Carrer d'en Perico Pomar 10; ⊙9am-2pm Mon-Fri) just north of the central grid, and the **other** (📞971 65 97 60; Avinguda de la Cala d'Or 4; ⊙10am-4pm Mon-Fri) inland from Cala Ferrera.

ℹ️ Getting There & Away

Bus 501 heads to Portopetro (€1.70, 15 minutes, up to eight times daily), then on to Palma (€8.45, 1¾ hours, up to 10 daily). Bus 441 runs along the eastern coast, stopping at all the major resorts.

WILDLIFE WATCHING

Birdwatchers have a ball with the varied species found in the area, which include falcons and turtledoves. Among those species that nest here are peregrine falcons and Audouin's gulls. Taking one of the walking trails that criss-cross the park will give you plenty of bird-watching opportunities. Also keep an eye out for Algerian hedgehogs, Hermann's tortoise and the Balearic toad.

Understand Mallorca

Mallorca Today

It's a mixed bag for sure, but Mallorca is looking sunny-side up. The island weathered the austerity storm better than many other parts of Spain and even recent corruption scandals have failed to deflate a generally buoyant mood. More than 23 million passengers touched down in Palma in 2014 and arrivals continue to break records, while the property market experienced 17% growth in 2015. New hotels are flinging open their doors and restaurant chefs hop to keep the tourist influx wined and dined.

Best on Film

The Night Manager (2016) Very popular BBC series based on the novel of the same name by John le Carré, with many locations filmed in Mallorca.

Woman of Straw (1963) Stars Sean Connery with Artà as the backdrop.

The Magus (1968) Anthony Quinn, Michael Caine and Candice Bergen with Mallorca standing in for a Greek island.

A Winter in Mallorca (1969) Relives Chopin and George Sand's ill-fated stay on the island.

Presence of Mind (*El Celo,* 2000) Sadie Frost, Harvey Keitel and Lauren Bacall; a tutor comes to the island to educate two orphaned children.

Best in Print

Mañana Mañana (Peter Kerr) The pick of the books about trying to live like a Mallorcan.

Bread and Oil: Majorcan Culture's Last Stand (Tomás Graves) Food-dominated book centred on traditional Mallorca's greatest passions.

British Travellers in Mallorca in the Nineteenth Century (eds Brian J Dendle and Shelby Thacker) Anthology of Mallorcan travellers' tales.

A Bull on the Beach (Anna Nicholas) One of several lively yarns about the life of an expat in rural Mallorca.

The Tourist Toll

With a registered population of just under 900,000, Mallorca's residents are outnumbered more than 10 to one by visitors, who annually constitute an army 9.5 million strong. That's a lot of sunscreen. Shunning the terrorist hot spots of Tunisia, Egypt and Turkey, holidaymakers have turned their attention to the sun-kissed Balearic Islands. Locals, however, complain the island is coming apart at the seams during the peak summer crush. Sewage systems have been overwhelmed. Water resources (sucked dry by golf courses and hotels) and electricity supplies have been pushed to their limits, while overflowing rubbish bins and congested roads add to the woes. The tourist tax, launched in 2016, is partly aimed at controlling the huge numbers of arrivals, but servicing the influx while protecting the island's resources, environment and infrastructure is an ongoing headache.

Corruption and Sleaze

Linked inextricably to the cash-cow tourist economy that feeds around 80% of Mallorca's GDP, corruption has a ceaselessly corrosive effect on good business practice and public confidence. Illegal property construction and infrastructure contracts for roads and flyovers to nowhere have long sapped public faith in political leadership, while corruption has worsened labour conditions at the pointy end where 45% of under-25s are unemployed (in the Balearic Islands as a whole). The left-wing, anti-austerity Podemos party has pledged to weed out corruption, but it's a tall order battling something so deeply ingrained within the island's business culture. In 2014, the former Balearic Islands' President and Popular Party minister Jaume Matas was sentenced to a six-year jail term for fraud. Since 2010, 16 former PP politicians have been jailed for corruption. Even Princess Cristina and husband Iñaki Urdangarin stood trial in 2016 in Palma, accused of tax fraud and corruption.

An Image Change

An image change for Mallorca – from the slightly seedy, booze-fuelled and resort-infested picture of yesteryear – has repositioned the island in the travelling consciousness. Mallorca is increasingly appealing to a broader cross-section of visitors, as hikers, cyclists and birdwatchers arrive in greater and greater numbers. The mushrooming population of *fincas* (farmsteads, or estates) converted to hotels has transformed holidaymakers' enjoyment of the island, while the Palma restaurant scene continues to refresh itself with new openings and an influx of creative chefs.

Despite the pressure of visitor arrivals, black vultures (*Aegypius monachus*), Europe's largest raptor, have established new records in their breeding season in the Serra de Tramuntana, where the species has been gradually growing over the last three decades, before which the bird almost disappeared from Mallorca.

Hemingway would have been appalled, but the pressure group *Mallorca Sense Sang* (Mallorca Without Blood) succeeded in having bullfighting banned in Palma and campaigners hope the ban will extend to the entire island.

Winter tourism is another big focus, with more hotels opening earlier and closing later every year to cater for growing numbers of out-of-season visitors. And it is working: more and more operators are adding outdoor-focused holidays to their portfolio. Boozy Magaluf still casts the occasional shadow, but the horizons are looking bright.

POPULATION: **869,067**

GDP PER CAPITA: **€24,394**

UNEMPLOYMENT RATE: **13.9%**

NUMBER OF PASSENGERS THROUGH PALMA AIRPORT (2015): **23.745 MILLION**

if Mallorca were 100 people

78 would be Mallorquin
9 would be from mainland Spain
3 would be German
10 would be Other

belief systems
(% of population)

95 — Roman Catholic
5 — Other

population per sq km

MALLORCA

USA

UK

≈ 30 people

History

Mallorca's position in the heart of Europe's most fought-over sea has placed it in the path of the great sweeps of Mediterranean history, and events in that wider theatre have transformed the island time and again. But for all its experience of invasion, war, prosperity and hunger, Mallorca has rarely been at the heart of great European affairs. It's the perfect blend of historical riches and contemporary getaway.

The Talayotic Period

The Balearic Islands were separated from the Spanish continent a mere eight million years ago. They were inhabited by a variety of animal life that carried on in splendid isolation until around 9000 to 10,000 years ago, when the first groups of Epipaleolithic people set out from the Spanish coast in rudimentary vessels and bumped into Mallorca.

The earliest signs of human presence on the island date to around 7200 BC. In the following 6000 years, the population, made up of disparate groups or tribes, largely lived as hunter-gatherers in caves or other natural shelters. Around 2000 BC they started building megalithic funerary monuments, but at the time the pyramids were being constructed in Egypt, Mallorca was home to only a basic civilisation.

Things were shaken up in Mallorca and Menorca around 1200 BC with the arrival of warrior tribes, probably from Asia Minor, who overwhelmed the local populace. They are known today as the Talayotic people, after the dry-stone *talayots* (towers) that are their chief material legacy, still scattered across many Mallorcan sites. The circular (and sometimes square- or hull-shaped) stone edifices are testimony to an organised and hierarchical society. The most common circular *talayots* could reach a height of 6m and had two floors. Their purpose is a matter of conjecture: were they symbolic of the power of local chieftains, or their burial places? Were they used for storage or defence? Or were they perhaps religious sites? There were at least 200 Talayotic villages across the island: simple ceramics, along with artefacts in bronze (swords, axes, necklaces), have been found on these sites.

TIMELINE	7200 BC	c 1200 BC	c 700 BC
	Archaeologists date the first human settlements in Mallorca to this time, based on carbon-dated findings in the southwest of the island in Cova de Canet, a cave near Esplores.	Warrior tribes invade Mallorca, Menorca, Corsica and Sardinia. Those in Mallorca and Menorca are known today as the Talayotic people because of the *talayots* (stone towers) they built.	Phoenician traders install themselves around the coast, extending their influence across Mallorca. Balearic slingers serve as mercenaries in Carthaginian armies.

The ancients knew Mallorca and Menorca as the Gymnesias Islands, from a word meaning 'naked' (it appears that at least some of the islanders got about with a minimum of covering). Talayotic society seems to have been divided into a ruling elite, a broad subsistence-farming underclass and slaves. It is not known if they had a written language.

Contact with the outside world came through Greek and Phoenician traders, although the Carthaginian Phoenicians attempted to establish a foothold in Mallorca and failed. They did, however, enrol Mallorcans as mercenaries: Balearic men were noted for their skill as slingers, having learned to use these simple weapons with deadly accuracy as children. These sling-wielding Mallorcan and Menorcan *foners* (Catalan for 'warriors') gave themselves the name 'Balears', possibly derived from an ancient Greek word meaning 'to throw'. And so their island homes also came to be known as the Balearics. These men weren't averse to payment, developing a reputation as slings for hire: in Carthaginian armies they would shower a deadly hail of stones on the enemy before the infantry advanced. Also carrying daggers or short swords for hand-to-hand combat, they wore virtually no protection. Balears played their part in the Carthaginian victory over the Greeks in Sicily in the 5th century BC, and again in the Punic Wars against Rome.

Romans, Vandals & Byzantines

When the Roman Consul Quintus Cecilius Metelus approached the shores of Mallorca in 123 BC, possibly around Platja des Trenc in the south, he did not come unprepared. Knowing that the island warriors were capable of slinging heavy stones at his ships' waterline and sinking them, he had come up with a novel idea. Using heavy skins and leather, he effectively invented the first armoured vessels. Stunned by their incapacity to inflict serious damage, the Mallorcan warriors fled inland before the advance of Metelus's legions. Within two years the island had been pacified.

Metelus had 3000 settlers brought over from mainland Iberia, and founded two military camps in the usual Roman style (with the intersecting main streets of the *decumanus* and *cardus maximus*). Known as Palmeria (or Palma) and Pol·lentia, they soon developed into Mallorca's main towns. Pol·lentia, neatly situated between the two northeast bays of Pollença and Alcúdia, was the senior of the two.

As Pol·lentia was embellished with fine buildings, temples, a theatre and more, some Roman citizens opted for the rural life, building grand country villas. None remain today, but it is tempting to see them as the precursor to the Arab *alqueries* (farmsteads) and Mallorcan *possessions* (country estates).

Talayotic Sites

Ses Païsses, Artà

Capocorb Vell, Cala Pi

Necròpolis de Son Real, Ca'n Picafort

Museu Arqueològic de Son Fornés, Montuïri

Es Figueral de Son Real, Ca'n Picafort

Illot dels Porros, Ca'n Picafort

123 BC	AD 426	534	707
On the pretext of ending Balearic piracy, the Roman general Quintus Cecilius Metelus, later dubbed Balearicus, storms ashore and takes control of Mallorca and Menorca.	Raids on Mallorca by the Vandals, central European Germanic tribes that had pillaged their way across Europe to North Africa, lead to the destruction of the Roman city of Pol·lentia.	Belisarius takes control of the Balearic Islands in the name of the Byzantine Emperor Justinian, who, until his death in 565, attempted to re-establish the Roman Empire across the Mediterranean.	Muslim Arabs from North Africa raid Mallorca for the first time. Four years later they begin the conquest of the Spanish mainland.

The indigenous population slowly adopted the Roman language and customs, but continued to live in its own villages. Plinius the Elder reported that Mallorcan wine was as good as that in Italy, and the island's wheat and snails were also appreciated.

Archaeological evidence of early Christianity – such as the 5th-century AD remains of a basilica at Son Peretó near Manacor – suggest that the new Roman faith had arrived on the island as early as the 4th century. By then storm clouds were gathering, breaking in the form of barbarian assaults on the Roman Empire from the 5th century. The Balearic Islands felt the scourge of the Vandals (an East Germanic tribe that plundered their way into Roman territory) in 426. Forty years later, having crashed across Spain to establish their base in North Africa, they returned to take the islands.

The Vandals got their comeuppance when Byzantine Emperor Justinian decided to try to rebuild the Roman Empire. His tireless general, Belisarius, vanquished the Vandals in North Africa in 533 and took the Balearic Islands the following year. After Justinian's death in 565, Byzantine control over territories in the western Mediterranean quickly waned. By the time the Muslims swept across North Africa in the first years of the 8th century, the Balearic Islands were an independent Christian enclave.

The Islamic Centuries

In 902 an Arab noble from Al-Andalus (Muslim Spain), Isam al-Jaulani, was forced by bad weather to take shelter in the port of Palma. During his stay he became convinced that the town could and should be taken, along with Mallorca and the rest of the Balearic Islands, and incorporated into the Caliphate of Córdoba. On his return to Córdoba, the Caliph Abdallah entrusted him with the task, and Al-Jaulani returned with a landing party in 902 or 903.

The port town fell easily but Al-Jaulani, now the Wāli (governor) of the territory dubbed 'the Eastern Islands of Al-Andalus' by the Arabs, was compelled to wage another eight years of war against pockets of Christian guerilla resistance throughout the islands. But by the time Al-Jaulani died in 913, the islands had been pacified and he had begun work to expand and improve its only city, now called Medina Mayurka (City of Mallorca).

The Muslims divided the island into 12 districts, and in the ensuing century Mallorca thrived. They brought advanced irrigation methods, allowing the *alqueries* – the farms they established – to flourish. Medina Mayurka became one of Europe's most cosmopolitan cities, and by the end of the 12th century it had a population of 35,000, on par with Barcelona and London. The *al-qasr*, or castle-palace (Palau de l'Almudaina),

Some historians claim the funny white, green and red clay figurine-whistles known as *siurells* were introduced to Mallorca by the Phoenicians and may have represented ancient deities. Classic figures include bulls, horse riders and dog-headed men.

869	903	1075	1114–15
Norman raiders sack Mallorca's population centres, just 21 years after an Arab raid from Muslim Spain, which Mallorca's leaders had agreed to in return for being left in peace.	Muslim forces take control of Mallorca in the name of the Caliph of Córdoba in Spain. Local Christian warriors resist for another eight years in redoubts across the island.	Mallorca becomes an independent *taifa* (small kingdom) in the wake of the civil conflicts that shattered the Caliphate of Córdoba into a series of *taifas* across Spain.	A Catalan–Pisan crusading force arrives to end the piracy that is damaging Mediterranean trade. They take Medina Mayurka (Palma) in 1115 and free 30,000 Christian slaves before leaving the island.

was built over a Roman fort, and the grand mosque stood where Palma Catedral now does. With the raising of walls around the new Rabad al-Jadid quarter (roughly Es Puig de Sant Pere), the city reached the extents it would maintain until the late 19th century. It was a typical medieval Muslim city, a medina like Marrakech or Fez. Few of the narrow streets that made up its labyrinth, now called *estrets* (narrows), remain. Medina Mayurka enjoyed close relations with the rest of the Muslim world in the western Mediterranean, although by 1075 the emirs (princes) of the Eastern Islands were independent of mainland jurisdiction.

Al-Jaulani's successors dedicated considerable energy to piracy, which by the opening of the 12th century was the islands' principal source of

THE JEWS IN MALLORCA

The first Jews appear to have arrived in Mallorca in AD 70, after the destruction of the Temple in Jerusalem. Under Muslim rule, a small Jewish minority thrived in Medina Mayurka; Christian Mallorca, following the 1229 conquest, was not so kind.

Although barred from most professions and public office, Mallorca's Jews were esteemed for their learning and business sense. Jewish doctors, astronomers, bankers and traders – generally fluent in Catalan and/or Spanish, Latin, Hebrew and Arabic – often played key public roles.

By the end of the 13th century, there were perhaps 2000 to 3000 Jews in Ciutat (Palma). They were evicted from the environment of Palau de l'Almudaina and moved to the Call (Catalan equivalent of a ghetto) in the streets around Carrer de Monti-Sion, in eastern Sa Calatrava. Here they were locked in at night and obliged to wear a red and yellow circular patch during the day. In 1315 their synagogue was converted into the Església de Monti-Sion, and they would not have another until 1373. In 1391, rioting farmers killed some 300 Jews in an anti-Semitic pogrom.

In 1435 the bulk of the island's Jews were forced to convert to Christianity and their synagogues were converted into churches. At the beginning of the 16th century they were forced to move from the Call Major to the Call Menor, centred on Carrer de Colom. Now officially Christian, they were nonetheless suspected of secretly practising Jewish rites. They were a particular target for the Inquisition, and the last auto-da-fé (trial by fire) of such so-called *judaizantes* took place in 1691, when three citizens were burned at the stake.

Known as *xuetes* (from *xua,* a derogatory term referring to pork meat), they continued to be shunned by many Christians, and couldn't breathe more easily until the 19th century. A veritable flurry of 19th-century Mallorcan writers and poets came from *xueta* families. During WWII, when the Nazis asked Mallorca to surrender its Jewish population, the religious authorities purportedly refused. Today the descendants of these families (who even in the mid-20th century could be shunned) are estimated to number between 15,000 and 20,000.

1148	1185	1203	1229
Mallorca signs a trade agreement with the Italian cities of Genoa and Pisa, opening Mallorcan markets to the Italians and reducing the threat of further Christian assaults on the island.	The Muslim governor of the island, Wāli Ishaq, dies, ending a period of unprecedented prosperity. His rule represents the high point of Almoravid control over Mallorca.	The Almohads in peninsular Spain defeat the Almoravid regime in Medina Mayurka and take control of the island, although life continues largely unchanged for most of Mallorca's inhabitants.	Under Jaume I, King of Aragón, Catalan troops land at Santa Ponça in Mallorca, defeat the Muslims and camp before the walls of Medina Mayurka.

PLAGUE

Mallorca's connection to the seafaring trade routes of the Mediterranean ensured that it was particularly vulnerable to the ravages of the plague, which hit the island repeatedly, decimating the population in the process.

revenue, arousing the wrath of Christian Europe's trading powers. In 1114, 500 vessels carrying a reported 65,000 Pisan and Catalan troops landed on Mallorca and launched a bloody campaign, entering Medina Mayurka in April the following year. Exhausted after 10 months' fighting, news of a Muslim relief fleet en route from North Africa persuaded the invaders to depart, laden with booty, prisoners and freed Christian slaves.

In 1116, a new era dawned in Mallorca, as the Almoravids (a Berber tribe from Morocco) from mainland Spain took control. The Balearics reached new heights in prosperity, particularly under the Wāli Ishaq, who ruled from 1152 to 1185. Then, in 1203, Mallorca fell under the sway of the Almohads, who had taken control of Al-Andalus.

The internecine strife between Muslim factions had not gone unnoticed in Christian Spain, where the Reconquista (the reconquest of Muslim-held territory by the Christian kingdoms) had taken on new impetus after the rout of Almohad armies in the Battle of Las Navas de Tolosa in 1212. By 1250 the Christians would take Valencia, Extremadura, Córdoba and Seville and the last Muslims would be expelled from Portugal. In such a context, it is hardly surprising that a plan should be hatched to take the Balearic Islands – especially as Mallorca continued to be a major source of piracy, seriously hindering Christian sea trade.

El Conqueridor

On 5 September 1229, 155 vessels bearing 1500 mounted knights and 15,000 infantry weighed anchor in the Catalan ports of Barcelona, Tarragona and Salou, setting sail for Mallorca. Jaume I (1208–76), the energetic 21-year-old king of Aragón and Catalonia, vowed to take the Balearic Islands and end Muslim piracy in the process. Later dubbed El Conqueridor (The Conqueror), Jaume landed at Santa Ponça and, after two swift skirmishes, marched on Medina Mayurka, to which he laid siege. Finally, on 31 December, Christian troops breached the defences and poured into the city, pillaging mercilessly. In the following months, Jaume I pursued enemy troops across the island, meeting only feeble resistance.

With the conquest of Mallorca complete, Jaume proceeded to divide it up among his lieutenants and allies. The Arab *alqueries, rafals* (hamlets) and villages were handed over to their new *senyors* (masters). Many changed name, but a good number retained their Arab nomenclature (places beginning with *bini* (meaning 'sons of') are notable examples). Many took on the names of their new lord, preceded by the possessive particle *son* or *sa* (loosely translated as 'that which is of...'). Jaume codified this division of the spoils in his *Llibre del Repartiment*.

Among Jaume's early priorities was a rapid program of church-building, Christianisation of the local populace and the introduction of set-

Dec 1229	1267	1276	1343
Jaume I enters the city, which his troops sack, leaving it in such a state that a plague the following Easter kills many of the inhabitants and invading soldiers.	Mallorcan icon Ramon Llull has a series of visions that will ultimately transform him into one of the most important Catalan cultural figures in history.	Jaume I dies, almost 50 years after bringing Christian rule to Mallorca. The territories under his rule are divided between his two sons, prompting decades of internecine conflict.	Pere III of the Crown of Aragón invades Mallorca and seizes the crown from Jaume III, who dies six years later in the Battle of Llucmajor, trying to reclaim it.

tlers from Catalonia (mostly from around the city of Girona). For the first century after the conquest, Ciutat (the city) held the bulk of the island's population. The Part Forana ('Part Outside' Ciutat) was divided into 14 districts, but all power in Mallorca was concentrated in Ciutat. Beneath the king, day-to-day governance was carried out by six *jurats,* or 'magistrates'.

The Christian Catalan settlers imposed their religion, tongue and customs on the island, while the bulk of the Muslim population was reduced to slavery. Those that did not flee or accept this destiny had only one real choice: to renounce Islam. The Jewish population would also have a troubling time of it.

In the Part Forana the farmsteads came to be known as *possessions* and were the focal point of the agricultural economy upon which the island would largely come to depend. The *possessions* were run by local managers who were faithful to their (frequently absentee) noble overlords, and were often well-off farmers themselves. They employed *missatges* (permanent farm labour) and *jornalers* (day wage labourers), both of whom generally lived on the edge of misery. Small-farm holders frequently failed to make ends meet, ceded their holdings to the more important *possessions* and themselves became *jornalers.*

THE EVANGELISING CATALAN SHAKESPEARE

Born in Ciutat (Palma) de Mallorca, mystic, theologian and all-round Renaissance man before his time Ramon Llull (1232–1316) started off on a worldly trajectory. After entering Jaume I's court as a page, Ramon was elevated to major-domo of Jaume II, the future king of Mallorca. In this enviable position he proceeded to live it up, writing love ditties and reputedly enjoying a wild sex life.

Then, in 1267, he saw five visions of Christ crucified and everything changed. His next five years were consumed with profound theological, moral and linguistic training (in Arabic and Hebrew). He founded a monastery (with Jaume II's backing) at Miramar for the teaching of theology and Eastern languages to future evangelists. His burning desire was to convert Jews and Muslims, and he began to travel throughout Europe, the Near East and North Africa to preach. At the same time he wrote countless tracts in Catalan and Arabic, and is considered the father of Catalan as a literary language. In 1295 he joined the Franciscans and in 1307 risked the ire of Muslims by preaching outside North African mosques. Some say he was lynched in Tunisia by an angry mob, while others affirm he died while en route to his native Mallorca in 1316. Certainly, he is buried in the **Basílica de Sant Francesc** (p54) in Palma. His beatification was confirmed by Pope John Paul II and the long, uncertain process of canonisation began in 2007.

1382	1391	1488	1521
Sac i Sort (Bag and Luck) is introduced, whereby the names of six candidates to be named *jurats* (magistrates) for the following 12 months are pulled out of four bags.	Hundreds of Jews die in a pogrom as farmers and labourers sack the Jewish quarter of Palma. Months later, those involved are released without sentence, for fear of causing greater unrest.	The Inquisition, which had operated from the mainland, is formally established in Mallorca. In the following decades hundreds would die, burned at the stake as heretics.	Armed workers and farm labourers rise up in the beginning of the Germania revolt against the nobles. In October 1522, Carlos V sends troops to Alcúdia to quell the revolt.

Crown of Aragón

On Jaume I's death in 1276, his territories were divided between his two sons, Jaume II and Pere II. In the succeeding years Mallorca was torn in the contest between the two, a dynamic that persisted under their heirs. By 1349, the previously independent Kingdom of Mallorca was tied into the Crown of Aragón, although it retained a high degree of autonomy.

The fortunes of Mallorca, particularly Palma, closely followed those of Barcelona, the Catalan headquarters of the Crown of Aragón and its trading hub. In the middle of the 15th century, both cities (despite setbacks such as outbreaks of the plague) were among the most prosperous in the Mediterranean. Palma had some 35 consulates and trade representatives sprinkled around the Med. The city's trade community had a merchant fleet of 400 vessels and the medieval Bourse, Sa Llotja, was an animated focal point of business.

One of the most beautiful descriptions written of the island was the Catalan painter Santiago Rusiñol's *Mallorca, l'Illa de la Calma* (*Mallorca, the Island of Calm*; 1922), in which he takes a critical look at the rough rural life of many Mallorcans.

But not all was rosy. In the Part Forana farm labourers lived on the edge of starvation, and crops occasionally failed to such an extent that people dropped dead in the streets, as in 1374. Frequent localised revolts, such as that of 1391 (the same year that furious workers sacked the Call in Ciutat), were stamped out mercilessly by the army. A much greater shock to the ruling classes was the 1521 Germania revolt, an urban working-class uprising largely provoked by crushing taxes imposed on the lower classes. The unrest forced the viceroy (by now Mallorca was part of a united Spain under Emperor Carlos V) to flee. In October 1522 Carlos sent in the army, but control was not re-established until the following March.

By then Mallorca's commercial fortunes had declined and by the 16th century its coast had become constant prey to the attacks of North African pirates. Around the island the building of 'fire-towers' (watchtowers communicating by bonfire) and fortifications, many of which stand today, testified to the urgency of the problem. Some of Mallorca's most colourful traditional festivals, such as Moros i Cristians in Pollença and Es Firó in Sóller, date to these times. From the 17th century Spain's fortunes declined and Mallorca slid into provincial obscurity. Backing the Habsburgs in the War of the Spanish Succession (1703–15) didn't endear Mallorca to the finally victorious Bourbon monarch, Felipe V. In 1716 he abolished all the island's privileges and autonomy.

Pirate attacks forced Mallorca to be on its guard throughout much of the 18th century, until the island received permission to retaliate without punishment in 1785. At the same time, Mallorcan Franciscan friar Fray Junípero Serra was in California, founding missions that seeded major cities, such as San Francisco and San Diego.

1706	1773	1809	1837
The Austrian pretender to the Spanish throne in the War of the Spanish Succession (1702–15) takes control of Mallorca. Nine years later, Mallorca is conquered by Felipe V.	King Carlos III orders that the Jews of Palma be allowed to live wherever they wish and that all forms of discrimination and mistreatment of the Jewish population be punished.	Thousands of French troops captured in battle in mainland Spain are sent to Illa de Cabrera, where they live in appalling conditions. The survivors would not be released until 1814.	A passenger steamer between Barcelona and Palma begins service, creating a regular link to the mainland. Among its first passengers, in 1838, were George Sand and Frédéric Chopin.

A RIGHT ROYAL DILETTANTE

As the first battles of the Italian campaign raged in 1915, Archduke Ludwig Salvator sat frustrated in Brandeis Castle in Bohemia, writing furiously, but impeded by the fighting from returning to his beloved Balearic Islands. He died in October that year of blood poisoning after an operation on his leg.

Ludwig had been born in 1847 in Florence, the fourth son of Grand Duke Leopold II. He was soon travelling, studying and visiting cities all over Europe. From the outset he wrote of what he saw. His first books were published one year after his first visit to the Balearic Islands in 1867. He returned to Mallorca in 1871 and the following year bought Miramar. He decided to make Mallorca his main base – a lifestyle choice that many northern Europeans would seek to imitate over a century later.

Salvator was an insatiable traveller. In his private steam-driven yacht *Nixe* (and its successors) and other forms of transport, he visited places as far apart as Cyprus and Tasmania. Hardly a year passed in which he didn't publish a book on his travels and studies, possibly the best known of which are his weighty tomes on *Die Balearen* (*The Balearics*). His love remained Mallorca (where royals and other VIPs visited him regularly) and, in 1877, local deputies awarded him the title of Adopted Son of the Balearic Islands. Four years later he was made an honorary member of the Royal Geographic Society in London.

The Napoleonic Wars of the early 19th century had repercussions for Mallorca – waves of Catalan refugees flooded the island, provoking economic and social unrest. The second half of the century saw the rise of the bourgeoisie, an increase in agricultural activity and, in 1875, the opening of the first railway, between Palma and Inca.

Mallorca in the Civil War

The 1931 nationwide elections brought unprecedented results: the Republicans and Socialists together won an absolute majority in Palma, in line with the results in Madrid. The Confederación Española de Derechas Autónomas (Spanish Confederation of the Autonomous Right) won the national elections in 1933 and all the left-wing mayors in Mallorca were sacked by early 1934. They were back again in a euphoric mood after the dramatic elections of 1936 gave a countervailing landslide victory to the left.

For many generals this was the last straw. Their ringleader, General Francisco Franco, launched an uprising against the central Republican government in July 1936. In Mallorca the insurrection found little resistance. On 19 July rebel soldiers and right-wing Falange militants burst into Cort (the town hall) and arrested the left-wing mayor, Emili

April 1912	June 1922	19 July 1936	1 April 1939
The train line linking Palma with Sóller opens; until then, poor mountain roads had made it easier for the people of Sóller to travel north by sea to France than south by land to Palma.	The first postal service flight takes place between Barcelona and Palma. The service would use flying boats parked in hangars at Es Jonquet in Palma.	The army and right-wing militias take control of Mallorca for General Franco as he launches his military uprising against the Republican government in Madrid.	Franco claims victory in a nationally televised radio speech, three days after Madrid had fallen to Nationalist troops, bringing to an end almost three years of conflict.

Darder (he and other politicians would be executed in February 1937). They quickly occupied strategic points across Palma with barely a shot fired. More resistance came from towns in the Part Forana, but that was soon bloodily squashed.

By mid-August battalions of Italian troops and war planes sent by Franco's fascist ally, Benito Mussolini, were pouring into Mallorca. The island became the main base for Italian air operations and it was from here that raids were carried out against Barcelona, with increasing intensity as the Civil War wore on.

On 9 August, 1936, a Catalan-Valencian force (apparently without approval from central command) retook Ibiza from Franco and then, on the 16th, landed at Porto Cristo. So taken aback were they by the lack of resistance that they failed to press home the advantage of surprise. A Nationalist counter-attack begun on 3 September, backed by Italian planes, pushed the hapless (and ill-equipped) invaders back into the sea. Soon thereafter, the Republicans also abandoned Ibiza and Formentera. Of the Balearic Islands, only Menorca remained loyal to the Republic throughout the war.

With Franco's victory in 1939, life in Mallorca mirrored that of the mainland: use of Catalan in public announcements, signs, education and so on, was banned. In 1940, rationing was introduced and stayed in place until 1952. Of the nine mayors the city had from 1936 to 1976, four were military men and the others staunchly conservative.

Boom Times

In 1950 the first charter flight landed on a small airstrip on Mallorca: no one could have predicted the implications. By 1955 central Palma had a dozen hotels, while others stretched along the waterfront towards Cala Major.

The 1960s and 1970s brought an extraordinary urban revolution, as mass tourism took off vertiginously. The rampant high-rise expansion around both sides of the Badia de Palma – and later along countless other beaches around Mallorca's coast – was the result of a deliberate policy by Franco's central government to encourage tourism in Spain's coastal areas. Many of the hotels built during this period have since been closed, or recycled as apartment or office blocks.

The islanders now enjoyed – by some estimates – the highest standard of living in Spain, but 80% of their economy was (and still is) based on tourism. For decades this led to thoughtless construction and frequent anxiety attacks whenever a season didn't meet expectations. The term *balearización* was coined to illustrate this short-term mentality and the avid overdevelopment of one of the island's most precious resources – its beautiful coastline.

AIR RAIDS

Between 16 and 18 March, 1938, Italian air-force bombers based in Mallorca launched 17 raids on Barcelona, killing about 1300 people. Apparently Mussolini ordered the raids without the knowledge of the Spanish Nationalist high command.

1952	1960	1983	May 2007
After almost 12 years, post–Civil War rationing finally ends on the island. Although many Mallorcans continue to live subsistence lives, the tourism boom will soon transform the island forever.	An estimated 500,000 tourists visit the island, marking the beginning of Mallorcan mass tourism. These figures would increase 50 times over during the decades that followed.	The autonomy statute for the Balearic Islands region (together with those of other Spanish regions) is approved, eight years after Franco's death.	Mallorcan Socialist Francesc Antich ends right-wing Partido Popular rule by forming a coalition government with promises to put a brake on construction projects.

A Change of Image

In recent years Mallorca's tourism weathervane has been slowly tilting, with an increasing focus on sustainability, eco-awareness and year-round activities.The island is waking up to the fact that thoughtless construction and anonymous package-holiday hotels are the past, not the future. While areas of Mallorca still offer the boozy resorts and cheap-as-chips English breakfasts that, for some, define the island, the true light of Mallorcan culture, cuisine, history and hospitality is increasingly emerging.

Agritourism has proven to be more than just a passing fad, and more and more *fincas* (working farms) are opening their doors to visitors, offering faultless accommodation in peaceful rural locations and meals that feature Mallorca's fantastic produce. Meanwhile, the urban counterparts to those handsome *fincas,* the venerable aristocratic manor houses of the towns and cities, are being sensitively restored as boutique hotels. If Mallorcan tourism has anything of an image problem, fixing it is simply a matter of accentuating these positives – the heritage, style and native pleasures the island has always boasted.

Though many resorts still go into winter hibernation, hotels in busier towns and villages are now staying open during the low season, mostly to cater for a growing number of travellers who come for the island's outdoor activities. Many of Europe's pro cycling teams rely on Mallorca for their winter training and increasing numbers of people are waking up to the richness and variety of outdoor pursuits the island offers. Adventure sports companies offering everything from guided hikes and mountain biking to canyoning, caving and coasteering are rising in number. Their message? Look beyond the beach – Mallorca has year-round substance, variety and appeal.

For an island that is banging the drum about its sustainable tourism, unique landscapes and outdoor activities, the Serra de Tramuntana's inscription on the Unesco World Heritage list of cultural landscapes in 2011 was the icing on the cake. The wild mountains rising in Mallorca's northwestern hinterland are now getting the measure of attention their beauty warrants.

2009
The Basque separatist group, ETA, detonates a series of bombs, killing two policemen and causing havoc at the height of Mallorca's July and August summer tourist seasons.

2011
The conservative Partido Popular (PP) storms back into power, winning an absolute majority in regional elections. The Unió Mallorquina, king-makers in 2007, loses all of its seats.

Landscape & Wildlife

All of the Balearics are beautiful, but Mother Nature really pulled out the stops for Mallorca. Whether you're slow-touring the wild west, where limestone cliffs drop suddenly to curvaceous bays and water 50 shades of blue; rambling through the hinterland, where hills rise steep and wooded above meadows cloaked in wildflowers, olive groves and citrus orchards; or lounging on flour-white beaches on the south coast, you can't help but feel that Mallorca's loveliness is often underrated. Trust us – it's stunning.

Mallorca's Landscape

Mallorca, shaped like a rough trapezoid, is the largest island of the Balearic archipelago. Technically, the island chain is an extension of mainland Spain's Sistema Penibético (Beltic mountain range), which dips close to 1.5km below the Mediterranean and peeks up again to form the islands of Mallorca, Menorca, Ibiza and Formentera. The stretch of water between the archipelago and the mainland is called the Balearic Sea.

The Coast

Mallorca's coastline is punctuated for the most part by small coves, save for three major bays. The Badia de Palma in the south is the most densely populated corner of the island. The two large, shell-shaped bays of the north, the Badia de Pollença and Badia d'Alcúdia, are enclosed by a series of dramatic headlands, Cap de Formentor, Cap des Pinar and Cap Ferrutx.

A series of plunging cliffs interspersed with calm bays marks the south, which is where you'll also find Mallorca's two main island networks: the Illa de Sa Dragonera (offshore from Sant Elm) and the 19-island Parc Nacional Marítim-Terrestre de l'Arxipèlag de Cabrera (from Colònia de Sant Jordi).

Mountains

The island's defining geographic feature is the 90km-long Serra de Tramuntana, a Unesco World Heritage Cultural Landscape since 2011. Spectacularly buckled and contorted, this range of peaks, gullies and cliffs begins close to Andratx in the southwest and reaches its dramatic finale in the northern Cap de Formentor. The highest summits are in the centre of the range, northeast of Sóller, but the steep-sided western flanks that rise abruptly from the Mediterranean shore and shelter numerous villages give the appearance of being higher than they really are. The range is for the most part characterised by forested hillsides (terraced with agriculture in some areas) and bald limestone peaks. A number of tributary ranges, such as the Serra d'Alfabia and Els Cornadors, both close to Sóller, are sometimes named separately.

On the other side of the island, the less-dramatic Serra de Llevant extends from Cap Ferrutx in the north to Cap de Ses Salines in the south; the offshore Illa de Cabrera is considered an extension of the range. The highest point is the easily accessible Santuari de Sant Salvador (509m), while the range dominates the Parc Natural de la Península de Llevant, north of Artà. Between the two, in the centre of the island, extends the vast fertile plain known as Es Pla.

Caves

Mallorca, particularly along its eastern and southern coasts, is drilled with caves created by erosion, waves or water drainage. The caves range from tiny well-like dugouts to vast kilometres-long tunnels replete with lakes, rivers and astounding shapes sculptured by the elements. Although underground, most of the caves actually sit above sea level. The best-known are the Coves del Drac (p162) and Coves dels Hams (p162), both outside Porto Cristo; Coves d'Artà (p159) in Canyamel; Coves de Campanet (p144) in Campanet; and Coves de Gènova (p87).

Wildlife

Mallorca's animal population is fairly modest in both numbers and variety, but this is more than compensated for by the abundant birdlife, which makes the island a major Mediterranean destination for twitchers.

Land Animals

The most charismatic (and easily visible) of Mallorca's land species is the Mallorcan wild goat *(Capra ageagrus hircus),* which survives in reasonable numbers only in the Serra de Tramuntana, Cap des Pinar and Parc Natural de la Península de Llevant.

Other mammals include feral cats (a serious threat to bird populations), ferrets, rabbits and hedgehogs. Lizards, turtles, frogs and bats make up the bulk of the native populations. Lizards thrive on Mallorca's islands due to the lack of human population and introduced species, particularly on the Illa de Sa Dragonera, where they have the run of the island, and the Illa de Cabrera; the latter provides a refuge for 80% of the last surviving Balearic lizards *(Podarcis lilfordi).* You'll also find spiders, more than 300 moth species and 30 kinds of butterflies.

Marine Life

Sperm whales, pilot whales and finback whales feed not far offshore. Also swimming here are bottlenose dolphins, white-sided dolphins and other species. Scuba divers often spot barracuda, octopus, moray eels, grouper, cardinal fish, damsel fish, starfish, sea urchins, sponges and corals.

MALLORCA'S PARKS

The creation of protected wildlife areas has helped stabilise Mallorca's wildlife and make it accessible to visitors. Now 40% of the island falls under official environmental protection.

PARK	FEATURES	ACTIVITIES	WHEN TO VISIT
Parc Nacional Marítim-Terrestre de l'Arxipèlag de Cabrera	Archipelago of 19 islands and islets; home to 130 bird species and marine life	Birdwatching, hiking, scuba diving, snorkelling, swimming	Easter–Oct
Parc Natural de S'Albufera	Vital wetland sheltering 400 plants and 230 species of birds,	Birdwatching (including 80% of the birds recorded on the Balearic Islands), cycling	Spring & autumn
Parc Natural de Mondragó	Rolling dunes, juniper groves, vibrant wetlands and unspoilt beaches	Hiking, picnicking, swimming	May–Sep
Parc Natural de la Península de Llevant	Flora and fauna	Walking, birdwatching	May–Sep
Parc Natural de Sa Dragonera	Two small islets and the 4km-long Dragonera Island; endangered gull population	Snorkelling, scuba diving	May–Sep

PLANTS

Plants of the Balearic Islands, by Anthony Bonner, is the definitive guide to Mallorca's flora and the ideal companion for budding botanists who plan to spend lots of time hiking.

Birds

As a natural resting point between Europe and Africa, and as one of the few Mediterranean islands with considerable wetlands, Mallorca is a wonderful birdwatching destination. Coastal regions in particular draw hundreds of resident and migratory species, especially during the migration periods in spring and autumn.

With more than 200 species it's all but impossible to predict what you'll see. The birds can be divided into three categories: sedentary (those that live on the island year-round), seasonal (those that migrate south after hatching chicks or to escape the cold winters in northern Europe) and migratory (those that rest briefly in Mallorca before continuing their journey).

Endangered Species

The populations of Mallorca's threatened species of Mediterranean birds, tortoises and toads are recovering thanks to the conservation and controlled breeding efforts of Mallorca's parks and natural areas.

Endangered species here include the spur-thighed tortoise and Hermann's tortoise, the only two tortoises found in Spain, and bird species such as the red kite. In 2006 the endemic Mallorcan midwife toad's status was changed to 'vulnerable' from 'critically endangered' on the IUCN Red List of Threatened Species. But there's not such good news about the Balearic shearwater, a water bird that has suffered greatly because of feral cats; IUCN listed it as 'critically endangered' in its 2013 report.

Plants

Mountains & Plains

On the peaks of the Serra de Tramuntana, Mallorca's hardy mountain flora survives harsh sun and wind. Thriving species tend to be ground-huggers or cliff species such as *Scabiosa cretica,* which burrow into rock fissures to keep their roots well drained and cool.

On Mallorca's rocky hillsides and flat plains, where oak forests once grew before being burned or destroyed to create farmland, drought-

BIRDWATCHING SITES

Parc Natural de S'Albufera (p135) A marshy birdwatchers' paradise where some 230 species, including moustached warblers and shoveler ducks, vie for your attention. The park is home to no less than two-thirds of the species that live permanently in, or winter on, Mallorca and is a Ramsar Wetland of International Importance.

Parc Nacional Marítim-Terrestre de l'Arxipèlag de Cabrera (p172) These protected offshore islands draw marine birds, migrants and birds of prey, including fisher eagles, endangered Balearic shearwaters, Audouin's gulls, Cory's shearwaters, shags, ospreys, Eleonora's falcons and peregrine falcons.

Parc Natural de la Península de Llevant (p154) Watch for cormorants and Audouin's gulls in this rugged promontory north of Artà.

Parc Natural de Mondragó (p175) Falcons, turtle doves and coastal species are the major draws here.

Embassament de Cúber In the shadow of the Puig Major de Son Torrella, watch for raptors and other mountain species.

Vall de Bóquer Near Port Pollença, this rocky valley is home to warblers, Eurasian Scops owls, red-legged partridges, peregrine falcons, and other mountain and migratory species.

Cap de Formentor (p127) Species on this dramatic peninsula include all manner of warblers, blue rock thrushes, crag martins, Eleonora's falcons, pallid swifts, migrating raptors and, if you're lucky, the Balearic shearwater.

resistant scrubland flora now thrives. Expect to see evergreen shrubs like wild olives and dwarf fan palms, as well as herbs such as rosemary, thyme and lavender. Other plants include heather, broom, prickly pear (which can be made into jam) and 60 species of orchid.

Endemic plants include the lovely *Paeonia cambessedesii,* a pink peony that lives in the shade of some Serra de Tramuntana gullies, and *Naufraga balearica,* a clover-like plant found on shady Tramuntana slopes.

Forests & Ferns

Where evergreen oak forests have managed to survive you'll find holly oaks, kermes oaks and holm oaks growing alongside smaller, less noticeable species such as violets, heather and butcher's broom. Most interesting to botanists are endangered endemic species like the shiny-leaved box *(Buxus balearica)* and the needled yew *(Taxus baccata),* a perennial tree that can grow for hundreds of years. A specimen in Esporles is thought to be more than 2000 years old.

Coastal Species

Along the shore, plants have had to adapt to constant sea spray, salt deposits and strong winds. One of Mallorca's most beloved coastal species is samphire *(fonoll marí),* a leafy coastal herb that was given to sailors as a source of scurvy-preventing vitamin C. These days it's marinated and used in salads. Other common species are the spiny cushion-like *Launaea cervicornis,* and *Senecio rodriguezii,* or *margalideta de la mar* (little daisy of the sea).

In the wetlands, marshes and dunes of Mallorca, a variety of coastal freshwater flora prospers. Duckweed is one of the most common plants here, though it is often kept company by bulrush, yellow flag iris, sedge and mint. These sand-dwelling species often have white or pale-green leaves and an extensive root system that helps keep them anchored in the shifting sands.

Environmental Threats

The uninhibited construction that began in the 1960s and 1970s has influenced everything from birds' nesting habits to plant habitats, rainwater run-off and water shortages. Although the government is more environmentally aware now than in decades past, the relationship between development and environmental protection remains uneasy.

One of the most pressing concerns for environmentalists is the prevalence of invasive plant species. Many destructive species were first introduced in local gardens but have found such a good home in Mallorca that they're crowding out endemic species. A good example is *Carpobrotus edulis,* called 'sour fig' in England and locally dubbed *patata frita* (French fry) or *dent de león* (lion's tooth) because of its long, slender leaves. A robust low-lying plant, it chokes native species wherever it goes.

A Green Future?

You need only take one look at Mallorca to see the island's potential for producing renewable energy. The island has an average of 300 days of sunshine a year, and steady winds prevail on the coast. Yet until fairly recently the island was dragging its heels when it came to clean energy, despite its natural resources.

Things are slowly changing. In 2011 Siemens set a precedent by introducing a high-voltage direct current (HVDC) in the form of a 244km submarine cable between Palma and Valencia. The HVDC provides renewable energy from the Spanish mainland. Though it is early days, it is hoped that the island will derive the vast majority of its power from renewable sources, including wind, solar and hydroelectric power.

POSEIDON GRASS

Sea grass (Poseidon grass or poseidonia), looks like rafts of algae but its presence is good for the maritime environment, hindering erosion on the seabed, attracting abundant sealife and absorbing carbon dioxide.

Mallorcan Architecture

For an overview of Mallorca's architectural spectrum, a visit to Palma should be high on your list. You'll glimpse Arab baths and Renaissance mansions where Mallorcan aristocrats once swanned around, baroque *patis* (patios) and Modernista mansions. And, of course, Palma's Gothic cathedral, as unique as it is vast. The next chapter is still to be written: the wave of innovation sweeping contemporary Spanish architectural circles is barely beginning to wash over Mallorca.

First Beginnings

Remains of the *talayots* (stone towers) of the first Balearic peoples are found at various sites around the island. Most settlements of these so-called Talayotic peoples were encircled by high stone walls, within which were numerous dwellings and the towers, which were built of stone, usually without the use of mortar. It is thought that some of the *talayots* may have served as watchtowers, others tombs, but little is known about these structures or the lives of those who built them. Although Talayotic cultures survived roughly until the Roman arrival of 123 BC, many of the structures seen today date back to 1000 BC. The best preserved sites are at Ses Païsses and Capocorb Vell.

Despite ruling over Mallorca for more than two centuries and despite their reputation as mighty builders, the Romans left behind surprisingly few signposts to their presence. This dearth of Roman ruins on Mallorca is most likely attributable to the fact that the Romans, unlike their predecessors, occupied the prime patches of coastal real estate, which was then built over by subsequent civilisations. The only meaningful extant Roman site in Mallorca – Pollèntia, in Alcúdia in the island's north – is also believed to have been its largest city.

Buildings of Muslim Mallorca

Banys Àrabs, Palma

Jardins d'Alfàbia, Serra de Tramuntana

Porta de l'Almudaina, Palma

Remnants of 12th-century Arab wall, Palma

Castell de Santueri, Felanitx

Muslim Mallorca

Mallorca has remarkably little to show for its three centuries of Muslim rule, not least because the mosques they built were invariably occupied by conquering Christian armies in the 13th century, and were subsequently converted into churches. Palma's Catedral and Església de Sant Miquel are two such examples – nothing of their original form survives. And mosques were not the only buildings to be appropriated by the new Christian rulers and transformed beyond recognition – the Palau de l'Almudaina was first built by the Romans, then adapted by a succession of Muslim governors, before becoming the seat of royal (Christian) power on the island.

Defensive fortresses on strategically sited hilltops were another feature of the Islamic occupation but, again, most were taken over and much modified by Christian forces in the centuries that followed. Castell de Capdepera is perhaps the most impressive example.

Mallorcan Gothic

The Catalan slant on the Gothic style, with its broad, low-slung, vaulting church entrances and sober adornment, inevitably predominated in Catalan-conquered Mallorca. Guillem Sagrera (c 1380–1456), a Catalan architect and sculptor who had previously worked in Perpignan (today in France), moved to Mallorca in 1420 to take over the direction of work on the Catedral, the island's foremost Gothic structure. Sagrera is considered to be the greatest architect and sculptor of the period in Mallorca. He designed one of the Catedral's chapels and the Gothic chapter house, and, more importantly, he raised Sa Llotja, Mallorca's other stand-out Gothic monument.

As in other parts of Spain, Islamic influences were evident in some aspects of building throughout the Gothic period. In Mallorca this Mudéjar style is not immediately evident in external facades, but a handful of beautiful *artesonados* (coffered wood ceilings) remain. Those in Palma's Palau de l'Almudaina are outstanding. The beautiful *artesonado* in the manor house at the Jardins d'Alfàbia appears to be an Islamic relic.

Renaissance & Baroque

Renaissance building had a rational impulse founded on the architecture of classical antiquity, but it seems to have largely passed Mallorca by. Some exceptions confirm the rule, such as the (later remodelled) main entrance to Palma's Catedral, the Consolat de Mar building and the mostly Renaissance-era sea walls. Although decorated in baroque fashion, the Monestir de Lluc is basically late Renaissance, and was designed by sculptor and architect Jaume Blanquer (c 1578–1636).

The more curvaceous and, many would say, less attractive successor to the Renaissance was a moderate, island-wide baroque that rarely reached the florid extremes that one encounters elsewhere in Europe. It is most often manifest in the large churches that dominate inland towns. In many of the churches, existing Gothic structures received a serious reworking, evident in such elements as barrel vaulting, circular windows, and bloated and curvaceous pillars and columns. Church exteriors are

The return to Christian rule in 1229 came too late for Romanesque architecture to truly make its mark on Mallorca. Perhaps only the Palau de l'Almudaina in Palma shows some traces of the style.

ARCHITECTURAL INSIGHT

Pollèntia (p128) Roman ruins in Alcúdia, with remnants of houses, temples and a theatre.

Patis (p63) Flit back to Renaissance and baroque times in the *patis* in Palma's historic centre.

Museu Regional d'Artà (p152) Take a brief trot through island history. Brush up on your knowledge of *talayots* here.

Palma Catedral (p51) The giant of Gothic, with its flying buttresses, soaring pinnacles and one of the world's largest rose windows.

Ses Païsses (p152) Close to Artà, this is one of Mallorca's largest and most impressive Talayotic sites.

Banys Àrabs (p57) Palma's Arab baths are the most important remaining monument to Muslim domination of the island.

Castell d'Alaró (p114) The enigmatic ruins of a medieval fortress.

Ca'n Prunera (p106) A classic example of a Modernista mansion in Sóller.

Es Baluard (p66) This contemporary gallery seamlessly merges with Palma's Renaissance seaward walls.

Old Alcúdia (p127) The medieval walls here are among the island's best-preserved.

PATIS

in the main sober (with the occasional gaudy facade). An exception can be found in the *retablos* (*retaules* in Catalan), the grand sculptural altarpieces in most churches. Often gilt and swirling with ornament, this was where baroque sculptors could let their imaginations run wild.

Yet perhaps the most pleasing examples of Mallorca's interpretation of the baroque style comes in the *patis* that grace old Palma's mansions. Drawing on Islamic/Andalusian and Roman influences, dictated by a warm Mediterranean climate, these courtyards represent one of Spain's most subtle baroque forms.

Although baroque is the predominant form, a handful of noble Palma houses betray Renaissance influences, such as the facade of the Cal Marquès del Palmer: standing in front of this building, you might for the briefest of moment think yourself transported to Medici Florence.

Modernisme

Palma

While you can peer into many of Palma's *patis* from the street, architecture buffs would do well to time their visit to Palma with Corpus Christi, when many of these otherwise private spaces are opened to the public. Or sign up for the 'Courtyards and Palaces' walking tour led by Mallorca Rutes.

Like most island-wide phenomena, Palma is the centrepiece of Mallorca's Modernista period. A contemporary of Gaudí, Lluís Domènech i Montaner (1850–1923) was another great Catalan Modernista architect who left his mark on the magnificent former Grand Hotel, now the CaixaForum.

The undulating facade of Can Casasayas, built for the wealthy Casasayas family, once known for the sadly lamented confectioner's Confitería Frasquet, is a typical feature of Modernisme. The site is now given over to one of Palma celebrity Marc Fosh's restaurants.

Another eminent and influential figure in the history of Mallorcan Modernisme was Gaspar Bennàssar (1869–1933). Unlike many other Catalan architects who worked on the island, Bennàssar was born in Palma and he played with various styles during his long career, including Modernisme. An outstanding example of this is the Almacenes El Águila, built in 1908 at the height of Modernisme's glory. Each of the three floors is different and the generous use of wrought iron in the main facade exemplifies the style. Next door the use of *trencadís* (ceramic shards) in the **Can Forteza Rey** facade is classic Gaudí-esque. **Can Corbella**, on the other hand, dates from roughly the same period, but is dominated by a neo-Mudéjar look.

The seat of the Balearic Islands' Parliament is located in the **Círculo Mallorquin**, a high-society club on Carrer del Conquistador that local Modernista architect Miquel Madorell i Rius (1869–1936) renovated in 1913.

Sóller

Provincial Sóller can't rival Palma for the breadth of its Modernista buildings, but it does have some outstanding examples of the genre. Most of it is attributable to Joan Rubió, an acolyte of Antoni Gaudí, and the most eye-catching example is the unusual early-20th-century Modernist facade he grafted onto the 18th-century Església de Sant Bartomeu. The adjacent and extravagant Banco de Sóller is a typically bold example of his approach. Nearby, the Can Prunera – Museu Modernista sports a typically delicate stone facade with muted wrought ironwork; it's also unusual on Mallorca in that it allows you to step beyond the Modernist facade and see the genre's influence upon early-20th-century interiors.

Arts & Crafts

Mallorca has been a source of inspiration for artists for centuries – Joan Miró felt such an affinity for his maternal homeland that he moved to Palma from his birth city, Barcelona, while local legend Miquel Barceló has added a vibrant splash of colour to galleries across the island. Today you can still encounter deep-rooted arts and crafts traditions, be they in the upbeat ballads sung at *festes* (festivals) or the leather-making factories in Inca, where funky footwear label Camper took its first steps.

Literature

Mallorca's many accomplished writers have not only created works of enduring significance, but have been instrumental in establishing Catalan and Mallorquin as literary languages. The works of many of Mallorca's leading writers, such as Llorenç Villalonga and Baltasar Porcel have now been translated, inviting outsiders into a rich literary scene little known beyond the Catalan-speaking world.

Those curious to find out more about authors writing in Catalan should check out www.escriptors.cat, the website of the Association of Catalan Language Writers.

The Early Centuries

In one sense Mallorcan literature began with the island's medieval conqueror, Jaume I (1208–76), who recorded his daring deeds in *El Llibre dels Fets* (*The Book of Deeds*). He wrote in Catalan, a language that the Palma-born poet and visionary evangeliser Ramon Llull (1232–1316) would elevate to a powerful literary tool. A controversial figure, who many feel should be declared a saint (he has made it to beatification), Llull has long been canonised as the father of the literary Catalan tongue.

Few Mallorcans grapple with Llull's medieval texts, but most know at least one poem by Miquel Costa i Llobera (1854–1922), a theologian and poet. His *El Pi de Fomentor* (*The Formentor Pinetree*, 1907), which eulogises Mallorcan landscapes through a pine on the Formentor peninsula, is *the* Mallorcan poem.

The 20th Century

One of the island's greatest poets was the reclusive Miquel Bauça (1940–2005). His *Una Bella Història* (1962–85) is a major achievement. Llorenç Villalonga (1897–1980), born into an elite Palman family and trained in medicine, was one of Mallorca's top 20th-century novelists. Many of his works, including his most successful novel, *Bearn* (1952), portray the decay of the island's landed nobility.

Baltasar Porcel (1937–2009) was the doyen of contemporary Mallorcan literature. *L'Emperador o l'Ull del Vent* (*The Emperor or the Eye of the Wind*, 2001) is a dramatic tale about the imprisonment of thousands of Napoleon's soldiers on Illa de Cabrera. Carme Riera (b 1948, Palma) has churned out an impressive series of novels, short stories, scripts and more. *L'Estiu de l'Anglès* (*The English Summer*, 2006), tells of a frustrated Barcelona estate agent's decision to spend a month learning English in a middle-of-nowhere UK town.

Anaïs Nin set an erotic short story, *Mallorca,* in Deià. It appeared in the volume *Delta of Venus* and deals with a local girl who gets into an erotic tangle with a pair of foreigners and pays a high price. Nin stayed in Deià for a year in 1941.

Guillem Frontera (b 1945, Ariany) has produced some engaging crime novels, particularly the 1980 *La Ruta dels Cangurs* (*The Kangaroo Route*), in which the murder of the detective's ex-girlfriend muddies his Mallorca holiday plans.

Music

Folk

Mallorca, like any other part of Spain, has a rich heritage in folk songs and ballads sung in Mallorquin. At many traditional *festes* in Mallorcan towns you'll hear the sounds of the *xeremiers,* a duo of ambling musicians, one of whom plays the *xeremia* (similar to the bagpipes) and the other a *flabiol* (a high-pitched pipe). Younger bands sometimes give these Mallorcan songs a bit of a rough-edged rock sound.

Contemporary

Los Valldemossa, who sang Mallorcan folk songs with a jazz feel in Palma's clubs, had some success overseas – they wound up playing the London circuit and, in 1969, won the Eurovision Song Contest, which actually meant something back then. They stopped playing in 2001, but their CDs still abound.

The island's best-known singer-songwriter is Palma's Maria del Mar Bonet i Verdaguer (b 1947). She moved to Barcelona at the age of 20 to join the Nova Cançó Catalana movement, which promoted singers and bands working in Catalan. Bonet became an international success and is known for her interpretations of Mediterranean folk music, French *chanson* and experiments with jazz and Brazilian music.

An altogether different performer is Concha Buika. Of Equatorial Guinean origins, she was born in Palma in 1972 and rose through the Palma club circuit with her very personal brand of music, ranging from hip-hop to flamenco to soul. Her second CD, *Mi Niña Lola,* came out in 2007, followed by *Niña de Fuego* a year later, and in 2009 *El Ultimo Trago,* a collaboration with Chucho Valdés, the renowned Cuban jazz pianist. She continues to release albums, most recently *Vivir Sin Miedo* in 2015.

WRITINGS ABOUT MALLORCA

➡ *A Lizard in my Luggage* (2006), *Goats from a Small Island* (2009), *Donkeys on my Doorstep* (2010), *A Bull on the Beach* (2012), *A Chorus of Cockerels* (2016) by Anna Nicholas

➡ *Snowball Oranges* (2000), *Mañana Mañana* (2001), *Viva Mallorca* (2004) and *A Basketful of Snowflakes* (2007), by Peter Kerr

➡ *Rafael's Wings: A Novel of Mallorca* (2006), *Von Ripper's Odyssey* (2016) by Sian Mackay

➡ *Tuning Up At Dawn* (2004) and *Bread and Oil: Majorcan Culture's Last Stand* (2006), by Tomás Graves, son of Robert Graves

➡ *Wild Olives: Life in Majorca With Robert Graves* (2001), by William Graves

➡ *Un Hiver à Mallorque* (*A Winter in Mallorca*, 1839), by the 19th-century French novelist George Sand (actually Amandine-Aurore-Lucille Dupin)

➡ *Jogging Around Mallorca* (1929), by Gordon West

➡ *British Travellers in Mallorca in the Nineteenth Century* (2006), edited by Brian J Dendle and Shelby Thacker

➡ *Letters From Mallorca* (1887), by Charles W Wood

➡ *Die Insel des Zweiten Gesichts* (*The Island of the Second Vision*, 1953), by German writer Albert Vigoleis Thelen

Argentine-born, Mallorca-based starlet Chenoa got her break when she stunned all in the TV talent show *Operación Triunfo*. Since 2002 she has churned out seven albums and has become one of the most popular voices in Spanish-Latin pop.

Painting & Sculpture

The Early Centuries

Absorbed after the 1229 conquest into the Catalan world of the Crown of Aragón, Mallorca nonetheless remained a Mediterranean crossroads, open to outside influences. Historically, artists and movements have long been attracted from the Spanish mainland to Mallorca.

The earliest works from this revival of Catalan culture, transmitted by Catalan artists, were influenced by the Gothic art of the Sienese school in Italy. Later, International Gothic began to filter through, notably under the influence of the Valencian artist Francesc Comes, who worked in Mallorca from 1390 to 1415.

Important artists around the mid-15th century include Rafel Mòger (c 1424–70) and Frenchman Pere Niçard, productive in Mallorca from 1468 to 1470. They created one of the era's most important works, *Sant Jordi*, now housed in Palma's Museu Diocesà. The outstanding sculptor of this time was Guillem Sagrera, who did much of the detail work on Sa Llotja.

Pere Terrencs (active c 1479–1528) returned from a study stint in Valencia with the technique of oil painting – the death knell for egg-based pigments. His was a transitional style between late Gothic and the Renaissance. In a similar category was Córdoba-born Mateu López (d 1581), who trained in the prestigious Valencia workshops of father and son Vicent Macip and Joan de Joanes (aka Joan Vicent Macip, 1523–79), both signal artists. In 1544 López landed in Mallorca.

Gaspar Oms (c 1540–1614) was Mallorca's most outstanding late-Renaissance painter. The Oms clan, from Valencia, dominated the Mallorcan art scene throughout the 17th and 18th centuries.

Miquel Bestard (1592–1633) created major baroque canvases for churches, such as the Convento de Santa Clara and the Església de Monte-Sion, in Palma. Guillem Mesquida i Munar (1675–1747) concentrated on religious motifs and scenes from classical mythology.

19th & 20th Centuries

The 19th century brought a wave of landscape artists to Mallorca. Many came from mainland Spain, particularly Catalonia, but the island produced its own painters, too. More than half a dozen notables were born and raised in Palma. Joan O'Neille Rosiñol (1828–1907) is considered the founder of the island's landscape movement. He and his younger contemporaries, Ricard Anckermann Riera (1842–1907) and Antoni Ribas Oliver (1845–1911), both from Palma, were among the first to cast their artistic eyes over the island and infuse it with romantic lyricism. The latter two concentrated particularly on coastal scenes.

From 1890 a flood of Modernista artists from Catalonia 'discovered' Mallorca and brought new influences to the island. Some of them, such as Santiago Rusiñol (1861–1931), had spent time in Paris, which was then the hotbed of the art world. Locals enthusiastically joined in the Modernista movement. Palma-born Antoni Gelabert Massot (1877–1932) became a key figure, depicting his home city in paintings such as *Murada i Catedral a Entrada de Fosc* (1902–04). Other artists caught up in this wave were Joan Fuster Bonnín (1870–1943) and Llorenç Cerdà i Bisbal (1862–1955), born in Pollença.

Meanwhile Llorenç Rosselló (1867–1902) was shaping up to be the island's most prominent sculptor until his early death. A handful of Rosselló's bronzes, as well as a selection of works by many of the painters mentioned here, can be seen in Es Baluard.

Best Niche Galleries

Es Baluard, Palma

Casa-Museu Dionís Bennàssar, Pollença

Ca'n Prunera – Museu Modernista, Sóller

By the 1910s and 1920s symbolism began to creep into local artists' vocabulary. Two important names from this period are Joan Antoni Fuster Valiente (1892–1964) and Ramón Nadal (1913–99), both from Palma.

Contemporary

Towering above everyone else in modern Mallorcan art is local hero and art icon, Miquel Barceló (b 1957, Felanitx). His profile has been especially sharp in his island home since the unveiling in 2007 of one of his more controversial masterpieces, a ceramic depiction of the miracle of the loaves and fishes housed in Palma's Catedral. Barceló, who divides his time between Paris and Mali's Dogon Country, has a studio in Naples and was a rising star by the age of 25. Although he is best known as a painter, Barceló has worked with ceramics since the late 1990s. The commission for the Catedral was on an unimagined scale for the artist.

Less well known but nonetheless prolific is Palma-born Ferran García Sevilla (b 1949), whose canvases are frequently full of primal colour and strong shapes and images. Since the early 1980s he has exhibited in galleries throughout Europe. Joan Costa (b 1961, Palma) is one of the island's key contemporary sculptors, who also indulges in occasional brushwork.

One cannot leave out 20th-century Catalan icon Joan Miró (1893–1983). His mother came from Sóller and he lived the last 27 years of his life in Cala Major.

Crafts

Tourism may have led to the overdevelopment of the Mallorcan coast, but it has enabled the revival of many traditional crafts.

Glasswork & Leatherwork

Glasswork was first produced on the island way back in the 2nd century BC and its artisans were part of a network of production and trade centred on Murano in Venice. Mallorcan glass manufacturing reached its high point in the 18th century, after which the industry fell into decline. But one family, the Gordiolas, who first entered the industry in its 18th-century heyday, have been almost single-handedly responsible for Mallorcan glass-making's revival in the mid- to late 20th century. Although you'll find smaller artisans working with glass, the Museu de Gordiola, outside Algaida, is the island's largest producer, and here you can watch traditional glass-blowing techniques.

Thanks to famous shoe manufacturers such as Camper, Mallorca's leather-making industries have become renowned worldwide for their quality. Although smaller traditional manufacturers tend to get drowned out by the larger companies, there's no denying that this industry is a stunning Mallorcan success story. Inca is the capital of Mallorcan shoe-making, with a host of factories and outlets open to the public.

MIRÓ & MALLORCA

Joan Miró grew up and spent most of his life in Barcelona, but Mallorca was his spiritual home and it became his permanent abode when he moved here in the mid-1950s. The island was an endless source of inspiration to the artist – the horizons, the 'eloquent silence', the pure brilliance of the light, and the vivid blues of the sea that were reflected in works such as *Bleu I, II, III* (1961), a three-part series of intensely hued paintings.

Here Miró could walk through the streets and listen to the organist in the cathedral unnoticed, and he relished this anonymity. His studio on the outskirts of the city gave him ample breathing space to fully immerse himself in his art. He lived there until his death in 1983, aged 90. You can visit his house and studio, and see many of his paintings, sketches and sculptures, at **Fundació Pilar i Joan Miró** (p86).

Survival
Guide

Directory A–Z

Customs Regulations

There are no duty-free allowances for travel between EU countries and no restrictions on the import of duty-paid items into Spain from other EU countries for personal use.

VAT-free articles can be bought at airport shops when travelling between EU countries.

Duty-free allowances for travellers entering Spain from outside the EU include 2L of wine (or 1L of wine and 1L of spirits) and 200 cigarettes, 50 cigars or 250g of tobacco.

Discount Cards

Students, seniors (over 65s), families and young people get discounts of 20% to 50% at many sights. Museum entry is often free for under 12s. From October to April, some 4-star hotels and car-hire companies offer discounts for over-55s.

City Cards Some Mallorcan centres offer discount cards entitling holders to entry to multiple attractions, and other perks. The most useful is the Palma Pass.

Senior's Cards Reduced prices at museums and attractions (sometimes restricted to EU citizens only) and occasionally reduced costs on transport.

Student Cards An ISIC (International Student Identity Card; www.isic.org) can save you up to 50% off stays, attractions and more.

Youth Card Travel, sights and youth hostel discounts with the European Youth Card (Carnet Joven in Spain; www.euro26.org).

Palma Pass Useful three-day pass (€33), one-day express pass (€16) or family pass (€92) includes entry to 35 museums and monuments, access to public transport, and discounts. See www.palmapass.com.

Electricity

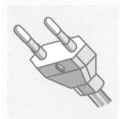

Type C
220V/50Hz

GLBTI Travellers

Homosexuality is legal in Spain. In 2005 the socialist president of Spain, José Luis Rodríguez Zapatero, gave the conservative Catholic foundations of the country a shake with the legalisation of same-sex marriage. In Mallorca, Palma is the natural epicentre of a proud and prominent gay culture.

Resources

➡ **Ben Amics** (⏰871 96 54 66; www.benamics.com; Carrer del General Riera 3; ◷9am–3pm) The island's umbrella association for gays, lesbians and transsexuals.

➡ **Gay Mallorca** (www.gay-mallorca.blogspot.com) Weekly events listings.

➡ **Guía Gay de España** (http://guia.universogay.com/palmademallorca) Useful listings of cafes, saunas, nightclubs and restaurants.

➡ **Mallorca Gay Map** (www.mallorcagaymap.com) A handy guide to gay-friendly venues; a printed version is available from some municipal tourist offices in Palma.

Health

Mallorca doesn't present any health dangers – your main gripes are likely to be sunburn, insect bites, mild stomach problems and hangovers.

Before You Go
HEALTH INSURANCE

➡ If you're an EU citizen, a European Health Insurance Card (EHIC), available from health centres or, in the UK, post offices, covers you for most medical care. It will not cover you for nonemergencies, emergency repatriation or procedures you've travelled specifically for.

➡ Citizens from other countries should find out if there is a reciprocal arrangement for free medical care between their country and Spain.

VACCINATIONS

No jabs are necessary for Mallorca but the WHO recommends that all travellers be covered for diphtheria, tetanus, measles, mumps, rubella and polio, regardless of their destination.

In Mallorca
AVAILABILITY & COST OF HEALTH CARE

➡ If you need an ambulance, call ☏061.

➡ Clinical standards and waiting times are among the best in Europe, and costs are equivalent to other Western European countries.

➡ For emergency treatment go straight to the *urgencias* (casualty) section of the nearest hospital. The island's main hospital is Palma's **Hospital Universitari Son Espases** (☏871 20 50 00; www.hospitalsonespases.es; Carretera de Valldemossa 79), but other important ones are based in Inca and Manacor.

➡ At the main coastal tourist resorts you will generally find clinics with English- and German-speaking staff.

➡ *Farmacias* (pharmacies) offer advice and sell over-the-counter medication. When a pharmacy is closed it posts the name of the nearest *farmacia de guardia* (duty pharmacies) on the door.

Climate

Palma de Mallorca

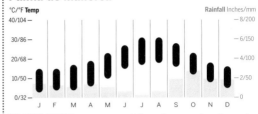

HEALTH RISKS

➡ Heat exhaustion occurs following excessive fluid loss. Symptoms include headache, dizziness and tiredness. Treat by drinking plenty of water and/or fruit juice.

➡ Heat stroke is much more serious, resulting in irrational and hyperactive behaviour and eventually loss of consciousness and death. Rapid cooling by spraying the body with water and fanning is ideal.

➡ If you have a severe allergy to bee or wasp stings, carry an EpiPen or similar adrenaline injection.

➡ In forested areas, watch out for the hairy reddish-brown caterpillars of the pine processionary moth. Touching the caterpillars' hairs sets off a severely irritating allergic skin reaction.

➡ Some Spanish centipedes have a very nasty, but nonfatal, sting. The ones to watch out for are those with clearly defined segments, for instance, black and yellow stripes.

➡ In summer, waves of stingers (jellyfish) can wash up on the island's beaches. Vinegar, ice and Epsom salts can soothe the pain of a sting. If unavailable, rub in salt water; fresh water can stimulate the sting. Head to a Red Cross stand

(usually present on the main beaches) if you are stung.

➡ Sandflies are found on many Mallorcan beaches. They usually cause only a nasty itchy bite but can occasionally carry a rare skin disorder called cutaneous leishmaniasis, a raised lesion at the site of the bite which can leave atrophic scarring.

TAP WATER

Tap water is safe to drink across Mallorca, but is often unpalatable because of high sodium or chlorine levels; bottled water is cheap to buy.

Insurance

Comprehensive travel-insurance to cover theft, loss, medical problems and cancellations is highly recommended. Read the fine print, as some policies exclude 'high risk' activities such as scuba diving and canyoning.

EU citizens are entitled to health care in public hospitals (present your European Health Insurance Card).

Check that the policy covers ambulances or an emergency flight home.

Keep all documents and bills if you have to make a claim.

Worldwide travel insurance is available at www.lonelyplanet.com/travel-insurance. You can buy, extend and claim online any time – even if you're already on the road.

Internet Access

➡ Numerous cafes and bars have free wi-fi. You may need to ask for the password when ordering.

➡ Most hotels have wi-fi, but in some cases the signal is weak beyond the lobby.

➡ Internet cafes are increasingly rare, but tourist offices should be able to point you to the nearest one. Typical rates are €2 to €3 per hour.

Legal Matters

➡ By law you are expected to carry some form of photographic identification at all times, such as a passport, national ID card or driving licence.

➡ The blood alcohol limit for driving in Spain is 0.05%. There are stiff fines (up to €1000) for anyone caught exceeding this limit. Levels of 0.12% and above carry a risk of imprisonment.

➡ Cannabis is legal but only for personal use and in very small quantities. Public consumption of any drug is illegal.

➡ If arrested, you will be allotted the free services of

a duty solicitor (abogado de oficio), who may speak only Spanish (and Mallorquin). You are entitled to have the nature of the accusation against you explained in a language you understand, and to make a phone call.

➡ If you end up in court, the authorities are obliged to provide a translator.

Maps

Among the better and clearer island maps:

➡ Freytag and Berndt's Mallorca (1:50,000)

➡ Michelin's No.579 Balears/ Balearics (1:140,000)

➡ Marco Polo's Mallorca (1:125,000)

➡ Bike Mallorca's Mallorca Bicycle Map (1:100,000)

Walking Maps

Walking maps must be at least 1:25,000 in scale; anything bigger is practically useless. Purchase your maps at hiking shops, or check out map specialists in other countries, for example Stanfords (www.stanfords.co.uk) in the UK.

➡ Alpina Editorial produces three maps to the Serra de Tramuntana range (Mallorca

Tramuntana Sud, Mallorca Tramuntana Central and Mallorca Tramuntana Nord). These come with detailed walk descriptions in a solid booklet. The third map is in Catalan and German only.

➡ Discovery Walking Guides publishes detailed guides to different regions of the island. Their Walk! Mallorca (North & Mountains), for example, is packed with walks, basic maps and GPS coordinates. You'll need to buy additional maps though.

➡ The Kompass Wanderführer 5910 Mallorca (in German), by Wolfgang Heizmann, comes with detailed walking maps.

➡ Spain's Centro Nacional de Información Geográfica (www.cnig.es) covers a good part of the island in 1:25,000 scale sheets.

Money

ATMs are widely available in towns and resorts. Credit cards are accepted in most hotels, restaurants and shops.

ATMs

➡ Most debit and credit cards, such as Visa, MasterCard and Cirrus, can be used to withdraw cash from cajeros automáticos (ATMs).

➡ ATMs are ubiquitous in towns and major resorts, and accessible 24/7.

➡ There is usually a charge (around 1.5% to 2%) on ATM cash withdrawals abroad.

Cash

➡ Cash is king for small purchases in Mallorca, and spare change is handy for coffee pit stops and spontaneous market buys.

➡ Avoid taking more money to the beach than you need for ice cream, drinks, and sunbed and parasol hire (€10 to €15 per day).

PRACTICALITIES

➡ **Weights & Measures** The metric system is used.

➡ **Newspapers** English- and German-language dailies are widely available in resorts. Major Spanish newspapers include centre-left El País (http://elpais.com) and centre-right El Mundo (www.elmundo.es). For Mallorca news, try Diario de Mallorca (www.diariodemallorca.es), Ultima Hora (http://ultimahora.es) or English-language Majorca Daily Bulletin (http://majorcadailybulletin.com).

➡ **Radio** Regional stations include Radio Balear (www.radiobalear.net) and English-speaking Radio One Mallorca (www.radioonemallorca.com).

➡ **Smoking** Many Mallorcans smoke, although the ban on smoking in all enclosed public places, once often flouted, is now enforced more rigorously.

➡ Most banks exchange major foreign currencies and offer the best rates. Ask about commissions and take your passport.

➡ Exchange bureaux (look for the sign 'cambio') tend to open longer hours but usually charge outrageous commissions.

Credit & Debit Cards

➡ Credit and debit cards are generally accepted in hotels, with the exception of some rural B&Bs.

➡ Small, family-run restaurants and cafes might insist on cash – check before ordering to be on the safe side.

➡ Cards can be used to pay for most other purchases. You'll sometimes be asked to show your passport or some other form of photo ID.

➡ Among the most widely accepted cards are Visa, MasterCard, American Express (Amex), Cirrus, Maestro, Plus, Diners Club and JCB.

Taxes & Refunds

Spain's IVA (VAT) goods-and-services tax of up to 21% is included in stated prices. Refunds are available on goods costing more than €90, if taken out of the EU within three months. Collect a refund form when purchasing and present it (together with the purchases) to the customs IVA refunds booth when leaving the EU. For more information, see www.globalblue.com.

Tipping

➡ **Hotels** Discretionary: porters around €1 per bag and cleaners €2 per day.

➡ **Cafes and bars** Not expected, but you can reward good service by rounding the bill to the nearest euro or two.

➡ **Restaurants** Service charge is included, unless 'servicio no incluido' is specified, but many still leave an extra 5% or so.

➡ **Taxis** Not necessary, but feel free to round up or leave a modest tip, especially for longer journeys.

Opening Hours

We've provided high-season hours; hours will generally decrease in the shoulder and low seasons. Many resort restaurants and hotels close from November to March.

Banks 8.30am–2pm Monday to Friday; some also open 4–7pm Thursday and 9am–1pm Saturday

Bars 7pm–3am

Cafes 11am–1am

Clubs midnight–6am

Post offices 8.30am–9.30pm Monday to Friday, 8.30am–2pm Saturday

Restaurants lunch 1–3.30pm, dinner 7.30–11pm

Shops 10am–2pm & 4.30–7.30pm or 5–8pm Monday to Saturday; big supermarkets and department stores generally 10am–9pm Monday to Saturday

Post

The Spanish postal system, Correos (www.correos.es), is generally reliable, if a little slow at times. Delivery times are erratic but ordinary mail to other Western European countries can take up to a week; to North America up to 10 days; and to Australia or New Zealand between 10 days and three weeks.

Sellos (stamps) are sold at most *estancos* (tobacconists' shops with 'Tabacos' in yellow letters on a maroon background), as well as post offices. A postcard or letter weighing up to 20g costs €1.15 from Spain to other European countries; rates are higher to other countries. For a full list of prices for certified (*certificado*) and express post (*urgente*) mail, check the 'Fee Calculator' on the Correos website.

Public Holidays

The two main periods when Spaniards (and Mallorcans are no real exception) go on holiday are Semana Santa (the week leading up to Easter Sunday) and August, which also happens to be when half of Europe descends on Mallorca. Accommodation can be hard to find and transport is put under strain.

There are 14 official holidays a year, to which most towns add at least one to mark their patron saint's day. Some places have several traditional feast days, not all of which are official holidays, but which are often a reason for partying. The main island-wide public holidays:

Cap d'Any (New Year's Day) 1 January

Epifania del Senyor (Epiphany) 6 January – in Palma, a landing of the Three Wise Men (Reis Mags) is staged in the port, followed by a procession

Dia de les Illes Balears (Balearic Islands Day) 1 March

Dijous Santa (Holy Thursday) March/April

Divendres Sant (Good Friday) March/April

Diumenge de Pasqua (Easter Sunday) March/April

Festa del Treball (Labour Day) 1 May

L'Assumpció (Feast of the Assumption) 15 August

Festa Nacional d'Espanya (Spanish National Day) 12 October

Tots Sants (All Saints) 1 November

Dia de la Constitució (Constitution Day) 6 December

L'Immacula da Concepció (Feast of the Immaculate Conception) 8 December

Nadal (Christmas) 25 December

Segona Festa de Nadal (Boxing Day) 26 December

Safe Travel

Mallorca is safe, but the usual precautions are advised. The main thing to be wary of is petty theft: keep an eye on your valuables and you should be OK.

Report thefts to the **national police** (☏902 10 21 12; www.policia.es). It is unlikely that you will recover your goods, but you need to make a formal *denuncia* for insurance purposes. To save time, you can make the report by phone (in various languages), or on online (search for 'denuncias').

Telephone

Mallorca's blue payphones are easy to use for international and domestic calls. They accept coins, *tarjetas telefónicas* (phonecards issued by the national phone company Telefónica) and, in some cases, credit cards. Calling using an internet-based service such as Skype is generally the cheapest option.

Mobile Phones

Local SIM cards are widely available and can be used in European and Australian mobile phones. Other phones may need to be set to roaming.

Phonecards

Cut-rate phonecards from private companies can be good value for international calls. They can be bought from *estancos*, news-stands and *locutorios* (call centres), especially in Palma and coastal resorts – compare rates if possible.

Telephone Numbers

➡ All telephone numbers in Mallorca (including mobile numbers) have nine digits.

➡ Almost all fixed-line telephone numbers in Mallorca begin with ☏971, although a small number begin with ☏871.

➡ Numbers starting with a '6' are for mobile phones.

➡ Numbers starting with 900 are national toll-free numbers, while those starting 901 to 905 come with varying costs. A common one is 902, which is a national standard rate number, but can only be dialled from within Spain. In a similar category are numbers starting with 800, 803, 806 and 807.

➡ It is possible to dial an operator in your country of residence at no cost to make a reverse-charge call (*una llamada a cobro revertido*) – pick up the number before you leave home. You can usually get an English-speaking Spanish international operator on ☏1008 (for calls within Europe) or ☏1005 (rest of the world).

Time

Mallorca runs on central European time (GMT/UTC plus one hour). Daylight saving time begins on the last Sunday in March and ends on the last Sunday in October.

UK, Ireland, Portugal & Canary Islands One hour behind mainland Spain.

USA Spanish time is USA Eastern Time plus six hours, or USA Pacific Time plus nine hours.

Australia During the Australian winter (Spanish summer), subtract eight hours from Australian Eastern Standard Time to get Spanish time; during the Australian summer, subtract 10 hours.

Toilets

Toilets are of the sit-down variety, although public toilets are rare to non-existent across the island. If you find yourself in need of the facilities, remember that most bars and restaurants will expect you to purchase something before or after you use the toilet.

Tourist Information

➡ Almost every town and resort in Mallorca has a walk-up tourist office (*oficina de turismo* or *oficina de información turística*) for local maps and information.

➡ Tourist offices in coastal areas usually open from Easter or May until October and keep surprisingly short hours. If you do find them open, they're usually helpful and overflowing with useful brochures.

➡ In Palma you'll find municipal tourist offices focussing on Palma and its immediate surrounds. There's also the **Consell de Mallorca Tourist Office** (Map p58; ☏971 17 39 90; www.infomallorca.net; Plaça de la Reina 2; ☺8.30am-8pm Mon-Fri, to 3pm Sat; ☏), which covers the whole island.

➡ For general information about the Balearic Islands, visit www.illesbalears.es.

Travellers with Disabilities

Mallorca is a long way from being barrier-free, but things are slowly improving. Disabled access to some museums, official buildings and hotels represents something of a sea-change in local thinking.

➡ Be circumspect about hotels advertising themselves as disabled-friendly, as this can mean as little as wide doors to rooms and bathrooms, a ramp into reception or other token efforts.

➡ Cobbled streets and flights of steps in hill towns can make getting around difficult.

➡ Palma city buses are equipped for wheelchair access, as are some of those that travel around the island. Some taxi companies run adapted taxis – they must be booked in advance.

➡ Download Lonely Planet's free Accessible Travel guide from http://lptravel.to/AccessibleTravel.

Visas

Generally not required for stays of up to 90 days; not required for members of EU or Schengen countries. Some nationalities will need a Schengen visa.

Visa Requirements

Spain is one of 26 member countries of the Schengen Convention, under which 22 EU countries (all but Bulgaria, Cyprus, Ireland, Romania and the UK) plus Iceland, Norway and Switzerland have abolished checks at common borders.

To work or study in Spain a special visa may be required – contact a Spanish embassy or consulate before you travel.

CITIZENS OR RESIDENTS OF	VISA REQUIRED?
EU & Schengen countries	No
Australia, Canada, Israel, Japan, NZ and the USA	Not required for tourist visits of up to 90 days
Other countries	Check the Foreign Office website (www.exteriores.gob.es).

Extensions & Residence

You can apply for no more than two visas in any 12-month period and they are not renewable once in Spain.

Nationals of EU countries, Iceland, Norway and Switzerland can enter and leave Spain at will and don't need to apply for a *tarjeta de residencia* (residence card), although they are supposed to apply for residence papers and must meet certain criteria.

People of other nationalities who want to stay in Spain longer than 90 days require one of two types of residence card – for less than or more than six months. Getting one can be a drawn-out process, starting with an appropriate visa issued by a Spanish consulate in their country of residence. Start the process well in advance.

Volunteering

Most volunteering opportunities in Spain are on the mainland, but it is worth checking Go Abroad (www.goabroad.com) for projects in Mallorca. *Fincas* (farms) and families offering work and board on a voluntary basis advertise on Work Away (www.workaway.info).

Women Travellers

Travelling in Mallorca is largely as easy as travelling anywhere else in the Western world. However, you may still occasionally find yourself the object of staring, catcalls and unnecessary comments. Simply ignoring them is usually sufficient. Eye-to-eye contact and flirting is part of daily Spanish life and need not be offensive.

Spanish women generally have a highly developed sense of style and put considerable effort into looking their best. While topless bathing and skimpy clothes are in fashion on the island's coastal resorts, people tend to dress more modestly in the towns and inland.

Work

Nationals of EU countries, Switzerland, Norway and Iceland may work freely in Spain, and hence, Mallorca. Virtually everyone else needs to obtain, from a Spanish consulate in their country of residence, a work permit and (for stays of more than 90 days) a residence visa.

Many bars (especially of the UK and Irish persuasion), restaurants and other businesses are run by foreigners and look for temporary staff in summer. Check any local press in foreign languages, which carry ads for waiters, nannies, chefs, babysitters, cleaners and the like.

Translating and interpreting could be an option if you are fluent both in Spanish and a language in demand. You can start a job search on the web, for instance at Think Spain (www.thinkspain.com).

Transport

GETTING THERE & AWAY

Most visitors to Mallorca fly into Palma's international airport, though it's possible to arrive by ferry from points along the Spanish coast (Alicante, Barcelona, Denia and Valencia). The neighbouring islands of Ibiza and Menorca are also linked to Mallorca by air and ferry.

Flights and tours can be booked online at lonely planet.com/bookings.

Entering the Country

Entry and exit procedures in Mallorca are generally smooth and not overly officious.

Passports

Citizens of most of the 28 European Union member states and Switzerland can travel to Spain with their national identity card. Citizens of countries that don't issue ID cards, such as the UK, need a full passport. All other nationalities must have a full valid passport, and a few even require visas. Full details can be found at the website of the Spanish Foreign Office (ww.exteriores.gob.es)

If applying for a visa, check that your passport's expiry date is at least six months away. Non-EU citizens must fill out a landing card. By law you are technically supposed to carry your passport or ID card with you at all times.

Air

Air is the most convenient and popular way of arriving in Mallorca, so much so that Palma airport is the third-busiest in Spain, with connections to 61 cities across Spain and Europe.

Airports & Airlines

Palma de Mallorca Airport (PMI;☑902 404704; www.aena-aeropuertos.es) is 8km east of Palma de Mallorca. Flying to 105 countries, it's Spain's third-largest airport, and one of the busiest in Europe. In summer especially, masses of charter and regular flights form an air bridge to Palma from around Europe, among them many low-cost airlines.

The arrivals hall is on the ground floor of the main terminal building, where you'll find a **tourist office** (☑971 78 95 56; Aeroport de Palma; ⊙8am-8pm Mon-Sat, to 2pm Sun), money-exchange offices, car hire, tour operators and hotel-booking stands. Departures are on the 2nd floor.

Nearly every European airline serves Mallorca, along with the majority of budget carriers. Airlines flying to the island include the following:

➡ **Air Berlin** (www.airberlin. com) From London (Stansted), dozens of cities all over Germany and elsewhere in mainland Europe.

CLIMATE CHANGE & TRAVEL

Every form of transport that relies on carbon-based fuel generates CO_2, the main cause of human-induced climate change. Modern travel is dependent on aeroplanes, which might use less fuel per kilometre per person than most cars but travel much greater distances. The altitude at which aircraft emit gases (including CO_2) and particles also contributes to their climate change impact. Many websites offer 'carbon calculators' that allow people to estimate the carbon emissions generated by their journey and, for those who wish to do so, to offset the impact of the greenhouse gases emitted with contributions to portfolios of climate-friendly initiatives throughout the world. Lonely Planet offsets the carbon footprint of all staff and author travel.

➡ **British Airways** (www.britishairways.com) From London.

➡ **easyJet** (www.easyjet.com) From 13 UK airports and nine in mainland Europe.

➡ **Germanwings** (www.germanwings.com) From dozens of UK and mainland Europe airports.

➡ **Iberia** (www.iberia.es) With its subsidiary Air Nostrum, flies from many mainland Spanish cities.

➡ **Jet2** (www.jet2.com) From Belfast, Leeds, Edinburgh and Newcastle.

➡ **Lufthansa** (www.lufthansa.com) From central European cities.

➡ **Monarch** (www.flymonarch.com) Scheduled and charter flights from London (Luton), Edinburgh, Birmingham and Manchester.

➡ **Ryanair** (www.ryanair.com) From numerous UK and mainland European airports.

➡ **Thomson Fly** (www.thomsonfly.com) From many UK cities.

Departure Tax

Departure tax is included in the price of a ticket.

Sea

Ferry services connect Mallorca to the Spanish mainland and to Menorca, Ibiza and Formentera. Most services operate only from Easter to late October, and those that continue into the winter reduce their departure times. Most ferry companies allow you to transport vehicles on longer routes and have car holds (this incurs an additional fee and advance bookings are essential). If you are travelling with your own vehicle, be sure to arrive at the port in good time for boarding.

Prices vary according to season; check routes and compare prices at Direct Ferries (www.directferries.com).

Ferry companies that operate to and from Mallorca include the following:

➡ **Acciona Trasmediterránea** (☎902 45 46 45; www.trasmediterranea.es)

➡ **Baleària** (☎902 16 01 80; www.balearia.com)

➡ **Iscomar** (☎902 119128; www.iscomar.com)

Tours

Joining an organised tour to Mallorca is certainly not necessary – it's an easy destination for independent travel. But some companies offer specialist tours that make it so much easier to indulge your passions, whatever they may be.

➡ **Mallorca Muntanya** (☎639 71 32 12; www.mallorcamuntanya.com) Trekking tours, mostly in the Serra de Tramuntana.

➡ **Tramuntana Tours** (Map p106; ☎971 63 24 23; www.tramuntanatours.com; Carrer de Sa Lluna 72; bicycle rental per day €12-75; ☉9am-1.30pm & 3-7.30pm Mon-Fri, 9am-1.30pm Sat) Guided hikes in the Serra de Tramuntana.

➡ **Mar y Roc** (☎680 32 21 71; www.mallorca-wandern.de) Group hiking tours in Mallorca.

FERRY SERVICES

TO	FROM	COMPANY	PRICE	FREQUENCY	DURATION (HR)	SLEEPER BERTH
Palma	Barcelona	Acciona Trasmediterránea, Baleària	seat from €59	1-2 daily	7½	yes
Palma	Denia	Baleària	seat from €82	2 daily	8	yes
Ibiza	Formentera	Baleària	seat from €18	numerous daily	45 min	no
Palma	Ibiza (Ibiza City)	Baleària	seat from €52	2 daily	4	yes
Palma	Mahon (Menorca)	Acciona Trasmediterránea	seat from €42	Sun	3½	no
Palma	Valencia	Acciona Trasmediterránea, Baleària	seat from €62	1 daily	8	yes
Port d'Alcúdia	Barcelona	Baleària	seat from €50	1 daily	7	yes
Port d'Alcúdia	Ciutatdella (Menorca)	Acciona Trasmediterránea, Baleària	seat from €32	2 daily	1-2	no

➡ **Naturetrek** (📞in UK 01962 733051; www.naturetrek.co.uk) Eight-day birdwatching tour.

➡ **Unicorn Trails** (📞in UK 01767 600 606; www.unicorntrails.com) Two week-long horse-riding tours.

➡ **Cycle Mallorca** (www.cyclemallorca.co.uk) Well-organised road cycling holidays.

➡ **Inntravel** (www.inntravel.co.uk) A slow-tour specialist offering walking and cycling holidays.

GETTING AROUND

Transport in Mallorca is reasonably priced, though buses and trains do not cover every corner of the island, and some services dwindle during the low season. For timetables throughout the island, head to **Transport de les Illes Balears** (TIB; 📞971 17 77 77; www.tib.org).

Bicycle

Pro cycling teams' fondness for Mallorca as a winter training ground have really put the island on the cycling map in recent years. It's now one of Europe's most popular destinations for road cycling. Although the uphill slog can be tough in mountainous areas, especially along the island's western and north-western coasts, much of the island is flat and can be easily explored by bike.

Wide shoulders, a decent number of bike paths and familiarity with and acceptance of cyclists by other road users make it all the more appealing. Signposts have been put up across much of rural Mallorca indicating cycling routes (usually secondary roads between towns and villages).

For an overview of cycling on the island, visit www.illesbalears.es and click on 'Sport Tourism'. It has numerous routes across the island. An-

other recommended website with routes graded according to difficulty is http://mallorcacycling.co.uk.

Hire

Bike-hire places are scattered around the main resorts of the island, including Palma, and are usually highly professional. Prices vary widely, but on average you'll pay between €10 and €15 per day for a city bike, and €20 to €30 per day for an aluminium or carbon road bike. The longer you hire the bike, the cheaper daily rates get, and many hire outfits will deliver to you.

Bus

The island is roughly divided into five bus zones radiating from Palma. Bus line numbers in the 100s cover the southwest, the 200s the west (as far as Sóller), the 300s the north and much of the centre, the 400s a wedge of the centre and east coast and the 500s the south. These services are run by a phalanx of small bus companies, but you can get route and timetable information for all by contacting **Transport de les Illes Balears** (TIB; 📞971 17 77 77; www.tib.org).

Most of the island is accessible by bus from Palma. All buses depart from (or near) Palma's **Estació Intermodal** (Map p54; 📞971 17 77 77; www.tib.org; Plaça d'Espanya) on Plaça d'Espanya. Not all lines are especially frequent, and some services slow to a trickle on weekends. Frequency to many coastal areas also drops from November to April and some lines are cut altogether (such as between Ca'n Picafort and Sa Calobra or Sóller).

Although services in most parts of the island are adequate, out-of-the-way places can be tedious to reach and getting around the Serra de Tramuntana by bus, while possible, isn't always easy. Bus 200 from Palma runs to

Estellencs via Banyalbufar for example, while bus 210 runs to Valldemossa and then, less frequently, on to Deià and Sóller. Nothing makes the connection between Estellencs and Valldemossa and all but the Palma–Valldemossa run are infrequent.

Distances are usually short, with very few services taking longer than two hours to reach their destinations.

Car & Motorcycle

Mallorca's roads are generally excellent, though there are a few coastal hair-raisers in the north and west of the island that are not for faint-hearted drivers (Sa Calobra and Formentor to name two). The narrow roads on these cliff-flanked coasts and the country roads through the interior are ideal for motorbike touring.

The island's main artery is the Ma13 motorway, which slices through the island diagonally, linking Palma in the west with Alcúdia in the north. The Ma1 loops southwest of Palma to Andratx.

While you can get about much of the island by bus and train, especially in high season, having a car will give you far greater freedom. With your own wheels you can seek out the nature parks, secluded coves and mountain retreats away from the crowds. If your car is not equipped with sat nav, it's worth investing in a decent road map to negotiate the island's more offbeat corners. Marco Polo produces a decent one at a 1:125,000 scale.

Automobile Associations

The Real Automóvil Club de España (www.race.es) is the national automobile club. They may well come to assist you in case of breakdown, but in any event you should obtain an emergency telephone number for Spain from your own insurer.

Bring Your Own Vehicle

Always carry proof of ownership of a private vehicle.

Every vehicle should display a nationality plate of its country of registration. It is compulsory in Spain to carry a warning triangle (to be used in case of breakdown) and a reflective jacket. Recommended accessories include a first-aid kit, spare-bulb kit and fire extinguisher.

Driving Licences

EU driving licences are recognised throughout Europe. Those with a non-EU licence are supposed to obtain a 12-month International Driver's Permit (IDP) from their home automobile association to accompany their national licence. In practice, national licences from countries such as Australia, Canada, New Zealand and the USA are usually accepted.

Fuel

You'll find petrol stations (*gasolineras*) in major towns and cities and most large resorts. Make sure you have a full tank if you're exploring rural areas off the beaten track. Choose between lead-free (*sin plomo*; 95 octane) and diesel (*gasóleo*). Petrol prices are on a par with the rest of Europe. You can pay with major credit cards at most service stations.

Hire

Car-hire rates vary, but you should be able to get an economy vehicle for between €40 and €70 per day; bear in mind that compact cars can be a tight fit for families. Additional drivers and one-way hire can bump up the cost. Extras like child seats (around €10 per day) should be reserved at the time of booking.

To rent a car you have to have a licence, be aged 21 or older and, for the major companies at least, have a credit card. A word of advice: some agencies try to make even more money by charging a hefty fee for fuel, instead of asking you to bring it back with a full tank. Always read the fine print carefully before signing off.

All the major car-hire companies are represented on the island. It can pay to shop around, and you might want to check a cost comparison site like www.travelsuper-market.com before going down the tried-and-trusted route. Branches at the airport include the following:

➡ **Avis** (☏ 902 110261; www.avis.com)

➡ **Europcar** (☏ 902 105055; www.europcar.com)

➡ **Gold Car** (☏ 902 119726; www.goldcar.es)

➡ **Hertz** (☏ 971 78 96 70; www.hertz.com)

➡ **Sixt** (☏ 902 49 16 16; www.sixt.com)

Insurance

➡ Third-party liability insurance is a minimum requirement in Spain and throughout Europe.

➡ Ask your insurer for a European Accident Statement form, which can simplify matters in the event of an accident.

➡ A European breakdown-assistance policy, such as the AA Five Star Service or RAC European Breakdown Cover, is a good investment.

➡ Car-hire companies provide third-party liability insurance, but make sure you understand what your liabilities and excess are, and what waivers you're entitled to in case of an accident or damage to the hire vehicle.

➡ Insurance that covers damage to the vehicle – Collision Damage Waiver (CDW) – usually costs extra, but driving without it is not recommended.

➡ Car-hire multiday or annual excess insurance can be cheaper online; try www.icarhireinsurance.com or http://insurance4carhire.com.

Road Rules

Blood-alcohol limit 0.05%. If found to be over the limit you can be judged, fined and deprived of your licence within 24 hours. Fines range up to around €1000 for serious offences, and you can even be jailed for a reading of 0.12% and above.

Legal driving age For cars, 18; for motorcycles and scooters, 16 (80cc and over) or 14 (50cc and under). A licence is required.

Motorcyclists Must use headlights at all times and wear a helmet if riding a bike of 125cc or more.

Overtaking Spanish truck drivers often have the courtesy to turn on their right indicator to show that the way ahead of them is clear for overtaking (and the left one if it is not and you are attempting this manoeuvre).

Roundabouts Vehicles already in the circle have the right of way.

Side of the road Drive on the right.

Speed limits In built-up areas, 50km/h; increases to 100km/h on major roads and up to 110km/h on the four-lane highways leading out of Palma.

Train

Four train lines run from Plaça d'Espanya in Palma de Mallorca; **Transport de les Illes Balears** (TIB; ☏ 971 17 77 77; www.tib.org) has details.

One heads north to Sóller and is a panoramic excursion in an antique wooden train; it's one of Palma's most popular day trips.

The other three lines head inland to Inca, where one terminates and the others shear off to serve Sa Pobla and Manacor. Prices are generally cheaper than buses and departures are frequent throughout the day. Mooted plans to extend the line from Manacor to Artà seem unlikely to come to fruition, now that the route has been turned into a cycle trail.

Language

Mallorca is a bilingual island, at least on paper. Since the Balearic Islands received their autonomy statute in the 1980s, the islanders' native Catalan (*català*) has recovered its official status alongside Spanish. This said, it would be pushing a point to say that Catalan, or its local dialect, *mallorquí*, had again become the primary language of Mallorca or the rest of the Balearic Islands. Today Spanish remains the lingua franca, especially between Mallorquins and other Spaniards or foreigners.

Spanish pronunciation is straightforward as most Spanish sounds are pronounced the same as their English counterparts. Note that the kh in our pronunciation guides is a guttural sound (like the 'ch' in the Scottish *loch*), ly is pronounced as the 'lli' in 'million', ny as the 'ni' in 'onion', th is pronounced with a lisp, and r is strongly rolled. In our pronunciation guides, the stressed syllables are in italics. If you follow our pronunciation guides given with each phrase in this chapter, you'll be understood just fine.

Spanish nouns (and the adjectives that go with them) are marked for gender – feminine nouns generally end with -a and masculine ones with -o. Where necessary, both forms are given for the words and phrases in this chapter, separated by a slash and with the masculine form first, eg *perdido/a* (m/f).

Also note that Spanish has two words for the English 'you': when talking to people familiar to you or younger than you, use the informal form, *tú*, rather than the polite form *Usted*. The polite form is used in the phrases provided in this chapter; where both options are given, they are indicated by the abbreviations 'pol' and 'inf'.

BASICS

Hello./Goodbye.	Hola./Adiós.	o·la/a·dyos
How are you?	¿Qué tal?	ke tal
Fine, thanks.	Bien, gracias.	byen gra·thyas
Excuse me.	Perdón.	per·don
Sorry.	Lo siento.	lo syen·to
Yes./No.	Sí./No.	see/no
Please.	Por favor.	por fa·vor
Thank you.	Gracias.	gra·thyas
You're welcome.	De nada.	de na·da

My name is ...
Me llamo ... — me *lya*·mo ...

What's your name?
¿Cómo se llama Usted? ko·mo se lya·ma oo·ste

Do you speak (English)?
¿Habla (inglés)? a·bla (een·gles)

I (don't) understand.
Yo (no) entiendo. yo (no) en·tyen·do

ACCOMMODATION

I'd like to book a room.
Quisiera reservar una habitación. kee·sye·ra re·ser·var oo·na a·bee·ta·thyon

How much is it per night/person?
¿Cuánto cuesta por noche/persona? kwan·to kwes·ta por no·che/per·so·na

air-con	aire acondicionado	ai·re a·kon·dee·thyo·na·do
bathroom	baño	ba·nyo
bed	cama	ka·ma
campsite	terreno de cámping	te·re·no de kam·peeng
double room	habitación doble	a·bee·ta·thyon do·ble
guesthouse	pensión	pen·syon
hotel	hotel	o·tel

single room	habitación individual	a·bee·ta·thyon een·dee·vee·dwal
window	ventana	ven·ta·na
youth hostel	albergue juvenil	al·ber·ge khoo·ve·neel

DIRECTIONS

Where's ...?
¿Dónde está ...? — don·de es·ta ...

What's the address?
¿Cuál es la dirección? — kwal es la dee·rek·thyon

Could you please write it down?
¿Puede escribirlo, por favor? — pwe·de es·kree·beer·lo por fa·vor

Can you show me (on the map)?
¿Me lo puede indicar (en el mapa)? — me lo pwe·de een·dee·kar (en el ma·pa)

behind ...	detrás de ...	de·tras de ...
far away	lejos	le·khos
in front of ...	enfrente de ...	en·fren·te de ...
left	izquierda	eeth·kyer·da
near	cerca	ther·ka
next to ...	al lado de ...	al la·do de ...
opposite ...	frente a ...	fren·te a ...
right	derecha	de·re·cha

EATING & DRINKING

I'd like to book a table.
Quisiera reservar una mesa. — kee·sye·ra re·ser·var oo·na me·sa

What would you recommend?
¿Qué recomienda? — ke re·ko·myen·da

What's in that dish?
¿Que lleva ese plato? — ke lye·va e·se pla·to

I don't eat ...
No como ... — no ko·mo ...

That was delicious!
¡Estaba buenísimo! — es·ta·ba bwe·nee·see·mo

Please bring the bill.
Por favor nos trae la cuenta. — por fa·vor nos tra·e la kwen·ta

Cheers!
¡Salud! — sa·loo

Key Words

appetisers	aperitivos	a·pe·ree·tee·vos
bar	bar	bar
bottle	botella	bo·te·lya
breakfast	desayuno	de·sa·yoo·no
cafe	café	ka·fe

KEY PATTERNS

To get by in Spanish, mix and match these simple patterns with words of your choice:

When's (the next flight)?
¿Cuándo sale (el próximo vuelo)? — kwan·do sa·le (el prok·see·mo vwe·lo)

Where's (the station)?
¿Dónde está (la estación)? — don·de es·ta (la es·ta·thyon)

Where can I (buy a ticket)?
¿Dónde puedo (comprar un billete)? — don·de pwe·do (kom·prar oon bee·lye·te)

Do you have (a map)?
¿Tiene (un mapa)? — tye·ne (oon ma·pa)

Is there (a toilet)?
¿Hay (servicios)? — ai (ser·vee·thyos)

I'd like (a coffee).
Quisiera (un café). — kee·sye·ra (oon ka·fe)

Could you please (help me)?
¿Puede (ayudarme), por favor? — pwe·de (a·yoo·dar·me) por fa·vor

children's menu	menú infantil	me·noo een·fan·teel
cold	frío	free·o
dinner	cena	the·na
food	comida	ko·mee·da
fork	tenedor	te·ne·dor
glass	vaso	va·so
highchair	trona	tro·na
hot (warm)	caliente	ka·lyen·te
knife	cuchillo	koo·chee·lyo
lunch	comida	ko·mee·da
main course	segundo plato	se·goon·do pla·to
market	mercado	mer·ka·do
menu (in English)	menú (en inglés)	me·noo (en een·gles)
plate	plato	pla·to
restaurant	restaurante	res·tow·ran·te
spoon	cuchara	koo·cha·ra
supermarket	supermercado	soo·per·mer·kado
with/without	con/sin	kon/seen
vegetarian food	comida vegetariana	ko·mee·da ve·khe·ta·rya·na

Meat & Fish

beef	carne de vaca	kar·ne de va·ka
chicken	pollo	po·lyo
duck	pato	pa·to

Signs

Abierto	Open
Cerrado	Closed
Entrada	Entrance
Hombres	Men
Mujeres	Women
Prohibido	Prohibited
Salida	Exit
Servicios/Aseos	Toilets

fish	*pescado*	pes·*ka*·do
lamb	*cordero*	kor·*de*·ro
pork	*cerdo*	*ther*·do
turkey	*pavo*	*pa*·vo
veal	*ternera*	ter·*ne*·ra

Fruit & Vegetables

apple	*manzana*	man·*tha*·na
apricot	*albaricoque*	al·ba·ree·*ko*·ke
artichoke	*alcachofa*	al·ka·*cho*·fa
asparagus	*espárragos*	es·*pa*·ra·gos
banana	*plátano*	*pla*·ta·no
beans	*judías*	khoo·*dee*·as
beetroot	*remolacha*	re·mo·*la*·cha
cabbage	*col*	kol
carrot	*zanahoria*	tha·na·o·rya
cherry	*cereza*	the·*re*·tha
corn	*maíz*	ma·*eeth*
cucumber	*pepino*	pe·*pee*·no
fruit	*fruta*	*froo*·ta
grape	*uvas*	*oo*·vas
lemon	*limón*	lee·*mon*
lentils	*lentejas*	len·*te*·khas
lettuce	*lechuga*	le·*choo*·ga
mushroom	*champiñón*	cham·pee·*nyon*
nuts	*nueces*	*nwe*·thes
onion	*cebolla*	the·*bo*·lya
orange	*naranja*	na·*ran*·kha
peach	*melocotón*	me·lo·ko·*ton*
peas	*guisantes*	gee·*san*·tes
(red/green) pepper	*pimiento (rojo/verde)*	pee·*myen*·to (*ro*·kho/*ver*·de)
pineapple	*piña*	*pee*·nya
plum	*ciruela*	theer·*we*·la
potato	*patata*	pa·*ta*·ta
pumpkin	*calabaza*	ka·la·*ba*·tha
spinach	*espinacas*	es·pee·*na*·kas

strawberry	*fresa*	*fre*·sa
tomato	*tomate*	to·*ma*·te
vegetable	*verdura*	ver·*doo*·ra
watermelon	*sandía*	san·*dee*·a

Other

bread	*pan*	pan
butter	*mantequilla*	man·te·*kee*·lya
cheese	*queso*	*ke*·so
egg	*huevo*	*we*·vo
honey	*miel*	myel
jam	*mermelada*	mer·me·*la*·da
oil	*aceite*	a·*they*·te
pepper	*pimienta*	pee·*myen*·ta
rice	*arroz*	a·*roth*
salt	*sal*	sal
sugar	*azúcar*	a·*thoo*·kar
vinegar	*vinagre*	vee·*na*·gre

Drinks

beer	*cerveza*	ther·*ve*·tha
coffee	*café*	ka·*fe*
(orange) juice	*zumo (de naranja)*	*thoo*·mo (de na·*ran*·kha)
milk	*leche*	*le*·che
tea	*té*	te
(mineral) water	*agua (mineral)*	*a*·gwa (mee·ne·*ral*)
(red) wine	*vino (tinto)*	vee·no (*teen*·to)
(white) wine	*vino (blanco)*	vee·no (*blan*·ko)

EMERGENCIES

Help!
¡Socorro! — so·*ko*·ro

Go away!
¡Vete! — *ve*·te

Call a doctor!
¡Llame a un médico! — *lya*·me a oon *me*·dee·ko

Call the police!
¡Llame a la policía! — *lya*·me a la po·lee·*thee*·a

I'm lost.
Estoy perdido/a. — es·*toy* per·*dee*·do/a (m/f)

I'm ill.
Estoy enfermo/a. — es·*toy* en·*fer*·mo/a (m/f)

Where are the toilets?
¿Dónde están los baños? — *don*·de es·*tan* los *ba*·nyos

Catalan – Basics

Good morning.	Bon dia.	bon dee·a
Good afternoon.	Bona tarda.	bo·na tar·da
Good evening.	Bon vespre.	bon bes·pra
Goodbye.	Adéu.	a·the·oo
Please.	Sisplau.	sees·pla·oo
Thank you.	Gràcies.	gra·see·a
You're welcome.	De res.	de res
Excuse me.	Perdoni.	par·tho·nee
I'm sorry.	Ho sento.	oo sen·to
How are you?	Com estàs?	kom as·tas
(Very) Well.	(Molt) Bé.	(mol) be

NUMBERS

1	uno	oo·no
2	dos	dos
3	tres	tres
4	cuatro	kwa·tro
5	cinco	theen·ko
6	seis	seys
7	siete	sye·te
8	ocho	o·cho
9	nueve	nwe·ve
10	diez	dyeth
20	veinte	veyn·te
30	treinta	treyn·ta
40	cuarenta	kwa·ren·ta
50	cincuenta	theen·kwen·ta
60	sesenta	se·sen·ta
70	setenta	se·ten·ta
80	ochenta	o·chen·ta
90	noventa	no·ven·ta
100	cien	thyen
1000	mil	meel

SHOPPING & SERVICES

I'd like to buy ...
Quisiera comprar ...   kee·sye·ra kom·prar ...

May I look at it?
¿Puedo verlo?   pwe·do ver·lo

How much is it?
¿Cuánto cuesta?   kwan·to kwes·ta

That's too/very expensive.
Es muy caro.   es mooy ka·ro

Can you lower the price?
¿Podría bajar un   po·dree·a ba·khar oon
poco el precio?   po·ko el pre·thyo

There's a mistake in the bill.
Hay un error en la cuenta.   ai oon e·ror en la kwen·ta

ATM   cajero automático   ka·khe·ro ow·to·ma·tee·ko

credit card   tarjeta de crédito   tar·khe·ta de kre·dee·to

post office   correos   ko·re·os

tourist office   oficina de turismo   o·fee·thee·na de too·rees·mo

TIME & DATES

What time is it?
¿Qué hora es?   ke o·ra es

It's (10) o'clock.
Son (las diez).   son (las dyeth)

Half past (one).
Es (la una) y media.   es (la oo·na) ee me·dya

morning	mañana	ma·nya·na
afternoon	tarde	tar·de
evening	noche	no·che
yesterday	ayer	a·yer
today	hoy	oy
tomorrow	mañana	ma·nya·na

Monday	lunes	loo·nes
Tuesday	martes	mar·tes
Wednesday	miércoles	myer·ko·les
Thursday	jueves	khwe·bes
Friday	viernes	vyer·nes
Saturday	sábado	sa·ba·do
Sunday	domingo	do·meen·go

TRANSPORT

I want to go to ...
Quisiera ir a ...   kee·sye·ra eer a ...

What time does it arrive/leave?
¿A qué hora llega/sale?   a ke o·ra lye·ga/sa·le

I want to get off here.
Quiero bajarme aquí.   kye·ro ba·khar·me a·kee

1st-class	primera clase	pree·me·ra kla·se
2nd-class	segunda clase	se·goon·da kla·se
bicycle	bicicleta	bee·thee·kle·ta
boat	barco	bar·ko
bus	autobús	ow·to·boos
car	coche	ko·che
cancelled	cancelado	kan·the·la·do
delayed	retrasado	re·tra·sa·do
motorcycle	moto	mo·to
one-way	ida	ee·da
plane	avión	a·vyon
return	ida y vuelta	ee·da ee vwel·ta
ticket	billete	bee·lye·te
ticket office	taquilla	ta·kee·lya
timetable	horario	o·ra·ryo
train	tren	tren

GLOSSARY

Most of the following terms are in Castilian Spanish which is fully understood around the island. A handful of specialised terms in Catalan (C) also appear. No distinction has been made for any Mallorcan dialect variations.

agroturisme (C) – rural tourism

ajuntament (C) – city or town hall

alquería – Muslim-era farmstead

avenida – avenue

avinguda (C) – see *avenida*

baño completo – full bathroom with toilet, shower and/or bath

bodega – cellar (especially wine cellar)

bomberos – fire brigade

cala – cove

call (C) – Jewish quarter in Palma, Inca and some other Mallorcan towns

cambio – change; also currency exchange

caña – small glass of beer

canguro – babysitter

capilla – chapel

carrer (C) – street

carretera – highway

carta – menu

castell (C) – castle

castellano – Castilian; used in preference to '*Español*' to describe the national language

català – Catalan language; a native of Catalonia. The Mallorcan dialect is Mallorquin

celler – (C) wine cellars turned into restaurants

cervecería – beer bar

comisaría – police station

conquistador – conqueror

converso – Jew who converted to Christianity in medieval Spain

correos – post office

cortado – short black coffee with a little milk

costa – coast

cuenta – bill, cheque

ensaïmada (C) – Mallorcan pastry

entrada – entrance, ticket

ermita – small hermitage or country chapel

església (C) – see *iglesia*

estació (C) – see *estación*

estación – station

estanco – tobacconist shop

farmacia – pharmacy

faro – lighthouse

fiesta – festival, public holiday or party

finca – farmhouse

gasolina – petrol

guardía civil – military police

habitaciones libres – literally 'rooms available'

hostal – see *pensión*

iglesia – church

IVA – *impuesto sobre el valor añadido*, or value-added tax

lavabo – washbasin

librería – bookshop

lista de correos – poste restante

locutorio – telephone centre

marisquería – seafood eatery

menú del día – menu of the day

mercat (C) – market

mirador – lookout point

Modernisme – the Catalan version of the art nouveau architectural and artistic style

monestir (C) – monastery

museo – museum

museu (C) – see *museo*

objetos perdidos – lost-and-found

oficina de turismo – tourist office; also *oficina de información turística*

palacio – palace, grand mansion or noble house

palau (C) – see *palacio*

pensión – small family-run hotel

plaça (C) – see *plaza*

platja (C) – see *playa*

playa – beach

plaza – square

port (C) – see *puerto*

possessió (C) – typical Mallorcan farmhouse

PP – Partido Popular (People's Party)

puente – bridge

puerto – port

puig (C) – mountain peak

rambla – avenue or riverbed

refugis (C) – hikers' huts

retablo – altarpiece

retaule (C) – see *retablo*

robes de llengües (C) – traditional striped Mallorcan fabrics

santuari (C) – shrine or sanctuary, hermitage

según precio del mercado – on menus, 'according to market price' (often written 'spm')

Semana Santa – Holy Week

serra (C) – mountain range

servicios – toilets

tafona (C) – traditional oil press found on most Mallorcan farms

talayot (C) – ancient watchtower

tarjeta de crédito – credit card

tarjeta de residencia – residence card

tarjeta telefónica – phonecard

terraza – terrace; pavement cafe

torre – tower

turismo – tourism or saloon car

urgencia – emergency

Behind the Scenes

SEND US YOUR FEEDBACK

We love to hear from travellers – your comments keep us on our toes and help make our books better. Our well-travelled team reads every word on what you loved or loathed about this book. Although we cannot reply individually to your submissions, we always guarantee that your feedback goes straight to the appropriate authors, in time for the next edition. Each person who sends us information is thanked in the next edition – the most useful submissions are rewarded with a selection of digital PDF chapters.

Visit **lonelyplanet.com/contact** to submit your updates and suggestions or to ask for help. Our award-winning website also features inspirational travel stories, news and discussions.

Note: We may edit, reproduce and incorporate your comments in Lonely Planet products such as guidebooks, websites and digital products, so let us know if you don't want your comments reproduced or your name acknowledged. For a copy of our privacy policy visit lonelyplanet.com/privacy.

OUR READERS

Many thanks to the travellers who used the last edition and wrote to us with helpful hints, useful advice and interesting anecdotes:

Andrew Gladstone, Anne Winstrup, Esther Hardman, Eva Kristénsen, Rocío Mora, Sylvie Dodwell.

WRITER THANKS

Hugh McNaughtan

I'd like to express thanks for the patience and support of Tasmin, Maise and Willa, the top-notch editorial and technical assistance of Lauren and the LP support team, and the kindness and generosity of many, many Mallorcans.

Damian Harper

Many thanks to Ann Harper, Richard Guy Hayward Harper, Daniel Hands, Emmanuelle Arbona, Robert Landreth, Amanda Godson, Norma Gray, Catalina and each and every one of the locals of Fornalutx (former inhabitants included), plus a round of applause for Daisy, Tim and Emma.

ACKNOWLEDGMENTS

Climate map data adapted from Peel MC, Finlayson BL & McMahon TA (2007) 'Updated World Map of the Köppen-Geiger Climate Classification', Hydrology and Earth System Sciences, 11, 1633–44.

Cover photograph: Steps of the Way of the Cross & Nostra Senyora dels Angels church, Pollenca, Doug Pearson/AWL

THIS BOOK

This 4th edition of Lonely Planet's *Mallorca* guidebook was researched and written by Hugh McNaughtan and Damian Harper. The 3rd edition was written by Kerry Christiani, the 2nd by Anthony Ham and the 1st by Damien Simonis, with contributions from Sally Schafer. This guidebook was produced by the following:

Destination Editor Lauren Keith

Product Editors Paul Harding, Catherine Naghten

Senior Cartographer Anthony Phelan

Book Designer Virginia Moreno

Assisting Editors Samantha Forge, Victoria Harrison, Anne Mulvaney, Lauren O'Connell, Kristin Odijk, Maja Vatric, Simon Williamson

Cover Researcher Naomi Parker

Thanks to Jennifer Carey, Jo Cooke, Daniel Corbett, Bruce Evans, Jane Grisman, Liz Heynes, Andi Jones, Alison Lyall, Karyn Noble, Claire Naylor, Kirsten Rawlings, Dianne Schallmeiner, Tom Stainer, Tony Wheeler, Dora Whitaker

Index

Map Legend

Sights

- Beach
- Bird Sanctuary
- Buddhist
- Castle/Palace
- Christian
- Confucian
- Hindu
- Islamic
- Jain
- Jewish
- Monument
- Museum/Gallery/Historic Building
- Ruin
- Shinto
- Sikh
- Taoist
- Winery/Vineyard
- Zoo/Wildlife Sanctuary
- Other Sight

Activities, Courses & Tours

- Bodysurfing
- Diving
- Canoeing/Kayaking
- Course/Tour
- Sento Hot Baths/Onsen
- Skiing
- Snorkelling
- Surfing
- Swimming/Pool
- Walking
- Windsurfing
- Other Activity

Sleeping

- Sleeping
- Camping

Eating

- Eating

Drinking & Nightlife

- Drinking & Nightlife
- Cafe

Entertainment

- Entertainment

Shopping

- Shopping

Information

- Bank
- Embassy/Consulate
- Hospital/Medical
- Internet
- Police
- Post Office
- Telephone
- Toilet
- Tourist Information
- Other Information

Geographic

- Beach
- Gate
- Hut/Shelter
- Lighthouse
- Lookout
- Mountain/Volcano
- Oasis
- Park
- Pass
- Picnic Area
- Waterfall

Population

- Capital (National)
- Capital (State/Province)
- City/Large Town
- Town/Village

Transport

- Airport
- Border crossing
- Bus
- Cable car/Funicular
- Cycling
- Ferry
- Metro station
- Monorail
- Parking
- Petrol station
- S-Bahn/Subway station
- Taxi
- T-bane/Tunnelbana station
- Train station/Railway
- Tram
- Tube station
- U-Bahn/Underground station
- Other Transport

Note: Not all symbols displayed above appear on the maps in this book

Routes

- Tollway
- Freeway
- Primary
- Secondary
- Tertiary
- Lane
- Unsealed road
- Road under construction
- Plaza/Mall
- Steps
- Tunnel
- Pedestrian overpass
- Walking Tour
- Walking Tour detour
- Path/Walking Trail

Boundaries

- International
- State/Province
- Disputed
- Regional/Suburb
- Marine Park
- Cliff
- Wall

Hydrography

- River, Creek
- Intermittent River
- Canal
- Water
- Dry/Salt/Intermittent Lake
- Reef

Areas

- Airport/Runway
- Beach/Desert
- Cemetery (Christian)
- Cemetery (Other)
- Glacier
- Mudflat
- Park/Forest
- Sight (Building)
- Sportsground
- Swamp/Mangrove

OUR STORY

A beat-up old car, a few dollars in the pocket and a sense of adventure. In 1972 that's all Tony and Maureen Wheeler needed for the trip of a lifetime – across Europe and Asia overland to Australia. It took several months, and at the end – broke but inspired – they sat at their kitchen table writing and stapling together their first travel guide, *Across Asia on the Cheap*. Within a week they'd sold 1500 copies. Lonely Planet was born.

Today, Lonely Planet has offices in Franklin, London, Melbourne, Oakland, Dublin, Beijing and Delhi, with more than 600 staff and writers. We share Tony's belief that 'a great guidebook should do three things: inform, educate and amuse'.

OUR WRITERS

Hugh McNaughtan

Palma & the Badia de Palma, The Interior, Eastern Mallorca, Southern Mallorca

A former English lecturer and food writer, Hugh moved to the UK with his young family in 2013, and took up travel writing full time. He's written (and eaten) his way through Mallorca, Maluku, Lithuania, Bulgaria and Britain, and still has a soft spot for the fabulous food of his home town, Melbourne. Hugh also updated the Understand chapters.

Damian Harper

Western Mallorca, Northern Mallorca

Ten years of British boarding school life gave Damian every incentive to explore new horizons beyond home. A degree in History of Art at Leeds University fortified this persuasion and Damian found himself living at the Shakespeare & Co bookshop in Paris, stacking shelves, fending off bedbugs and falling in love with books. Damian has been working largely full time as a travel writer (and translator) since 1997 and has also written for *National Geographic Traveler*, the *Guardian*, the *Daily Telegraph*, Abbeville Press (Celestial Realm: *The Yellow Mountains of China*), *Lexean*, *Frequent Traveller*, *China Ethos* and various other magazines and newspapers. Damian also updated the Plan Your Trip section.

Published by Lonely Planet Global Limited
CRN 554153
4th edition – Jul 2017
ISBN 978 1 78657 547 0
© Lonely Planet 2017   Photographs © as indicated 2017
10 9 8 7 6 5 4 3 2 1
Printed in Singapore